Child Study Research

Child Study Research

Current Perspectives and Applications

Genevieve Clapp
San Diego Research Consultants

Lexington Books
D.C. Heath and Company/Lexington, Massachusetts/Toronto

Library of Congress Cataloging-in-Publication Data

Clapp, Genevieve.
    Child study research.

    Includes index.
    1. Child development—United States. 2. Child rearing—United States.
3. Child mental health—United States. I. Title.
HQ792.U5C55   1988   305.2'3   86-45882
ISBN 0-669-14507-6

Published simultaneously in Canada
Printed in the United States of America
International Standard Book Number: 0-669-14507-6
Library of Congress Catalog Card Number: 86-45882

The paper used in this publication meets the minimum requirements of American National
Standard for Information Sciences—Permanence of Paper for Printed Library Materials,
ANSI Z39.48-1984.   ∞™

88 89 90 91 92 8 7 6 5 4 3 2 1

This book is dedicated to all those involved in child-related professions, who are being asked each year to perform in more dimensions and in more depth; to the children whose lives will be enriched because of a well-informed professional; and to two very special children, Gary and Karen.

Contents

Preface and Acknowledgments   ix

1. **The Controversial Early Years: Do They Map the Future?**   1

   Evidence Supporting the Permanent Influence of Early Experience   2
   Evidence Questioning the Permanent Influence of Early Experience   4
   The Controversy Continues   16
   Consistency and Change in Development: Important Factors   18
   Implications of the Research   21

2. **Employed Mothers and Day Care**   27

   Maternal Employment   28
   Day Care   33

3. **Television: Today's Most Important Socializer?**   57

   Amount and Content of Viewing   57
   A Child's Television Experience   58
   A Child's Perceptions of the World: Does Television Bias Them?   60
   Television Violence: Does It Instigate Aggression?   62
   Music Videos: A New Kind of Television Influence?   69
   Television: Educational Enrichment or Detraction?   71
   Mitigating Television's Negative Effects   74

4. **Parental Discord and Divorce**   85

   Divorce: The Experience   85
   Divorce: Long-Term Consequences for Children   88
   Divorce: Why Children Adjust Successfully or Poorly   90
   Parental Conflict: Should We Stay Together for the Children's Sake?   98
   Buffering Children from the Negative Consequences of Divorce   99

5. **Childhood Stress and Youth Suicide 111**

Childhood Stress 111
Stress-Resistant Children 118
Depression in Children and Adolescents 123
Youth Suicide 125
Intervention 132
Recurring Themes in the Literature 135

6. **Child Abuse 143**

Child Abuse and Its Occurrence 143
Risk Factors Leading to Abuse 144
The Abuse 155
The Sequelae of Abuse 156
Intervention 160
The Social Problem of Child Abuse 169

7. **Learning Disabilities: What Has Been Learned? 181**

A Brief Look Back 181
Learning Disabled Children 183
Causes of Learning Disabilities 186
The Search for Subtypes of Learning Disabilities 201

8. **Learning Disabilities: Steps to Remediation 211**

The Process Training Approach to Remediation 212
The Holistic Approach to Remediation 213
The Direct Skills Approach to Remediation 215
The Neuropsychological Approach: Fine-Tuning Remediation 230
There Are No Remedial Shortcuts 231
Learning Disabilities Subtypes Revisited 235

Index 243

About the Author 251

Preface and Acknowledgments

This book is not a traditional survey of the literature, either in content, emphasis, or style. Its purpose is to enable the reader to quickly become informed in each surveyed area, its current issues, and its latest research results, even if the reader is generally unfamiliar with an area and its jargon. The book's intended audience is professionals who are involved with children or families, directly or indirectly: college course instructors, family and child therapists, social workers, training directors in education or mental health disciplines, consultants, school psychologists and school counselors, classroom teachers, pediatricians, pastoral counselors, day care providers, and so forth.

Currently, many child study researchers are focusing their efforts in areas that reflect societal needs—areas in which practicing professionals are being asked to perform. Exciting, relevant, and useful information is emerging from our universities. Although no *single* piece of research may be critically important to practicing professionals, when results are integrated, consistent patterns emerge that would help practitioners to function more effectively: to answer the wide range of changing questions they are asked on a daily basis, to make more effective recommendations, to update class lectures or revise course content, and to learn about new programs and new treatment and teaching approaches.

Unfortunately, this research is scattered in over 200 journals, and there are limited resources to help practitioners keep abreast of new developments in a wide range of areas. Any single journal provides an insignificant fraction of published studies, and most available books limit their coverage to a single topic. There are some books that are broader in scope, but usually they are compilations of academic literature reviews. Generally these are more appropriate for researchers than for practitioners because of their emphasis on lengthy analyses of individual studies, research methodology, and theoretical issues. At present, there is an unfortunate communication gap between child study researchers, who are doing an exemplary job increasing available knowledge about children and their problems in today's society, and practicing professionals, who could be applying this new information.

It is my hope that this book will be a step toward bridging the existing communication gap, by enabling practicing professionals to extract succinct and useful information in a wide range of critical areas. Not only do the surveyed topics reflect practitioners' concerns, but also the coverage of each topic is specifically geared to their needs. Each chapter provides: (1) a broad perspective of an area; (2) a synthesis of current research findings (integrated with relevant findings from other areas); (3) the current thought of the leading experts in the area; (4) the implications and applications of the research; and (5) where relevant, the latest programs and treatment approaches developed. The book is written from an interdisciplinary approach, avoiding the jargon of any one discipline. Thus, it is easily readable to all those in child- or family-related professions, whether their training was in psychology, psychiatry, social work, education, home economics, or pediatrics.

The literature reviews in each chapter have been carried out somewhat differently than most literature reviews. Because the book is designed to reflect current thought rather than my personal biases, chapters survey the academic literature reviews on each topic. These reviews generally are written by highly specialized academicians with particular expertise and interest in the area. Therefore, the conclusions and the implications presented in each chapter are based upon those of the most professionally competent people in each field. Where controversy exists, both sides are presented. Additionally, because the book is designed to be interdisciplinary, chapters also survey the journals in all child-related disciplines: psychology, psychiatry, social work, education, and pediatrics. (References to reviews as opposed to original research are distinguished by a "see" before the author[s] name[s].)

My sincere thanks to the many people who assisted me at each stage of this book: to Dr. Marion Potts, Dr. Barbara Jean Shea, Dr. Kay W. Wilder, Jerry Clapp, and Diane Murdoch for their critical review of chapters and the insightful suggestions they offered; to the hundreds of researchers throughout the country who sent me copies of their publications and kept me informed of the progress of their current research; to the libraries at the University of California at San Diego and San Diego State University; to my editor, Margaret Zusky; and to my family for their bottomless reserve of support, patience, understanding, and humor throughout the course of this project.

1

The Controversial Early Years: Do They Map the Future?

> The most pervasive western model for human development . . . is the view that the first few years of life necessarily have crucial effects upon later development and adult characteristics. . . . Such a view must be challenged in the light of growing evidence.
>
> —Clarke & Clarke 1976

The idea that a child's early years have a permanent impact on his psychological development has been so widely accepted, it virtually has gone unchallenged—until recently. Such unquestioned acceptance is not surprising: the idea has appeared in Western thought since the days of Plato. Some 400 years B.C., in *The Republic*, he wrote:

And the first step, as you know, is always what matters most, particularly when we are dealing with those who are young and tender. That is the time when they are taking shape and when any impression we choose to make leaves a permanent mark (Clarke & Clarke 1976).

Various philosophers replanted the notion throughout the centuries. For example, in 1916, James Mill wrote:

As soon as the infant, or rather the embryo, begins to feel, the character begins to be formed; and . . . the habits, which are then contracted, are the most pervasive and operative of all (Clarke & Clarke 1976).

Freud was, perhaps, most influential in cementing the idea in millions of minds. Throughout his career, he stressed the importance of the first five years of life—an assumption he derived from theory and his subjective observation of patients, rather than from objective research. In 1910, Freud wrote:

The very impressions which we have forgotten have nevertheless left the deepest traces in our psychic life, and acted as determinants for our whole future development (Clarke & Clarke 1976).

Whether or not a child's early years have permanent consequences for his future development is, of course, a crucial issue. Only in "recent" history have we had the benefit of research to evaluate the long-held assumption that a child's early years are his most critical ones, with consequences lasting a lifetime. This research and its implications have stirred a recent and heated controversy.

Evidence Supporting the Permanent Influence of Early Experience

Research supporting the critical nature of early experience has been publicized widely for many years. Therefore, only a brief historical overview with some examples will be given. An extensive review has been written by Hunt (1979).

Although the enduring nature of early experience had been assumed for centuries, the assumption had no great impact in this country—socially, educationally, or politically—until after World War II (Hunt 1979). At this time, numerous psychological studies reported that institutionally reared infants were severely retarded in all areas of development—physical, motor, intellectual, and social (e.g., Goldfarb 1943, Spitz 1946). The fate of these infants became widely publicized in 1951 as a result of a very influential report to the World Health Organization by John Bowlby (1951). The picture depicting limp, listless, retarded babies was so terrifying that most of the country replaced institutional care for infants with foster care (Hunt 1979).

The work of Goldfarb was influential in this early stream of research. One frequently quoted study (Goldfarb 1943) followed two groups of fifteen children: one group institutionalized from six months to three years before being placed in foster homes, the other group placed in foster homes immediately. When followed up between the ages of 10 to 14, those in the early institutionalized group were markedly inferior in intelligence, maturity, speech, and the ability to form relationships.

The assumption that early experience is critical gained further support and momentum from animal research conducted in the fifties and sixties. Experiments conducted by Harry Harlow (e.g., 1958) at the University of Wisconsin became classics. Harlow raised monkeys in isolation and observed how their development was affected. The fate of "Harlow's monkeys" became ingrained in the minds of every beginning student of psychology. The monkeys had developed into social vegetables that were unable to relate, mate, or mother in any normal fashion. The effects of early experience on animal development were demonstrated in numerous other situations (see Hunt 1979). A few examples follow. Cats that had spent their early lives with rats would not, in adulthood, kill rats even if hungry. Animals that were reared in the dark at an early age experienced degenerative changes in parts of the eye and brain. Animals that were raised in isolation developed into very inferior problem solvers. Other research, conducted at the University of California, demonstrated what an enriched early environment could do for young rats: it altered both the chemistry and anatomy of their brains (see Hunt 1979).

In the sixties, a separate stream of research contributed additional momentum to the strong early influence thesis. At this time, a flood of experiments and social programs emerged that attempted to alter the early environment of disadvantaged children. In the mid-sixties, behavioral scientists and politicians joined forces to create Project Head Start under President Johnson's Anti-Poverty Bill. Head Start programs reached hundreds of thousands of preschool children and reported substantial gains in IQ after just one year of intervention (see Bronfenbrenner 1976).

More recently, several studies have suggested that the lack of opportunity to form attachments early in life may interfere with children's later social development (see MacDonald 1985; Rutter 1979, 1985a). Children who had been denied this opportunity have been found to be attention seeking, indiscriminately friendly, socially inept, and unpopular with peers. One study suggested that this missed opportunity was associated with later antisocial behavior (Cadoret & Cain, cited in MacDonald 1985).

Research had clearly demonstrated that early experience could have serious consequences for both humans and animals, and it was widely assumed that these consequences were permanent. The idea of permanency had been given scientific credibility by earlier research that had studied the phenomenon of critical periods (see Columbo 1982). This research had found that, for many animals, there were limited periods of time in their life span during which environmental events had a profound, and apparently permanent, influence on some aspect of development, such as binocular vision or the formation of attachments. For example, experiments had found that there was a critical time period during which a precocial bird (one capable of moving when first hatched) would follow and form an attachment to the most prominent moving object it encountered (a phenomenon called imprinting). In nature, of course, the most prominent object would be the mother. But in experimental laboratories, attachments (which appeared to be permanent) were formed to people, purple cubes, or whatever object was prominent during this critical time period.

What occurred in the animal's development during these specific periods to make its timing so critical? Researchers hypothesized that during these critical periods, some aspect of development was proceeding at a very rapid rate, and the speed with which it was progressing made that part of development particularly sensitive to influences from the environment. Once the rapid growth ceased, the role played by the environment faded.

Because critical periods had been found in animal development, it was a small jump to hypothesize that there were critical periods in human development too (Hunt 1979). After all, children have periods of particularly rapid growth and change: their early years. Isn't it logical that a child's development should be most influenced by environmental events during her period of most rapid growth? This certainly would have explained the severity of retardation found in institutionally reared infants.

Thus, during the two decades after World War II, Western society's long-held assumption—that the early years necessarily have a rather permanent impact on later development—gained scientific credibility.

Evidence Questioning the Permanent Influence of Early Experience

Although the case supporting the overriding importance of early experience was mounting, bits and pieces of data were being reported that suggested the consequences of early experience may not be as permanent as most people assumed. A number of the early institutional studies had been riddled with methodological flaws, and so their results were questioned (Clarke & Clarke 1976). Other studies reported remarkable improvements shown by individuals who had experienced early severe deprivation but, later, were removed to better environments (e.g., Clarke, Clarke & Reiman 1958; Davis 1947; Dennis & Najarian 1957; Koluchova 1972, 1976; Skeels & Dye 1939; Skeels 1966). And in the early sixties, points out Featherman (1983), two influential personality studies were published that had been in progress since before World War II (Kagan & Moss 1962, Macfarlane 1963). Their authors had been studying the development of a large group of individuals throughout the previous two decades. Both studies reported finding poor predictability of adult personality from early childhood personality and events.

Clarke and Clarke (1976) suggest that it was easy to disregard these fragments of evidence because they were contrary to what had become accepted dogma. It was not until 1967 that Dr. A.D.B. Clarke, as the invited speaker for the 42nd Maudsley Lecture, first publicly questioned whether the research actually supported the alleged permanent influence of early experience.

The next decade witnessed an explosion of interest in the area. Between 1968 and 1977, over 1,500 articles and investigations were published that dealt with the effects of early experience in some way; most of these involved research with animals (Hunt 1979).

New Research Designs

The animal research conducted earlier had been limited in its scope because it had been demonstrational rather than exploratory or analytical (Cairns & Hood 1983). It demonstrated that the effects of early experience could be detected, but generally it went no further. New experiments were designed to go beyond demonstration—to explore and to analyze the properties of early experience and its effects (Cairns & Hood 1983). Issues addressed by new research included the feasibility of reversing early experience and the role played by later experience.

Harlow, for example, continuing to experiment with monkeys, found that the debilitating effects of early isolation were reversible. These maladjusted monkeys emerged with social skills indistinguishable from other monkeys when moved to a type of therapeutic environment (e.g., Suomi & Harlow 1972). Impressive resiliency was found in other species as well (see Cairns, Green & MacCrombie 1980; Cairns & Hood 1983). New experiments found that imprinting and other behaviors learned during critical periods were alterable (see Cairns & Hood 1983, Columbo 1982). Changes in brain chemistry that were produced by early enrichment were not necessarily permanent either; they were lost if the subsequent environment was a deprived one (see Simmel & Baker 1980). Furthermore, experiments found that it was not necessary for rats to experience enrichment at an early age for brain changes to occur. The brains of adult rats were also modified by enriched environments, although not as quickly as the brains of very young animals (e.g., Rosenzweig, Bennett & Diamond 1972).

Follow-up studies of Head Start, finding that the impressive IQ gains made by program children diminished over time once the special intervention stopped, were very disappointing (see Bronfenbrenner 1976, Clarke-Stewart & Fein 1983). There was some encouragement in the fact that not all the benefits of these programs faded. Program children repeated grades less frequently and were placed in special education classes less frequently. Additionally, mothers had higher aspirations for program children than did mothers of control children (Lazar & Darlington 1982). But, the interpretation of these positive findings was open to debate. Some argued that the program experience did not "inoculate" the children against failure, as initially expected. Rather, the experience may have begun a chain of events in which each positive school experience made the next more likely (see Clarke & Clarke 1986, Clarke-Stewart & Fein 1983, Scarr & Weinberg 1986). It could be argued that these children's school success was due to the continuation of good experiences throughout childhood rather than to any lasting effects of the early experience per se.

During the seventies and eighties, reviews were published that attempted to organize, assess, and draw conclusions from the massive amount of research examining the issue (e.g., Brim & Kagan 1980, Clarke & Clarke 1976, Hunt 1979, Rutter 1980, Sameroff 1975). The conclusions of many reviewers cast further doubt on the validity of the assumption that the early years set the course for future psychological development. For example, in his 1975 review, Sameroff concluded:

> Despite the reasonableness of the notion that one should be able to make long-range predictions based on the initial characteristics of a child or his environment, the above review has found little evidence for the validity of such predictions (p. 285).

In 1976, Clarke and Clarke wrote:

> The view that the first few years of life necessarily have crucial effects upon later development and adult characteristics . . . *must* be challenged in the light of growing evidence . . . (p. 4).

In 1980, Rutter concluded:

> Continuities between infancy and maturity undoubtedly exist, but the residual effects of early experience on adult behaviour tend to be quite slight because of

the maturational changes that take place during middle and later childhood, and because of the effects of beneficial and adverse experiences during all the years after infancy (p. 811).

Also in 1980, Orville Brim and Jerome Kagan concluded:

> The view that emerges from this work is that humans have a capacity for change across the entire life span. . . . the consequences of the events of early childhood are continually transformed by later experiences, making the course of human development more open than many have believed (p. 1).

That early experience plays a critical role in later development has been a central concept in many theories of development to which we have long ascribed. It is hardly surprising that conclusions such as these have stirred a heated controversy, particularly when no single piece of evidence is convincing by itself. It is the totality of the data that these reviewers found compelling. This was expressed eloquently by Kagan and his colleagues (1978): "but individual strands of evidence, each too weak to bear the burden of proof alone, can be woven into a fabric with some persuasive power" (p. 141).

It is impossible to survey all the research that led these reviewers to their conclusions, but we will look at some examples.

Early Trauma Studies

The long-term influence of early experience generally has been studied in one of two ways. The first looks at children who have undergone trauma or severe deprivation early in life. If early experience has permanent effects on a child, these effects should be evident in her subsequent development, even if conditions markedly improve in her later life.

The Iowa Studies. One such investigation was a study, conducted by Skeels and Dye (1939), of thirteen retarded children who were transferred at the average age of 19 months from a poor-quality state orphanage to a state school for the mentally retarded. At their new home, each of the children became the "favorite" of an older resident and received large doses of special attention. These retarded youngsters thrived in their new environment. In time (one and one-half years on the average), their IQs increased enough for them to be adopted. The average IQ of these children had soared from 64 to 91.8, an average gain of 27.8 points. (Average IQ ranges from 90 to 110.)

Skeels and Dye also studied a similar age contrast group that remained in the orphanage, receiving good physical care but little else. During the two and one-half-year period they were studied, their average IQ fell from 86 to 60.5, an average loss of 25.5 points.

More than twenty years later, Skeels (1966) conducted a follow-up study. What had happened to these two groups of children? Both had had similar deprived infancies, but due to little more than chance, each group had gone in separate directions in their toddler years. The transferred group had completed an average of twelve grades in school. Their occupations included a vocational counselor, sales manager, Air Force staff sergeant, teacher, nurse, and airline stewardess. The contrast group, on the other hand, had completed an average of four grades in school, and those who were employed were unskilled manual laborers. There was only one exception in the contrast group, a child who had been moved later to a better-quality institution because of a hearing loss.

In reviewing Skeels's investigations, Clarke and Clarke (1976) contended that these children's development was influenced more by their long-term environment than by their early deprivation in infancy or by their experiences as toddlers and preschoolers. They cited many examples to support this conclusion. The exceptional child in the contrast group was one. Left in his deprived early environment, his IQ had been only 67 at the age of 3-1/2. Yet, as an adult, he became a typesetter with some college education. He had a stable marriage and four children, described as intelligent. His adult success presumably was due to his later removal to a better institution because of his hearing loss. Another example of long-term environmental influence was the only child in the transferred group to be adopted by a middle-class family, rather than a lower-middle-class one. This child had been at risk genetically (his natural mother had been mentally retarded) and environmentally (he had spent a full twenty-six months in the deprived orphanage before being transferred). He had had an IQ of 75 at the time of transfer and only 82 at the age of 4. Yet, as an adult, he had not only graduated from college but had continued on to graduate school. In spite of the obvious testing issues, his academic achievements certainly could not have been predicted based upon his early childhood.

The Guatemalan Study. In 1972, a fascinating study was reported by Harvard's Jerome Kagan in an address to the American Association for the Advancement of Science. Kagan and his colleague, Robert Klein, had just finished studying children from an isolated village of Guatemala (Kagan & Klein 1973). Kagan described the first year of these children's lives as spent in a small, dark, windowless hut, with few objects for play and manipulation. Although the mothers were close by, they rarely talked to their babies, played with them, or even allowed them to crawl. By the time the infants were 1 year old, not only were they intellectually retarded (by American standards), but they were extremely passive, quiet, unalert, fearful, and unsmiling.

What happens to the children in this culture as they grow older and experience the world beyond the small, dark hut? Kagan and Klein tested the children of various ages; all apparently had been raised similarly in infancy. The investigators used their own tests (designed to be as free from cultural bias as possible) to measure memory, perceptual analysis, conceptualization, and the ability to make inferences. Not surprisingly, the 5- and 6-year-old children scored far behind both American middle-class youngsters and urban Guatemalan children. But the test scores of the 11-year-olds from these isolated villages were very surprising. The 11-year-olds had caught up to both their American and Guatemalan counterparts on these tests.

It was not only children's intellectual functioning that responded to an improved environment. In contrast to the infants, who were passive, unalert, and fearful, Kagan and Klein described the 11-year-olds as gay, alert, active, and full of expression. According to Kagan, examples such as these and the Iowa studies do not illustrate the impotence of the early environment but the potency of the environment in which the child is living presently.

The Kagan and Klein study caused a stir in the popular press and was greeted with skepticism by some in the scientific community. How could the Guatemalan children perform on a par with middle-class American youngsters when there were such differences between the two culturally, educationally, and experientially? Others were concerned about the political implications of the report. Since the Guatemalan children needed no special intervention to realize their potential, would special intervention programs in this country, designed to raise the intellectual functioning of disadvantaged children, be thought unnecessary and canceled?

Kagan and Klein, however, interpreted their findings as support for intervention programs in this country. They pointed out that, unlike the Guatemalan society, our society generally does not provide a more stimulating environment for children who experience early deprivation. Instead, our children are labeled and rank-ordered from an early age and frequently are offered or denied further experience on this basis. Say Kagan and Klein (1973), "We live in a society in which the relative retardation of a four-year-old seriously influences his future opportunities because we have made relative retardation functionally synonymous with absolute retardation" (p. 960). Kagan believed that his research signaled educators and congressmen, "Look . . . that poor black child isn't doomed, his resilience is enormous. Do not erase him from the book of life" (Senn 1975, p. 81).

There is another chapter to the Kagan and Klein study, one that makes their findings even less easy to interpret. Six years after the original study, they returned to Guatemala and retested the youngsters in the original village of San Marcos (Kagan, Klein & Finley 1979). They also tested children in a less-isolated Guatemalan town that was larger, more complex, and more modern (San Pedro). This time, the investigators designed tests that were much more difficult than the original tests had been. On the more complex tests, each age group of San Marcos children performed far below their American middle-class counterparts and scored two to three years behind their San Pedro counterparts. The original tests designed by Kagan and Klein had been too easy and had not tapped more advanced skills.

There is no clear-cut interpretation of this new data, as there was no clear-cut interpretation of the older data. Those believing in the critical nature of early experience could argue that early deprivation was responsible for the poorer performance of the San Marcos children. But the argument that the present environment was responsible is also compelling; compared to San Pedro, San Marcos lacked variety and challenge, provided poor nutrition, placed little value on learning, and offered inferior and inconsistent schooling (Kagan, Klein & Finley 1979).

In support of this latter interpretation is data from developing countries which have clearly demonstrated that cognitive performance improves as a result of schooling, even if that schooling is delayed until middle childhood or adolescence (see Rutter 1980).

The Lebanese Studies. The ability of the later environment to compensate for an earlier one was supported by a study conducted in a poor-quality Lebanese orphanage by Dennis and Najarian (1957). Nothing unusual was reported about the infants in this orphanage. As in previous institutional studies, these babies were severely retarded. Startling, however, was the functioning of the older children (above age 5 or 6) in this same orphanage. At the age of 4, children were routinely placed in the more stimulating environment of a kindergarten. By the time these children were tested again at age 6, their functioning on performance tests of development and mental ability (memory, maze-solving, and the Goodenough Draw-A-Man Test) was not very different from that of children living in normal environments.

In a different study, Dennis reported that children gained thirty IQ points after being moved at age 6 from a poor-quality to a better-quality orphanage (see Rutter 1980).

The Canadian Study. In 1966, Flint reported on a group of 2- to 4-year-old children who had been raised in a barren, overcrowded, understaffed institution. Flint and his colleagues tackled the job of rehabilitating the institution, increasing its staff, and educating them. Following is Flint's description of the older children (who had had two and one-half to four years of severe adversity and deprivation).

> These inarticulate, undeveloped youngsters who had formed no relationships in their lives, who were aimless and without capacity to concentrate on anything, had resembled a pack of animals more than a group of human beings. We had predicted a long and disappointing period of treatment before there would be any adequate response at all. . . . When affection was displayed towards them, consistent care given, and encouragement offered in such activities as eating, dressing, and washing, they responded with surprising intensity. They seemed to yearn insatiably for adult contacts and attention (p. 138).

After a year, the apathetic behavior which had previously characterized the institution had almost disappeared. According to Flint, the children were developing self-confidence and self-reliance, their activities had direction and purpose, and they were reaching out to new people and new interests.

The Czechoslovakian Twins. A case of Czechoslovakian twin boys, reported in the seventies, powerfully demonstrates just how potent the later environment can be and how resilient some children are (Koluchova 1972, 1976). These twins had spent most of their first eighteen months in an orphanage and then went to live with their father and stepmother. For the next six years, they were beaten and kept in isolation (either in a small, unheated closet or in a barren cellar, where they were forced to stay seated at an empty table). The neighbors were unaware of their existence but reported hearing "inhuman shrieks resembling howling" from the cellar. When the twins were discovered at the age of 7, they suffered from rickets and could barely walk. They were timid, mistrustful, fearful, had no speech, and played very primitively; their mental age was estimated to be that of a 3-year-old's.

A follow-up seven years later, when they were 14, found the twins thriving in a loving foster home. Each had a normal IQ (100 and 101); each had adjusted well in school; each had developed typical interests and skills, such as reading, riding bicycles, swimming, and playing the piano.

MacDonald (1986) hypothesized that the children's companionship throughout their appalling early lives may have played a role in their dramatic recovery.

Late Adoptions. A frequently quoted study is Alfred Kadushin's 1970 report on long-term adoption outcomes for ninety-one older children who had been physically, emotionally, socially, and intellectually deprived during their early years (see Kadushin 1976). The children ranged in age from 5 to 12 at the time of adoption (7.2 years on the average), and all had been in at least one foster home. They had spent an average of three and one-half years with their natural parents, who perhaps could be described as parental disasters, characterized as they were by promiscuity, alcoholism, imprisonment, mental deficiency, mental illness, poverty, and marital conflict. In all cases, the children had been removed from their parents legally (a step usually taken only as a last resort by the courts) because of physical neglect or abuse.

Kadushin interviewed adoptive parents, focusing on their own satisfactions, dissatisfactions, problems, and adjustment. How satisfying a life did these parents have with their older adopted children? Transcripts of the interviews, analyzed by three independent judges, revealed that adoptive parents, as a group, had expressed four times more discrete satisfactions than dissatisfactions.

All the adoptions were not successful. Success was less likely the older the child (some were already 12), the more homes a child had lived in, and the more behavioral problems a child had when adopted. However, it might surprise many to learn that 78 percent of these older adoptions were judged successful (as determined by a composite of parents', interviewer's, and judges' ratings); 13 percent were judged unsuccessful; and 9 percent were judged mixed. These outcomes were only slightly poorer than those generally found in infant adoptions. Kadushin concluded from his data that "older children can be placed for adoption with expectations that the placement will work out to the satisfactions of the adoptive parents" (p. 193).

Kadushin was aware that his results and conclusions were contrary to popular expectations. He also was concerned about the tendency for many social workers and mental health professionals to "overemphasize" the power of the past. He therefore cited nine other studies that had found impressive social and emotional resiliency in adopted or foster children in spite of early trauma and neglect. Most typically, the investigators of these studies also had expressed surprise at their findings. In the words of one such investigator, "No one who has read the records of some of these lives and pondered on them can escape a profound sense of awe at the biological toughness of the human species" (Roe & Burks, cited in Kadushin 1976, p. 195).

Perinatal Trauma. Trauma sometimes strikes a child before, during, or shortly after the birth process. Does this trauma influence later development? Many developmental problems have been attributed to such perinatal traumas, and for good reason. Early investigations that retraced the histories of children who had a wide range of problems (including epilepsy, learning disabilities, and behavioral disorders) had found that these children had experienced more birth complications than had the general population (see Sameroff 1975, Sameroff & Chandler 1975). These birth complications included prematurity, anoxia, and a variety of pregnancy (toxemia, maternal bleeding) and delivery complications. Furthermore, children who had the most serious problems were more likely to have had the greatest number of obstetrical complications.

But were the perinatal traumas responsible for the subsequent problems? To answer this question, more sophisticated research was conducted prospectively. Rather than looking back at the history of children who had developed problems, this new research followed the development of infants who had birth complications to see what, if any, problems they would develop. The results of these prospective studies do not support the implications of the earlier research. After reviewing the research, Sameroff and Chandler (1975) concluded that the majority of infants born with birth complications do not experience long-term difficulties. Often the effects of early birth trauma are apparent throughout infancy and even later. But generally, by elementary school age, there are minimal, if any, differences between the functioning of these children and their age-mates. (The exception may be prematurity. Although intellectual deficits decrease with age, small deficits seem to remain in children born prematurely. Generally, the lower the birth weight, the more serious the deficit.)

Interestingly, Sameroff and Chandler identified a critical factor that generally differentiated the children who had later difficulties and those who did not. This critical factor was the environment in which they were raised. Environments that were compensatory and supportive dissipated the effects of early perinatal trauma. Environments that were stressful and deprived amplified the effects of the early trauma.

Kopp and Krakow (1983) reviewed the research on perinatal trauma more recently and drew conclusions similar to those of Sameroff and Chandler.

Bonding Research. During the seventies, when a growing number of researchers were questioning the critical nature of early experience, new formulations began to be published that reasserted the importance of early events, but this time in a new way (see Chess & Thomas 1982). These formulations concern "bonding" (the formation of deep attachments between parent and infant). The concept of bonding implies an enduring and special relationship. On the part of the parent, it implies a responsible attachment and unique capability to care for the child (Herbert, Sluckin & Sluckin 1982).

The most influential of the bonding formulations was published by pediatricians Klaus and Kennell (1976). It played an important role in changing hospital procedures to allow parents greater contact with their newborns (even premature, low-birth-weight, and ill infants). Klaus and Kennell asserted that bonding is very important to future parent-child relationships and to a child's optimal development. Furthermore, they suggested that there is an optimal time for bonding: *immediately* after delivery. According to this formulation, close and extended contact between parents and child is vitally important during a child's first hours and days.

The concept of bonding has been enthusiastically embraced by the media, the layperson, and some communities of professionals as well. It has been hypothesized that the parent-child relationship is irreparably damaged if separation continues for a matter of weeks immediately after delivery, which commonly is necessary in cases of prematurity, illness, or low birth weight (see Herbert, Sluckin & Sluckin 1982). Furthermore, a failure to bond has been implicated as a cause of later child abuse (see Herbert, Sluckin & Sluckin 1982; Myers 1984).

To what extent has research supported the various assertions of the bonding thesis? Although numerous studies have been cited to support bonding (see Klaus & Kennell 1976), this research has been highly criticized by many reviewers (e.g., Chess & Thomas 1982; Goldberg 1983; Herbert, Sluckin & Sluckin 1982; Lamb 1982; Myers 1984). Many of the studies are animal investigations with questionable applicability to humans. And most of those that studied human mothers and infants have been criticized for at least one of several reasons: they looked at only short-term effects of bonding, they were inconclusive, or they contained numerous methodological flaws or confounding variables. Although some studies found differences in maternal behavior for mothers who had extended early contact with their infants (such as more affection or eye contact initiated), generally differences were short-lived. Other studies found no differences at all. There also is poor support for the hypothesis that early mother-infant separation is a cause of child abuse (see Oates 1986, chapter 6).

The bonding thesis has had positive influences. Changed hospital policies, allowing greater contact between parent and child, provide a more realistic model of how infants should be cared for at home and allow new parents to develop early confidence in caring for their babies.

However, bonding formulations (or perhaps misinterpretations of them) have raised other issues that cause serious concern for many (see Chess & Thomas 1982; Herbert, Sluckin & Sluckin 1982). One such issue is the possibility that "bonding failure" could be used as a catchall explanation for future parent-child problems.

Parent-child difficulties are likely to have multiple causes, and most are more responsive to change than is "bonding failure." It is a sobering thought that once a bonding failure explanation is used, it could possibly deter mental health professionals from pursuing the lengthy process of teasing out other factors that are contributing to current difficulties. The second concern is that it is a disservice to millions of parents to imply that post-delivery separation will impair their relationship with their child. (Many hospitals still allow only limited contact between parents and infant in the days after delivery.)

Klaus and Kennell have recently addressed this last concern (Kennell & Klaus 1984, Klaus & Kennell 1982). Their current writing is more moderate than is the interpretation generally given their original work. They write:

> Obviously, in spite of a lack of early contact experienced by mothers in hospital births in the past 20 to 30 years, almost all these parents became bonded to their babies. The human is highly adaptable, and there are many fail-safe routes to attachment. Sadly, some parents who missed the bonding experience have felt that all was lost for their future relationships. This was (and is) completely incorrect (Klaus & Kennell 1982, p. 55).

Longitudinal Studies

Besides observing the long-term effects of early trauma or deprivation, researchers have investigated the importance of early experience by studying large numbers of people over the course of many years, beginning in infancy. If a person's basic personality is really formed early in life, as a result of some combination of genetic makeup and early experience, there should be a strong relationship between the personality of the child and her personality as an adult. What have these longitudinal studies found? Is personality set in early childhood and consistent over long periods of time? How predictable is the adult based upon our knowledge of her as a child? The following are three longitudinal studies that are widely cited in the literature.

The Berkeley Growth Study. A study conducted at the University of California at Berkeley followed a group of 250 people (randomly selected from birth certificate registrations) for the first three decades of their lives. IQ tests, personality and projective measures, and school records were systematically obtained for each child until the age of 18. Throughout this time, interviews were conducted with the children, as well as with parents, teachers, and siblings. Interviewers were clinical psychologists and pediatricians. Each individual under study was again interviewed at the age of 30.

It was reasoned that if early experience had exerted a strong role upon these individuals' lives, their adult personality and functioning should be predictable from their childhood personality and experiences. Predictions were made by a team of researchers at Berkeley's Institute of Human Development. When the director of the investigation, Dr. Jean Macfarlane (1963), reported the study's findings, her surprise was evident: " . . . seeing them as adults some twelve years later occasioned dramatic shock after shock" (p. 338). Almost 50 percent of this large sample had grown into "more stable and effective adults" than had been predicted by the Berkeley team, which consisted of professionals with "differing theoretical biases." Another 20 percent were "less substantial" as adults than the team had predicted.

Why were their predictions, based on volumes of information about each individual from infancy through adolescence, so inaccurate? Macfarlane cited numerous reasons. Most people were surprisingly able to alter attitudes and patterns of behavior (even long-established ones) that became either counterproductive or ineffective. Some individuals seemed to convert childhood needs into the opposite patterns of behavior in adulthood (for example, many overly dependent children became highly nurturant adults). Some were simply "late bloomers," giving no indication of their eventual good adjustment and success until adulthood. For some, intensely difficult problems acted as growing experiences rather than as handicaps, as had been predicted. (See chapter 5 for relevant discussions.) Finally, there were a number of subjects who had breezed through a carefree childhood and adolescence showing great potential, but as adults, they were discontented and not living up to that potential. In this last group were many of those who had been "overindulged" with status, popularity, and easy success throughout childhood and adolescence. Macfarlane hypothesized that they may have invested too much energy in their images rather than in developing depth. Because of their basic ability, she believed that many still might achieve fulfilling lives.

The researchers did make some accurate predictions (slightly less than one-third). Who were these people whose adult functioning was predictable from childhood and adolescence? Primarily they could be placed into three categories. One category consisted of people who had received extremely inconsistent parental treatment throughout their childhood (for example, overindulgence alternated with severe harshness). This inconsistency, says Macfarlane, seemed responsible for a poor adjustment that was never overcome. The second category was the mentally retarded, and the third consisted of individuals who had developed very strong defenses. Individuals in this latter group essentially had built a barrier around themselves which protected them from the outside world. However, it insulated them from many new learning experiences as well. Consequently, their early behavior and approaches to life perpetuated themselves throughout childhood and adolescence and continued into adulthood.

The Fels Study. Jerome Kagan and H.A. Moss (1962) studied a population of Caucasian middle-class subjects from birth to adulthood. This study, which employed naturalistic observations during childhood and interviews during adulthood, found virtually no relationships (with one exception) between personality in early childhood and personality in adulthood. The one exception? Kagan (1976) reported:

The sole support for long-term continuity (in the rank-order meaning of the word) was the tendency for passive infant males to be more dependent as adults on their wives or sweethearts than less passive infants (p. 120).

It was not until the children in this study had reached middle childhood (6 to 10 years old) that some moderately strong relationships between childhood and adult personality were found. Kagan (1976) has suggested that the early elementary years may be more critical to adult personality than are the first five years, as has been traditionally believed.

The New York Longitudinal Study. Alexander Thomas and Stella Chess focused on the stability of early temperament in their longitudinal study of 133 children (Thomas & Chess 1977, 1984; Chess & Thomas 1977). These investigators identified temperamental differences in infants, such as activity level, adaptability, responsiveness, persistence, intensity of reactions, quality of moods (e.g., friendliness, pleasantness), and the extent to which infants approached or avoided new situations. Do these basic temperamental differences, obvious even at birth, continue throughout a child's development? Thomas and Chess (1984) reported:

> Continuity over time of one or another temperamental characteristic . . . has been strikingly evident in a number of our subjects . . . In other subjects, striking and even dramatic psychological changes have occurred—changes that appear fundamental and not superficial, and changes which could not have been predicted from earlier life data (pp. 146,153).

Thomas and Chess concluded that it was impossible to look at temperament without looking at the complex interaction between it and the environment. While following this study group over many years, they recurrently observed that consistency in temperament could not be attributed to stable attributes within the person as much as it could be attributed to continuity in the way the person interacted with his environment. Likewise, discontinuity in temperament appeared to stem from changes in the way the person interacted with his environment. These changes were sometimes instigated by unpredictable changes in life situations or sometimes by changes within the person himself (Thomas & Chess 1984). The following case illustrates this point.

Nancy was a temperamentally difficult child from infancy, who was intense, slow to adapt, and generally negative. Her father, a rigid and demanding person, consistently criticized her and labeled her a "rotten kid." By age 6, she was an explosive child who sucked her thumb and related poorly to other children. Psychotherapy was only mildly beneficial. In the fourth grade, the youngster began to show dramatic and musical talent that earned her considerable recognition, praise, and attention at school. This led her father to see her differently, to have pride in her, and to make allowances for her temperament, which he now believed was a reflection of her "artistic" nature. By the time she was a teenager, there was no evidence of her previous neurotic functioning. Instead, she was lively with an active social life and good school grades. As an adult, she was still functioning well.

In their review of longitudinal studies, Moss and Sussman (1980) report that there are some continuities that emerge during the preschool years and continue throughout development. These continuities are in stylistic behaviors, such as expressiveness, introversion-extroversion, and activity level.

Although few continuities are found between early childhood and adulthood, longitudinal studies find greater consistency between middle childhood and adulthood (Moss & Sussman 1980). Additionally, Rutter (1984) points out that continuity over time is found for some characteristics more so than for others. As examples, he reports that "aggression and conduct disturbance show stronger consistencies over time than do emotional difficulties or temperamental features other than aggressivity" (p. 47).

The Controversy Continues

The results of both longitudinal investigations and early trauma studies challenge the long-held assumption that early experience necessarily maps the course of future psychological development.

But the issue is far from settled. Just how critical those early years are remains a subject of controversy.

The Strong Early Influence Position

There still are many adherents to the strong early influence position, maintaining that the early years are the years most critical to development. This school of thought no longer takes the position that behavior is fixed at an early age (MacDonald 1985). However, they point out that the early years are the time during which a child develops her self-concept, her perceptions and expectations of the world, and her patterns for interpersonal relationships. It is logical, they contend, that these should act as a foundation which directs the child's future psychological development. Once the foundation is laid, the child shapes and interprets her later experiences within the context of her earlier ones. Throughout development, these basic foundations are elaborated upon (see Stroufe 1977, 1979).

The fact that strong links between the early years and later development have not been found may be due, supporters of the strong early influence position say, to the inadequacies of our research rather than to reality (see, e.g., Block 1981, Stroufe 1979). (This possibility is not denied by those who now question the importance of early experience [see Kagan 1986].) The inadequacies in research could lie in poor research designs, insensitive measures of personality, or inadequate conceptualizations or analyses.

Even the startling resiliency shown by many people after their removal from early deprived conditions does not disprove the strong early influence position. Did any of these studies establish conclusively that these individuals' early experience did not influence their later lives dramatically? Were they seriously affected in ways we could not measure? Were they able to maximize their full potential? What might they have become had their early years not been so traumatic or deprived (Stroufe 1977)?

Some support for this latter contention comes from studies of later adoptees. There is a recurrent finding that children adopted later in life have slightly lower IQ scores than do children adopted in infancy (see Rutter 1980). Additionally, a few studies have found that some older adopted children, although able to adjust well in their new home and form strong attachments to their adoptive parents, have social problems at school. They are rated as attention seeking, overfriendly, socially inept, and unpopular—problems that are characteristic of children who remain in orphanages. Generally, children who develop these social problems have had a great many caretakers early in life. It is hypothesized that the lack of opportunity to form early attachments to consistent parent figures interferes with their later social development (see Rutter 1985a).

The lasting influence of the early years may emerge in very subtle ways, too, points out Stroufe (1979). Early experience may play an important role in a person's later response to life stress—either increasing or decreasing his vulnerability. (This is discussed more fully in chapter 5.) Or, says Stroufe, the effects of inadequate early experience may emerge only in special contexts, such as adult intimate relationships or parenting children.

The Other Side of the Controversy

On the other side of the controversy, there are a growing number of scientists who believe that the accumulating evidence is very impressive (e.g., Brim & Kagan 1980; Cairns, Green & MacCrombie 1980; Clarke 1978; Clarke & Clarke 1976, 1986; Featherman 1983; Goldhaber 1979; Kadushin 1976; Rutter 1980; Sameroff 1975; Simmel & Baker 1980). "There are at least 60 careful studies," say Clarke and Clarke (1986), "which indicate that *by itself* early experience does not set for the child an invariant path" (p. 743).

Many of these scientists agree that the evidence does not disprove the traditional strong early influence view, but they argue that the evidence is strong enough to shift the burden of proof to those who adhere to the strong early influence position (Brim & Kagan 1980).

Supporters of this newer school of thought suggest that we have *assumed* the critical nature of the early years for too long and that this assumption has colored our thinking, social decisions, theories, and the questions we ask in research. They point out that the critical nature of the early years is not a fact nor can it be an assumption. Instead, it is a hypothesis, still in need of scientific evaluation (Brim & Kagan 1980, Simmel & Baker 1980).

Throughout the seventies and eighties, a growing number of scientists have been attracted to a life-span approach of human development. As yet, there is no theory of life-span development (Brim & Kagan 1980). Rather, it is an approach or perspective in which development is viewed as an ongoing process, with change continuing throughout life. The past, according to this approach, is only *one* determinant in development because the outcomes of the past are continually transformed by new experiences. It is not that the past is unimportant. Rather, the present is so potent that it acts as a continuous and powerful force pressuring each person to come to terms with it (e.g., see Brim & Kagan 1980, Clarke 1978, Featherman 1983, Kadushin 1976, Sameroff 1975).

A Key Difference

It is tempting to form a mental image of the two developmental models as diametrically opposed to one another—with the life-span position viewing the early years as unimportant and the strong early influence position viewing them as critical. But such a mental image would be incorrect. Those who view development as an ongoing process do not argue that the early years are unimportant (e.g., Cairns, Green & MacCrombie 1980; Goldhaber 1979; Kagan 1976). One look at the apathy and retardation of the institutionally reared infants would dispel any such notion. This newer view of development contends that the early years can have serious consequences. But subsequent years can be just as important or sometimes more important. Later environments can heal old wounds and compel adaptation and change—the more different the later environment, the more likely is change.

In contrast, those adhering to a strong early influence position generally believe that the early years are of overriding importance. They believe it is very difficult—although not necessarily impossible—to alter the effects of early experience (see Brim & Kagan 1980).

These two viewpoints, then, are not diametrically opposed on this issue; their difference, says Kagan (1976), is the degree to which it is believed that the outcomes of early experience are modifiable.

Consistency and Change in Development: Important Factors

It is clear that early experience can have serious effects. But it is clear, too, that many children make impressive recoveries from adverse early experiences (Rutter 1980). Some researchers, therefore, have tried to identify the conditions under which the effects of early experience are likely to continue or to fade. Some of these conditions follow.

Environmental Continuity

Many researchers point out that most children experience continuity in their environment over time. It is this continuity, they say, which is responsible for the persistence of psychological attributes developed during the early years (see Cairns & Hood 1983; Clarke & Clarke 1976; Kagan, Kearsley & Zelazo 1978; Rutter 1980, 1985a; Wachs 1986). In other words, if the early circumstances continue (for example, highly stimulating environment, good parent-child relationships, inconsistent discipline, family conflict, neglect, abuse), then one would expect that the child's early psychological attributes would persist as well (for example, personality characteristics, sense of security, emotional problems, IQ, and so forth). One could argue that it is the cumulative effects of rearing conditions or even the current rearing conditions that are responsible for the child as she is today, rather than the persistence of any early experience effects. Some scientists suggest that the psychological structures developed during the early years must be reinforced by the later environment if they are to persist over time (see Kagan, Kearsley & Zelazo 1978; Wachs 1986). Otherwise, it is likely that there will be dramatic changes in the child.

Although children usually experience a good deal of continuity, life is not static, and some change is likely. Some youngsters are cast on unpredicted courses by chance encounters or by unforseen crises. And all children face discontinuities as each new phase of development and life is reached. Milestones (such as leaving the security of the home, achieving new levels of cognitive development, entering adolescence) demand change, adaptation, and a certain amount of personal restructuring.

The changing nature of each new level of development may be one reason why children's early deficits or assets sometimes appear to fade over time; the demands of a new level of maturity may be different from those of a former level. Hence, we find low correlations between "intelligence" in infancy and later "intelligence," and the successful student is not always a success in the work force.

Chains of Events

One way that early experience can have long-term effects is by setting into motion a chain of events, each event making the next more likely (Clarke & Clarke 1986). For example, adverse early environments are likely to provide children with fewer coping skills, thereby increasing their vulnerability to future stress and adversity. Self-concepts and perceptions are likely to bias future interactions and interpretations of events. Early school success is likely to set the stage for future success, and so forth.

Chains of events can be quite complex, as illustrated by the following example, taken from the literature. It is a recurrent finding that individuals who experience the death of a parent in early childhood are at greater risk to experience depression in adulthood (see Rutter 1985b). However, recent research indicates that the early childhood loss per se is not the critical factor in determining increased vulnerability to adult depression. It appears that early parental loss leads to adult psychiatric problems only when the loss results in long-term inadequate care for the child or long-term emotional instability in the child's family (see Rutter 1985b). The younger the child, the more likely he will be affected by these adverse conditions and the longer he will experience them.

Thus, early parental death sometimes leads to chronically unsatisfactory family circumstances. It begins a chain of events which combine to increase a child's vulnerability to later adversity. Rutter (1985b) points out that the chain of events is not inevitable; neither are the consequences. Each link in the chain can be altered along the way by any number of events.

About these chains of events, Rutter (1983) writes:

> The question of how far early experiences have long-term effects extending into later childhood or even adult life has proved remarkably difficult to answer. However, it is clear that the links between infancy and adulthood are complex, indirect, and uncertain (p. 2).

Individual Differences

It is evident that children differ markedly in their reactions to life events and in their malleability and resiliency. Even in the adoption studies that suggested some lasting consequences of early experience, only a portion of the children developed social problems later in development (see MacDonald 1985). Undoubtedly many factors contribute to children's individual differences. Some have been identified, including the following.

Biological Makeup. Because genetic and hormonal factors can influence children's reactions to environmental events, a child's biological makeup can influence her malleability and contribute to her consistency throughout development (Cairns & Hood 1983, Kadushin 1976). One child adapts easily to recurrent changes, another is resistant to even minor changes. What is challenging to one is a catastrophe to another.

However, even biological makeup is not cast in concrete. Especially in humans, biological makeup can be modified (either intensified or diminished) through interactions with the environment (Cairns, Green & MacCrombie 1980; Cairns & Hood 1983; Chess & Thomas 1977; Clarke, Clarke & Reiman 1958). This was clearly demonstrated in the New York Longitudinal Study, which focused on the stability of temperament.

Environmental Protective Factors and Risk Factors. Research has found that one reason children respond differently to adversity is because of factors within their environment. The environments of some children buffer them from the adversities they encounter, whereas the environments of others increase their vulnerability to similar adversities.

The environmental buffers enjoyed by some children have been labeled protective factors. Examples are close relationships with warm loving parents and positive experiences outside the family. These relationships and positive experiences can go a long way in protecting a child from the negative consequences of whatever adversity life deals him. Children who are buffered by many protective factors can show marked recovery from severe adversity as well as positive adaptations throughout their lifetime (see Garmezy 1985, Rutter 1985b, Werner 1986).

The environments of other children, however, are not so kind. They contain numerous risk factors which increase the child's vulnerability to whatever adversities he encounters. Examples of risk factors are poor relationships with parents, prolonged parental conflict, and poverty and overcrowded living conditions. The more environmental risk factors to which children are chronically exposed, the less likely they are to cope successfully with new adversities they encounter (see Garmezy 1985, Rutter 1985b, Werner 1986).

Protective factors and risk factors are discussed more fully in chapter 5.

Age. A child's malleability seems to decline gradually with age (Clarke 1978, Kadushin 1976, MacDonald 1985). Related to age is the length of time she spends in an environment. The longer she remains in an adverse environment (and the more adverse it is), the more likely it will have some enduring effects on her (Clarke 1978; MacDonald 1985, 1986).

One argument often used to support the strong early influence view is that intervention with an older child is less effective than intervention with a younger one. Rutter (1980) points out, however, that one cannot equate a child who has experienced two years of adversity with a child who has had six, nine, or twelve years of adversity. Of course, effective intervention is more difficult with the latter.

Implications of the Research

In spite of many unanswered questions, our current state of knowledge has implications to evaluate and incorporate into everyday dealings with children and their parents.

Remove Some of the Pressure from the Early Years

The assumption that a child's early experiences have permanent consequences has made the early years a time of intense concern for many parents and society in general. Some parents feel so much pressure to prepare their child for his future, they have neither the time nor perspective to relax and enjoy this period for its own sake. Psychologist Edward Zigler's (1973) anecdote of the "mobile syndrome" reflects the pressure so often felt. Zigler recalls that for a long time after it was publicized that placing a mobile over infants' cribs improved their later performance on certain tasks, he encountered anxiety-laden mothers who were concerned whether there was anything they could do to make up for their not having had a mobile for their child as a baby. Many of the children involved were already teenagers!

Zigler's anecdote illustrates the deep concern, anxiety and guilt experienced by many parents who believe that the early years are a one-shot deal and that mistakes made then have consequences throughout life. Parents would be comforted to know that "mistakes" will be made but they can be rectified. Jerome Kagan (1979) noted that:

> Even though the behaviors of parents influence young children, often dramatically, and the child's profile at one year might predict his or her behavior 6, 12, or 18 months later, it has been difficult to demonstrate that most of the child's early attributes have an indefinite life. It appears that some problems observed during the first year continue for two or three years and they gradually vanish due, we suppose, to the therapeutic effect of new experiences (p. 888).

And for the professional, psychiatrists Stella Chess and Alexander Thomas (1982) write:

> We now have a much more optimistic vision of human development. The emotionally traumatized child is not doomed, the parents' early mistakes are not irrevocable, and our preventive and therapeutic intervention can make a difference at all age-periods (p. 221).

The term *critical period* in human development has now been replaced with the softer terms *sensitive* or *optimal periods*. These terms imply that although it *may* be easier for environmental events to influence a child during certain periods of development, the child retains degrees of plasticity after that period (Columbo 1982, Myers 1984, Rutter 1980).

A number of researchers believe the research has major implications for social policy (e.g., Brim & Kagan 1980, Lerner & Hood 1986, McCarthy 1986). Although intervention during the early years may be the most cost-effective approach, they argue that the research makes a good case that social services can begin at later ages with a reasonable expectation of success—assuming the services are good enough (Brim & Kagan 1980, Lerner & Hood 1986). The research also indicates that services should continue over time. It can no longer be assumed that a brief intervention during the early years will have long-term effects. A child's circumstances must be improved throughout development (Lerner & Hood 1986).

Continuity: The Key?

Just as it can no longer be assumed that a brief early intervention will have long-term effects, it can no longer be assumed (as it commonly is) that starting early is the whole key to success. It is often heard that if a child is given a good early start emotionally, it will assure her later adjustment; if she is given a stimulating early environment, it will assure her high IQ; if a child is taught to read early, she will always be ahead. But it now appears that continuity of those good early experiences may be the crucial link to success, the link we often fail to consider (see Goldhaber 1979). Giving a child a good early start may give her an edge in successfully coping with the chance encounters and calamities of life, but the quality of her environment in middle childhood and in adolescence is also important (Rutter 1979, 1980). Similarly, providing a child with a stimulating early environment may not guarantee that she will always have a high IQ. IQ has been found to drop when later environments take a turn for the worse (Fogelman & Goldstein 1976). And teaching a preschooler to read will not guarantee that she will always maintain her early lead over her age-mates. It appears that such gains are lost unless children are given continued opportunities to build on those early skills at a faster rate than their age-mates (see Teale & Jeffries 1982). Once again, it is not that the early environment is impotent but that the current one often is so potent (Kagan 1976).

After reviewing the research, J. McVicker Hunt (1979) concluded, "A major share of early losses can be made up if the development-fostering quality of experience improves, and a great deal of early gain can be lost if the quality of experience depreciates" (p. 136).

Children's early problems and difficulties will not necessarily continue into later life, but neither will their early strengths necessarily continue into later life. This implies that some of the intense concern usually focused upon the early years should be distributed throughout development: the quality time, the enriched environments, the interest, and the tender care given children as infants, toddlers, and preschoolers, should be continued throughout their development. All stages of development appear to be important. It appears that good starts can be lost and poor starts, with careful effort, can be remedied.

References

Block, J. 1981. "The Many Faces of Continuity." *Contemporary Psychology* 26: 746–50.

Bowlby, J. 1951. *Maternal Care and Mental Health.* N.Y.: Columbia University Press.

Brim, O.G., Jr. and Kagan, J. 1980. "Constancy and Change: A View of the Issues," in O.G. Brim, Jr. & J. Kagan, eds., *Constancy and Change in Human Development.* Cambridge, Mass.: Harvard University Press.

Bronfenbrenner, U. 1976. "Is Early Intervention Effective? Facts and Principles of Early Intervention: A Summary," in A.M. Clarke & A.D.B. Clarke, eds., *Early Experience: Myth and Evidence.* N.Y.: The Free Press.

Cairns, R.B., Green, J.A., & MacCrombie, D.J. 1980. "The Dynamics of Social Development," in E.C. Simmel, ed., *Early Experience and Early Behavior.* N.Y.: Academic Press.

Cairns, R.B. & Hood, K.E. 1983. "Continuity in Social Development: A Comparative Perspective on Individual Difference Prediction," in P.B. Baltes & O.G. Brim, Jr., eds., *Life-Span Development and Behavior.* Vol. 5. N.Y.: Academic Press.

Chess, S. & Thomas A. 1977. "Temperamental Individuality from Childhood to Adolescence." *Journal of the American Academy of Child Psychiatry* 16: 218–26.

———. 1982. "Infant Bonding: Mystique and Reality." *American Journal of Orthopsychiatry* 52: 213–22.

Clarke, A.D.B. 1978. "Predicting Human Development: Problems, Evidence, Implications." *Bulletin of the British Psychological Society* 31: 249–58.

Clarke, A.D.B., Clarke, A.M. & Reiman, S. 1958. "Cognitive and Social Changes in the Feebleminded—Three Further Studies." *British Journal of Psychology* 49: 144–57.

Clarke, A.M. & Clarke, A.D.B. 1976. "The Formative Years?" in A.M. Clarke & A.D.B. Clarke, eds., *Early Experience: Myth and Evidence*. N.Y.: The Free Press.

———. 1986. "Thirty Years of Child Psychology: A Selective Review." *Journal of Child Psychology and Psychiatry* 27: 719–59.

Clarke-Stewart, K.A. & Fein, G.G. 1983. "Early Childhood Programs," in P.H. Mussen, ed., *Handbook of Child Psychology*. 4th ed. Vol. 2. N.Y.: John Wiley and Sons.

Columbo, J. 1982. "The Critical Period Concept: Research, Methodology, and Theoretical Issues." *Psychological Bulletin* 91: 260–75.

Davis, K. 1947. "Final Note on a Case of Extreme Isolation." *American Journal of Sociology* 45: 554–65.

Dennis, W. & Najarian, P. 1957. "Infant Development Under Environmental Handicap." *Psychological Monographs* 71. No. 7.

Featherman, D.L. 1983. "Life-Span Perspectives in Social Science Research," in P.B. Baltes & O.G. Brim, Jr., eds., *Life-Span Development and Behavior*. Vol. 5. N.Y.: Academic Press.

Flint, B.M. 1966. *The Child and the Institution*. Toronto: University of Toronto Press.

Fogelman, K.R. & Goldstein, H. 1976. "Social Factors Associated with Changes in Educational Attainment Between 7 and 11 Years of Age." *Educational Studies* 2: 95–109.

Garmezy, N. 1985. "Stress-Resistant Children: The Search for Protective Factors," in J.E. Stevenson, ed., *Recent Research in Developmental Psychopathology*. Oxford: Pergamon Press.

Goldberg, S. 1983. "Parent-Infant Bonding: Another Look." *Child Development* 54: 1355–82.

Goldfarb, W. 1943. "The Effects of Early Institutional Care on Adolescent Personality." *Journal of Experimental Education* 12: 106–29.

Goldhaber, D. 1979. "Does the Changing View of Early Experience Imply a Changing View of Early Development?" in L. Katz, ed., *Current Topics in Early Childhood Education*. Norwood, N.J.: Ablex Publishing Corp.

Harlow, H.F. 1958. "The Nature of Love." *American Psychologist* 13: 673–85.

Herbert, M., Sluckin, W. & Sluckin, A. 1982. "Mother to Infant 'Bonding'. " *Journal of Child Psychology and Psychiatry* 23: 205–21.

Hunt, J.M. 1979. "Psychological Development: Early Experience." *Annual Review of Psychology*. Vol. 3. Palo Alto, Calif.: Annual Reviews, Inc.

Kadushin, A. 1976. "Adopting Older Children: Summary and Implications," in A.M. Clarke & A.D.B. Clarke, eds., *Early Experience: Myth and Evidence*. N.Y.: The Free Press.

Kagan, J. 1976. "Resilience and Continuity in Psychological Development," in A.M. Clarke & A.D.B. Clarke, eds., *Early Experience: Myth and Evidence*. N.Y.: The Free Press.

———. 1979. "Family Experience and the Child's Development." *American Psychologist* 34: 886–91.

———. 1986. "Rates of Change in Psychological Processes." *Journal of Applied Developmental Psychology* 7: 125–30.

Kagan, J., Kearsley, R.B. & Zelazo, P.R. 1978. *Infancy: Its Place in Human Development.* Cambridge, Mass.: Harvard University Press.

Kagan, J. & Klein, R.E. 1973. "Cross-Cultural Perspectives on Early Development." *American Psychologist* 28: 947–61.

Kagan, J., Klein, R.E., Finley, G.E., Rogoff, B. & Nolan, E. 1979. "A Cross-Cultural Study of Cognitive Development." *Monographs of the Society for Research in Child Development* 44 (5, Serial No. 180).

Kagan, J. & Moss, H.A. 1962. *Birth to Maturity.* N.Y.: John Wiley and Sons.

Kennell, J.H., & Klaus, M.H. 1984. "Mother-Infant Bonding: Weighing the Evidence." *Developmental Review* 4: 275–82.

Klaus, M. & Kennell, J. 1976. *Maternal-Infant Bonding.* St. Louis, Mo.: C.V. Mosby.

———. 1982. *Parent-Infant Bonding.* St. Louis, Mo.: C.V. Mosby.

Koluchova, J. 1972. "Severe Deprivation in Twins. A Case Study." *Journal of Child Psychology and Psychiatry* 13: 107–14.

———. 1976. "A Report on the Further Development of Twins After Severe and Prolonged Deprivation," in A.M. Clarke & A.D.B. Clarke, eds., *Early Experience: Myth and Evidence.* N.Y.: The Free Press.

Kopp, C. & Krakow, J.B. 1983. "The Developmentalist and the Study of Biological Risk: A View of the Past with an Eye Toward the Future." *Child Development* 54: 1086–1108.

Lamb, M.E. 1982. "Early Contact and Maternal-Infant Bonding: One Decade Later." *Pediatrics* 70: 763–68.

Lazar, I. & Darlington, R.B. 1982. "Lasting Effects of an Early Education." *Monographs of the Society for Research in Child Development* 47: (2–3, Serial No. 195).

Lerner, R.M. & Hood, K.E. 1986. "Plasticity in Development: Concepts and Issues for Intervention." *Journal of Applied Developmental Psychology* 7: 139–52.

MacDonald, K.B. 1985. "Early Experience, Relative Plasticity and Social Development." *Developmental Review,* 5: 99–121.

———. 1986. "Early Experience, Relative Plasticity, and Cognitive Development." *Journal of Applied Developmental Psychology* 7: 101–24.

Macfarlane, J. 1963. "From Infancy to Adulthood." *Childhood Education* 39: 336–42.

McCarthy, J.M. 1986. "Educational Implications of Developmental Problems in the Preschool Years," in B.K. Keogh, ed., *Advances in Special Education.* Vol. 5. Greenwich, Conn.: JAI Press.

Moss, H.J. & Sussman, E.J. 1980. "Longitudinal Study of Personality Development," in O.G. Brim, Jr. & J. Kagan, eds., *Constancy and Change in Human Development.* Cambridge, Mass.: Harvard University Press.

Myers, B.J. 1984. "Mother-Infant Bonding: The Status of This Critical-Period Hypothesis." *Developmental Review* 4: 240–74.

Oates, K. 1986. *Child Abuse and Neglect: What Happens Eventually?* N.Y.: Brunner/Mazel Publ.

Rosenzweig, M.R., Bennett, E.L. & Diamond, M.C. 1972. "Chemical and Anatomical Plasticity of Brain: Replications and Extensions," in J. Gaeto, ed., *Macromolecules and Behavior.* 2d ed. N.Y.: Appleton-Century-Crofts.

Rutter, M. 1979. "Maternal Deprivation, 1972–1978: New Findings, New Concepts, New Approaches." *Child Development* 50: 283–305.

———. 1980. "The Long-Term Effects of Early Experience." *Developmental Medicine and Child Neurology* 22: 800–15.

Rutter, M. 1983. "Stress, Coping, and Development: Some Issues and Some Questions," in N. Garmezy & M. Rutter, eds., *Stress, Coping, and Development in Children.* N.Y.: McGraw-Hill Book Co.

———. 1984. "Continuities and Discontinuities in Socioemotional Development: Empirical and Conceptual Perspectives," in R.N. Emde & R.J. Harmon, eds., *Continuities and Discontinuities in Development.* N.Y.: Plenum Press.

———. 1985a. "Family and School Influences: Meanings, Mechanisms and Implications," in A.R. Nicol, ed., *Longitudinal Studies in Child Psychology and Psychiatry.* Chichester: John Wiley and Sons.

———. 1985b. "Resilience in the Face of Adversity: Protective Factors and Resistance to Psychiatric Disorder." *British Journal of Psychiatry* 147: 598–611.

Sameroff, A.J. 1975. "Early Influences on Development: Fact or Fancy?" *Merrill-Palmer Quarterly* 21: 267–94.

Sameroff, A.J. & Chandler, M.J. 1975. "Reproductive Risk and the Continuum of Caretaking Casualty," in F.D. Horowitz, M. Hetherington, S. Scarr-Salapatek, & G. Siegel, eds., *Review of Child Development Research.* Vol. 4. Chicago: University of Chicago Press.

Scarr, S. & Weinberg, R.A. 1986. "The Early Childhood Enterprise: Care and Education of the Young." *American Psychologist* 41: 1140–46.

Senn, M.J.E. 1975. "Insights on the Child Development Movement in the United States." *Monographs of the Society for Research in Child Development* 40 (3–4, Serial No. 161).

Simmel, E.C. & Baker, E. 1980. "The Effects of Early Experiences on Later Behavior: A Critical Discussion," in E.C. Simmel, ed., *Early Experience and Early Behavior.* N.Y.: Academic Press.

Skeels, H.M. 1966. "Adult Status of Children with Contrasting Early Life Experiences: A Follow-Up Study." *Monographs of the Society for Research in Child Development* 31 (3, Serial No. 105).

Skeels, H.M. & Dye, H.B. 1939. "A Study of the Effects of Differential Stimulation on Mentally Retarded Children." *Proceedings of the American Association on Mental Deficiency* 44: 114–36.

Spitz, R.A. 1946. "Anaclitic Depression." *Psychoanalytic Study of the Child* 2: 313–42.

Stroufe, L.A. 1977. "Early Experience: Evidence and Myth." *Contemporary Psychology* 22: 878–80.

———. 1979. "The Coherence of Individual Development." *American Psychologist* 34: 834–41.

Suomi, S.J. & Harlow, H.F. 1972. "Social Rehabilitation of Isolate-Reared Monkeys." *Developmental Psychology* 6: 487–96.

Teale, W.H. & Jeffries, L.E. 1982. "Reading in Early Childhood: A Selected Annotated Bibliography." *The Exceptional Child* 29: 127–36.

Thomas, A. & Chess, S. 1977. *Temperament and Development.* N.Y.: Brunner/Mazel.

———. 1984. "Genesis and Evolution of Behavioral Disorders: From Infancy to Early Adult Life." *American Journal of Psychiatry* 141: 1–9.

Wachs, T.D. 1986. "Understanding Early Experience and Development: The Relevance of Stages of Inquiry." *Journal of Applied Developmental Psychology* 7: 153–65.

Werner, E.E. 1986. "The Concept of Risk From a Developmental Perspective," in B.K. Keogh, ed., *Advances in Special Education.* Vol. 5. Greenwich, Conn.: JAI Press.

Zigler, E. 1973. "On Growing Up Learning and Loving." *Human Behavior* (March): 65–67.

2
Employed Mothers and Day Care

The Journal of the American Academy of Child Psychiatry recently published results of a survey that assessed health professionals' attitudes toward maternal employment (Martin, Burgess & Crnic 1984). The great majority of those surveyed were pediatricians and family practitioners (some in private practice, others in academia). Forty percent of these professionals believed it preferable for mothers not to work outside of the home, and 19 percent reported they actively tried to influence mothers not to do so. Over 50 percent believed a mother's outside employment would have a negative impact on a child under the age of 2. Twenty percent believed it would have a negative impact on children as old as 6 to 12.

However, over the past three decades, economic and social conditions have sent increasing numbers of mothers into the work force: 45 percent of mothers with infants under a year old, 50.8 percent of mothers with children under the age of 3, and 59.9 percent of women with 3- to 5-year-olds are now employed outside the home (World Almanac 1986, Young & Zigler 1986).

What has research revealed about the effects of maternal employment and day care on children? Why is there such a broad range of opinions among the professionals whose advice parents seek on this issue?

After reviewing the research, Bronfenbrenner and Crouter (1982) recently concluded, "Taken by itself, the fact that a mother works outside the home has no universally predictable effects on the child" (p. 51). A mother's employment is likely to have some ramifications (both positive and negative) for herself, for family relationships, and for children. However, the specific effects of her employment will differ, depending upon her satisfaction with her employment status, the nature of her employment, her social class, the sex and age of a child, and the quality of supplemental care the child receives.

In this chapter, both the maternal employment and the day care literature will be surveyed. The two are not synonymous. Not all children of employed mothers are in day care, and not all day care children have employed mothers (Hoffman 1984a).

Maternal Employment

Ramifications for Mothers

Many studies have reported that employed mothers are happier with their lives, feel more competent, have greater self-esteem, and are less depressed than are their nonemployed counterparts (see Baruch, Biener & Barnett 1987; Hoffman 1984b; Rutter 1982; Scarr & Weinberg 1986). In contrast, stay-at-home mothers appear to have a growing morale problem in today's social climate (Hoffman 1984b). Although women with high-status jobs enjoy the greatest benefits, even low-status jobs offer women social ties, positive feedback, structure, and stimulation (Baruch, Biener & Barnett 1987).

Employment has its costs to mothers, however. Studies consistently have found that mothers shoulder the major burden of both child care and household responsibilities (see Gilbert & Rachlin 1987, Lamb 1982, Piotrkowski & Repetti 1984, Scanzoni & Fox 1980, Szinovacz 1984). Although precise estimates vary from study to study, a representative example is that husbands of working wives do roughly 32 percent of the total family work, compared to 21 percent done by husbands of full-time homemakers (see Stein 1984). As spouses' salaries approach equality, husbands increase their contribution to household chores. However, even in high-level dual-career families, the division of labor generally is rather traditional, despite professed beliefs of equality (see Gilbert & Rachlin 1987, Piotrkowski & Repetti 1984, Rachlin 1987). (In defense of husbands, several studies have found that men think they make a more significant contribution to household chores than they actually do, and they underestimate their wives' stress and work overload. Additionally, husbands generally spend more time on the job than do their spouses [see Stein 1984].)

Not surprisingly, complaints about work overload frequently emerge in studies of employed mothers (see Hoffman 1984b, Skinner 1982). Complaints about the problems of dual roles are also common (see Hoffman 1984b, Skinner 1982). Generally, women are affected adversely when they experience conflict between family and work roles. Such conflict is associated with increased levels of depression, anxiety, and psychiatric symptoms (Krause & Geyer-Pestello 1985, Parry 1987). Interestingly, Light (1984) found that women who placed career over family had significantly higher anxiety and depression scores than did women who placed family over career.

Ramifications for Family Relationships

A common coping strategy in employed-mother families is compromise—of career aspirations, household standards, and social life (Piotrkowski & Repetti 1984, Skinner 1982). Is the time with children compromised as well? Carew (1978) points out that for most employed mothers, daily interaction with children must take place in the context of a few crowded hours before and after work, along with cooking, dishes, laundry, shopping, housecleaning, and essential child care tasks. Several researchers have investigated parent-child relationships in dual-earner families. The findings of these studies are as follows.

Mother-Child Relationships. In a large-scale survey, parents were asked to keep diaries of the amount of time they spent teaching, reading, talking, and playing with their children, as well as in physical and medical care. Mothers who were employed more than twenty hours per week spent considerably less time in these activities, regardless of the age of their children. However, for college-educated employed mothers, the time difference narrowed: they spent only 25 percent less time involved in these activities than did their nonemployed counterparts (Hill & Stafford, cited in Hoffman 1984b).

What of quality time? Several studies have reported that employed mothers increase the intensity of their interaction with their children, setting aside special times for them or organizing specific activities (see Hoffman 1984b). A study conducted by Goldberg (see Lamb 1982) focused on the amount of one-to-one interaction between middle-class mothers and preschool children. Goldberg found no differences in the amount of one-to-one interaction employed and nonemployed middle-class mothers had with their preschoolers. (Total time spent with children was less for employed mothers, however.) After reviewing the research, Hoffman (1984a) concluded there was no evidence that employed mothers had poorer quality interactions with their children than did stay-at-home mothers.

Father-Child Relationships. Recently, a few investigators have turned their attention to other family relationships in dual-earner families. Several studies have reported provocative results which converge to form a pattern: it may be father-child relationships that are most affected in employed-mother families. The following is a brief look at some of these studies.

An often quoted study, conducted by Pederson and others (1982), observed mothers' and fathers' interactions with their infants in the early evening hours after work. In nonemployed-mother homes, it was fathers who interacted intensely with their infants during these after-work hours. But in employed-mother families, it was mothers who interacted with infants during after-work hours; fathers spent less time with their infants than did either fathers or mothers in single-earner families. The investigators suggested that employed mothers, attempting to compensate for their absence all day, "squeezed" their husbands out of parent-child interactions.

By the time these infants were a year old, fathers were spending more time with them (Zaslow et al., cited in Easterbrooks & Goldberg 1985). However, a study conducted by Chase-Lansdale (1981) found a different problem between fathers and this age child in employed-mother families. One-year-old sons had significantly less secure attachments to their fathers than did sons of stay-at-home mothers. No differences were found for daughters.

Insecure attachments between fathers and infant sons may be transitory. In a study of 2-year-olds, no evidence of insecure father-son attachments was found in dual-earner families (Easterbrooks & Goldberg 1985). But this study reported new difficulties between fathers and toddlers in these families. Fathers interacted less sensitively with their toddlers and generally were more aggravated with them, compared to fathers in single-earner families. The investigators pointed out that fathers in two-earner families took more responsibility for child care tasks, which may have taken time away from more pleasurable interactions with their children.

Fathers' relationships with older children may also be affected by a mother's employment. Fathers in two-earner families have been found to spend significantly less free time with their adolescents (Montemayor 1984), and they are perceived by their college-age daughters to be less friendly and supportive (Jensen & Borges 1986), compared to fathers in nonemployed-mother families. Shortly it will be shown that in low-income dual-earner families, father-son relationships are strained.

At this point, conclusive statements cannot be made about maternal employment effects on father-child relationships, but the potential of troubled relationships between fathers and children should be kept in mind. A great deal of research on this issue is certain in the future.

Ramifications for Children

Hoffman (1984b) points out that the situational demands created by a mother's employment usually force adaptations within the family that can have positive consequences for children. Fathers generally spend more time interacting with children (Easterbrooks & Goldberg 1985, Hoffman 1984a, Lamb 1982), with the exception of adolescents and infants (Montemayor 1984, Pederson et al. 1982). School-age children generally are expected to do more household chores. This can be beneficial since responsibility for chores is associated with enhanced self-esteem in children (see Hoffman 1984b, Lamb 1982). Two-earner families model less stereotyped sex roles. And, not surprisingly, less stereotyped sex role attitudes are found in both preschool and school-age children of employed mothers (see Hoffman 1984b, Lamb 1982). Interestingly, however, differences in sex role attitudes fade in adolescence, perhaps because of peer group pressure at this age for attitudinal conformity (see Montemayor & Clayton 1983). Finally, lower-class youngsters with employed mothers experience more structured and enforced rules, undoubtedly to compensate for the absence of personal supervision.

Is children's overall adjustment affected by their mother's employment? This issue has been investigated in many studies. Reviewers of the research agree that maternal employment per se does not importantly influence children's overall adjustment (see Belsky, Lerner & Spanier 1984; Hoffman 1984b; Lamb 1982; Piotrkowski & Repetti 1984; Rutter 1982). Much more critical, they point out, is a mother's satisfaction with her employment status, whether it be employed or nonemployed. When mothers are satisfied with their roles, they are more likely to have positive interactions and relationships with children, and children are more likely to be adjusted and competent.

Perhaps the most interesting findings reported in this literature are the differential effects of a mother's employment on sons and daughters. Compared to daughters of stay-at-home mothers, those of employed mothers often are more independent, outgoing, personally and socially adjusted, and have higher achievement aspirations. Generally they have a greater admiration for their mothers and for women's competence (see Hoffman 1984a, Lamb 1982). It is believed that working mothers provide daughters a role model of initiative and achievement, which in turn positively affects their daughters' development (Bronfenbrenner & Crouter 1982).

Although mothers' employment shows benefits for girls, benefits for boys have been found less consistently (see Bronfenbrenner & Crouter 1982). Furthermore, some boys seem to be at risk for negative consequences. Reviewers of the literature note an often reported finding that middle-class sons of employed mothers are lower achievers than are sons of stay-at-home mothers (Bronfenbrenner 1986, Bronfenbrenner & Crouter 1982, Hoffman 1984a, Lamb 1982, Montemayor & Clayton 1983). Lower IQ scores, lower grade point averages, and lower achievement test scores have all been found, although all studies have not found this pattern of lower achievement. The reason for boys' poorer achievement is not clear (Lamb 1982), although many speculations have been offered (Hoffman 1984b). Bronfenbrenner & Crouter (1982) suggest that, compared to their employed counterparts, middle-class stay-at-home mothers may supervise their sons more closely—overseeing schoolwork, monitoring television viewing, and encouraging selective friendships.

Interestingly, poorer achievement is not found for sons of employed mothers in low-income families. However, these boys generally have different problems. As a group, they are more poorly adjusted, have strained relationships with their fathers, and have lower levels of respect and admiration for their fathers (Hoffman 1984a, Lamb 1982). These boys' difficulties probably have their roots in their subculture, in which sex role attitudes are still very traditional. A boy from a lower socioeconomic background is more likely to interpret his mother's working as an indication of his father's failure to provide for his family (Lamb 1982).

Other negative consequences for boys may have been uncovered by Montemayor (1984), who found that arguments between adolescent sons and mothers were significantly more frequent, intense, and of longer duration when mothers were employed. And we already saw that 1-year-old sons (but not daughters) were less likely to have secure attachments to their fathers in employed-mother families.

It is not clear why a mother's outside employment should have different consequences for sons and daughters. Several hypotheses have been proposed. Some authors point to the recurring finding that boys are more likely to be affected by environmental events than girls (e.g., Bronfenbrenner & Crouter 1982). Boys' greater vulnerability has been found in the divorce literature (see chapter 4), the stress literature (see chapter 5), the maternal employment literature, and some trends have been found in the day care literature as well (see Howes & Olenick 1986, Rutter 1982). A second reason for the observed sex differences is suggested by several studies that found differential treatment of boys and girls in one-earner and two-earner families (see Hoffman 1984a). In employed-mother homes, daughters tend to receive more attention and to be described more positively than are sons. In contrast, in nonemployed-mother families, it is boys who receive more attention and who are described more positively. It is not clear why this should be the case. According to Hoffman (1984a), evidence indicates that families typically interact with boys more so than with girls. However, speculates Hoffman, mothers who are juggling dual roles may find sons stressful, since they are more likely than girls to be active and noncompliant. A third hypothesis for the observed sex differences found in children of employed mothers has been offered by Montemayor and Clayton (1983). They suggest that having a role model of competence and achievement may be an advantage for girls that compensates for the disadvantages that a mother's employment may have. Sons, on the other hand, experience only the disadvantages.

Caveats and Conclusions

Before drawing any conclusions from the maternal employment literature, a number of issues must be raised.

1. It must be remembered that the data is correlational. Families of employed and nonemployed mothers are compared, but differences are not necessarily caused by a mother's employment. Mothers who are employed and nonemployed are likely to differ in ways other than their employment status. Obvious differences, such as marital status and socioeconomic status, can be controlled in research. More subtle differences, such as attitudinal and personality differences, are more difficult to control. For example, there is some evidence that mothers who are employed while their children are infants tend to be more career-oriented and to value motherhood less than do mothers who stay at home with their infants (see Lamb 1982). Mothers' attitudinal and personality differences are likely to influence children's development as much as their employment status does.

2. Most of the research in this area has been conducted with school-age children. Less is known about maternal employment effects on infants and toddlers, for whom mothers' employment is a fairly recent phenomenon. Most research with infants, toddlers, and preschoolers has focused on the effects of day care.

3. Whether a mother's employment is part-time or full-time may prove to be an important variable when considering maternal employment effects. Unfortunately, researchers have often failed to make distinctions between the two, and no consistent standards have been used in studies to define "employment" (Baruch, Biener & Barnett 1987; Parry 1987). Although part-time employment has not been extensively studied as a separate entity, a few studies have compared the two and have found important differences. Maternal part-time employment seems to have more positive outcomes for children (see Hoffman 1984b). Youngsters whose mothers work part-time have higher self-esteem, better social adjustment, and more positive attitudes toward parents than do children whose mothers work full-time. Hoffman (1984b) attributes these better child outcomes to less role strain among

part-time employed mothers. Interesting differences in daughters of part-time and full-time employed mothers were found in one large-scale national study conducted with adolescents (Douvan and Adelson 1966). On several dimensions, adolescent daughters of full-time and part-time employed mothers fell at the extremes, with those of nonemployed mothers falling in the middle. Daughters whose mothers worked part-time were the most independent, spent the most leisure time with their parents, and had the most mature relationships with parents. Next came daughters of nonemployed mothers, and last, the adolescent daughters of full-time employed mothers. Douvan and Adelson speculated that part-time employed mothers provided a model of achievement and competence, yet still had time to spend with their offspring.

In concluding their reviews of the literature, several authors have pointed out that maternal employment and nonemployment each has its costs and benefits for children (Hoffman 1984b, Piotrkowski & Repetti 1984). Although some of these costs and benefits have been identified, reviewers make no claims that current research evidence represents a complete picture in this area. There may be effects of either maternal employment or nonemployment that are not accessible to measurement and evaluation (Hoffman 1984b). There also may be "sleeper effects" (Easterbrooks & Goldberg 1985), that is, influences that are not apparent for many years. For example, perhaps relationships between grown children and parents are different, depending upon whether mothers were at home or employed while those children were growing up.

The relationships that have been identified are complex ones that defy simple generalizations (Montemayor and Clayton 1983). Clearly, when one looks at maternal employment "effects," one must also consider other variables: a mother's satisfaction, which influences the quality of mother-child interactions; the sex and age of the child; social class; father-child relationships; the number of hours a mother is employed; and the quality of the supplemental care received by the child.

This last variable, supplemental care, will now be discussed. It may prove to play the most influential role in the effects of maternal employment.

Day Care

Alison Clarke-Stewart (1984) has called day care effects "one of the most complex environmental issues developmental psychologists have yet faced" (p. 61). Not only do complex family variables enter into the picture, but so do numerous factors associated with variable day care situations.

Basically, there are three types of supplemental day care: home care (with a sitter), family day care (in a caregiver's home, along with a relatively small group of children and one or two caregivers), and center day care (usually a commercial building with larger numbers of children and caregivers).

Each type of day care is likely to offer children a different set of experiences (Belsky, Steinberg & Walker 1982). Center day care often has a school-like atmosphere, generally with superior play materials, equipment, and physical space. Family day care has a home atmosphere, generally with more individual attention. Home care with a sitter provides a familiar environment. However, the variability in day care situations is so enormous that differences within types of day care can be as large as differences between types (Belsky, Steinberg & Walker 1982).

The largest share of day care research has been conducted in university-based, high-quality day care centers with infants, toddlers, and preschoolers. It is this kind of care which we know most about. Less is known about average- or poor-quality centers and about family day care. Within the last decade, however, significant progress has been made toward rectifying this void. Least is known about home care with sitters, which is highly dependent upon the competence of individual caregivers.

Day Care Effects

Research studying day care effects has investigated day care's influence on children's emotional, intellectual, and social development.

Emotional Development. Most of the research studying emotional development has focused on children's attachment to their mothers. This emphasis has been sparked by fears that long periods of daily separations would prevent youngsters from forming their primary attachments to parents. The concern has been for children under 2, for whom attachments are forming and becoming well established.

There is wide agreement among those who have reviewed this research that day care children do form their primary attachments to mothers rather than to caregivers (Belsky, Steinberg & Walker 1982; Bradley 1982; Clarke-Stewart & Fein 1983; Etaugh 1980; Gamble & Zigler 1986; Lamb 1982; Rutter 1982). Infants' and toddlers' attachments are inferred from their behavior. Day care children prefer mothers over caregivers when distressed, bored, or in need of help. Day care children are more distressed at separations from mothers than separations from caregivers and respond more enthusiastically to reunions with mothers than to reunions with caregivers (see Clarke-Stewart & Fein 1983, Rutter 1982).

Recently, concerns have shifted from whether day care disrupts the formation of attachments to whether day care influences the quality of those attachments (Belsky 1984, Clarke-Stewart & Fein 1983, Gamble & Zigler 1986, Lamb 1982, Rutter 1982). In assessing quality, researchers have looked at older infants' and toddlers' responses in three situations: their separation distress when mothers leave them unexpectedly and without warning in a strange situation; their proximity seeking in an anxiety-provoking situation (that is, their attempts to stay close to mothers in an unfamiliar setting that includes a stranger); and their response to reunion with their mothers after a separation (Clarke-Stewart & Fein 1983).

Generally, securely attached older infants and toddlers are secure in their mothers' presence (freely exploring their environments), they seek contact with mothers in anxiety-provoking situations, and they seek closeness with mothers after a separation. There are two types of insecure attachments shown by some older infants and toddlers. An *anxiously* attached child appears to be less secure in his mother's presence, acutely distressed during separations from her, and responds both with anger and proximity seeking when reunited with her. A child who has an *avoidant* attachment, on the other hand, actively avoids his mother when reunited after a separation (Rutter & Garmezy 1983).

Clarke-Stewart and Fein (1983) analyzed twenty-eight attachment studies in the day care literature and found some clear patterns. Day care infants and toddlers tend to seek less proximity with their mothers in strange situations and are more likely to ignore or to actually avoid their mothers when reunited after separations. These behavioral patterns are not found in all day care children and have been found only in some studies (Clarke-Stewart & Fein 1983).

However, avoidance of mothers and less proximity seeking has been found often enough among day care youngsters for researchers to search for the conditions that cause this behavior. The fact that this behavior is not characteristic of most day care children suggests that it is not day care per se, but day care in conjunction with other conditions, that may raise the risk of disturbed mother-child relationships. The following conditions have been identified.

Early starts. Evidence is emerging that the likelihood of insecure attachments is increased when day care begins during the infant's first year (see Barglow, Vaughn & Molitor 1987; Belsky 1984; Clarke-Stewart & Fein 1983; Gamble & Zigler 1986; Young & Zigler 1986). Note that early starts do not inevitably lead to insecure attachments. Most infants who begin day care before their first birthday do form secure attachments. However, early day care starts may make a child more vulnerable if she encounters other negative environmental events.

Poor-quality day care is an example of a negative environmental event. Infants placed in poor-quality or unstable care prior to their first birthday are more likely to develop insecure attachments (see Belsky 1984). The issue of quality will be discussed shortly.

Family stress also increases the risks that day care will have a negative impact on parent-infant attachments (see Gamble & Zigler 1986). In unstable caretaking environments, the quality of attachments fluctuates in response to family stress. In stable caretaking environments, on the other hand, the quality of attachments remains fairly stable (see Gamble & Zigler 1986). Gamble and Zigler (1986) suggest that stress absorbs a mother's energy, rendering her less emotionally available and responsive to her infant. Daily separations from the mother for day care may then exacerbate the stress the infant is already encountering.

Individual differences are likely to influence children's response to day care, say several authors (Bradley 1982, Gamble & Zigler 1986, Rutter 1982). Boys, in fact, have been more likely to display avoidant responses toward mothers than have girls.

This may reflect differential treatment of boys and girls by employed mothers (Clarke-Stewart & Fein 1983). Other likely candidates of influence area are a child's prior experiences and temperament, either of which may increase a child's vulnerability to the effects of different caretaking patterns (Rutter 1982).

An Additive Model of Environmental Impact. In assessing the effects of day care on attachments and emotional development of infants and toddlers, Gamble and Zigler (1986) concluded that the data fit an additive model of environmental impact: as the number and strength of negative environmental encounters increase, there is a greater likelihood of negative impact on a child. For example, poor-quality day care places a child at risk for negative outcomes. (This will be discussed in more detail shortly.) His risks increase if he begins such care in his first year. The risk of negative outcomes rises further if he also comes from a stressful home. His risks grow further, still, if his parents are neglectful, and so on.

Older Day Care Children. Few studies have looked at the emotional adjustment of older day care children. Those that have suggest that age of entry and quality of day care are, once again, important factors. Based upon the limited available data, Belsky (1984) warned that children who begin poor-quality or unstable care during their first year seem more likely to display social and emotional problems in subsequent years.

It appears that early center care may place a child at greater risk than do other forms of day care. McCartney and her colleagues (1982) found poorer emotional adjustment among preschoolers who had been placed in center care during their first year, compared to children who had been in family day care or sitter home care during their first year (before entering center care at a later age). The centers in this study varied in quality.

Intellectual Development. Early concerns about day care effects on intellectual development stemmed from the absence of one-to-one adult-child interactions in day care settings. It was feared that day care would provide inadequate verbal and intellectual stimulation and result in impaired cognitive development (Ruopp & Travers 1982). A large number of studies have investigated this issue.

Reviewers of the research generally have concluded that day care has neither negative nor beneficial effects on children's intellectual development. However, for economically disadvantaged children, day care appears to attenuate the decline in test scores typically found in their home-reared counterparts (Belsky & Steinberg 1978; Belsky, Steinberg & Walker 1982; Bradley 1982; Etaugh 1980). Reviewers often add the caveat that most research has been conducted in high-quality day care settings.

Clarke-Stewart and Fein (1983) came to a different conclusion about day care effects on intellectual development. In their review, they analyzed research according to whether it was conducted in day care centers or in family day care. This analysis revealed that children in day care centers outperformed both parent-care and family day care children on a wide range of intellectual measures. This was true for both lower-class children and middle-class children. And it was true whether children attended centers full-time or part-time.

Why should center-care children outperform home-reared children? These findings are, perhaps, not surprising, given that the high-quality centers most frequently studied in research generally design their programs to foster cognitive development. Do day care center children maintain their early intellectual advantage? The answer, report Clarke-Stewart and Fein, is no. Particularly for middle-class youngsters, by the time parent-care children are 5 (and themselves in school environments), they catch up to their more precocious day care center counterparts.

Social Development. Belsky (1984) concluded that findings about the social development of day care children offer both good and bad news. Day care experience is likely to increase children's positive interactions with peers, but it is likely to increase their negative interactions as well. A common conclusion among those who have reviewed this research is that day care children tend to be more peer-oriented, more assertive, and often more aggressive than are their home-reared counterparts (e.g., Belsky, Steinberg & Walker 1982; Bradley 1982; Gamble & Zigler 1986).

In a very extensive review, Clarke-Stewart and Fein (1983) once again analyzed research conducted in day care centers separately from that conducted in family day care. Once again, they found significant differences in center-care children compared to children in either family day care or parent care. Center children, they say, generally are found to be more self-assured, outgoing, assertive, independent, more comfortable in new situations, and better adjusted when they begin school. At the same time, center-care children generally are found to be more aggressive, less polite, less agreeable, less respectful of others' rights, and less compliant with mothers' and teachers' directives. According to Clarke-Stewart and Fein, these behavioral patterns have been rather consistently found—in both model and mediocre day care center programs, whether children are in centers full-time or part-time, and regardless of how long children have been in center care. These reviewers concluded that center-care children are more socially mature and competent, since most of these behaviors, positive and negative, typically are found in older children. Perhaps a more precise label would be socially precocious.

Clarke-Stewart and Fein report that most of these differences between center children and their peers decrease by the primary grade years. However, the only longitudinal study to continue to adolescence (conducted in London) found that adolescent boys who had been in day care were more peer-oriented, more liked by peers, more aggressive, less conforming to parental requirements, and less influenced by punishment. The home-reared adolescent boys, on the other hand, were more adult-oriented, more conforming to adult standards, more self-controlled, and more interested in academics. No consistent differences were found for girls (Moore

1975). It is unlikely that the sharp contrasts between the day care and home-reared group reflected only their earlier care experiences because the mothers of the two groups were quite different in personality (Rutter 1982). However, some researchers believe more longitudinal research is needed to determine whether there are "sleeper effects" of day care that are not evident for many years (e.g., Belsky, Steinberg & Walker 1982; Cochran & Robinson 1983; Young & Zigler 1986).

Belsky and his colleagues suggest that the behavioral pattern found in center day care children is probably a phenomenon specific to our society (Belsky & Steinberg 1978; Belsky, Steinberg & Walker 1982). Group care, they point out, can have many different sequelae, as evidenced by outcomes in the United States, the Soviet Union, and Israel. According to these authors, day care effects on social development must be viewed within two contexts: (1) American values, which stress aggressiveness, impulsiveness, and egocentrism, and (2) practices of day care center programs. Compared to parents, the staffs at day care centers are found to be more permissive and tolerant of aggressiveness and disobedience, and less likely to set firm standards of behavior (Ambron, cited in Belsky, Steinberg & Walker 1982).

Conclusions and Caveats. Reviewers of day care research generally have been cautiously optimistic in their conclusions. For example, Etaugh (1980) concluded:

> Under optimal conditions, nonmaternal care does not appear to have adverse effects on development (p. 405).

Rutter's review, in 1982, concluded:

> It would be wrong to conclude that day care, any more than home care, is without effects, and it would be misleading to assume that it carries no risks (even though these have been greatly exaggerated in the past) (pp. 22–23).

Clarke-Stewart and Fein (1983), the reviewers who found day care center children to be intellectually and socially advanced, wrote:

> The message suggested by the available data is basically reassuring. If children are placed in a decent program after 2 years of age, effects, if any, are likely to be positive (p. 980).

As is evident from this last statement, the most serious concern still remains with infants and toddlers, which is the fastest growing type of day care. Gamble and Zigler (1986) warn:

> The phenomenon of infant day care is simply too new, and the stakes too high, for either layman or scientist to risk premature conclusions about its effects (p. 27).

Have the findings of day care research warranted such cautious conclusions? The problem, as virtually every reviewer has pointed out, is the limitations of the research in this field. The following are major concerns:

1. Researchers have only assessed a narrow range of psychological outcomes. Do these appropriately reflect total development? Or are there day care effects that are incapable of being measured or that researchers have not had the foresight to measure? Even those outcomes that have been assessed have been done so with rather "gross measures," which may have been insensitive to subtle effects of day care (Brazelton 1986, Clarke-Stewart & Fein 1983, Rutter 1982).

2. Because of the absence of longitudinal studies, research has only looked at the immediate effects of day care, which could be transitory. We have no idea if there are "sleeper effects" which appear later in development (Belsky, Steinberg & Walker 1982; Bradley 1982; Cochran & Robinson 1983).

3. All reviewers have warned that the majority of research has been conducted in high-quality, university-based day care centers, which have programs designed to foster emotional, intellectual, and social development. For many years, researchers have added this caveat and pointed out that this type of care is quite different from that experienced by the average day care child.

The assumption in the day care literature always has been that the quality of care would affect day care outcomes. Recent research, which has focused on the issue of quality, has borne out this assumption. This critical issue of quality will now be discussed.

The Critical Element: Quality

For many years, quality in day care was a rather elusive concept. Although everyone agreed it was important, little attempt was made at precise specifications. Today, however, we have a much clearer picture of at least some of the conditions that define quality. We know how these conditions influence children's day care experience. And we are beginning to learn how these conditions affect children's development.

The single largest contributor to precise conceptualizations of quality day care was the National Day Care Study (Ruopp et al. 1979, Ruopp & Travers 1982, Travers & Ruopp 1978). This was a large-scale national study, designed to determine how specific *regulatable* characteristics of day care affected children's daily experiences and development. Staff-to-child ratios, group size, caregiver qualifications, and other center characteristics were manipulated and investigated. Sixty-seven centers, 200 caregivers, and approximately 1,000 children were studied. A separate study, the National Day Care Home Study (Fosburg & Hawkins 1981), took the same approach with family day care.

The results of the National Day Care Study (NDCS) were "clear and consistent across sites" (Ruopp & Travers 1982). For the first time, it was conclusively demonstrated that there were specifiable characteristics of day care programs that affected children's emotional, social, and cognitive development (Collins 1983). Following are the major findings.

Group Size. One of the most significant findings coming out of the NDCS was the importance of group size, a previously unappreciated variable. It was critically important for all age groups studied—infants, toddlers, and preschoolers.

Interestingly, for preschool children (ages 3 to 5), group size emerged as the single most important variable (Belsky 1984). When groups were relatively small (less than fifteen to eighteen), children made greater gains in standardized tests and were more cooperative, more responsive, and more involved in tasks. There was less conflict and hostility in the room and less aimless wandering. Perhaps the better outcomes which were found in small groups can be explained by the differential care received by children in small groups compared to large ones. When groups were small, teachers were more involved with children—questioning, responding, praising, and comforting.

Group size emerged as an important index of quality in the National Day Care *Home* Study too, influencing caregiver behavior, children's daily experiences, and children's development (Fosburg & Hawkins 1981).

Staff-to-Child Ratios. Although group size was critically important for all groups, an equally important factor for infant and toddler groups was staff-to-child ratio. As the number of children per caregiver decreased: (1) infants and toddlers showed fewer signs of overt distress and apathy, (2) caregivers spent more time interacting with youngsters and less time managing/controlling them, and (3) children were exposed to fewer potential physical threats.

For preschool children, a favorable staff-to-child ratio was important but not as important as small group size. Group size and staff-to-child ratios are quite separate issues because centers often will have large groups of children with several caretakers. Hence staff-to-child ratios can be favorable whereas group size is large. Why is staff-to-child ratio less important than group size for preschool-age children? The NDCS found that when preschool groups were large with many caregivers, the staff spent more time talking with one another and engaging in routine chores, such as working with materials (Ruopp & Travers 1982). Even when adults were interacting with children, the lead teacher typically was responsible for most children, whereas aides worked with only a few. Hence, in large groups, preschool children do not directly benefit from added staff.

Caregiver Training. The third critical variable found by the NDCS was the importance of caregiver training. For youngsters to benefit, however, training had to be in areas related to children, such as child development, early childhood education, or day care. Education in other areas was unrelated to child outcomes (regardless of years of schooling or academic degrees).

When caregivers had child-related training, they were more involved with children—interacting, comforting, responding, questioning, and teaching. The children of trained caregivers were more cooperative and more involved in tasks. They made larger gains on standardized tests, and they interacted more with one another.

Caregiver training was found to be important in family day care too, influencing both caregiver behavior and the quality of children's daily experience.

Further Indices of Quality. The National Day Care Study did not evaluate all aspects of day care settings, and it should not be assumed that group size, staff-to-child ratios, and caregiver training are the only variables involved in quality care. Research conducted since the NDCS has supported the importance of these three variables and has identified others as well (see Belsky 1984). Not surprisingly, characteristics of caregivers and the physical setting are also important.

Involvement of caregivers has frequently emerged as an important determinant of quality (see Belsky 1984). Many hints of its importance were observed in the NDCS. But a large-scale project, conducted by Yale and Harvard University researchers, has demonstrated just how important caregiver involvement is (McCartney et al. 1982, McCartney 1984). These researchers looked at centers which were good in overall quality but which provided limited verbal interaction with caregivers. The children in these centers were reported by their caregivers to be anxious, hyperactive, and aggressive. In fact, these children had higher maladjustment scores than did children attending centers with poorer overall quality but a greater amount of verbal interaction with caregivers (McCartney et al. 1982). Less surprising were findings that children's scores on language tests were significantly higher in centers where children had more verbal interaction with caregivers. Interaction with peers was unrelated to language development (McCartney 1984).

More recently, Phillips, McCartney, and Scarr (1987) found that higher amounts of verbal interaction between caregivers and children were predictive of children's sociability, task orientation, and consideration of others.

Caregiver stability is widely assumed to be an important element of quality, particularly for infants and toddlers (see Gamble & Zigler 1986). Although there is a paucity of data on caregiver stability, Cummings (1980) found that day care infants were less distressed by their mothers' daily departure when left with a stable caregiver with whom they had had consistent contact.

Physical space (both indoor and outdoor) has been found by several studies to be important (see Belsky, Steinberg & Walker 1982). For example, Rohe and Patterson found an interesting correlation: children's aggressiveness, destructiveness, and unoccupied behavior increased as the number of children per square foot increased (see Belsky, Steinberg & Walker 1982).

Minimal Standards for Quality Day Care. Within the past few years, there have been three major efforts to precisely specify minimal acceptable standards for day care (Child Welfare League of America 1984, HEW 1980, National Association for the Education of Young Children 1984). Groups of child development specialists have been involved in each effort, drawing upon empirical evidence as their guides. These standards are not ideal but represent a balance between what appears to be necessary for positive child outcomes and what is economically feasible. Phillips (1986) points out that the guidelines are remarkably similar in all three documents, reflecting the rather strong consensus in the field about the *minimal* acceptable standards for quality day care. Phillips (1986) refers to these minimal standards as thresholds of quality. Following are the *maximum* group size and staff-to-child ratios allowed in these three sets of guidelines. In some cases, there is a range because of differences in standards specified by the three documents. (This data was reported by Phillips 1986.)

	Group Size	*Staff-to-Child Ratios*
Infants	6–8	1:3
Toddlers	12	1:3–1:5
Preschoolers	16–18	1:7–1:9
School-age	24	1:10–1:16

Other guidelines address staff qualifications (some training in early childhood education or child development), health and safety requirements, developmentally appropriate materials and equipment, and unrestricted access to day care settings so parents can observe their children (Phillips 1986).

The Department of Health, Education, and Welfare also developed the following minimal standards for staff-to-child ratios in family day care (see Young & Zigler 1986):

1:6—if all children are over 2 years of age

1:5—if any child is under the age of 2. However, a maximum of two children under age 2 are allowed with this ratio.

1:3—for children under age 2

Outcomes of Poor-Quality Care. Well-controlled studies, designed to compare day care settings of varying quality, paint a picture of negative experiences and outcomes associated with poor-quality day care.

For preschoolers low-quality care is associated with decreased test scores, aimless wandering, conflict and hostility, less sociability, less cooperation, and less consideration of others (McCartney et al. 1982, 1985; Phillips, McCartney & Scarr 1987; Ruopp & Travers 1982; Travers & Ruopp 1978). Poor-quality care may also affect preschoolers' relationships with parents. Peterson and Peterson (1986) reported that preschoolers in poor-quality care were less compliant with mothers' requests and engaged in limited, single-sentence verbal exchanges with mothers, rather than in sustained dialogue as was characteristic of children in high-quality care or parent care.

For infants and toddlers, poor-quality care is associated with overt distress, apathy, limited attention spans, behavioral deviancy, hyperactivity, poor coordination, and limited verbal expressiveness (McCartney et al. 1982, 1985; Ruopp et al. 1979; Ruopp & Travers 1982; Schwarz et al., cited in Belsky 1984; Travers & Ruopp 1978). The greater likelihood of poor-quality attachments for infants who are in poor-quality care has already been discussed.

Quality is clearly the critical element in the day care setting. As Belsky (1984) concluded: "What this analysis suggests is that it is not where the child is reared that is of principal importance but how he or she is cared for. . . . This is as true in a day care milieu as it is in a family environment" (p. 27).

Minimal Acceptable Standards versus State Regulations

The responsibility for day care regulations and licensing lies not with the federal government but with state and local governments. Except for basic health and safety issues, licensing standards vary widely from state to state (Kendall & Walker 1984). Since quality day care has proved so important and since there are now empirically determined minimal standards for group size and staff-to-child ratios, some authors have compared these minimal acceptable standards to those required by each of the states. Young and Zigler (1986) made these comparisons for infants and toddlers, and Collins (1983) did so for 4-year-olds.

Table 2–1 compares the maximum group size allowed by the three sets of professional guidelines with the maximum size allowed by regulations in the fifty states. Few states comply with professional guidelines. Note that most states have no maximum limit to the number of children who can be grouped together. Young and Zigler (1986) point out that in most states, day care centers can comply with staff-to-child ratios while providing assembly line care to large numbers of children in large noisy areas where chaos prevails.

Table 2–1
Maximum Group Size Allowed

	Professional Guidelines[a]	*State Regulations*[b]	
Infants	6–8	6–8	(10 states)
		9–20	(8 states)
		No limit	(32 states)
Toddlers	12	12 or under	(10 states)
		14–16	(5 states)
		20 or above	(4 states)
		No limit	(31 states)
Preschool	16–18	Under 20	(5 states)
		20–45	(12 states)
		No limit	(33 states)

Source: (a) adapted from Phillips (1986); (b) infant and toddler data adapted from Young and Zigler (1986), preschool data adapted from Collins (1983).

Table 2–2 compares staff-to-child ratios allowed by the professional guidelines with those allowed by state regulations. The comparisons are rather startling. Again, few states comply with empirically determined guidelines. Many states allow a single caregiver to be responsible for double and triple the acceptable number of children. Scarr and Weinberg (1986) pointedly illustrate the insurmountable task of one person in complete charge of eight infants or twelve to fifteen toddlers. Even if one were not concerned about the psychological needs of these youngsters, what of the logistics of one person evacuating eight infants or twelve toddlers in an emergency?

Both Young and Zigler (1986) and Collins (1983) obtained their data about state regulations from the Comparative Licensing Study (Johnson and Associates, Inc. 1982). The obvious question is whether states have since changed their regulations to be more compatible with empirically determined guidelines. To determine this, Kendall and Walker (1984) surveyed each state about its changes in day care licensing regulations. Thirty-four states reported changes. However, rather than improving quality, the changes repeatedly involved reduction in staff, additional staff responsibilities, and poorer staff-to-child ratios. For family day care, many states had replaced licensing with registration. (Requirements for registration generally are limited to providing basic health and safety conditions.) The one improvement in regulations made by states was in the area of staff qualifications. At the time of the Comparative Licensing Study, staff qualifications were rather minimal (Young & Zigler 1986). For example, the most common requirement for directors of day care centers was a high school diploma and a minimum age of 18 or 21. For caregivers, thirty-one states did not require even a high school diploma, and nine states

Table 2–2
Staff-to-Child Ratios Allowed

	Professional Guidelines[a]	State Regulations[b]	
Infants	1:3	1:3	(3 states)
		1:4	(18 states)
		1:5–1:8	(21 states)
		No limit	(8 states)
Toddlers	1:3–1:5	1:4–1:5	(13 states)
		1:6–1:7	(7 states)
		1:8–1:10	(21 states)
		1:12–1:15	(6 states)
		No limit	(3 states)
Preschool	1:7–1:9	Under 1:10	(4 states)
		1:10	(20 states)
		1:11–1:18	(22 states)
		1:20 or more	(4 states)

Source: (a) adapted from Phillips (1986); (b) infant and toddler data adapted from Young and Zigler (1986), preschool data adapted from Collins (1983).

allowed 16-year-olds to be a child's primary caregiver (Young & Zigler 1986). By the end of 1983, twenty-six states required some staff to have a Child Development Associate Credential, and other states were considering this change (Collins 1983). By the end of 1984, thirty-six states required in-service training for day care staff as opposed to nineteen states in 1981 (Snow & Creech 1986). Why are states moving in the direction of fewer but better trained staff? The answer is a simple one—cost. If one person is in charge of only three to four infants or six to eight toddlers, her salary must be paid by a small number of parents. Gamble and Zigler (1986) estimate that the cost of high-quality infant day care (small group size, high staff-to-child ratios, trained and stable caregivers, and so on) could exceed $150 per week. Relatively few parents can afford such costs, particularly if they have a number of children in day care. Yet better trained caregivers are comparatively inexpensive because day care traditionally has been an extremely low paid profession. According to Ruopp and Travers (1982), salaries of day care personnel fall in the bottom 5 percent of all wage earners, which is probably one reason for the high turnover rate found among day care personnel.

The Day Care Decision

The renowned child psychiatrist Michael Rutter (1982) has posed two questions. His first question is whether it is essential during children's early years for one parent to remain at home. He responds that the answer must be "no," given that no substantial emotional or social problems are commonly found as a result of day care. His second question is whether it is usually desirable for one parent to remain at home. To which he responds that no general statement is sensible, given the diversity of individual circumstances.

Research suggests that a mother's satisfaction is a critical variable in children's adjustment. Satisfied mothers are more likely to have positive interactions and relationships with children than are dissatisfied mothers. However, Rutter cautions, many other factors must be considered if day care is to have positive outcomes. Minimally, day care must be of good quality, children's needs must be met, there must be time after work for pleasurable interaction between parent and child (when neither is too fatigued to enjoy the other), and parents' working hours and work commitments must be flexible enough so that they can be available when children need them. For the preceding to be feasible, Rutter points to the probable necessity of *both* parents sharing household chores. He suggests that part-time employment may be preferable to full-time when children are under the age of 3.

The American Academy of Pediatrics (1984) made very similar points in responding to the question, Is a mother's working harmful to her children? The variables they focused upon as essential were: a warm, caring, safe, and stimulating day care environment, sufficient vitality at day's end for mothers to nurture children, a mother's satisfaction with her work, and family support and sharing of child care and household work.

Individual Differences. Any day care decision must take children's individual differences into account (Rutter 1982). Some children may not do as well in supplementary care as others. Examples are children with difficult temperaments or insecure attachments. Young children who have had unhappy separation experiences or who must cope with other family stresses may do more poorly as well (Rutter 1982). Additionally, boys may warrant more caution than do girls because day care has been found more likely to affect boys (see Clarke-Stewart & Fein 1983, Gamble & Zigler 1986, Howes & Olenick 1986, Rutter 1982). Interestingly, the effects of day care on boys have not been consistent from study to study. The data are consistent with data obtained in other areas (stress, divorce, maternal employment) that boys are more likely than girls to be affected in some way by environmental events (Bronfenbrenner 1979).

The way in which the individual child responds to day care and separations should be the guiding factor, says Rutter (1982). Relevant here, however, are some findings reported by Blanchard and Main (1979). These investigators found evidence that many young children go through a stressful adaptation period when placed in day care, characterized by emotional and social problems. These problems tend to decrease, however, the longer children remain in supplementary care. (It should be noted that the day care settings in this study were good-quality ones). Belsky (1984) reported that young children generally adapt successfully to supplementary care in six months' time. This, of course, assumes that the care is good.

Age of Entry. The age at which day care is initiated has been the subject of much concern. Several well-respected names in the child development field have suggested that regular supplementary care not begin during the infant's first three to six months (e.g., Brazelton 1986; Zigler & Muenchow 1983). Jerome Kagan and his colleagues (1978) suggest that day care begin either before 7 months or after 18 months. They point out that 7 to 18 months is the time when infants generally become distressed at separations and fearful of unfamiliar people and places. It is also the time attachments are forming and becoming well established (Rutter 1982). Findings reported by Benn (1986) offer support for this recommendation. Benn found that boys were more likely to have insecure attachments when they began day care during the latter part, rather than the earlier part, of their first year. (The youngsters were between 17 and 21 months when tested.)

Concern about day care generally extends to children under the age of 3, according to Rutter (1982). This concern has a number of bases. Children under 3 are highly dependent upon adults. There is a greater likelihood of their responding negatively to repeated separations and to long days away from home. It is generally considered essential, by child development specialists, for children under 3 to receive a great deal of individual attention. (This position has been borne out by studies finding that higher staff-to-child ratios were needed for infants and toddlers if positive outcomes were to be obtained.) Inconsistent caregivers, a common problem in day care, is also a concern for children under 3. If a child does not form attachments to supplementary caregivers, it is feared that no one will be capable of providing her comfort when she is afraid, hurt, sick, or otherwise distressed.

Family Day Care versus Day Care Centers. Of primary importance in day care decisions is the type of day care best suited for the child—home care with a sitter, family day care, or center day care. Although the variations within each type of care are so great that no simple generalizations can be made, each is likely to provide a different set of experiences for children (Belsky, Steinberg & Walker 1982).

Sandra Scarr's research finds that children under the age of 3 generally fare better in family day care (or with sitters at home), where they are likely to receive more adult attention. Preschoolers, she finds, benefit more from a high-quality center with educational opportunities and a larger peer group (Scarr 1984). A look at day care settings may shed some light on her findings. (Attention will be focused on family day care and center care, since home care is so dependent upon caregiver competence that it has seldom been studied. More detailed comparisons can be found in Clarke-Stewart [1982].)

Family Day Care. Family day care offers children a home environment and contact with typical daily living experiences. This is the environment in which much early learning usually takes place (Belsky, Steinberg & Walker 1982). Additionally, it is likely to provide small groups, an important determinant of positive day care outcomes (Bradley 1982). Research comparing this form of care with center care indicates that family day care usually provides children with more adult attention, assistance, and conversation than does center care (see Belsky, Steinberg & Walker 1982; Clarke-Stewart 1982). Although this is a clear advantage, family day care has been found to be unstable over long periods of time, as caregivers lose interest or turn to better paying jobs (see Belsky, Steinberg & Walker 1982; Long, Peters & Gardieque 1985). This, of course, is a clear disadvantage.

Although there are tremendous variations in the quality of family day care, quality appears to be related to the type of family day care involved (Ruopp & Travers 1982). Three distinct types exist (Belsky, Steinberg & Walker 1982). *Unregulated* homes, by far the most prevalent, are not licensed, registered, or supervised. *Licensed* (or regulated) homes are licensed by a government agency and comply with state regulations about group size, health, and safety measures. *Sponsored* homes are not only licensed but are affiliated with a larger administrative agency which provides caregivers with training and other child support services, such as play materials, advice, and emergency backup caregivers.

Studies have found significant differences in these three types of family day care, and these differences affect youngsters' day care experience (see Belsky, Steinberg & Walker 1982; O'Connell 1983; Ruopp & Travers 1982). Sponsored homes generally have better trained caregivers who engage in more positive and stimulating interaction with children. Groups tend to be larger in these settings (often caregivers join forces), but they are small compared to centers. Compared to sponsored homes, licensed homes generally provide less caregiver-child interaction. Usually unregulated homes provide the least caregiver involvement. This perhaps explains findings that toddlers tend to have the most difficulty in unlicensed settings, as shown by more overt signs of unhappiness, less involvement, and more antisocial behavior, compared to toddlers in licensed or sponsored homes (see Belsky, Steinberg & Walker 1982).

Scarr (1984) points out that parents can learn a great deal about an individual family day care situation by detailed interviews with providers—what she believes her job to be, what a typical day in the home would be, the number and ages of other children, activities and experiences provided, and so forth.

Center Day Care. Center care often resembles a preschool program. Belsky and his colleagues (1982) suggest that centers are environments scaled down to a "child sized world," but one which detaches children from typical everyday living experiences found in the home and neighborhood. Compared with family day care, centers usually have poorer caregiver-to-child ratios and larger groups, composed of a narrow age range of children (Clarke-Stewart 1982).

Center care has many advantages, however. It is more likely to provide superior facilities, trained caregivers, educational programs, a rich variety of materials and activities, and a wide variety of peers (Clarke-Stewart 1982, Scarr 1984). Preschool children, says Scarr (1984), are more likely to benefit from these advantages than are infants or toddlers.

Centers vary widely in quality, however, and can be as poor as they can be excellent. Poorly run centers, says Scarr (1984), can resemble prison camps at one extreme and chaos at the other. Generally, smaller centers (with between thirty and sixty children) have more positive outcomes for children. Larger centers (over sixty) offer less sensitivity to individual needs, fewer opportunities for child-initiated activities, and place a heavier emphasis on control (see Belsky, Steinberg & Walker 1982).

Checklists for determining the quality of center care have been provided by Clarke-Stewart (1982), Endsley and Bradbard (1981), and Scarr (1984). These checklists provide parents with very detailed and specific characteristics to look for when selecting day care for their children. The characteristics encompass the physical setting, materials, activities, caregiver behavior, children's behavior, and health and safety features.

The Future of Day Care: Issues and Actions

The most pressing issue facing this country today, write Scarr and Weinberg (1986), is the care and development of children. These investigators believe that our current day care situation is approaching a national crisis. There are three major problems: availability, affordability, and quality.

Presently there is not enough day care for the children who need it. And it is projected that the number of children in need of care will be as high as 10.5 million by 1990 (Schindler, Moely & Frank 1987). Even now, waiting periods for day care centers are long, sometimes eighteen to twenty-four months (Szantin, cited in Phillips 1986). The child care that is available is not affordable for many parents, and it is often poor quality, far below standards considered necessary for positive outcomes (Rutter 1982).

One of the consequences of the current day care crisis is an increased number of latchkey children. Presently, approximately 7 percent of the preschool children of working parents fend for themselves for part or all of the day. This translates into an excess of half a million preschool youngsters (Scarr & Weinberg 1986). A recent study suggested that 40 percent of the children in self-care became latchkey children between the ages of 8 and 10 (Kuchak, cited in Powell 1987). As yet, we know little about the consequences for children, if any, of self-care (Rodman & Cole 1987).

Scarr and Weinberg believe the current day care crisis has been caused by our society's ambivalence about the roles of women and the appropriateness of out-of-home care for young children. However, these no longer are the issues demanding our immediate attention. The burgeoning trend of working mothers is not likely to reverse itself. And as Chess and Thomas (1985) concluded, "The data are abundant and the conclusion clearcut: The children of mothers working outside the home are hot harmed if a satisfactory substitute caretaker (or caretakers) is provided" (p. 223).

The critical issues today are: (1) providing good quality care that will have positive outcomes for children and (2) making it affordable for parents. Many child development specialists have suggested courses of future action. Examples follow.

An immediate step is greater parent involvement in children's day care. According to Young and Zigler (1986), parent involvement up to now generally has been minimal. Yet, parents have tremendous power to influence their child's day care experiences. Parents need to become aware that placing their child in day care is "purchasing an environment" that will affect that child's development (Young & Zigler 1986).

Scarr (1984) suggests the best way to assure good quality day care is for parents to join forces with others in their community, raise money, find a facility, and choose caregivers themselves. Community groups (Rotary, Lions Club, Junior League, PTA, and so on) could be natural allies in a joint effort to increase public consciousness about day care issues and to work towards establishing acceptable standards of child care in their communities.

Some suggest the public schools hold the answer to high-quality affordable day care (e.g., Blank 1984, Caldwell, n.d.). Caldwell points out that school schedules originally were established to accommodate a society in which children were needed for daily early morning and late afternoon chores and for summer field work. Different social realities now face the families which public schools serve. Yet, says

Caldwell, public schools have not risen to meet this need for extended days and summer programs. Interestingly, private schools have. Caldwell points out that public school facilities could be used for younger children as well as for school-age children.

Overwhelmingly, however, child development specialists look to federal government intervention as a necessity for the future of day care. Ruopp and Travers (1982) suggest that government has a responsibility to foster the sound development of its children who represent the future of the nation. Why should government step in once children reach the age of 5 (providing public education) but remain detached from their needs for those first five years? During those years, point out Caldwell and Boyd (1984), a child must learn some of the most important tasks he will ever learn—to trust people, to enjoy learning, how to form friendships, and so forth. Although the home remains the dominant influence in these areas, the day care environment can either reinforce or counter home learning (Caldwell & Boyd 1984).

Many in the field point out that the United States, unlike other Western nations, has no national child care policy (e.g., Brazelton 1986, Scarr 1984, Gamble & Zigler 1986). Brazelton (1986) believes it is the responsibility of mental health and child care professionals to work towards a national policy for child care. Scarr (1984) encourages parents and community groups to become advocates as well. The problem, says Scarr, is the lack of any distinct constituency that supports a single policy.

What national policies have been suggested? Zigler and his colleagues (e.g., Zigler & Muenchow 1983) have long advocated paid infant care leave for a minimum of the first few months after a baby's birth. They believe the evidence warrants this alternative to infant day care. Interestingly, the United States is the only industrialized Western nation that does not make such an option available (Gamble & Zigler 1986). In contrast to other nations, this country seems to encourage early separation, writes Friedman (1984), by such policies as employer-paid incentives for a new mother's early return to work. Additionally, legislators can be pressured to require minimal acceptable standards of quality for day care programs purchased with federal funds (either with direct subsidies or through tax breaks). Scarr (1984) points out the ludicrousness of tax dollars paying for substandard care in which children are "warehoused" in large groups, receiving only custodial care. Better-quality care, of course, is more expensive care. Larger child care subsidies for the poor are needed. Scarr also suggests that all forms of child care be made a fully tax deductible business expense.

The professional community is taking its own steps to improve day care in the future. The National Association for the Education of Young Children (NAEYC) has established a national accreditation program (see Scarr & Weinberg 1986). And innovative and economical techniques to provide in-service training for day care personnel have been developed (Snow & Creech 1986). Examples include videotaped courses on child care and child development (Beeby 1984, Stratton 1983), computer-assisted training, and teleconferencing (telephone hookups, with and without video, between trainers and trainees).

Researchers have already provided us with an abundance of information on day care effects and the conditions under which day care can have positive outcomes for children. Studies must continue to refine our knowledge. Longitudinal research is needed. And many thought-providing issues, raised by child development specialists, need to be addressed (Belsky & Steinberg 1978, Caldwell 1984). How is development affected by inconsistencies between home and day care philosophy and training? Do parents who use day care lose some of their influence in rearing their children? Will early experience in groups lead to more acceptance of different ethnic groups or to more altruistic adults? Belsky and Steinberg (1978) point out that the day care center environment is an age-segregated and child-oriented one, offering limited contact with adult non-caregiver models and few off-limit areas compared to most homes. Does sequestering children in such environments eight to ten hours a day differentially affect development in some ways? Finally, Clarke-Stewart and Fein (1983) point out that day care settings require children to deal with "an adultlike world" of regulations and schedules at an early age. Does such early exposure, they wonder, deny day care children the idyllic period that we have previously associated with childhood?

References

American Academy of Pediatrics Committee on Psychosocial Aspects of Child and Family Health. 1984. "The Mother Working Outside the Home." *Pediatrics* 73: 874–75.

Barglow, P., Vaughn, B.E. & Molitor, N. 1987. "Effects of Maternal Absence Due to Employment on the Quality of Infant-Mother Attachment in a Low-Risk Sample." *Child Development* 58: 945–54.

Baruch, G.K., Biener, L. & Barnett, R.C. 1987. "Women and Gender in Research on Work and Family Stress." *American Psychologist* 42: 130–36.

Beeby, E. 1984. *Orientation to Child Care.* Stillwater, Okla.: Oklahoma Training for Child Care Careers.

Belsky, J. 1984. "Two Waves of Day Care Research: Developmental Effects and Conditions of Quality," in R. Ainslie, ed., *The Child and the Day Care Setting.* N.Y.: Praeger.

Belsky, J., Lerner, R.M. & Spanier, G.B. 1984. *The Child in the Family.* Reading, Mass.: Addison-Wesley Publ. Co.

Belsky, J. & Steinberg, L.D. 1978. "The Effects of Day Care: A Critical Review." *Child Development* 49: 929–49.

Belsky, J., Steinberg, L.D. & Walker, A. 1982. "The Ecology of Day Care," in M.E. Lamb, ed., *Nontraditional Families: Parenting and Child Development.* Hillsdale, N.J.: Lawrence Erlbaum Assoc. Publ.

Benn, R. 1986. "Factors Promoting Secure Attachment Relationships Between Employed Mothers and Their Sons." *Child Development* 57: 1224–31.

Blanchard, M. & Main, M. 1979. "Avoidance of the Attachment Figure and Social-Emotional Adjustment in Day Care Infants." *Developmental Psychology* 15: 445–46.

Blank, H. 1985. "Early Childhood and the Public Schools: An Essential Partnership." *Young Children* 40: 52–55.

Bradley, R.H. 1982. "Day Care: A Brief Review." *Physical and Occupational Therapy in Pediatrics* 2: 73–81.

Brazelton, T.B. 1986. "Issues for Working Parents." *American Journal of Orthopsychiatry* 56: 14–25.

Bronfenbrenner, U. 1979. *The Ecology of Human Development.* Cambridge, Mass.: Harvard University Press.

Bronfenbrenner, U. 1986. "Ecology of the Family as a Context for Human Development: Research Perspectives." *Child Development* 22: 723–42.

Bronfenbrenner, U. & Crouter, A. 1982. "Work and Family Through Time and Space," in S.B. Kamerman & C.D. Hayes, eds., *Families that Work: Children in a Changing World.* Washington, D.C.: National Academy Press.

Caldwell, B.M. n.d. "Day Care and the Public Schools—Natural Allies, Natural Enemies." Unpublished manuscript.

Caldwell, B.M. 1984. "What Is Quality Child Care?" *Young Children* 39: 3–8.

Caldwell, B.M. & Boyd, H.W. 1984. "Effective Marketing of Quality Child Care." *Journal of Children in Contemporary Society* 17: 25–39.

Carew, J.V. 1978. "The Care of Young Children. Some Problems with Research Assumptions, Methods, and Findings," in J.H. Stevens, Jr. & M. Mathews, eds., *Mother/Child, Father/Child Relationships.* Washington, D.C.: The National Association for the Education of Young Children.

Chase-Lansdale, P.L. 1981. "Maternal Employment and Quality of Infant-Mother and Infant-Father Attachment." *Dissertation Abstracts International* 42 (2562B).

Chess, S. & Thomas, A. 1985. "Maternal Employment Outside the Home." in S. Chess & A. Thomas, eds., *Annual Progress in Child Psychiatry and Child Development.* N.Y.: Brunner/Mazel.

Child Welfare League of America. 1984. *Standards for Day Care Service.* Rev. ed. Washington, D.C.: Child Welfare League of America.

Clarke-Stewart, A. 1982. *Daycare.* Cambridge, Mass.: Harvard University Press.

Clarke-Stewart, A. 1984. "Day Care: A New Context for Research and Development," in M. Perlmutter, ed., *Parent-Child Interaction and Parent-Child Relations in Child Development. The Minnesota Symposia on Child Psychology.* Vol. 17. Hillsdale, N.J.: Lawrence Erlbaum Assoc. Publ.

Clarke-Stewart, K.A. & Fein, G.G. 1983. "Early Childhood Programs," in P.H. Mussen, ed., *Handbook of Child Psychology.* 4th ed. Vol. 2. N.Y.: John Wiley and Sons.

Cochran, M. & Robinson, J. 1983. "Day Care, Family Circumstances and Sex Differences in Children." *Advances in Early Education and Day Care* 3: 47–67.

Collins, R.C. 1983. "Child Care and the States: The Comparative Licensing Study." *Young Children* 38: 3–11.

Cummings, F. 1980. "Caretaker Stability and Day Care." *Developmental Psychology* 16: 31–37.

Douvan, E. & Adelson, J. 1966. *The Adolescent Experience.* N.Y.: John Wiley and Sons.

Easterbrooks, M.A. & Goldberg, W.A. 1985. "Effects of Early Maternal Employment on Toddlers, Mothers, and Fathers." *Developmental Psychology* 21: 774–83.

Endsley, R.C. & Bradbard, M.R. 1981. *Quality Day Care: A Handbook of Choices for Parents and Caregivers.* Englewood Cliffs, N.J.: Prentice-Hall.

Etaugh, C. 1980. "Effects of Nonmaternal Care on Children: Research Evidence and Popular Views." *American Psychologist* 35: 309–19.

Fosburg, S. & Hawkins, P. 1981. *Final Report of the National Day Care Home Study.* Vol. 1. Cambridge, Mass.: Abt Books.

Friedman, D.E. 1984. "The Challenge of Employer-Supported Child Care: Meeting Parent Needs," in L.G. Katz, ed., *Current Topics in Early Childhood Education.* Vol. 5. Norwood, N.J.: Ablex Publ. Corp.

Gamble, T.J. & Zigler, E. 1986. "Effects of Infant Day Care: Another Look at the Evidence." *American Journal of Orthopsychiatry* 56: 26–41.

Gilbert, L.A. & Rachlin, V. 1987. "Mental Health and Psychological Functioning of Dual-Career Families." *The Counseling Psychologist* 15: 7–49.

Health, Education, and Welfare (HEW). 1980. "Day Care Regulations." *Federal Register* 45 (55): 17870–85.

Hoffman, L.W. 1984a. "Maternal Employment and the Young Child," in M. Perlmutter, ed., *Parent-Child Interaction and Parent-Child Relations in Child Development. The Minnesota Symposia on Child Psychology.* Vol. 17. Hillsdale, N.J.: Lawrence Erlbaum Assoc. Publ.

Hoffman, L.W. 1984b. "Work, Family and the Socialization of the Child," in R.D. Parke, ed., *Review of Child Development Research.* Vol. 7. Chicago: University of Chicago Press.

Howes, C. & Olenick, M. 1986. "Child Care and Family Influences in Toddlers' Compliance." *Child Development* 57: 202–16.

Jensen, L. & Borges, M. 1986. "The Effect of Maternal Employment on Adolescent Daughters." *Adolescence* 21: 659–66.

Johnson, L. and Associates, Inc. 1982. *Comparative Licensing Study: Profiles of State Day Care Licensing Requirements.* Washington, D.C.: Office of Program Development, Office of Developmental Services, Administration for Children, Youth and Families, Office of Human Development Services.

Kagan, J., Kearsley, R. & Zelazo, P. 1978. "The Effects of Infant Day Care on Psychological Development," in J. Kagan, ed., *The Growth of the Child.* N.Y.: Norton.

Kendall, E.D. & Walker, L.H. 1984. "Day Care Licensing: The Eroding Regulations." *Child Care Quarterly* 13: 278–90.

Krause, N. & Geyer-Pestello, H.F. 1985. "Depressive Symptoms Among Women Employed Outside the Home." *American Journal of Community Psychology* 13: 49–67.

Lamb, M.E. 1982. "Maternal Employment and Child Development: A Review," in M.E. Lamb, ed., *Nontraditional Families: Parenting and Child Development.* Hillsdale, N.J.: Lawrence Erlbaum Assoc. Publ.

Light, H.K. 1984. "Differences in Employed Women's Anxiety, Depression, and Hostility Levels According to Their Career and Family Role Commitment." *Psychological Reports* 55: 290.

Long, F., Peters, D.L. & Gardieque, L. 1985. "Continuity Between Home and Day Care: A Model for Defining Relevant Dimensions of Child Care," in I.E. Sigel, ed., *Advances in Applied Developmental Psychology.* Norwood, N.J.: Albex Publ. Corp.

Martin, H.P., Burgess, D. & Crnic, L.S. 1984. "Mothers Who Work Outside of the Home and Their Children: A Survey of Health Professionals' Attitudes." *Journal of the American Academy of Child Psychiatry* 23: 472–78.

McCartney, K. 1984. "The Effect of Quality Day Care Environment Upon Children's Language Development." *Developmental Psychology* 20: 244–60.

McCartney, K., Scarr, S., Phillips, D. & Grajek, S. 1985. "Day Care as Intervention: Comparisons of Varying Quality Programs." *Journal of Applied Developmental Psychology* 6: 247–60.

McCartney, K., Scarr, S., Phillips, D., Grajek, S. & Schwarz, J.C. 1982. "Environmental Differences Among Day Care Centers and Their Effects on Children's Development," in E.F. Zigler & E.W. Gordon, eds., *Day Care: Scientific and Social Policy Issues.* Boston: Auburn House.

Montemayor, R. 1984. "Maternal Employment and Adolescents' Relations with Parents, Siblings, and Peers." *Journal of Youth and Adolescence* 13: 543–57.

Montemayor, R. & Clayton, M.D. 1983. "Maternal Employment and Adolescent Development." *Theory Into Practice* 22: 112–18.

Moore, T. 1975. "Exclusive Early Mothering and Its Alternatives: The Outcome to Adolescence." *Scandinavian Journal of Psychology* 16: 255–72.

National Association for the Education of Young Children (NAEYC). 1984. *Accreditation Criteria and Procedures of the National Academy of Early Childhood Programs.* Washington, D.C.: NAEYC.

O'Connell, J.C. 1983. "Research in Review. Children of Working Mothers: What the Research Tells Us." *Young Children* 38: 63–70.

Parry, G. 1987. "Sex-Role Beliefs, Work Attitudes, and Mental Health in Employed and Non-Employed Mothers." *British Journal of Social Psychology* 26: 47–58.

Pederson, F.A., Cain, R., Zaslow, M. & Anderson, B. 1982. "Variation in Infant Experience Associated With Alternative Family Roles," in L. Laosa & J. Sigel, eds., *Families as Learning Environments for Children.* N.Y.: Plenum Press.

Peterson, C. & Peterson, R. 1986. "Parent-Child Interaction and Day Care: Does Quality Day Care Matter?" *Journal of Applied Developmental Psychology* 7: 1–15.

Phillips, D. 1986. "The Federal Model Child Care Standards Act of 1985: Step in the Right Direction or Hollow Gesture?" *American Journal of Orthopsychiatry* 56: 56–64.

Phillips, D., McCartney, K. & Scarr, S. 1987. "Child-Care Quality and Children's Social Development." *Developmental Psychology* 23: 537–43.

Piotrkowski, C.S. & Repetti, R.L. 1984. "Dual Earner Families." *Marriage and Family Review* 7: 99–124.

Powell, D.R. 1987. "After-School Child Care." *Young Children* 42: 62–66.

Rachlin, V.C. 1987. "Fair vs Equal Role Relations in Dual-Career and Dual-Earner Families: Implications for Family Interventions." *Family Relations* 36: 187–92.

Rodman, H. & Cole, C. 1987. "Latchkey Children: A Review of Policy and Resources." *Family Relations* 36: 101–5.

Ruopp, R. Travers, J., Glantz, F. & Coelen, C. 1979. *Children At the Center. Final Report of the National Day Care Study.* Cambridge, Mass.: Abt Books.

Ruopp, R. & Travers, J. 1982. "Janus Faces Day Care: Perspectives on Quality and Cost," in E.F. Zigler & E.W. Gordon, eds., *Day Care: Scientific and Social Policy Issues.* Boston: Auburn House.

Rutter, M. 1982. "Social-Emotional Consequences of Day Care for Preschool Children," in E.F. Zigler & E.W. Gordon, eds., *Day Care: Scientific and Social Policy Issues.* Boston: Auburn House.

Rutter, M. & Garmezy, N. 1983. "Developmental Psychopathology," in P.H. Mussen, ed., *Handbook of Child Psychology.* 4th. ed. Vol. 4. N.Y.: John Wiley and Sons.

Scanzoni, J. & Fox, G.L. 1980. "Sex Roles, Family, and Society: The Seventies and Beyond." *Journal of Marriage and the Family* 42: 743–56.

Scarr, S. 1984. *Mother Care/Other Care.* N.Y.: Basic Books.

Scarr, S. & Weinberg, R.A. 1986. "The Early Childhood Enterprise: Care and Education of the Young." *American Psychologist* 41: 1140–46.

Schindler, P.J., Moely, B.E., & Frank, A.L. 1987. "Time in Day Care and Social Participation of Young Children." *Developmental Psychology* 23: 255–61.

Skinner, D.A. 1982. "The Stressors and Coping Patterns of Dual-Career Families," in H.I. McCubbin, A.E. Cauble & J.M. Patterson, eds., *Family Stress, Coping, and Social Support.* Springfield, Ill.: Chas. C. Thomas Publ.

Snow, C.W. & Creech, S.H. 1986. "Designing In-Service Training," in K. Vander Ven & E. Tittnich, eds., *Competent Caregivers—Competent Children.* N.Y.: The Haworth Press.

Stein, P.G. 1984. "Men in Families." *Marriage and Family Review* 7: 143–62.

Stratton, B. 1983. *Child Development.* Stillwater, Okla.: Oklahoma Training for Child Care Careers.

Szinovacz, M.E. 1984. "Changing Family Roles and Interactions." *Marriage and Family Review* 7: 163–201.

Travers, J. & Ruopp, R. 1978. *National Day Care Study: Preliminary Findings and Other Implications.* Cambridge, Mass.: Abt Books.

World Almanac and Book of Facts, 1987. 1986. N.Y.: Newspaper Enterprise Association, Inc.

Young, K.T. & Zigler, E. 1986. "Infant and Toddler Day Care: Regulations and Policy Implications." *American Journal of Orthopsychiatry* 56: 43–55.

Zigler, E., & Muenchow, S. 1983. "Infant Day Care and Infant Care Leaves." *American Psychologist* 38: 91–94.

3
Television: Today's Most Important Socializer?

I n 1982, the National Institute of Mental Health published a two-volume government report entitled "Television and Behavior: Ten Years of Scientific Progress and Implications for the Eighties" (NIMH 1982; Pearl, Bouthilet, Lazar 1982). In the ten-year period covered by this report, more than 2,500 research projects had been published that studied some facet of television's influence.

The report put an end to any illusion that television is just mere entertainment. Rather, it concluded that television's influence on children, both short- and long-term, is almost comparable to that of family and school (NIMH 1982, p. 87). Other specialists in the field have not been so "conservative" in their appraisal. For example, in a major reference tome for pediatricians, Lisbeth Schorr (1983) wrote that television "must now be considered a major agent—perhaps *the* major agent—in the socialization of children" (p. 305).

An examination of both the NIMH report and research published since that time will clarify why social scientists currently attribute such importance to television. Much of this research points to television's negative influence, but it also demonstrates how this formidable medium can be made to work for children rather than against them.

Before looking at television's influence, one should first look at children's viewing habits and at their television experience—it is very different than one might expect.

Amount and Content of Viewing

It has been estimated that upon completion of twelve years of schooling, the average child will have spent 11,000 hours in school but 22,000 hours watching television (e.g., Hutchinson 1979). This translates into 3 to 4 hours daily, which is consistent with Nielsen statistics. For example, the 1985 Nielsen estimates of the average amount of television watched weekly by different ages were (*World Almanac* 1986):

Age	Television per Week
2 to 5 years old	28 hours, 15 minutes
6 to 11 years old	27 hours, 22 minutes
Teens	23 hours, 33 minutes

A comparison of these statistics with 1983 estimates reveals that elementary school-age children increased their TV viewing by 2-1/2 hours per week during this two-year period. However, other groups' viewing fluctuated only about an hour (*World Almanac* 1984).

Research conducted at the University of Massachusetts suggests that children's involvement may not be as consuming as these statistics suggest. Researchers there have used video cameras to assess the time children visually attend to the television set during viewing time. They found that both school-age children and adolescents spend roughly one-third of their viewing time doing other things—playing with toys, reading, interacting with others, leaving the room, and so forth. This was true regardless of how much TV children watched (Anderson et al. 1985, 1986). The time that preschool children attend to television is less. It dramatically increases each year from ages 1 through 5 and levels off at about 70 percent at school age (Anderson et al. 1986).

What do children watch during these hours? According to Nielsen reports, the majority of this time is spent viewing adult-oriented commercial television. Educational and news programs do not occupy a large percentage of viewing time. Surprisingly, children's programs occupy only 11 percent of viewing time for youngsters between the ages of 2 and 11 (see Abelman 1987).

A Child's Television Experience

The image of the mesmerized child, vegetating in front of the television set and passively consuming prepackaged trivia, is inconsistent with current research evidence (Anderson & Lorch 1983, Anderson & Smith 1984, Wright & Huston 1983). There are two aspects of a child's television experience that generally are unappreciated. The first is the active processing in which she must engage before she can make sense of her television viewing. The second is the marked differences between a child's perceptions of television programs and those of an adult.

Look, for a moment, at television from a child's perspective. For children, the content of television generally is both complex (with intertwining plots) and unfamiliar (due to children's limited experiences). Most typically, this content is presented at a fairly rapid pace, with abrupt shifts in time, location, characters, and complex camera angles. (In the once-popular "Dukes of Hazzard," there were shifts in either scene or visual perspective every five seconds on the average [Anderson & Smith 1984].) Any single half-hour television program can be filled with zooms, pans, cuts, inserts, fades, flashbacks, sound effects, voice-overs, and so forth.

Yet a child must make sense of this barrage of stimulation, differentiate between important and incidental information, and integrate events in their proper sequence and time frame. Not only that, he must infer events that were never actually shown, he must make connections between widely spaced events to detect cause and effect, and he must infer the motives and feelings of television characters (Anderson & Smith 1984, Wright & Huston 1983). All this from a child with limited cognitive processing abilities and limited experiences about the world!

The evidence indicates that children approach television viewing actively. They select, integrate, and interpret information based upon their cognitive abilities and their knowledge of situations and events (see Anderson & Smith 1984; Wright & Huston 1983; Rice, Huston & Wright 1986). Furthermore, their attention is guided by an active attempt to comprehend what they see (Anderson & Smith 1984; Lorch, Bellack & Augsbach 1987). They are not, as is often charged, interested only in being entertained by television's fast pacing and flashy techniques. In fact, when children are shown "Sesame Street" in Greek, their attention is reduced significantly (Anderson et al. 1981).

Despite their active attempts to process television content, children's comprehension of commercial television is meager. According to the evidence, preschoolers' understanding is fragmentary. Children's understanding and comprehension is still very poor as late as third grade. Even by eighth grade, their comprehension has not yet reached the level of adults' (Collins 1979, 1982).

Children's television experience is further influenced by their difficulty distinguishing television from reality. Children progress from equating TV with reality, to believing TV events probably happen in reality, to becoming gradually more sophisticated with age (see Greenfield 1984). The confusion of young children between television and reality is pointedly demonstrated in a study conducted by Quarforth (1979). He found that middle-class kindergarten children had difficulty distinguishing between human, animated, and puppet television characters. They also believed TV characters were inside the set, perhaps lowered by ropes. Primary grade children still accept much of what they see on television as real (Garry 1967). Some types of programs pose more of a problem to this age child than do others. For example, they can judge Westerns as unreal, but they are not so sure about crime and detective stories which are closer to real life (Garry 1967). School-age children still have difficulty deciding about the reality of adult-oriented prime time programs because of their realistic nature (Abelman 1984b). Even many preadolescents believe popular television characters, such as Fonzie, are real rather than characters portrayed by actors (see Singer 1982). What of televised violence? Children's ability to detect the unrealistic nature of television violence increases over time as they progress from grade one through grade five (Eron & Huesmann 1986).

For many years then, "children do not see and hear and understand the same things on a television show that adults see, hear, and understand" (NIMH 1982,

p. 23). Sometimes this can have important implications. For example, because of television's complexity, children are more likely to focus on the obvious features of a program (such as violence), and they often miss the relationship between cause and effect (such as between motives and behavior and between crime and later punishment) (NIMH 1982, p. 89).

A Child's Perceptions of the World: Does Television Bias Them?

Research has left little doubt that television can be an important influence on a child's perceptions of the world (see Greenfield 1984; Hawkins & Pingree 1982; NIMH 1982; Huesmann & Eron 1986b; Signorielli, Gross & Morgan 1982; Singer & Singer 1983). This has prompted researchers to analyze the kind of world that television portrays. Through statistical analyses of program content, studies have determined that television programs portray many aspects of life inaccurately, such as violence, sex, families, occupations, race, old age, and the consequences of reckless driving (NIMH 1982).

How seriously is a child's view of the world distorted by such misrepresentations? All children are not equally affected by television content. The data indicate that at least two factors (and probably more) play a role in determining their vulnerability. The first factor is the amount of exposure to television. Heavy viewers are more likely to accept what they see on television. The second is the extent to which a child relies on television, as opposed to other sources, for information. The narrower her knowledge base about a topic, the more likely she is to accept TV's version of reality on that topic. She simply has less information with which to balance or counteract her TV experience (see Greenfield 1984, NIMH 1982). Some specific examples will be illustrative.

Perceptions of Violence in the World

Study after study conducted in this country has found that heavy and light TV viewers (both children and adults) have different perceptions of the amount of violence in the world: heavy viewers perceive the world to be a more violent place (NIMH 1982). (Heavy viewers generally are defined as those watching an excess of four hours of TV a day, whereas light viewers are those watching one hour or less daily.) Whose perceptions are accurate and whose are inaccurate? Comparisons with crime statistics reveal that it is heavy viewers who are inaccurate; they perceive the world as more violent than it actually is.

Not only are the perceptions of heavy viewers affected, so are their attitudes and feelings. When compared to their light-viewing counterparts, heavy viewers are more mistrustful, feel more alienated, are more fearful of being involved in violence, and more often feel the need for weapons (NIMH 1982).

In short, it appears that heavy viewers perceive that television's excessive portrayal of violence reflects reality. Some intriguing evidence, reported by Bryant, Carveth, and Brown (1981), suggests it takes only a short time for television's impact on perceptions to be noticeable. These investigators randomly assigned college students to a schedule of light viewing or heavy viewing of violent programs. After only six weeks, students in the heavy viewing group had become more anxious and fearful.

Perceptions of Sex Roles

Children who watch TV heavily generally have more stereotyped perceptions of males and females than do other youngsters, and this tendency is evident as early as at 3 years of age (see Greenberg 1982). Analyses of television program content has revealed that men typically are depicted as rational, competent, stable, and dominant, whereas women are more emotional, warm, sensitive, and submissive. The emphasis for men is on performance, for women on attractiveness, family, romance, and social relationships (NIMH 1982).

Some programs are now aimed at counteracting these stereotypes, but these comprise a small percentage of TV fare, particularly when reruns of older shows are taken into account. Interestingly, analyses of many of these newer shows reveal that stereotyped sex roles are still present. They are just more subtle. For example, many programs portray women in exciting, difficult, and daring jobs, but the women are more emotional than men and often depend upon men in some capacity (Himmelweit & Bell 1980). For the television writer and director, sex role stereotypes serve a useful purpose. They help to develop a believable character and situation in a very brief period of time.

Sex role stereotypes are further perpetuated by television commercials, and commercials bombard children far more than any single program. There are, of course, the obvious examples of women advertising household cleansers and men advertising beer. But other commercials perpetuate stereotypes in more subtle ways. Research at the University of Kansas, for example, found commercials for girls' and boys' toys to have different clusters of features associated with them. Commercials for boys' toys generally had loud music, action, sound effects, and frequent cuts, whereas commercials for girls' toys had fades, dissolves, and background music (see Greenfield 1984).

Perceptions of Other Aspects of Life

Television's inaccurate portrayals of other aspects of life are a concern among social scientists (NIMH 1982). Sexual behavior, alcohol consumption, and reckless driving are three examples. Television's references to extramarital sex are five times more frequent than to marital sex (NIMH 1982). Alcohol is the most common beverage visible on television, according to program analyses. And usually it is shown as a pleasurable and fun aspect of social life, without risk or consequence, even among heavy or chronic drinkers (NIMH 1982). Fast and reckless driving is a favorite television theme but is seldom shown with consequential accident or injury, even though traffic accidents are a leading cause of death among young adults (NIMH 1982).

Research has not specifically investigated television's impact on children's perceptions in each of these areas. But there is ample evidence of its influence on perceptions in many other areas. Writing for the NIMH report, Signorielli and her colleagues (1982) concluded:

> Over the past decade, and across a large number of samples of all ages, substantial evidence has been accumulated that heavy viewers are more likely than are light viewers to hold perspectives and outlooks which are more congruent with television imagery (p. 170).

Television's Potential for Positive Influence

The bulk of studies point to television's negative influence, but this formidable medium has the potential for positive influence as well. Just as it can create inaccurate perceptions of the world, it can function to develop accurate perceptions. Television programs do not uniformly transmit inaccurate or objectionable messages. There are a variety of accurate, positive messages available if one actively seeks them out and selects programs that foster them.

Similarly, just as television can perpetuate stereotypes, it can alter them. An example was provided by "Freestyle," a public television thirteen-part series, developed to reduce sex-role stereotypes in 9- to 12-year-olds. Pre- and post-testing of 7,000 children who watched the series revealed some changes in attitudes toward nontraditional work and family roles (Johnston & Ettema 1982).

Early "Sesame Street" research further demonstrated television's ability to alter stereotypes, this time racial stereotypes. Follow-ups of children who had watched the program for two years reported that white children had developed more positive attitudes toward minorities, and minority children had gained in self-confidence and racial pride (see Greenfield 1984).

Television Violence:
Does It Instigate Aggression?

The concern about television violence dates back more than thirty years—at least to 1952 when the first congressional hearing on television programming was conducted. Yet over the years, in spite of increasing concern by Congress and citizens' groups, violence on TV has continued. In fact, since the mid-sixties, TV violence has increased. (The percentage of violent shows are the same, but the amount of violence depicted on these shows has been on the rise [NIMH 1982].) And the

NIMH (1982) reports that more violence is shown on children's weekend programs than on prime-time television (five violent acts per hour on prime-time programs and eighteen violent acts per hour on children's weekend programs).

What is the answer to the often-posed question, Does TV violence cause aggression? According to the NIMH report, the great bulk of evidence points to the conclusion that *television violence does cause later aggressive behavior among viewers* (p. 89). The more violence watched, the more likely is subsequent aggressive behavior. Many researchers and reviewers have since supported this conclusion (e.g., Eron & Huesmann 1986; Friedrich-Cofer & Huston 1986; Geen & Thomas 1986; Huesmann & Malamuth 1986; Rule & Ferguson 1986; Turner, Hesse & Peterson-Lewis 1986). It should be noted that a minority of researchers (e.g., Freedman 1984, 1986; Milavsky et al. 1982) believe that the evidence is inconclusive. Usually methodological problems with field studies and the "irrelevancy" of laboratory research are cited as reasons.

However, the frequency and consistency with which the relationship is found is impressive. The relationship between TV violence and subsequent aggressiveness has been demonstrated in children of both sexes, ranging from preschoolers to older adolescents, both in laboratory and in field studies, using many different measures of aggression (Eron & Huesmann 1986, NIMH 1982). The relationship has been found for children in the United States as well as in other countries, including England, Australia, Finland, the Netherlands, Israel, and Poland (see Eron & Huesmann 1986, Huesmann & Eron 1986b). The correlations found between television violence and aggression are as high as any correlations ever found with personality variables (Eron & Huesmann 1986). What about violent cartoons, assumed by many adults to be harmless? At least in younger children, these cartoons also increase aggressiveness (NIMH 1982, p. 47). And a recent study, conducted in Italy, suggests that commercials that show violence and aggression also increase the likelihood of subsequent aggressive behavior (Caprara et al. 1987).

Most researchers believe there is little doubt that the relationship between television violence and aggressive behavior is one of cause and effect (e.g., Eron & Huesmann 1986, NIMH 1982, Singer & Singer 1983). An alternative hypothesis is that it is the children who are already aggressive who choose violent programs. However, this hypothesis cannot explain the fact that a relationship between television violence and aggression is found *regardless* of children's initial level of aggressiveness (Eron & Huesmann 1986).

It does appear, however, that the relationship may be a *bidirectional* one, in which television violence increases aggressive behavior and aggressive behavior stimulates a greater amount of violence viewing (Eron 1982; Friedrich-Cofer & Huston 1986; Huesmann, Lagerspetz, & Eron 1984).

Television Violence and Aggression Research

A few examples will provide the flavor of the variety of research in this area.

T.M. Williams (1978) had the unique opportunity of studying children's aggressiveness before and after television was introduced into their small Canadian communities. In one community, children became more aggressive, both verbally and physically, once TV was brought into their homes. After television was brought into the second community, the children who became heavy viewers became more behaviorally aggressive.

A CBS (Columbia Broadcasting System)-sponsored study (Belson 1978), conducted in London, found (much to the dismay of CBS) that teenage boys were more likely to participate in "serious violence" after viewing TV violence.

E.D. McCarthy and his associates (1975) found an interesting relationship when they studied 732 children over a five-year period. As the total amount of time that children watched TV increased, so did their fighting, conflict with their parents, and delinquency.

Over the period of a year, Singer and Singer (1981) kept records of the behavior of 3- and 4-year-old children at their day care centers and the amount of violent TV programs they watched at home. They found that the two were related: as the time spent watching violent TV increased, so did the acts of "unwarranted aggression" at the day care centers.

Longitudinal studies indicate that television violence not only causes immediate aggression, but it has cumulative or long-lasting effects. The evidence suggests that early television viewing contributes to aggressiveness at a later age (Eron et al. 1972, Huesmann 1986a, Singer & Singer 1983). Discussion of the cumulative effects of TV violence will be returned to shortly.

The evidence linking television violence and subsequent aggressiveness is so consistent that research is now shifting from investigating whether a relationship exists to investigating the conditions that attenuate or exacerbate the relationship.

Variables in the Relationship between Television Violence and Aggression

Television violence does not affect all children and it does not affect children to the same degree (Eron & Huesmann 1986). Some researchers are now working to identify the conditions under which exposure to television violence promotes aggression. Foremost among these researchers are Leonard Eron and L. Rowell Huesmann of the University of Illinois at Chicago (e.g., Eron 1982; Eron & Huesmann 1986; Huesmann 1986a,b; Huesmann & Eron 1986a,b). Following are some of the variables identified.

Age. Although a relationship between television violence and aggression has been observed in children as young as 3 (Singer & Singer 1981), longitudinal data suggest that the relationship is much more consistent and substantial for children in middle childhood than at earlier ages (Eron & Huesmann 1986). Perhaps even more interesting is the finding that aggression in early adulthood is also related to the amount of violence watched in middle childhood, although it is not related to the amount watched in early adulthood (Eron et al. 1972).

On the basis of such findings, Eron and Huesmann (1986) propose that there is a sensitive period (between ages 8 and 12) during which children are particularly susceptible to the influence of television violence. They specifically pinpoint the age of 8 as the most vulnerable period for children in the United States, although the sensitive age range seems to vary somewhat from country to country.

A number of separate developmental trends merge in middle childhood that may create this sensitive period to television violence: (1) an increase in the amount of television violence that children in this age range generally watch, (2) the poor ability at this age to detect the unrealistic nature of television violence, and (3) the tendency of children to become increasingly more aggressive as they progress through middle childhood (which may stimulate additional violence viewing).

Amount of Television Watched. Some studies have found aggressive behavior to be related to the total amount of television watched, not only to the amount of violent television watched (see Eron & Huesmann 1986). Why should nonviolent programming increase children's aggressive behavior? Studies suggest that aggressive behavior can be stimulated not only by aggressive content but by frenetic, hectic programming that creates a high level of arousal in children (see Eron & Huesmann 1986, Wright & Huston 1983). There are, therefore, two variables operating within television that function to increase aggression: (1) the aggressive nature of TV content and (2) the frenetic pacing of TV programs, which increases children's arousal level.

Identification with Television Personalities. Some children identify heavily with TV personalities and the characters they play. Especially for boys, identification with a character substantially increases the likelihood that the character's aggressive behavior will be modeled (Huesmann & Eron 1986b; Huesmann, Lagerspetz, & Eron 1984). Significant relationships between aggressive behavior and identification with TV characters have been found for American, Finnish, and Polish boys and for Finnish and Polish girls. For many children, their identification with aggressive characters seems to be as important as the amount of violence they watch (Huesmann 1986a).

Belief That Television Violence Is Realistic. Believing in the realism of television violence exacerbates the effect that televised violence has on aggressive behavior. Significant relationships have been found between children's belief that TV violence is realistic, their aggressive behavior, and the amount of violence they watch (see Huesmann 1986b, Huesmann & Eron 1986b).

Intellectual Achievement. Children of lower intellectual achievement generally (1) watch more television, (2) watch more violent television, (3) believe violent TV reflects real life, and (4) behave more aggressively (Huesmann 1986b).

Low intellectual achievement seems to exacerbate the effect that television violence has on behavior. Perhaps children who are not successful in school turn to TV for gratification. Perhaps because of their lower intellectual capacity they are attracted to the easier solutions to social problems (that is, aggression) provided by violent TV programs. And perhaps, because of their lower intellectual competence, they are more frustrated and their learned aggressive responses are stimulated more easily (Huesmann 1986a,b).

Although it may seem reasonable to conclude that low intellectual functioning leads both to increased TV viewing and to increased levels of aggressiveness, a recently reported 22-year longitudinal study with 600 subjects suggests that the relationship between intellectual achievement and aggression is far more complex (Huesmann, Eron & Yarmel 1987). Huesmann and his colleagues found that "whatever effect intelligence has on aggressive behavior, it appears to have occurred by age 8." After age 8, early intelligence was no longer able to predict changes in aggressiveness. Instead, the data indicated that by middle childhood, a child's aggressiveness interfered with further intellectual functioning and achievement. In fact, childhood aggressiveness was predictive of poorer intellectual functioning in adulthood. Why should aggressiveness interfere with intellectual functioning and achievement? The researchers suggest that a highly aggressive child may be more likely to attend to social stimuli in the classroom than to learning. Moreover, his aggressive behavior may create a generalized negative attitude on the part of his teachers which may focus teacher-child interaction on discipline rather than on learning. It may even decrease the likelihood of teachers responding positively to the aggressive child's academic performance.

Summary. The majority of researchers believe the evidence leaves little doubt that television violence causes subsequent aggression. The relationship has been found for both boys and girls, living in this country as well as many others. The relationship may very well be a circular or bidirectional one, in which viewing television violence encourages aggression, and aggression stimulates additional violence viewing. There are some variables that exacerbate the relationship, including age, amount of television viewing, identification with aggressive television characters, belief in the realism of TV violence, and poor intellectual achievement. Other variables that exacerbate the effects television violence has upon a child, which were not discussed, are a child's unpopularity with his peers and a child's fantasizing about aggression (Eron & Huesmann 1986, Huesmann 1986b).

Explanations for the Relationship between
Television Violence and Aggression

The question still remains, *Why* does the relationship between TV violence and aggressive behavior exist? *Why* does television violence lead to aggression? The NIMH report (1982) suggested that two theoretical explanations were best supported by available evidence. The first explanation proposes that children learn to behave aggressively by observing it, just as they learn social skills by observing their parents and others. The more they watch programs that are aggressive in nature, the more likely they are to learn that life's problems are best solved by taking the offensive.

The second explanation suggests that continual exposure to violence modifies children's attitudes about aggression. The more they watch aggression, the more they accept it as normal; the more they accept it as normal, the more likely they are to eventually behave aggressively themselves. Drabman and Thomas (1974), for example, found that children were more willing to accept aggressive behavior in other children after only a brief exposure to violent scenes.

Recently, some researchers have turned to a more complex explanation of the relationship between television violence and aggressive behavior (e.g., Berkowitz 1984; Huesmann 1986b; Huesmann & Eron 1984, 1986a). Taking an information processing perspective, this new approach encompasses many previous explanations. The main points, as presented by Huesmann (1986b), Huesmann and Malamuth (1986), and Huesmann and Eron (1984, 1986a), will be briefly covered.

1. The evidence suggests that during the first decade of life, children generally develop a characteristic level of aggression that tends to persist, even into adulthood. It is proposed that during this time, children are learning cognitive scripts which then guide their behavior in social situations. These cognitive scripts can be thought of as rules or strategies of behaving. The child learns them in a variety of ways, including the television she watches.

2. Children are not necessarily influenced by the TV violence they watch. To be influenced, they must store a mental representation of the aggression in their memory. They are not likely to do this if the violence is not salient or understandable to them. Even more important, they are unlikely to store it in memory if it has no subjective utility for them, that is, if they do not perceive it as a potential strategy that can be used by them in the future. However, the more children see violence, the more they perceive it as reflecting real life, the more they identify with aggressive characters, then the more likely they are to store aggressive strategies in memory for possible future use.

3. Of course, many things are forgotten. To maintain an aggressive script, it must be rehearsed in some way, for example, by thinking or fantasizing about it. In fantasy, the original script is often elaborated upon and expanded.

4. Even if stored and rehearsed, the child still may never engage in the aggressive strategy. It must first be retrieved. The closer the characteristics of the present situation are to the situation in which the strategy was stored, the more likely it can be retrieved and used *if* deemed appropriate.

5. Aggressive children are children who regularly store and retrieve scripts that emphasize aggression. The television violence they watch is only one factor contributing to their aggressive behavior. TV can contribute in several ways. It can provide new aggressive scripts. It can provide cues for the retrieval and use of aggressive scripts already acquired, in any manner. It can increase the likelihood

that a child will maintain aggressive scripts in memory (because of the repeated exposure to aggression). It can contribute to the child's belief that aggression is a reasonable and justified solution to social problems (again because of repeated exposure).

6. This approach does not imply that family influences are unimportant. "Nothing could be further from the truth," says Huesmann (1986b). The data indicate that parents play a role both in children's television viewing and in children's aggressiveness. Children's aggressiveness is correlated with parental television habits, with parents' aggression, and with parents' child rearing habits (Huesmann 1986b). (Children who are primarily disciplined by coercion, such as physical punishment and threats, are more influenced by the antisocial behavior they see on television than are children who are primarily disciplined by reason and explanation [see Abelman 1985].)

Huesmann stresses that childhood aggression is *not* transitory and it should be a concern. A number of correlations found in research conducted by Huesmann and his colleagues (Huesmann, Eron, Lefkowitz & Walder 1984) are sobering. In a 22-year longitudinal study, aggressiveness at age 8 (for example, starting fights, shoving, pushing, being regularly in trouble) was significantly correlated with adult aggressive behavior, specifically, spouse and child (physical) abuse, conviction of crimes, and convictions of moving traffic violations, including drunk driving.

An intervention found to be effective in reducing television's negative effects on high violence viewers will be discussed later in the chapter.

The Other Side of the Coin: Television's Potential to Increase Prosocial Behavior

Given the consistent relationship found between television violence and subsequent aggressiveness, one might question whether the other side of the coin holds true: What happens when children observe television characters behaving in prosocial ways? (For example, being cooperative, considerate, friendly, or dealing with frustration and problems calmly and rationally.) Are children likely to imitate this positive behavior too? What happens when they observe people behaving altruistically or selflessly? Will children follow this example? According to the NIMH report (1982), the evidence suggests that they will, particularly when adults point out the prosocial behavior to them. The NIMH report concluded:

> The clear and simple message derived from the research . . . is that children learn from watching television and what they learn depends on what they watch. The programs they see on television change their behavior. If they look at violent or aggressive programs, they tend to become more aggressive and disobedient. But if they look at prosocial programs, they will more likely become more generous, friendly, and self-controlled. Television can have beneficial effects; it is a potential force for good (p. 51).

There is only limited research in this area, however. Additionally, the relationship between televised prosocial programs and prosocial behavior has not been found as consistently as that between television violence and aggressive behavior (Eron & Huesmann 1986). The reason for inconsistent findings may be that prosocial behavior is not as salient or as obvious to children as is television aggression. This explains the NIMH recommendation to point out examples of prosocial behavior to children.

The relationship between prosocial television and behavior has been found often enough, however, to take heed and use it as a guide for children's television viewing. The relationship has, in fact, been found not only in the United States but in England, Australia, New Zealand, Canada, the Netherlands, and Finland (Eron & Huesmann 1986). Eron and Huesmann (1986) write:

> The child who has been watching programs with primarily prosocial content will learn that the way to solve problems is through deference, consideration, cooperation, and kindness and that the world is a place where problems can be worked through (p. 310).

Music Videos: A New Kind of Television Influence?

On 1 August 1981, Music Television ("MTV") was launched and beamed into two million homes. Just three years later, it was deemed a success. Its revenue exceeded sixty million dollars and it was available in more than twenty-two million homes (Sherman & Dominick 1986). A nationwide study estimated that 43 percent of the adolescent population watch MTV (see Sun & Lull 1986), although the percentage of viewers is much higher in areas with easy access. Sun and Lull (1986) found that among their large and diverse sample of teens in San Jose, California, 80 percent watched "MTV" for an average of two hours per day.

Music videos have been the subject of concern and criticism. It is claimed they are heavily loaded with violent, sexist, sexual, and antiestablishment themes (see Aufderheide 1986, National Coalition on Television Violence 1984, Sherman & Dominick 1986). The National Coalition on Television Violence has been very vocal about the senseless violence of music videos. It has been pointed out that violence is used quite differently in these videos than in commercial television. Rather than used for the purpose of action, it is random, used for atmosphere and aesthetics (Aufderheide 1986).

Other criticism is focused on sexist themes, claiming men commonly are cast in images of sailors and gang members, women, as prostitutes, temptresses, virginal princesses, and servants (see Aufderheide 1986, Sherman & Dominick 1986). The portrayal of sexual behavior is also a concern. Critics point to the large number of videos that link sex with violence and to videos that contain innuendos of prostitution, homosexuality, and other nontraditional forms of sexual behavior.

Still another concern (see Aufderheide 1986, Sherman & Dominick 1986) is antiestablishment themes, in which teens are persecuted by establishment adults—a judge called Julius Hangman, a principal with a stocking mask, a school guard with a Doberman (Aufderheide 1986). And, it is pointed out, the retaliation of teens against authority is sometimes portrayed in bizarre fantasies of power, such as a girl incinerating her parents because of restrictions placed upon her (Aufderheide 1986).

In light of the large body of research that has found television to be an important influencer of behavior, perceptions, and attitudes, it is no wonder that music videos have created such a stir. Researchers have not yet studied the specific influence of music videos on children and teens, but several investigators have conducted content analyses of them so their content and messages can be assessed objectively (Brown & Campbell 1986, National Coalition on Television Violence 1984, Sherman & Dominick 1986). How valid is the concern over music videos? Are critics merely focusing on a few objectionable videos and generalizing their objections to all? Or are they heavily loaded with violence, sex, sexism, and antiestablishment themes? The results of these content analyses follow.

Violence in Music Videos

In 1984, The National Coalition on Television Violence (NCTV) analyzed 100 hours of music videos appearing on "MTV," "Night Tracks," and "Night Flight" over a seven-month period (see Sherman & Dominick 1986). Both performance and concept videos were analyzed. (Performance videos are those in which more than 50 percent of the video is devoted to shots of the group performing. Concept videos are those in which more than 50 percent of the video is devoted to a dramatization [Sherman & Dominick 1986].) The NCTV analysis found that during each hour of music videos, there was an average of eighteen acts which they defined as violent or hostile.

Sherman and Dominick (1986) analyzed 42 hours of concept music videos, appearing over a seven-week period on "MTV," "Night Tracks," and "Friday Night Videos." These investigators reported that violence was portrayed in 56 percent of the concept videos analyzed.

Sexual Behavior in Music Videos

Themes of sexual content seem to be prevalent. Sherman and Dominick (1986) reported an average of four sexual activities per video; only 25 percent of the videos were devoid of sexual content. However, sexual behavior was usually implied (flirting, nonintimate touching, and so on) rather than overt. Usually it was casual and devoid of emotional commitment (Sherman & Dominick 1986).

Sex frequently was linked with violence. The NCTV analysis found 39 percent of all violence shown to be sexually related. Seventy percent of sexual activities fell within the boundaries of heterosexuality. Homosexuality was implied in about 25 percent of sexual episodes; overtly nontraditional sexual behavior (transsexuality, bondage, and so forth) made up less than 3 percent of the episodes (Sherman & Dominick 1986).

Differences were found in video programs. "MTV" programming was more highly sexual in nature and more likely to portray nontraditional sexual behavior than either "Night Tracks" or "Friday Night Videos" (Sherman & Dominick 1986).

Sexism in Music Videos

Most frequently, the centers of attention and power in music videos are white men, and their behavior is more often aggressive and hostile than helpful and cooperative. Women, who generally are in the background, are dressed provocatively approximately one-half the time. Women are frequently represented as upper-class sex objects for whom lower-class males harbor fantasies of sexual conquests. An interesting twist found in these videos is that women are more likely to be the perpetrators of violence than its victims (Brown & Campbell 1986, Sherman & Dominick 1986).

Antiestablishment Themes in Music Videos

Brown and Campbell (1986) reported that approximately half the behavior in the videos they analyzed was what they termed "antisocial" in nature. Twenty percent of the themes focused on social protest (for example, nuclear war, the business establishment, oppression of workers), but only 5 percent had themes of actual social alienation.

Looking at the positive and negative portrayals of social institutions, such as marriage, work, and home, Brown and Campbell reported the following:

1. *Marriage* is portrayed negatively 57 percent of the time and positively 29 percent.
2. *Work* is portrayed negatively 46 percent of the time and positively 38 percent.
3. *Home* is portrayed negatively 33 percent of the time, positively 42 percent, and "mixed" 25 percent.
4. *Courtship and dating* is portrayed negatively 21 percent of the time, positively 58 percent, and "mixed" 21 percent.

Television: Educational Enrichment or Detraction?

Television has opened to children worlds that have been inaccessible to previous generations. Science, history, literature, music, art, and life in other countries are available at the press of a button. Has television contributed to children's intellectual development and educational enrichment? Researchers have looked at television's relationship to IQ scores and to achievement scores.

IQ Scores

Studies have found that light viewers vary considerably in IQ scores. However, among heavy viewers, there is a rather narrow range of scores and a rather consistent relationship found: in general, the more TV watched, the lower the IQ (NIMH 1982). This does not mean that heavy doses of TV necessarily lead to lower IQ scores. Lower IQ could lead to a preference for TV. Or some third factor may lead to increases in television viewing *and* decreases in intellectual functioning. We saw previously that a child's aggressiveness may operate in this way. So might the absence of interesting and stimulating activities in a child's life.

School Achievement

What has television's influence been on school achievement? In an analysis of 23 studies, P.A. Williams and colleagues (1982) found that school achievement generally increases slightly for children who watch up to 10 hours per week. However, beyond this point, achievement decreases as the amount of time viewing television increases. (This holds true for up to 35 to 40 hours per week, after which television's deleterious effects level off.)

Why does moderate to heavy viewing interfere with school achievement? Bronfenbrenner (1979) writes that the real danger of television is in the "behavior it prevents—the talks, the games, the family activities and the arguments through which much of a child's learning takes place." Another activity television seems to replace is reading (Gadberry 1980; Furu, cited in NIMH 1982; Williams, cited in NIMH 1982).

The relationship between television viewing and school achievement that was just described has been found for children in general. However, if one looks at children by age or by IQ, one finds that the relationship between amount of television viewing and school achievement is different within different groups of children. Consistent with much of the data is the idea that TV displaces other valuable activities.

School Achievement and Age. Focusing on age, one finds that a moderate amount of television (1 to 2 hours per day) is positively related to reading achievement scores for younger children only. By preadolescence, any beneficial effects TV may have disappear. At this point, reading scores decline as the amount of TV viewing increases. In other words, beginning in preadolescence, those who watch the least TV are the best readers, and those who watch the most TV are the poorest readers (NIMH 1982).

Why 1 to 2 hours of television per day is related to better reading achievement in younger children is a matter of speculation. Morgan and Gross (1982) point out that children who are very light viewers comprise a small population (usually no more than 5 percent of study samples). This small group might be the children who lack interest not only in TV but in many other activities, including school.

School Achievement and IQ. What about children with high IQ's? Are their achievement scores also hurt by long hours of TV viewing or does their high IQ immune them from the deleterious effects of heavy TV viewing? Unfortunately, high-IQ children are not immune. In fact, they are more adversely affected than are other children (Williams 1982). This is obvious not only in their reading comprehension but in their general school achievement and language usage as well (NIMH 1982). Perhaps the reason that high-IQ heavy viewers do so poorly is that their light viewing counterparts (with whom they are compared) spend the extra hours reading, studying, and in other active pursuits.

In contrast to high-IQ children, those with low IQ scores may derive some benefit from heavy TV viewing. These children reportedly enjoy a broader variety of reading materials than do their lighter viewing counterparts. Since their reading preference reflects television themes (for example, stories about movie stars, love, and teenagers), it could be that television may stimulate reading in low IQ children (NIMH 1982). At least for girls with low IQ scores, heavy viewing is associated with better reading comprehension and vocabulary scores than is lighter viewing.

Television's Potential for Educational Benefits

Unquestionably, television can be a powerful learning tool. Studies investigating the effectiveness of educational programs, such as "Sesame Street" and "The Infinity Factor," find that they can result in significant learning (see Ball, Palmer & Millward 1986). And in a review of 100 studies comparing science instruction by TV with conventional instruction, children instructed by television did as well if not better in 86 percent of the studies (Chu & Schramm 1975).

Television may be uniquely capable of reaching a wide range of children effectively. Abelman (1987) calls it the "great cultural common denominator" about which all children are enthusiastic. Some children may be more easily reached by TV than by other sources. Examples are some disadvantaged children who are uncomfortable with print and classrooms or children whose information processing abilities may be better suited to television than to reading or listening, the usual mode of classroom instruction (Greenfield 1984). Television can also benefit the very brightest students. In fact, evidence suggests that these children gain more from television instruction than do other populations (Abelman 1984b, Fortner 1985).

Mitigating Television's Negative Effects

Adult Intervention: A Powerful Mediator

By now it may appear that fighting television's influence is a losing battle. Although television can be beneficial, are we in a position to control its positive and negative influence? The answer is "yes." Research has clearly demonstrated that adult intervention can minimize any negative effects television may have on children. In fact, adult intervention can turn television into an ally, with benefits for youngsters. Before examining specific steps that can be taken, consider a few examples from the research.

Johnston and Ettema (1982) investigated whether the program "Freestyle" was successful in changing children's attitudes about traditional sex roles. (Recall that "Freestyle," discussed previously, was the public education series developed to change sex role stereotypes.) It was found that children who both watched the program *and* participated in class discussions about it benefited more than children who merely watched it.

Corder-Bolz and O'Bryant (1978) had preschool children watch an episode of "Adam-12" (its topic, truancy) with an adult who either made explanatory or neutral comments about the show. One week later, the children in the explanation group (as compared to the control group) had developed more positive attitudes about policemen and knew more details about truancy (a word they hadn't heard previously).

Ball and Bogatz (1970) found that children learned more from "Sesame Street" when they watched it with a mother who talked with them about it than when they watched it alone.

Leonard Eron (1986) reported an intervention that mitigated the effect that television violence had on high violence viewers. Through demonstration and discussion, children were helped to see the unrealistic nature of television violence and learned that most people do not solve problems in this way. Then they were asked to develop arguments and to write a paragraph about why TV violence is unrealistic and why viewing too much of it is bad. Children were videotaped reading their arguments ("so that older children who had been fooled by TV could be helped"). They also watched themselves reading their arguments on videotape. When followed up four months after the conclusion of the intervention program, these high violence viewers had not changed their TV habits. However, they were rated by their peers to be significantly lower in aggressive behavior than were control children who had not received the intervention—both groups had been equally aggressive initially! It appears that once these children no longer perceived the television violence to be realistic and appropriate, their behavior was less influenced by it. In support of this interpretation is the finding that children who continued to be aggressive, despite the intervention, were those who continued to believe that TV was a realistic depiction of life and who continued to identify with TV characters.

The preceding studies are only examples. There is considerable evidence demonstrating that adults can influence the kind and amount of information which children gain from television, their acceptance of information, their interpretation of information, and the behavior they learn (Abelman 1984a). In other words, adult intervention can reduce TV's potential harm and increase its benefits.

The Role of Parents

Obviously parents are in the best position to mediate the effects of television on their children. An excellent resource book for parents who wish to intervene in their youngsters' television viewing has been written by Singer, Singer, and Zuckerman (1980). Many other professionals (e.g., Abelman 1984a, NIMH 1982, O'Bryant & Corder-Bolz 1977, Schorr 1983) also have made specific suggestions to help parents increase television's positive effects while mitigating its potential negative effects. Some of these recommendations follow.

Limit Viewing Time. If parents do nothing else, limits should be placed on children's viewing time. The research on perceptions, aggressive behavior, intellectual functioning, and academic performance all points to the fact that the average 3 to 4 hours a day children spend with television is too much for most children. Children may need encouragement to become involved in alternative activities (physical activity, reading, hobbies, clubs, friends, solitary play, and so forth).

Monitor Program Selection. Television is a formidable educator and has as much potential to teach desirable attitudes and accurate information as it does the undesirable and inaccurate. There are television programs that can teach children academic subjects and expand their words. There are programs that expose them to realistic depictions of life, to positive attitudes of love, sex, and family life, and to models of prosocial and nonstereotyped behavior. With active involvement in program selection, parents can transform television from a liability to an asset.

O'Bryant and Corder-Bolz (1977) recommend a policy of purposeful viewing, that is, making decisions about programs to be watched before the set is turned on.

Provide Explanation and Interpretation. Even if parents were to view TV *passively* with children, evidence suggests that their presence during exciting programs should dampen youngsters' arousal level (see Abelman 1984a). Recall that heightened arousal is one instigator of aggression.

Parents who comment during their children's viewing, however, can significantly impact television's effects on their offspring in a variety of ways. By highlighting and integrating information, parents can influence what children learn. By pointing out prosocial behavior, they can provide desirable models. By helping children make connections between behavior and its consequences, parents can ensure that youngsters perceive the negative consequences of aggression and the positive consequences of prosocial behavior.

O'Bryant and Corder-Bolz (1977) recommend using television content to reinforce family values. These investigators found that parents usually respond to objectionable television content with silence. But, they point out, *silence implies consent*. Instead, these researchers advise parents to respond strenuously (even hissing) when they find content objectionable.

These same investigators suggest television content can be used as a springboard, to stimulate discussions on sensitive issues, such as sexual abuse, drugs, rape, and teenage pregnancy.

Teach Critical Viewing Skills. If children must see a popular TV program with objectionable content, its negative effects can be minimized by teaching them to view television critically. Basically, this involves teaching youngsters to question and to evaluate what they see on television, rather than to accept it passively. Some examples follow.

Parents can help children evaluate the accuracy of television's version of the world by providing experiences and examples to counteract inaccurate portrayals. They can also discuss the reasons that television portrays people in stereotypes and life in extremes (for example, exciting, violent, optimal, funny, and so on).

Parents can help children distinguish between television fantasy and reality by teaching them about special effects and by asking them questions to stimulate thinking. (What would probably happen if a person were to drive that way in real life? If that situation had really taken place, what other outcomes could it have had?)

Children can be taught to question commercials so they will be less influenced by them. When children are taught the purpose of commercials and how products are made appealing, they are less likely to perceive commercials as credible and products as desirable (see Greenfield 1984). The May 1987 issue of the magazine *Instructor* provides many ideas and fun exercises to help children become more sophisticated about TV advertising.

Critical viewing skills can be taught directly. They can also be modeled (that is, parents can discuss programs critically with another person in the child's presence). O'Bryant and Corder-Bolz (1977) recommend this indirect method for teens who might interpret more direct methods as "lectures."

Studies on Parent Involvement. Although parents are the most likely candidates to mitigate the negative effects of television on their children, research has found that most parents are not involved in their offsprings' television viewing. Generally parents place few restrictions on television and they seldom provide explanations or interpretations of television content (see Abelman 1984a, Schorr 1983, Greenfield 1984).

Furthermore, studies suggest that many parents are not easily convinced of the need to intervene. Singer and Singer (1983), for example, conducted consciousness-raising sessions to encourage parents to limit their children's viewing; they had little success. Cohen, Abelman, and Greenberg (see Abelman 1984a) created special viewing guides and materials to help parents become effectively involved with their children's viewing; these investigators also found little success with enlisting parental intervention.

Partly because of the lack of parental mediation and partly because of the important role television plays in children's socialization, professionals are currently becoming more actively involved in children's television viewing.

The Involvement of Professionals

Professional involvement primarily has come in four forms: research, advising parents (increasing their awareness of television's potential influence on children), teaching television literacy skills to children, and influencing social policy. These last two will be briefly discussed.

Teaching TV Literacy Skills. In recent years, many programs have been developed to teach children what is called TV literacy (e.g., Abelman, 1987; Abelman & Courtright 1983; Dorr, Graves & Phelps 1980; Rapaczynski, Singer & Singer 1982; Singer, Zuckerman, & Singer 1980). Lesson plans, workbooks, video programs, and comprehensive packaged programs are available (Abelman 1984a). The rationale behind TV literacy programs is that if children are to be raised with a medium that influences their perceptions, attitudes, and behavior, they should understand how it affects them (Singer & Singer 1983).

What are TV literacy skills? TV literacy programs differ, but one by Singer, Zuckerman, and Singer (1980), provides a good example. This program develops children's ability to distinguish between reality and fantasy and increases their sophistication about the medium of television. They learn about special effects, commercials, television's use of stereotypes, how television influences feelings and ideas, and so forth. Children are also encouraged to be selective viewers and to control their own viewing. Lesson plans, videotaped demonstrations, and homework assignments are used in instruction.

Many busy teachers may question whether it is their job to teach television literacy. Schools are being assigned the responsibility to educate children in an increasingly greater number of areas. Many teachers already are required to set time aside for programs in sex education, AIDS, drug abuse, and suicide prevention. However, an impressive case can be made that teaching TV literacy skills benefits not only children but educators too (Abelman 1984a). Television is a natural motivator for children and can be used as a springboard to teach many academic skills. The television literacy program of Singer and her colleagues, for example, is tied in with a language arts program. It is specifically designed to develop skills in reading, vocabulary, writing, punctuation, critical thinking, analogies, summary skills, and so forth (Singer & Singer 1983). How many children would find the work boring when it evolves around television?

Using television as a springboard has been found to enrich class discussion, improve children's critical thinking skills, and motivate serious thought and analyses (see Abelman 1984a). Television has also been used to increase *reading* comprehension by using television stories to practice comprehension skills, such as focusing on main ideas, determining cause and effect, sequencing events, and using context cues to make inferences (see Abelman 1984a, Greenfield 1984). Tips on choosing a TV literacy program that meets the needs of both teacher and students are offered by Abelman (1987).

Social Policy Involvement. In addition to public statements made by professional organizations about television's hazards to children, some social scientists have become individually involved in social policy. Social scientists serve on policymaking committees and as consultants to television writers and producers. They therefore provide a direct link between researchers and the television industry (Singer & Singer 1983).

Although television producers have long received negative feedback about their focus on violence, they are now being offered constructive suggestions for alternatives. A good example is recent research examining whether it is violence or action that attracts and sustains children's attention (see Wright & Huston 1983). Researchers have separated the two—violent content from nonviolent high-action content. Is violence an important contributor to maintaining children's attention, as producers and writers have assumed? When violence and action are separated, it is the action, not the violence, that attracts and maintains youngsters' attention. This is valuable information for writers and producers to have. (True, fast pacing per se also increases the likelihood of aggression, but when both are presented together, children must receive a double whammy.)

Television's potential to foster desirable behavior in children is also being emphasized by social scientists. Writers and producers are being encouraged to reduce the portrayals of unsafe and undesirable behavior and to find opportunities to model positive behavior (Singer & Singer 1983). As Dorothy and Jerome Singer (1983) point out, it is just as easy to have a television character refuse an alcoholic drink as to take one. At times, even a single television event can have dramatic effects, such as an episode in which the popular TV character Fonzie applied for a library card. The next day libraries across the nation had a rush of young library card applicants at their desks (Greenfield 1984). However, even though writers and producers are becoming aware that they can create positive benefits for children without subtracting from television's "appeal," they will need to hear it enough times that they automatically incorporate positive models and positive behavior into story lines.

Television is a fact of life, and in most American homes, it is here to stay. Its impact on children is also a fact of life. But we can shape the nature of that influence. If a passive role is assumed and no attempt is made to intervene in children's viewing, its influence is likely to be a negative one. On the other hand, by increasing the amount of adult intervention in children's viewing, this powerful medium can be channeled in a positive direction.

References

Abelman, R. 1984a. "Children and TV: The ABC's of Literacy." *Childhood Education* 60: 200–5.

——. 1984b. "Television and the Gifted Child." *Roeper Review* 7: 115–18.

——. 1985. "Styles of Parental Disciplinary Practices as a Mediator of Children's Learning from Prosocial Television Portrayals." *Child Study Journal* 15: 131–46.

——. 1987. "Television Literacy for Gifted Children." *Roeper Review* 9: 166–69.

——. 1987. "TV Literacy II: Amplifying the Affective Level Effects of Television's Prosocial Fare Through Curriculum Intervention." *Journal of Research and Development in Education* 20: 40–49.

Abelman, R., & Courtright, J. 1983. "Television Literacy: Amplifying the Cognitive Level Effects of Television's Prosocial Fare through Curriculum Intervention." *Journal of Research and Development in Education* 17: 46–57.

Anderson, D.R., Field, D.E., Collins, P.A., Lorch, E.P. & Nathan, J.G. 1985. "Estimates of Young Children's Time with Television: A Methodological Comparison of Parent Reports with Time-Lapse Video Home Observation." *Child Development* 56: 1345–57.

Anderson, D.R. & Lorch, E.P. 1983. "Looking at Television: Action or Reaction?" in J. Bryant & D.R. Anderson, eds., *Children's Understanding of Television: Research on Attention and Comprehension.* N.Y.: Academic Press.

Anderson, D.R., Lorch, E.P., Field, D.E., Collins, P.A. & Nathan, J.G. 1986. "Television Viewing at Home: Age Trends in Visual Attention and Time with T.V." *Child Development* 57: 1024–33.

Anderson, D.R., Lorch, E.P., Field, D.E. & Sanders, J. 1981. "The Effects of TV Program Comprehensibility on Preschool Children's Visual Attention to Television." *Child Development* 52: 151–57.

Anderson, D.R. & Smith, R. 1984. "Young Children's TV Viewing: The Problem of Cognitive Continuity." *Applied Developmental Psychology.* Vol. 1. N.Y.: Academic Press.

Aufderheide, P. 1986. "Music Videos: The Look of the Sound." *Journal of Communication* 36: 57–78 .

Ball, S., Palmer, P. & Millward, E. 1986. "Television and Its Educational Impact: A Reconsideration," in J. Bryant & D. Zillmann, eds., *Perspectives on Media Effects.* Hillsdale, N.J.: Lawrence Erlbaum Assoc. Publ.

Ball, S.J. & Bogatz, G.P. 1970. *The First Year of Sesame Street: An Evaluation.* Princeton, N.J.: Educational Testing Service.

Belson, W. 1978. *Television Violence and the Adolescent Boy.* London: Saxon House.

Berkowitz, L. 1984. "Some Effects of Thoughts on Anti- and Prosocial Influences of Media Events: A Cognitive-Neoassociation Analysis." *Psychological Bulletin* 95: 410–27.

Bronfenbrenner, U. 1979. *The Ecology of Human Development.* Cambridge, Mass.: Harvard University Press.

Brown, J.D. & Campbell, K. 1986. "Race and Gender in Music Videos: The Same Beat but a Different Drummer." *Journal of Communication* 36: 94–106.

Bryant, J., Carveth, R. & Brown, D. 1981. "Television Viewing and Anxiety: An Experimental Examination." *Journal of Communications* 31: 106–19.

Caprara, G.V., D'Imperio, G., Gentilomo, A., Mammucari, A., Renzi, P. & Travaglia, G. 1987. "The Intrusive Commercial: Influence of Aggressive TV Commercials on Aggression." *European Journal of Social Psychology* 17: 23–31.

Chu, G.C. & Schramm, W. 1975. *Learning from Television: What the Research Says.* Washington, D.C.: Dept. of Health, Education, and Welfare.

Collins, W.A. 1979. "Children's Comprehension of Television Content," in E. Wartella, ed., *Children Communicating: Media and the Development of Thought, Speech, Understanding.* Beverly Hills, Calif.: Sage.

———. 1982. "Cognitive Processing in Television Viewing," in D. Pearl, L. Bouthilet & J. Lazar, eds., *Television and Behavior: Ten Years of Scientific Progress and Implications for the Eighties.* Vol. 2. Washington: U.S. Government Printing Office.

Corder-Bolz, C.R. & O'Bryant, S.L. 1978. "Teacher vs. Program." *Journal of Communication* (Winter).

Dorr, A., Graves, S.B. & Phelps, E. 1980. "Television Literacy for Young Children." *Journal of Communication* 30: 71–83.

Drabman, C.S. & Thomas, M.H. 1974. "Does Media Violence Increase Children's Toleration of Real-Life Aggression?" *Developmental Psychology* 10: 418–21.

Eron, L.D. 1982. "Parent-Child Interaction, Television Violence, and Aggression in Children." *American Psychologist* 37: 197–211.

———. 1986. "Interventions to Mitigate the Psychological Effects of Media Violence on Aggressive Behavior." *Journal of Social Issues* 42: 155–69.

Eron, L.D. & Huesmann, L.R. 1986. "The Role of Television in the Development of Prosocial and Antisocial Behavior," in D. Olweus, J. Block & M. Radke-Yarrow, eds., *The Development of Antisocial and Prosocial Behavior: Research, Theories, and Issues.* N.Y.: The Academic Press.

Eron, L.D., Huesmann, L.R., Lefkowitz, M.M. & Walder, L.D. 1972. "Does Television Violence Cause Aggression?" *American Psychologist* 27: 253–63.

Fortner, R.W. 1985. "Relative Effectiveness of Classroom and Documentary Film Presentations on Marine Mammals." *Journal of Research in Science Teaching* 21: 115–26.

Freedman, J. 1984. "Effect of Television Violence on Aggressiveness." *Psychological Bulletin* 96: 227–46.

———. 1986. "Television Violence and Aggression: A Rejoinder." *Psychological Bulletin* 100: 372–78.

Friedrich-Cofer, L. & Huston, A.C. 1986. "Television Violence and Aggression: The Debate Continues." *Psychological Bulletin* 100: 364–71.

Gadberry, S. 1980. "Effects of Restricting First Graders," TV Viewing on Leisure Time Use, I.Q. Change, and Cognitive Style." *Journal of Applied Developmental Psychology* 1: 45–57.

Garry, R. 1967. *Television's Impact on the Child.* Washington: Association for Childhood International.

Geen, R.G. & Thomas, S.L. 1986. "The Immediate Effects of Media Violence on Behavior." *Journal of Social Issues* 42: 7–27.

Gerbner, G. & Gross, L. 1980. "The Violent Face of Television and Its Lessons," in E. Palmer and M. Dorr, eds., *Children and the Faces of Television: Teaching, Violence, Selling.* N.Y.: Academic Press.

Greenberg, B.S. 1982. "Television and Role Socialization: An Overview," in D. Pearl, L. Bouthilet, & J. Lazar, eds., *Television and Behavior: Ten Years of Scientific Progress and Implications for the Eighties.* Vol. 2. Washington: U.S. Government Printing Office.

Greenfield, P.M. 1984. *Mind and Media: The Effects of Television, Video Games, and Computers.* Cambridge, Mass.: Harvard University Press.

Hawkins, R.P. & Pingree, S. 1982. "Television's Influence on Social Reality," in D. Pearl, L. Bouthilet, & J. Lazar, eds., *Television and Behavior: Ten Years of Scientific Progress and Implications for the Eighties.* Vol. 2. Washington: U.S. Government Printing Office.

Himmelweit, H.T. & Bell, N. 1980. "Television as a Sphere of Influence on the Child's Learning about Sexuality," in E.J. Roberts, ed., *Childhood Sexual Learning: The Unwritten Curriculum.* Cambridge, Mass.: Ballinger.

Huesmann, L.R. 1986a. "Cross-National Communalities in the Learning of Aggression from Media Violence," in L.R. Huesmann & L.D. Eron, eds., *Television and the Aggressive Child: A Cross-National Comparison.* Hillsdale, N.J.: Lawrence Erlbaum Assoc. Publ.

———. 1986b. "Psychological Processes Promoting the Relation Between Exposure to Media Violence and Aggressive Behavior by the Viewer." *Journal of Social Issues* 42: 125–39.

Huesmann, L.R. & Eron, L.D. 1984. "Cognitive Processes and the Persistence of Aggressive Behavior." *Aggressive Behavior* 10: 243–51.

———. 1986a. "The Development of Aggression in Children of Different Cultures: Psychological Processes and Exposure to Violence," in L.R. Huesmann & L.D. Eron, eds., *Television and the Aggressive Child: A Cross-National Comparison.* Hillsdale, N.J.: Lawrence Erlbaum Assoc. Publ.

———. 1986b. *Television and the Aggressive Child: A Cross-National Comparison.* Hillsdale, N.J.: Lawrence Erlbaum Assoc. Publ.

Huesmann, L.R., Eron, L.D. Lefkowitz, M.M. & Walder, L.O. 1984. "Stability of Aggression Over Time and Generations." *Developmental Psychology* 20: 1120–34.

Huesmann, L.R., Eron, L.D. & Yarmel, P.W. 1987. "Intellectual Functioning and Aggression." *Journal of Personality and Social Psychology* 52: 232–40.

Huesmann, L.R., Lagerspetz, K. & Eron, L.D. 1984. "Intervening Variables in the Television Violence-Aggression Relation: Evidence from Two Countries." *Developmental Psychology* 20: 746–75.

Huesmann, L.R. & Malamuth, N.M. 1986. "Media Violence and Antisocial Behavior: An Overview." *Journal of Social Issues* 42: 1–6.

Hutchinson, L.F. 1979. "Since They're Going to Watch T.V. Anyway, Why Not Connect It To Reading?" *Reading World* 18: 236–39.

Johnston, J. & Ettema, J. 1982. *Positive Images: Breaking Stereotypes with Children's Television.* Beverly Hills, Calif.: Sage.

Lorch, E.P., Bellack, D.R. & Augsbach, L.H. 1987. "Young Children's Memory for Televised Stories: Effects of Importance." *Child Development* 58: 453–63.

McCarthy, E.D., Langner, T.S., Gersten, J.C., Eisenberg, J.G. & Orzeck, L. 1975. "Violence and Behavior Disorders." *Journal of Communication* 25: 71–85.

Milavsky, J.R., Kessler, R.C., Stipp, H.H. & Rubens, W.S. 1982. *Television and Aggression: A Panel Study.* N.Y.: Academic Press.

Morgan, M. & Gross, L. 1982. "Television and Educational Achievement and Aspiration," in D. Pearl, L. Bouthilet & J. Lazar, eds., *Television and Behavior: Ten Years of Scientific Progress and Implications for the Eighties.* Vol. 2. Washington: U.S. Government Printing Office.

National Coalition on Television Violence. 1984. "Rock Music and MTV Found Increasingly Violent." Press release, Champaign, Illinois, 14 Jan. 1984 (cited in Sherman & Dominick 1986).

National Institute of Mental Health. 1982. *Television and Behavior: Ten Years of Scientific Progress and Implications for the Eighties.* Vol. 1. Washington: U.S. Government Printing Office.

O'Bryant, S.L. & Corder-Bolz, C.R. 1977. "Tackling 'the tube' with Family Teamwork." *Children Today* 7: 21–24.

Pearl, D., Bouthilet, L. & Lazar, J., eds. 1982. *Television and Behavior: Ten Years of Scientific Progress and Implications for the Eighties.* Vol. 2. Washington: U.S. Government Printing Office.

Quarforth, J.M. 1979. "Children's Understanding of the Nature of Television Characters." *Journal of Communication* 29: 210–18.

Rapaczynski, W., Singer, D.G. & Singer, J.L. 1982. "Teaching Television: A Curriculum for Young Children." *Journal of Communication* 32: 46–55.

Rice, M.L., Huston, A.C. & Wright, J.C. 1986. "Replays as Repetitions: Young Children's Interpretation of Television Forms." *Journal of Applied Developmental Psychology* 7: 61–76.

Rule, B.G. & Ferguson, T.J. 1986. "The Effects of Media Violence on Attitudes, Emotions, and Cognitions." *Journal of Social Issues* 42: 29–50.

Schorr, L.B. 1983. "Television," in M.D. Levine, W.B. Carey, A.C. Crocker, & R.T. Gross, eds., *Developmental-Behavioral Pediatrics.* Philadelphia: W.B. Saunders Co.

Sherman, B.L. & Dominick, J.R. 1986. "Violence and Sex in Music Videos: TV and Rock 'n' Roll." *Journal of Communication* 36: 79–93.

Signorielli, N., Gross, L. & Morgan, M. 1982. "Violence in Television Programs: Ten Years Later," in D. Pearl, L. Bouthilet & J. Lazar, eds., *Television and Behavior: Ten Years of Scientific Progress and Implications for the Eighties.* Vol. 2. Washington: U.S. Government Printing Office.

Singer, D.G. 1982. "Television and the Developing Imagination of the Child," in D. Pearl, L. Bouthilet & J. Lazar, eds., *Television and Behavior: Ten Years of Scientific Progress and Implications for the Eighties.* Vol. 2. Washington: U.S. Government Printing Office.

Singer, D.G., Singer, J.L. & Zuckerman, D. 1980. *Teaching Television: How to Use Television to Your Child's Advantage.* N.Y.: Dial.

Singer, D.G., Zuckerman, D. & Singer, J.L. 1980. "Helping Elementary School Children Learn About TV." *Journal of Communication* 30: 84–93.

Singer, J.L. & Singer, D.G. 1981. *Television, Imagination and Aggression: A Study of Preschoolers Play.* Hillsdale, N.J.: Lawrence Erlbaum Assoc. Publ.

———. 1983. "Psychologists Look at Television: Cognitive, Developmental, Personality, and Social Policy Implications." *American Psychologist* 38: 826–34.

"Smart Kids' Guide to TV Advertising." 1987. *Instructor* 46: 88–92.

Sun, Se-Wen & Lull, J. 1986. "The Adolescent Audience for Music Videos and Why They Watch." *Journal of Communication* 36: 115–25.

Turner, C.W., Hesse, B.W. & Peterson-Lewis, S. 1986. "Naturalistic Studies of the Long-Term Effects of Television Violence." *Journal of Social Issues* 42: 51–73.

Williams, P.A., Haertel, E.H., Haertel, G.D. & Walberg, H.J. 1982. "The Impact of Leisure Time Television on School Learning: A Research Synthesis." *American Educational Research Journal* 19: 19–50.

Williams, T.M. 1978. *Differential Impact of TV on Children: A Natural Experiment in Communities with and without TV.* Paper presented at the meeting of the International Society for Research on Aggression, Washington.

World Almanac and Book of Facts, 1985, 1987. 1984, 1986. N.Y.: Newspaper Enterprise Association, Inc.

Wright, J.C. & Huston, A.C. 1983. "A Matter of Form: Potentials of Television for Young Viewers." *American Psychologist* 38: 835–43.

4
Parental Discord and Divorce

Divorce is far more than a single crisis in a family's life. Research has found it to be a multiple-stage process that disrupts family members for many years. Often, the decisive marital rupture is preceded by years of tension and conflict. Most typically, it is followed by an extended aftermath, marked by family transition and stress. During this aftermath, both the family's life and the long-established relationships of its members with one another undergo dramatic changes, which frequently are unanticipated and painful (Hetherington 1979, 1981).

Yet, available evidence indicates that children in divorcing families receive extraordinarily little support during this critical time. Family support collapses and outsiders are fearful of intruding. Generally, there is poor awareness of the plight of the child in the divorcing family and how his adjustment can best be facilitated.

The research studying divorce has yielded a wealth of information with compelling implications. It has examined how divorce has affected large numbers of families, why some children successfully adjust whereas others adjust poorly, and whether children whose parents stay together in a marriage filled with conflict fare better or worse than those whose parents divorce. This research indicates that most of the negative outcomes experienced by children in divorcing families arise not from the divorce itself but from events that surround divorce—events that, in many cases, are avoidable.

Divorce: The Experience

A child's experiences during the divorce process are so intertwined with those of her parents that it is impossible to examine the effects of divorce on children without first looking at its typical effects on both mother and father.

E. Mavis Hetherington and her colleagues (1978a) found that many couples they studied expected divorce to bring them a new lifestyle—one of greater freedom, less conflict, new experiences, and self-discovery. Their perceptions did not seem unrealistic to them. The book market, after all, is rampant with titles that encourage, perhaps partially create, such expectations (*Creative Divorce: A New Opportunity for Personal Growth; The Hundred Forty-Nine Ways to Profit from Your Divorce; Getting Unstuck: Moving on After Divorce*). But Hetherington and her colleagues found few couples prepared for the road to postdivorce adjustment that they actually encountered. For most people they studied, divorce was full of trauma and stress. Even many of those who initially felt an "ebullient sense of freedom" reported feeling anxious, depressed, or apathetic after several months.

Why should adjustment to divorce have been so difficult, even though the marriages had been so poor? Most people expect family conflict to end with divorce. Instead it generally escalates, at least during the first year and often longer (see Emery 1982, Hetherington 1981, Wallerstein & Kelly 1980). During this time, parent contact typically is consumed by battles about finances, support, visitation, child rearing differences, and intimate relationships with others (Hetherington, Cox & Cox 1978a). Stress within the family also heightens as parents and children face dramatic and unanticipated changes in their lives. Learning to cope with these changes is a slow process, its early stages often dominated by loneliness, failures, and conflicts (Hetherington, Cox & Cox 1978a; Wallerstein & Kelly 1980).

Divorced mothers find themselves spread thin at a time when emotional problems leave them little energy. They usually have custody of the children and must assume full child rearing responsibilities along with all the tasks formerly performed by their husbands (Hetherington 1979, Wallerstein & Kelly 1980). Financial worries, caused by the inevitably reduced economic resources, frequently are reported as a major source of stress (e.g., Albrecht 1980). Many women must return to full-time employment outside the home, adding to their overload. To make matters worse, divorced mothers often lose the social life they once had, as the initial concern of married friends turns to silence after a few months (Hetherington, Cox & Cox 1978a). Many divorced mothers find the stress overwhelming. Mixed feelings of failure, incompetence, depression, anger, and self-involvement are common. Typically, both their households and day-to-day lives are in a state of disorganization, and their parenting becomes erratic (Hetherington 1979; Hetherington, Cox & Cox 1978a; Wallerstein & Kelly 1980).

Divorced fathers are no less affected. Most have lost their home and steady contact with their children. They complain of feeling rootless, shut out, at loose ends, guilty, and anxious. During the first year, they report sleeping less, eating erratically, developing physical symptoms, having difficulty running a household, burying themselves in work, and having a frenzied rather than a satisfying social life. Similar to their former spouses, divorced fathers commonly are found to be self-involved and to experience strong feelings of failure, incompetence, depression, or anger (Grief 1979; Hetherington, Cox & Cox 1976).

Problems for divorced parents are most severe during the first year, often reaching a peak at about the one-year mark. At this point, new lifestyles are not yet satisfactory and parents wonder whether they should have tried harder to make the marriage work (Hetherington, Cox & Cox 1982; Wallerstein & Kelly 1980). Interestingly, both spouses, the initiator of the divorce and the noninitiator, appear to experience equal levels of stress and emotional trauma, although the timing of their peak stress levels may not be synchronized (Buehler 1987).

Most parents seem to need a two- to three-year period of adjustment after the decisive separation, but for some, the crises and stress of the postdivorce period continue for many years (Hetherington, Cox & Cox 1982; Johnston, Campbell & Tall 1985; Stolberg & Cullen 1983; Wallerstein 1983a). Even after the initial crisis is over, many divorced individuals continue to experience more health and emotional problems than do their married counterparts (see Bloom, Asher & White 1978). These long-term problems are, perhaps, not surprising if divorce is conceptualized as a compound (rather than a single) stressor that affects many aspects of the divorced person's life (Chiriboga, Catron & Weiler 1987).

How do the children fare? To the typical child, divorce creates a number of serious changes to which he must somehow try to adapt. His family is disrupted, and he always seems to be missing one or another of his parents. Yet, the unpleasant parental conflict still continues. His parents' behavior often seems unfamiliar and unpredictable. Not only are they less available to him, but wide mood swings, lethargy, sleep disturbances, and increased drinking, smoking, and drug use are common (see Hetherington & Camara 1984). Usually less money is available since two households must now be maintained. The youngster may suddenly find himself spending long hours in day care or alone because his mother has returned to full-time employment. He may even have to move and, consequently, lose contact with friends and familiar school. It is, understandably, a time during which children need extra doses of support, understanding, and love. However, the two comprehensive and intensive longitudinal studies that have been conducted (Hetherington, Cox & Cox; Wallerstein & Kelly) report a distressing picture of the child's life in the divorcing family (Hetherington 1981; Hetherington, Cox & Cox 1976, 1978a, 1985; Wallerstein 1984, 1985a,b, 1987; Wallerstein & Kelly 1980).

These studies found that parents (because of their own distress, depression, and self-involvement) generally were insensitive to their children's problems, needs, and stress during the first year following divorce or longer. Poor parenting was the rule. Parents offered children less attention, less affection, less support, less communication, and erratic discipline. Homes were chaotic, and inappropriate outbursts of parental anger were common (Hetherington, Cox & Cox 1978a; Wallerstein & Kelly 1980). Older children felt neglected; younger children feared abandonment (Wallerstein 1983b). Support from outside the family, even from grandparents, was lacking too. Most people simply were hesitant to intrude (Wallerstein 1983b).

How do children react to all this stress in their lives? Children's most common early responses are anxiety, fear, depression, guilt, rejection, loneliness, anger, yearning for the missing parent, and fantasies of parent reconciliations (Hetherington 1979, Hetherington & Camara 1984, Wallerstein & Kelly 1980). Difficulties in schoolwork have been reported (Guidubaldi, Perry & Cleminshaw 1984; Kinard & Reinherz 1986; Wallerstein & Kelly 1980). Perhaps most upsetting to parents are the new behavioral problems their offspring, particularly their sons, so often develop both at home and at school, such as aggressiveness, noncompliance, and negativeness (e.g., Emery 1982, Felner et al. 1981, Hetherington 1981, Stolberg & Anker 1984, Wallerstein 1983a). Children's problems, similar to the problems of their parents, are most pronounced during the first year, often peaking at about one year (Hetherington, Cox & Cox 1978a; Wallerstein 1983a).

It is easy to see how such reactions of both parents and children would exacerbate each others' stress. Not surprisingly, both intensive longitudinal studies found that parent-child relationships progressively deteriorated during the first year following divorce (Hetherington, Cox & Cox 1978a; Wallerstein 1983a). Hetherington and her colleagues (1978a) reported that relationships between mothers and young sons were particularly poor, often reflecting a vicious cycle: sons became increasingly more aggressive and noncompliant and mothers became increasingly more restrictive and negative, while offering less support and nurturance. Other studies have also reported the predominance of power-assertive and restrictive patterns of discipline in divorced homes (see Hetherington 1981).

The postdivorce situation, of course, is not equally bleak for all families. In fact, in a different study, Kurdek and Siesky (1980) reported a tendency among older children to report improved relationships with parents.

Divorce: Long-Term Consequences for Children

After reviewing the research, Hetherington and Camara (1984) concluded that most children and their families adjust to the short-term crisis of divorce within a few years, *providing* that additional stress and adversity do not continue in their lives. For example, Hetherington, Cox, and Cox (1978a) found that the second year of divorce generally was one of recovery and adjustment for members of the study families. By the end of two years, most families were over the hump. Parent-child relationships, which had been so stormy, were greatly improved. (Although, generally, there still was more conflict in postdivorce families than in intact families.) Boys' problematic behaviors (such as aggressiveness, noncompliance, and difficulties relating to others) were markedly reduced, although still evident. (A six-year follow-up of these children found that boys were more likely than girls to have some long-term adjustment problems in response to the divorce [Hetherington, Cox & Cox 1985].) By the end of two years, girls' social and emotional difficulties had mostly disappeared (Hetherington 1979).

The most ambitious attempt to study long-term consequences of divorce on children has been made by Judith Wallerstein and Joan Kelly (Wallerstein 1984, 1985a,b, 1987; Wallerstein & Kelly 1980). Their data suggest that the number of children having long-term difficulties may be rather significant. Their's is an in-depth study, which has continued for ten years, of 113 children who ranged from preschoolers to adolescents at the time their parents filed for divorce. A team of clinicians conducted extensive individual interviews with children and parents shortly after the decisive separation and at several follow-up periods. At the five-year follow-up, Wallerstein and Kelly (1980) reported that only one-third (34 percent) of these children were happy and thriving; their self-esteem was high, and they were coping well at home, at school, and with their peers. Boys and girls were equally represented in this resilient group, even though at the eighteen-month follow-up, there had been fewer boys who qualified as resilient. About one-third (29 percent) were doing "reasonably well," although they still were experiencing some loneliness or anger, as well as lowered self-esteem. The remaining one-third (37 percent), however, were intensely unhappy; even after five years, depression, loneliness, and anger occupied a significant part of their emotional lives.

Interestingly, the clinicians could not accurately predict a child's long-term adjustment based upon her initial adjustment. One-third of the children who originally had coped very well developed problems after about a year and a-half. Other children who initially had functioned very poorly showed later marked improvement. This was particularly true for children who previously had been neglected or who had come from homes marked by strife. In these cases, the divorce often improved their lives. The greatest change and unpredictability was seen in the group of children who initially functioned moderately well. Most of these children's adjustment either materially improved or deteriorated, so that by the end of the five-year follow-up, they either were very well adjusted or very poorly adjusted.

Data from other sources also suggest that a number of children from divorced homes continue to have long-term problems. For many boys, behavioral problems appear to become long-standing. There is ample evidence that boys living in divorced-mother-headed homes generally are more aggressive, impulsive, and rebellious than are boys from intact families (see Belsky, Lerner & Spanier 1984; Crouter, Belsky & Spanier 1984; Hetherington & Camara 1984; Hetherington, Cox & Cox 1978b).

For some girls, problems may reappear during adolescence, in the area of heterosexual relationships. Evidence of adolescent heterosexual difficulties have been found in several studies. A few examples follow. Hetherington (1972) found that lower- and lower-middle-class adolescent girls living in divorced-mother-headed homes had difficulty relating appropriately to the opposite sex. For example, while interacting with men and boys, these girls were more anxious, more attention-seeking, inappropriately assertive, and more provocative than were girls from nuclear families. Hetherington suggested that these girls may have missed developing confidence and social skills with the opposite sex because of their limited opportunity to interact with their fathers. In a follow-up study, Hetherington found that these girls (compared to a control group) had married younger, were more likely to have been pregnant before marriage, and had married men who tended to be immature, poorly educated, unstably employed, and who felt ambivalence or hostility toward their wives and children (Hetherington, Cox & Cox 1978b). In a ten-year follow-up of a different study group, Wallerstein (1985a) found evidence of problem heterosexual relationships in one-third of her sample of women whose parents had divorced during the women's preadolescent or adolescent years. These women, who were primarily middle-class, revealed several different patterns of troubled relationships, including sexual promiscuity during adolescence, drifting from one live-in relationship to another in adulthood, and strong fears of heterosexual attachments and betrayal. Although Wallerstein's study group was fairly small, other studies also suggest troubled heterosexual relationships for girls from divorced families. With a large study population, Mueller and Pope (1977) found that girls from divorced homes tended to be younger and less educated when they married, married lower-status men, and were more likely to have their marriages end in divorce, compared to girls from intact homes. The differences could not be explained by parents' socioeconomic level. Other studies have found that girls who have grown up without fathers have less satisfying sexual relationships than do girls from nuclear families (see Hetherington, Cox & Cox 1978b).

There is additional evidence that a number of children from divorced homes experience long-term problems. Consider the following findings. Children with divorced parents are overrepresented in the population of children who are referred for counseling. This is not crisis counseling at the time of the divorce. The average time of referral is five years after the divorce. The most common problems are conduct disorders: for example, aggressiveness, lying, destructiveness, defiance, and so forth (see Emery, Hetherington & Dilalla 1984). Children with divorced parents are overrepresented in the population of youths who attempt or commit suicide (see chapter 5). Many studies have reported that elementary school-age children of divorce, particularly boys, do less well academically than do their peers (see Belsky, Lerner & Spanier 1984; Emery, Hetherington & Dilalla 1984; Hodges 1986). And in a large-scale national study, boys from divorced homes, as a group, not only had more problems behaviorally, socially, and academically, but had more troubled relationships with parents than did their counterparts from intact homes (Guidubaldi, Perry & Cleminshaw 1984).

Divorce: Why Children Adjust Successfully or Poorly

Although a number of children appear to have long-term difficulties, the majority do seem to adjust successfully to their parents' divorce. Some even emerge with greater strength. Why do some children adapt well, whereas others do so poorly? Why do some adjust well initially but develop problems after a lapse of time? To what degree can the stage be set to assure children's successful adjustment?

Researchers in the divorce field have been able to identify a number of conditions that substantially affect children's adjustment to their parents' divorce. Many researchers find it difficult to assign a greater importance to one factor or to another. Lawrence Kurdek (1981) proposes that there may be many paths to good adjustment and that the absence of some of the right conditions can perhaps be compensated for by the presence of others. Negative consequences of divorce are not inevitable.

It will be obvious that these conditions are not totally independent from one another but overlap and interact with each other.

Relationships with Both Parents

Over and over again, research focusing on children's adjustment to divorce has demonstrated the prominent role played by a reliable and good relationship between a child and *each* of his parents (Emery 1982, Hess & Camara 1979, Hetherington 1979, Peterson & Zill 1986, Steinman 1981, Wallerstein & Kelly 1980). If a child has close and stable ties with both parents, she can have most of the emotional benefits offered by an intact family; any negative effects divorce may have on her can be mitigated. A study by Robert Hess and Kathleen Camara (1979) found that the best predictor of children's adjustment after divorce, both socially and academically, was the quality of the relationships they had with each parent. In fact, the quality of these relationships was a better predictor of children's adjustment than whether their parents were divorced or together. Hess and Camara maintain that the largest threat divorce has for children is the change or loss of these relationships.

The relationship between a child and his parent without custody is, of course, the one most vulnerable. Unfortunately, studies find that noncustodial fathers generally become less available to their children as time goes on, especially to their daughters (Hetherington 1981; Hetherington & Camara 1984; Peterson & Zill 1986; Santrock, Warshak & Elliott 1982; Wallerstein & Kelly 1980). For example, in one large-scale study, almost half the children from divorced families had had "virtually no contact" with their noncustodial parent during the previous year (Peterson & Zill 1986).

Even many fathers who were close to their children before the divorce withdraw from them afterward. There is no single reason for their unavailability. Some find the separation painful, some find the artificiality of visits awkward and unsatisfying, some find it difficult to overcome the barriers constructed by their former spouses (Ahrons 1983, Wallerstein & Kelly 1980). Many fathers do not take their withdrawal from their children lightly. They feel depressed and a sense of loss but can find no other way to handle their pain and stress (Grief 1979; Hetherington, Cox & Cox 1982). Other fathers find it easier to withdraw from their children, as indicated by the Weitzman and Dixon (1979) finding that less than half of the fathers under study were paying any child support one year after the divorce.

The unavailability of the noncustodial parent is distressing to children. In a study conducted by Hingst (1981), 50 percent of the children said that the worst thing about their parents' divorce was missing their father, and 77 percent wished for more time with him. Children's adjustment also suffers when their noncustodial parent is unavailable (Hetherington 1979, Jacobson 1978, Wallerstein & Kelly 1980).

In the Wallerstein and Kelly (1980) sample, even five years after the divorce, children with an indifferent noncustodial parent still felt anguished, depressed, and rejected. These children felt both unloved and unlovable, and generally they had low self-esteem.

Quality of Parenting in the Custodial Home

One often hears that if the custodial parent successfully adjusts to divorce, so will the children. It is true that it is easier on children if custodial parents can quickly handle the divorce themselves, create continuity in the new home situation, and establish stable patterns of living for the family (Hetherington 1979). However, parents' good adjustment to divorce is of no value to children if the quality of their parenting is poor (Stolberg & Bush 1985, Wallerstein & Kelly 1980).

The parenting of the child typically does break down in the divorcing family, but it is most important that it be resumed as quickly as possible. Ample evidence indicates that good parenting is an important predictor of a child's postdivorce adjustment. In fact, in their review of the literature, Crouter, Belsky, and Spanier (1984) suggested that poor parenting is the main cause of the negative effects that divorce has upon children.

Not surprisingly, studies have found that the custodial parent has a greater impact on children's adjustment than does the noncustodial parent (see Hetherington 1979, Lowery 1985). The quality of the relationship between the child and this parent is particularly crucial because the nonresident parent is not there to act as a buffer. For some children, an exceptionally good relationship with a sensitive, nurturant, and very caring custodial parent can compensate (although usually not totally) for an indifferent noncustodial parent. On the other hand, a good relationship with a nonresident parent does not seem to compensate for an immature or rejecting resident parent (Hetherington, Cox & Cox 1982; Wallerstein & Kelly 1980).

Good parenting may be important not only to the child's adjustment but to the custodial parent's adjustment as well. Hetherington, Cox, and Cox (1978b) reported that divorced mothers' self-esteem and happiness were increased more by a program in which they learned better parenting skills than by dynamic insight therapy.

Some researchers have identified conditions in the custodial home that facilitate children's adjustment. These can serve as guidelines to custodial parents. All children need warmth, sensitivity, nurturance, support, and good parent-child communication during the postdivorce period (Hetherington 1979, Hetherington & Camara 1984, Wallerstein 1983a). This cannot be overstressed. Additionally, different age children seem to require a somewhat different emphasis in the home during this time.

Preschoolers show better adjustment when their environment is highly structured, organized, and predictable and when rules are clearly defined and consistently enforced (Hetherington 1979). Hetherington points out that young children have difficulty with self-control during times of stress and so need external controls. Part of the preschool pattern is to regress to inappropriately immature behavior, and most parents seem to feel that it is best to make no demands on their young children during this difficult time. Contrary to their instincts, Hetherington advises parents to make appropriate maturity demands of preschoolers, firmly but lovingly.

Although school-age children do not need a highly structured environment, they do need well-organized routines, clearly defined rules, and consistent discipline. They also need a good deal of communication and verbal give and take (Hetherington & Camara 1984; Santrock, Warshak & Elliott 1982).

With school-age children and adolescents, parents often fall into the trap of making too many maturity demands. Children are pushed into assuming adult roles and responsibilities at too early an age. Many children care for the house and younger siblings and must emotionally support the parent as well. Not surprisingly, these children often feel overwhelmed, overburdened, and resentful (Hetherington & Camara 1984, Wallerstein 1985b). Hetherington and Camara (1984) report that these children frequently withdraw from the family and/or become sexually precocious. Researchers and clinicians agree that it is fine for school-age children to have some increased responsibilities and some sharing of a parent's concerns and plans, if not excessive (Hetherington 1979, Messinger & Walker 1981, Wallerstein 1985b). In fact, often this new role seems to create new relationships between parent and children that are companionate, loving, and sensitive (Wallerstein & Kelly 1980). How can a parent judge whether maturity demands are excessive or reasonable? The key, according to Messinger and Walker (1981), is realizing that children are still children and have both a right and a need to mature at their own rate. Requiring them to take on additional responsibilities is unlikely to harm them, but requiring them to function as little adults may.

Stress and Environmental Change

The amount of stress in the postdivorce period is yet another important factor in children's adjustment. Research suggests that a child usually can handle a single stress (such as divorce) without real risk of long-term negative consequences, but the risks multiply if she is faced with additional stresses (see Hetherington 1979, Hetherington & Camara 1984, Rutter 1979). In other words, a single stress places a child in a vulnerable position but one which is not insurmountable. If she must deal with an additional source of stress at the same time, she receives a double whammy. Each additional source of stress she encounters compounds her already difficult task of reconstructing her life and increases her perceptions that she has little control over her world (see chapter 5).

Environmental changes during the postdivorce period operate as additional sources of stress for children. A series of investigations conducted by Arnold Stolberg and his associates (1983, 1984, 1985) has found that the greater the amount of change in the home environment, the more likely that the child will develop maladaptive behavior, such as poor prosocial skills, aggressiveness, depression, or withdrawal. Unfortunately, divorce generally goes hand in hand with changes in the home environment: loss of one parent from the home, less parent involvement and availability, heightened conflict, uncertainty, financial problems, moving, remarriage, and so forth.

The stress factor probably explains the Hodges and Bloom (1984) finding that children fare better when their parents divorce rather than continue in a long separation. According to these researchers, a long separation leaves the child in a stressful state of limbo—hoping for a reconciliation, fearing the divorce, and unable to get on with his life.

Parental Conflict

Conflict is really a form of stress for families, but its continued presence or alleviation is so important to children's postdivorce adjustment that it warrants special attention. Escaping from parental conflict is one of the few positive aspects of divorce for children (Hetherington 1981, Wallerstein & Kelly 1980). However, when parents continue emotional warfare for many years following the divorce, very often the end result is youngsters' poor adjustment (e.g., Emery 1982; Jacobson 1978; Johnston, Campbell & Tall 1985; Kurdek & Blisk 1983; Wallerstein 1985b; Wallerstein & Kelly 1980). For these children, not only was the marriage a failure but so was the divorce. They are bewildered, angry, and can't begin to understand or to justify the suffering they have experienced (Wallerstein & Kelly 1980).

Overt bickering or fighting is the most obvious form of conflict in postdivorce families but, as Hetherington (1979) points out, not the only one. Some parents, due to their own bitterness and anguish, openly criticize and degrade their divorced spouse. This causes children to question, revise, and de-idealize their own perceptions of the criticized parent. This process is both painful and full of conflict. Other parents, says Hetherington, interpret a child's love for the divorced spouse as a personal rejection, as if a youngster could love only mother or father but not both. Because of this insecurity, a parent often resorts to pressuring a child for her sole allegiance, her rejection of the other parent, or her joining in an alliance against the other parent. Whether this pressure is overt or subtle, it is harmful. Most children want a relationship with both parents and have difficulty coping with conflicting loyalties.

A Child's Temperament and Predivorce Adjustment

Few would find it surprising that children's temperament and general adjustment play a role in their adjustment to divorce. Children with difficult temperaments (as compared to easygoing children) have been found to be less adaptable and less able to cope with adversity. To make matters worse, children with difficult dispositions are more likely to provoke anger and to elicit criticism from already distraught parents. These children not only have more difficulty coping with the divorce situation, but they have a more difficult situation to adapt to than do their easier going siblings (see Hetherington 1979, 1981).

What role does predivorce adjustment play? A child's adjustment prior to divorce does not necessarily predict his postdivorce adjustment, but there are trends in that direction. Two-thirds of the Wallerstein and Kelly (1980) sample who were judged to be well adjusted initially continued to function well. And children with histories of maladjustment were more likely to develop long-term emotional disturbances. For these children the divorce, undoubtedly, compounded the problems already in their lives.

A Child's Gender

Boys (particularly younger boys) are much more overtly affected by divorce than are girls. Boys' greater difficulties extend to all areas—emotional, social, behavioral, and academic (see Emery 1982; Hetherington 1979, 1981; Hodges & Bloom 1984; Wallerstein & Kelly 1980). Adjustment to divorce is also slower for boys.

For many boys, some problems continue. Many studies indicate that boys in divorced-mother-headed homes tend to be less self-controlled and more antisocial, impulsive, and rebellious than are boys from intact families (see Belsky, Lerner & Spanier 1984; Crouter, Belsky & Spanier 1984; Hetherington, Cox & Cox 1978b; Hetherington & Camara 1984).

Why boys have a more difficult time with divorce is not clear. However, research suggests that boys experience a more difficult postdivorce environment than do girls. Compared to girls, boys are more likely to be exposed to parental battles. Boys encounter more opposition, negative sanctions, and inconsistency from parents. Boys receive less support, sensitivity, and nurturance from parents, teachers, and peers (see Hetherington & Camara 1984). Of course, it is difficult to say how much this treatment by others might contribute to boys' problems and how much boys' aggressive and noncompliant behavior contributes to their treatment. Most probably, boys are caught in a vicious cycle—one that may be broken if others are more attuned to the special difficulties boys are having.

A series of investigations, conducted by Santrock and his colleagues (1982), may shed additional light on the sex differences usually found in the divorce literature. In their samples of middle-class elementary school children, they have found that boys who are in the custody of their fathers are more mature, independent, sociable and less demanding than are boys in the custody of their mothers. Similarly, better adjustment has been found for girls in mother custody than in father custody. Along the same lines, Peterson and Zill (1986) found that problem behavior was less likely in adolescents living with the same sex parent.

It may be that children adjust better when they live with their parent of the same sex. Why? Santrock and his colleagues (1982) suggest that parents may be more likely to show warmth, set clear rules, and talk openly with a child of the same sex. With a child of the opposite sex, parents may be more likely to be authoritarian or permissive.

The most common arrangement in the country is still mother custody, and certainly the research has focused on mother-custody families because of their availability. Custody arrangements may contribute to the more severe problems observed in boys. However, it is important to point out that the number of children in these studies was very small. Future research is required before enough confidence can be placed in these findings to influence custody decisions.

The possibility has been raised that girls also may be seriously affected by their parents' divorce, but their problems may be less noticeable than the behavior problems characteristic of boys (Emery, Hetherington & Dilalla 1984). A number of studies have found that girls are more likely to be depressed, withdrawn, and anxious during the postdivorce period (Emery, Hetherington & Dilalla 1984; Hetherington & Camara 1984; Reynolds 1985). However, these problems have not been found consistently, as have boys' problems. The troubled heterosexual relationships experienced by some girls during adolescence and young adulthood were discussed earlier.

A Child's Age

Frequently it is asked whether older or younger children have an easier time with divorce. The data is inconclusive. Some studies have indicated that it is the preschool child who is more affected (see Longfellow 1979). Others have suggested that it is the elementary school-age child (Stolberg & Cullen 1983). Still others have found age to be unrelated to adjustment (see Emery 1982). From their intensive longitudinal study, Wallerstein and Kelly (1980) noted that children of all ages are affected dramatically by divorce. However, each age group, because of its particular level of development, experiences a unique set of problems.

The Preschooler. The preschooler, because of her intellectual stage of development, perceives that she is the center of the world and that everything revolves around her. It is not surprising, then, to find this age child blaming herself for the divorce and believing it to be a personal rejection (Neal 1983, Wallerstein & Kelly 1980). She is both fearful and bewildered, and fantasies of abandonment are common. Typical responses are acting-out behavior and regressions in behavior, such as lapses in toilet training, masturbation, and reliance on security blankets (Hetherington, Cox & Cox 1978b; Wallerstein & Kelly 1980).

Some researchers believe that children in this age group are the most vulnerable during the postdivorce period (Kurdek 1981, Longfellow 1979). Preschoolers are the most dependent upon their parents and experience the most dramatic changes in their lives (Stolberg & Bush 1985, Wallerstein 1984). Additionally, they are the most visibly troubled, and the severity of their problems worsens over the first eighteen months (Hodges & Bloom 1984, Wallerstein 1984).

At the time of their five-year follow-up, however, Wallerstein and Kelly (1980) found preschoolers' adjustment to be no poorer than that of older children. And when followed up after ten years, this youngest age group seemed to have the fewest scars. They had little or no memory of the intact family, its strife, the divorce, or their feelings at the time (Wallerstein 1984).

The 6- to 8-Year-Old. Wallerstein and Kelly (1980) report that 6- to 8-year-olds do not blame themselves for the divorce as do preschoolers, but they do respond with a great sense of personal loss. More able to express their feelings than are their younger counterparts, children in this age group typically display pervasive sadness, feelings of rejection and abandonment, and a belief that the intact family is necessary for their well-being (Wallerstein & Kelly 1980). This age child believes that if he tries hard enough, his parents will reconcile (Neal 1983).

In Wallerstein's ten-year follow-up of this age group (1987), one-half of the boys and one-quarter of the girls were judged to be poorly adjusted. Typically observed were an overall sense of powerlessness, feelings of having been inadequately nurtured, and intense worries about relationships, commitments, and betrayal.

The 9- to 12-Year-Old. Although expressions of anger are not prevalent in 6- to 8-year olds, the 9- to 12-year-old child is likely to express intense anger at one or both parents, depending upon whom he blames for the divorce (Wallerstein & Kelly 1980). This age child is apt to align himself with one parent against the other, often turning on a parent with whom he had been close at one time. The 9- to 12-year-old believes that parents can reconcile their differences if only they try hard enough. Failure to do so is interpreted as selfishness (Neal 1983). Better able to perceive his situation from another's point of view, this age child commonly expresses shame and embarrassment about the divorce. He also experiences a shaken sense of who he is, who he will become, and what is right and wrong. Feelings of loneliness and somatic symptoms (headaches, stomachaches) are typical (Wallerstein & Kelly 1980).

In her ten-year follow-up, Wallerstein (1985a) grouped these children together with adolescents in her analysis. Both groups will be discussed together in the following section.

The Adolescent. Among adolescents, anger, intense sorrow, and acute depression are common responses to parental divorce (Wallerstein & Kelly 1980). Teens may be uniquely affected by divorce in several ways. It is difficult for some adolescents to deal with their parents' vulnerability and sexuality when they are struggling with their own. For some, concerns about their own futures and future marriages become intense. Additionally, many are forced to grow up very quickly. Wallerstein and Kelly found that many adolescents can meet these challenges, becoming helpful and compassionate in the process. But others, who still need the secure base of the family, show disruption in the normal tasks of growing up.

Adolescents who coped best were able to distance themselves emotionally and observe their parents and the divorce objectively.

In Wallerstein's ten-year follow-up, those who had been older children (ages 9 to 12) or adolescents when parents parted generally believed that the divorce had been a major influence in their lives (Wallerstein 1985a). Most felt that life had been more difficult for them than for their peers, but many felt that they had become stronger because of the experience. As a group, they were highly committed to a lasting marriage. However, one-third of the women had troubled heterosexual relationships, as discussed previously. Additionally, 30 percent (12 out of 40) of this predominantly middle-class group had become involved in illegal activities that were moderately serious to serious (burglary, assault, drug dealing, drunk driving, and so on). Perhaps the lack of discipline and structure, so typical in the postdivorce family, is especially harmful to older children and adolescents.

Parental Conflict: Should We Stay Together for the Children's Sake?

Since the road to postdivorce adjustment for both parents and children generally is not an easy or quick one, would it be better for children if their parents stayed together rather than divorced? Robert Emery (1982) reviewed the research that studied children who live in homes full of conflict and discord. He found the following: (1) These children are more likely to have behavioral and adjustment problems than are children from conflict-free families. (Problems of undercontrol, for example, aggression, poor self-control, and noncompliance, are found rather consistently. Problems of overcontrol, for example, anxiety and withdrawal, are found less consistently.) (2) The negative effects of parental conflict are more pronounced in boys than in girls. (3) Parental conflict is more detrimental to children the more it is openly hostile and the longer it continues. (4) The harmful consequences of marital conflict can be lessened for a child if he has very good relationships with his parents. However, there is a catch: parent-child relationships generally are poorer in discordant families (see Emery 1982, Peterson & Zill 1986). If all this sounds familiar, it is because there is a great deal of similarity between children from divorced families and children from discordant families.

This similarity led Emery to pose an interesting question. Which is more responsible for the behavioral problems so often found in children of divorce—the physical disruption of the family or marital conflict? He teased out some interesting findings from the literature. He discovered that children were more likely to have behavioral problems in the following situations: if they were separated from a parent by divorce rather than by death; if their divorced parents were still in conflict rather than coexisting harmoniously; if they were living in discordant intact homes as compared to conflict-free broken homes. Emery concluded that it is parental conflict, rather than the disruption of the family, that plays the more dominant role in the continuing behavioral problems so often found in children during the postdivorce years. (This does not imply that parental conflict is responsible for *all* problems experienced by children in postdivorce families.)

Additional support for Emery's conclusion comes from a longitudinal study published by Jeanne Block and her associates (1986) which suggests that many of the behavioral problems found in boys following divorce, such as aggression and poor self-control, actually may begin many years prior to the divorce—presumably due to the conflict and stress in the predivorce family.

The relationship between discordant homes and children's behavioral problems is a puzzling one. It is a relationship consistently found for boys, less so for girls. A possible explanation offered in the literature is that battling parents model a good deal of angry, hostile, and uncooperative behavior which children then adopt (Felner, Stolberg & Cowen 1975). The fact that aggression is more pronounced in boys from discordant homes than in girls from discordant homes may reflect the fact that aggression is more socially acceptable in boys than in girls. It may also reflect the fact that boys are exposed to more parental conflict than are girls (Hetherington & Camara 1984).

In a review of the research, O'Leary and Emery (1984) discovered that the relationship between behavior problems and discordant homes is much stronger in children referred for counseling than for the general population of children from discordant homes. They suggest that children may be able to handle parental discord if it is the only stress in their lives. But when combined with other stresses, marital conflict is more likely to have a significantly negative impact on youngsters.

Discordant homes may result in additional problems for children. Long and others (1987) found that parental conflict was the critical variable associated with lower levels of social and cognitive competence in adolescents. Interestingly, recent parental divorce in the absence of conflict was not related to low levels of functioning.

A number of researchers have concluded that divorce may offer a better environment to a child whose alternative is living in a discordant home—providing that marital conflict does not continue after the divorce (e.g., Emery 1982; Hetherington, Cox & Cox 1982; Longfellow 1979).

Buffering Children from the Negative Consequences of Divorce

The research studying divorce has clear and compelling implications. It is not necessarily better for children if parents remain together. And if parental conflict is severe and chronic, their staying together may do their children more harm than good (Emery 1982; Hetherington, Cox & Cox 1982; Longfellow 1979). Furthermore, the divorce itself does not negatively affect children as much as the conditions frequently associated with divorce, such as loss of the relationship with the noncustodial parent, parental conflict, diminished parenting, and the overwhelming changes in the child's life (see Crouter, Belsky & Spanier 1984).

Once the decision to divorce is made, it is crucial for children's adjustment that parents make every effort to accomplish the following:

1. Develop and maintain close and stable relationships with each of their children.
2. Make every effort to minimize their conflict with one another, at least in the children's presence.
3. Provide a stable, nurturant, and supportive environment in which each child's stress and difficulties are sensitively recognized, in which children are encouraged to talk about their feelings, and in which rules are consistently made and enforced.
4. Minimize any other changes in their children's environment, maintaining as much continuity between the old and new environments as possible.

Of course, knowing what is good for a child is very different from knowing how it can be achieved. Sometimes external conditions form barriers that parents feel are insurmountable. How does a father maintain a close relationship with his children during semimonthly visits to a park and restaurant? How can parents terminate their conflict when each relies heavily on lawyers who, interested only in their client's "winning," frequently give advice that escalates conflict?

Based both on research findings and clinical observations, mental health professionals have recommended different strategies to buffer the negative consequences of divorce for children. Many specific resource programs have been developed for members of divorcing families (e.g., Bronkowski, Bequette & Boomhower 1984; Faust 1987; Stolberg & Cullen 1983; Warren & Amara 1984; Pedro-Carroll & Cowen 1985; Pedro-Carroll et al. 1986). The following are two examples. The limited research that has looked at the effectiveness of each of these programs is encouraging.

The Divorce Adjustment Project (Stolberg & Cullen 1983) works with both children and parents (independently), teaching new skills and replacing lost social support systems. In the children's component of the program, youngsters (ages 8 to 12) meet for twelve sessions in children's support groups which can be held in their schools. In a supportive group atmosphere, children discuss divorce-related feelings and problems. They are also taught communication skills, impulse control skills, anger control skills, and relaxation techniques. Modeling and role-playing are used to teach ways of handling problems stemming from the divorce.

A program developed by Pedro-Carroll and her associates (1985, 1986) also can be conducted in school-based support groups. The program helps children to express divorce-related feelings and to share common experiences; it emphasizes enhancing self-esteem; it builds skills in communication, problem-solving, and anger control; and it works to clarify lingering misconceptions. Filmstrips, role-playing, and experiential exercises are used.

Families in the crisis of divorce can obtain assistance from community mental health facilities, family service agencies, community-sponsored programs, and counselors in the private sector. Most help is offered on a short-term basis (Hetherington & Camara 1984). Mental health professionals working with divorcing persons are referred to the special fall/winter 1986 issue of *Journal of Divorce*. It is titled "The Divorce Process: A Handbook for Clinicians."

In addition to formal kinds of help, researchers and mental health professionals offer more general suggestions that may be helpful to divorcing families. Some of these follow.

Establishing Support Systems

An increasing number of researchers are pointing out that divorcing families need extrafamilial support systems (Hetherington, Cox & Cox 1978b; Kurdek 1981; Longfellow 1979; Stolberg & Cullen 1983; Wallerstein 1983b). In the longitudinal study conducted by Hetherington, Cox, and Cox, a mother's outside support systems were related to her effectiveness as a parent (Hetherington 1981). Yet, generally, divorced women are found to have fewer contacts (friends, social organizations, and recreational activities) than do their married counterparts. Feelings of loneliness and social isolation are common. Both have been found to increase divorced mothers' vulnerability to acute depression (Longfellow 1979). Unfortunately, family ties (which divorced women tend to maintain) seem less effective in reducing feelings of loneliness than do social networks of friends and intimate relationships (Hetherington, Cox & Cox 1978b).

Wallerstein (1983b) reported that children who received outside support benefited from the concern of others. Yet, she reported that the children in her large-scale study received extraordinarily little support; their loneliness was striking. Only 25 percent of the children received support from members of their extended family, including grandparents. And less than 10 percent received support from an adult outside the family (teachers, pediatricians, members of their church or synagogue, and so on). People were afraid of intruding.

Wallerstein (1983b) makes a strong case for people to become more cognizant of the stress and loneliness of the child in the divorcing family. Particularly during the first year of divorce, when so many parents are psychologically unavailable to their children, the support of outside adults can be vitally important to a child who feels lost in the shuffle. Even minor efforts can make a difference: grandparents spending extra time with him, a teacher paying him special attention or offering a project that will bring him recognition and pleasure, a minister offering some special words of compassion and caring, a pediatrician talking with him about his feelings and concerns.

Establishing Continuity and an Atmosphere of Open Discussion

Children should be told about the impending divorce before one parent physically leaves the home. Based upon her longitudinal study, Wallerstein (1983b) suggests that time be given for several discussions about the divorce during which children's questions can be answered and their concerns and feelings openly expressed. Wallerstein suggests that the following points be made clear to youngsters: (1) the divorce is strictly between the parents, entirely separate from the children; (2) each child will be loved and cared for; (3) children can continue to love both parents, without taking sides. Additionally, the changes that will occur in the youngsters' lives should be discussed.

The more that parents help children deal with the separation, the better children adjust to the divorce, according to research reported by Jacobson (1978). Furthermore, open discussion should not end with the divorce but continue throughout the divorce adjustment period. Jacobson found that children's adjustment was better if discussion was encouraged *after* the divorce as well as before.

The point at which one parent physically leaves the home is a particularly stressful time. Children's primary fear seems to be the loss of their relationship with the departing parent (Hess & Camara 1979). Not only do children need reassurance that this parent will remain a part of their lives, but they need to understand the logistics of how this will be accomplished. In other words, it is important to their adjustment that specific plans for future visits and relationships be discussed and agreed upon before the parent leaves (Ahrons 1980, Messinger & Walker 1981). Then, the agreed-upon arrangements should begin immediately. A lapse of time before the first visit is often encouraged by either the parent with custody or by the legal system, supposedly to help children adjust to the separation (Messinger & Walker 1981). But is this really in the best interests of children? It breaks the continuity in the relationship between child and separated parent and creates a psychological distance between them. It may also heighten children's fear of abandonment. All of these are counterproductive to youngsters' adjustment (Messinger & Walker 1981).

Ending Open Marital Conflict

That marital conflict negatively affects children's functioning has been a recurrent theme throughout this chapter. Consistently, studies have demonstrated that it lays the groundwork for children's poor adjustment and intensified behavioral problems (see Emery 1982).

Yet, family conflict generally does escalate in the first year of divorce and frequently continues for many years (Hetherington 1979, Wallerstein 1983a). In their longitudinal study, Wallerstein and Kelly found that one-third of the children were still experiencing open conflict between their parents a full five years after the divorce (Wallerstein 1983a).

The importance of parents' reducing their open conflict with one another cannot be overstressed. This requires them to compartmentalize their negative feelings towards one another, so that they do not spill over into their parenting. Lillian Messinger and Kenneth Walker (1981) suggest that details about future parenting roles should be worked out before parents seek legal advice, since the legal system often serves to escalate conflict or to create a greater impasse between divorcing spouses.

Presently, divorce mediation is being championed as an effective method of resolving disputes between divorcing parties (see, e.g., Elkin 1987; Johnston, Campbell & Tall 1985). Divorce mediation is not therapy or marital counseling (Elkin 1987, Kressel 1985). In mediation, a professionally trained and neutral third party helps the divorcing spouses to arrive at decisions through a process of rational decision making, negotiation, and compromise. All divorce-related decisions can be dealt with—custody, visitation, child support, spousal support, division of property, and so forth. Mediation offers divorcing spouses the possibility of determining their own futures rather than leaving decisions to the courts. Examples of divorce mediation models can be found in Cooglar (1978) or Haynes (1981).

Studies report that divorce mediation is successful in increasing the number of out-of-court settlements and reducing the number of relitigations (see Hetherington & Camara 1984).

There are some divorcing spouses for whom divorce mediation is ineffective. Johnston and her colleagues (1985) believe that some couples must resolve their emotional conflicts before they can function at the more rational level required for mediation. Johnston and her associates (1985) have developed a model to work with these couples over a ten-week period within which their emotional and interpersonal conflicts are addressed before the mediation process begins.

Shared Parenting and the Issue of Joint Custody

A growing number of mental health professionals are recommending that parents try to arrange some type of shared parenting (see Elkin 1987; Messinger & Walker 1981; Wolchik, Braver & Sandler 1985). The term is not necessarily used in a legal sense but in a psychological one. It means only that both parents participate in their children's lives and both assume the responsibility of child rearing, decision making, and meeting their children's needs (Messinger & Walker 1981). There can be many different shared parenting arrangements. Most often, children maintain a strong presence in two homes, alternating on a daily, weekly, monthly, or even yearly basis, depending upon the proximity of the parents and the needs of the child. In some cases, a child primarily resides with one parent, but the nonresident parent maintains a strong psychological presence in the child's life and in decisions concerning her.

Potentially, shared parenting can have many advantages for children. Generally, a child's adjustment is facilitated when both parents participate in her life (Ahrons 1980, Hetherington 1979, Wallerstein & Kelly 1980). The child can maintain a close relationship with each parent and with the extended family of each. Because she is involved with a greater number of concerned adults, she is likely to receive greater emotional support and cognitive stimulation. Additionally, if it proves true that children adjust better in the custody of their same-sex parent, joint custody may be particularly beneficial for boys rather than sole custody with the mother, which is still the most common custody arrangement (Shiller 1986).

However, the idea of joint custody is a controversial one (see Wolchik, Braver & Sandler 1985). Critics argue that it is more likely to expose children to parental conflict, and it places children at greater risk of experiencing serious conflicting loyalties. Discontinuity in care and in physical and social environment is also cited as a disadvantage.

Although joint custody is a growing trend, arguments for or against it are theoretically based rather than empirically supported (Derdeyn & Scott 1984, Elkin 1987, Felner et al. 1985, Wallerstein 1983b). To date, there is a dearth of systematic research evaluating its viability, and findings have been mixed. Furthermore, studies primarily have used middle-class white populations, and the generalizability of findings has been questioned (Hagen 1987). A few examples of available studies follow.

Wolchik and others (1985) found that children in joint custody had higher self-esteem and reported having more positive experiences than did children in exclusive custody. However, neither this study nor one conducted by Luepnitz (1986) found any differences in children's psychological functioning in either form of custody. Luepnitz reported that it was parental conflict, not the form of custody, which was associated with children's poor adjustment. However, she found that joint custody did have distinct benefits. Children in joint custody maintained their relationships with both parents, whereas half the children in sole custody never saw their noncustodial parent. None of the joint-custody families had relitigated, despite the fact that only one-half of the families had agreed on joint custody initially. In contrast, 56 percent of the sole-custody families returned to court. Luepnitz concluded that "joint custody at its best is superior to single parent custody at *its* best." However, she made no sweeping recommendations.

A study conducted by Judith Grief (1979) suggested that joint parenting could work, even when the relationship between parents was poor. A number of parents in her study had angry and hostile relationships with one another but were successfully co-parenting their children, often using the school as an exchange point to limit their contact with one another. Their love for the child was the overriding issue for these couples, and they were able to separate their parenting of the child from their problems with one another.

In an intensive longitudinal study of thirty-two children in joint custody, Steinman (1981) concluded that shared parenting provided mixed blessings. Children's self-esteem was enhanced by the realization that both parents wanted them and both were willing to put forth considerable effort on the child's behalf. Seventy-five percent of the children seemed able to maintain two homes and complex schedules rather easily. However, the other 25 percent experienced confusion and anxiety about their schedules and switching homes. Not surprisingly, all the children placed great importance on the continuity of friendships and attending a single school.

Were these children troubled with conflicting loyalties? As a group, they were not. However, they did have an unusually strong empathy for each parent and seemed to assume the responsibility of maintaining fairness and equality for each. This was a responsibility judged (by clinical interviewers) to be burdensome to some. On the issue of parental conflict, children whose parents were in conflict were greatly troubled. However, since there was no control group, it could not be determined if these children were more troubled than are children in exclusive custody whose parents are in conflict. (Luepnitz's data [1986] would suggest not.)

According to Steinman, her data indicated that the success of joint custody rested not on children spending equal time with parents but on parents' cooperative and respectful relationship with one another, at least in the area of child rearing. She concluded that joint custody was not a simple solution, appropriate to every child and to all parents.

Agreeing with Steinman's conclusions, Wallerstein (1983b) has specified several conditions under which she believes that joint custody is beneficial to children: when parents place high priority on their parenting roles and are willing to accommodate their children's needs and priorities; when parents respect one another as parents and can communicate effectively; and when children can shift between two homes without disrupting their adjustment or their activities (which she believes is easier for school-age children than for preschoolers or adolescents). The success of joint custody, she warns, is very dependent on the individual child.

Pointing out that courts now sometimes impose joint custody on parents, Zemmelman and his colleagues have developed a program to help parents implement a joint custody arrangement (see Zemmelman, Steinman & Knoblauch 1987).

Redefining the Noncustodial Parent-Child Relationship

In exclusive-custody families, the parent without custody has unique problems in trying to establish or maintain a good relationship with his or her children. In fact, this can be one of the most difficult tasks he or she must face. Why? Regardless of how much continuity parents try to give their children, there is always discontinuity in this particular relationship. The nonresident parent (still usually the father) must take on a new role that is strange and unclear, with constraints on time, space, and flexibility. Noncustodial fathers and children often have the feeling of not knowing what to do, where to go, what to say, and how to act when they are together. Some fathers become "Disneyland fathers," always arranging some scheduled activity to fill their allotted time. Some become "Santa Claus fathers," showering their children with presents. Often both children and fathers are dissatisfied with visiting because it is neither natural nor comfortable.

How can fathers (and noncustodial mothers) overcome these artificial barriers to their relationships with their offspring? Messinger and Walker (1981) recommend as much continuity between the old and new relationship as possible. Rather than always spending their time together in planned activities, they suggest that children find a comfortable niche within their noncustodial parent's new home, perhaps even incorporating some belongings there. Spending good quality time together in the newly created home can be interspersed with outside planned activities. This combination is a more natural and comfortable situation for most children and parents.

In their longitudinal study, Wallerstein and Kelly (1980) found some noncustodial parents to be particularly successful in creating and maintaining good relationships with their children, despite the divorce. They found that shortly after the divorce, the parents and children who had good-quality relationships spent frequent and regular time together. The children also had input in how visits would be spent. This initial period seemed important in laying the foundation for the new relationship that would emerge. By the time of the five-year follow-up, the quality of the relationship was related to the attitudes and feelings of the noncustodial parent and children, rather than to the amount of time spent together.

Who were these nonresident parents who were able to maintain good relationships with their children throughout this difficult five-year period? They were not necessarily those who had been close to their children before the divorce. For many, the relationship was established afterwards. They were the parents who got to know their children as individuals, sometimes seeing them together and sometimes separately. They were willing to be flexible in their visiting schedules to accommodate their children's desires and needs (and sometimes the barriers created by their former spouses); sometimes visits were even as short as a few hours. They were willing to give visits with their children a top priority in their own busy schedules but not respond with anger or hurt when children canceled visits. Between visits, they had spontaneous communication with their children to keep abreast of their lives. These noncustodial parents refrained from competition, interference, or conflict with their former spouses. Finally, they accepted the restraints of the role of a parent without custody; they accepted that their impact on their children's lives would not be as great as the impact of their former spouse. Yet, these parents did manage to have a continuing influence on their children's lives and to create a satisfying relationship with them. They also acted as a separate resource for their offspring to draw upon, thereby contributing an additional dimension to their children's lives. In short, in spite of the divorce, these parents without custody of their children accomplished what some parents in intact homes never accomplish.

References

Ahrons, C.R. 1980. "Divorce: A Crisis of Family Transition and Change," *Family Relations* 29: 533–40.

———. 1983. "Predictors of Paternal Involvement Post Divorce: Mothers' and Fathers' Perceptions." *Journal of Divorce* 6: 55–69.

Albrecht, S.L. 1980. "Reactions and Adjustments to Divorce: Difference in Experiences of Males and Females." *Family Relations* 29: 59–68.

Belsky, J., Lerner, R.M. & Spanier, G.B. 1984. *The Child in the Family.* Reading, Mass.: Addison-Wesley Publ. Co.

Block, J.H., Block, J. & Gjerde, P.F. 1986. "The Personality of Children Prior to Divorce: A Prospective Study." *Child Development* 57: 827–40.

Bloom, B.L., Asher, S.J. & White, S.W. 1978. "Marital Disruption as a Stressor: A Review and Analysis." *Psychological Bulletin* 85: 867–984.

Bronkowski, S.E., Bequette, S.Q. & Boomhower, S.J. 1984. "A Group Design to Help Children Adjust to Parental Divorce." *Social Casework* 65: 131–37.

Buehler, C. 1987. "Initiator Status and the Divorce Transition." *Family Relations* 36: 82–86.

Chiriboga, D., Catron, L. & Weiler, P. 1987. "Childhood Stress and Adult Functioning During Marital Separation." *Family Relations* 36: 163–67.

Cooglar, O. 1978. *Structured Mediation in Divorce Settlements: A Handbook for Marital Mediators.* Lexington, Mass.: D.C. Heath.

Crouter, A.C., Belsky, J. & Spanier, G.B. 1984. "The Family Context of Child Development: Divorce and Maternal Employment," in G.J. Whitehurst, ed., *Annals of Child Development.* Greenwich, Conn.: JAI Press.

Derdeyn, A.P. & Scott, E. 1984. "Joint Custody: A Critical Analysis and Appraisal." *American Journal of Orthopsychiatry.* 54: 199–209.

Elkin, M. 1987. "Joint Custody: Affirming that Parents and Families Are Forever." *Social Work* 32: 18–24.

Emery, R.E. 1982. "Interparental Conflict and the Children of Discord and Divorce." *Psychological Bulletin* 92: 310–30.

Emery, R.E., Hetherington, E.M. & Dilalla, L.F. 1984. "Divorce, Children, and Social Policy," in H.W. Stevenson & A.E. Siegel, eds., *Child Development Research and Social Policy.* Vol. 1. Chicago: University of Chicago Press.

Faust, R.G. 1987. "A Model of Divorce Adjustment for Use in Family Service Agencies." *Social Work* 32: 78–79.

Felner, R.D., Ginter, M.A., Boike, M.F. & Cowen, E.L. 1981. "Parental Death or Divorce and the School Adjustment of Young Children." *American Journal of Community Psychology* 9: 181–91.

Felner, R.D., Stolberg, A., & Cowen, E.L. 1975. "Crisis Events and School Mental Health Referral Patterns of Young Children." *Journal of Consulting and Clinical Psychology* 43: 305–10.

Felner, R.D., Terre, L., Farber, S., Primavera, J. & Bishop, T.A. 1985. "Child Custody: Practices and Perspectives of Legal Professionals." *Journal of Clinical Child Psychology* 14: 27–34.

Grief, J.B. 1979. "Fathers, Children and Joint Custody." *American Journal of Orthopsychiatry* 49: 311–19.

Guidubaldi, J., Perry, J.D. & Cleminshaw, H.K. 1984. "The Legacy of Parental Divorce: A Nationwide Study of Family Variables on Children's Academic and Social Competencies," in B.B. Lahey & A.E. Kazdin, eds., *Advances in Clinical Child Psychology.* Vol. 7. N.Y.: Plenum Press.

Hagen, J.L. 1987. "Proceed With Caution: Advocating Joint Custody." *Social Work* 32: 26–30.

Haynes, J. 1981. *Divorce Mediation.* N.Y.: Springer.

Hess, R.D. & Camara, K.A. 1979. "Post-Divorce Family Relationships as Mediating Factors in the Consequences of Divorce for Children." *Journal of Social Issues* 35: 79–96.

Hetherington, E.M. 1972. "Effects of Paternal Absence on Personality Development in Adolescent Daughters." *Developmental Psychology* 7: 313–26.

———. 1979. "Divorce, A Child's Perspective." *American Psychologist* 34: 851–58.

———. 1981. "Children and Divorce," in R.W. Henderson, ed., *Parent-Child Interaction: Theory, Research and Prospects.* N.Y.: Academic Press.

Hetherington, E.M. & Camara, K.A. 1984. "Families in Transition: The Process of Dissolution and Reconstitution," in R. Parke, ed., *Review of Child Development Research.* Vol. 7. Chicago: University of Chicago Press.

Hetherington, E.M., Cox, M. & Cox, R. 1976. "Divorced Fathers." *The Family Coordinator* 25: 417–28.

———. 1978a. "The Aftermath of Divorce," in J.H. Stevens & M. Mathews, eds., *Mother-Child, Father-Child Relations.* Washington, D.C.: National Association for the Education of Young Children.

———. 1978b. "The Development of Children in Mother-Headed Families," in D. Reiss & H. Hoffman, eds., *The American Family: Dying or Developing?* N.Y.: Plenum Press.

———. 1982. "Effects of Divorce on Parents and Children," in M. Lamb, ed., *Nontraditional Families: Parenting and Child Development.* Hillsdale, N.J.: Lawrence Erlbaum Assoc. Publ.

———. 1985. "Long Term Effects of Divorce and Remarriage on the Adjustment of Children." *Journal of the American Academy of Child Psychiatry* 24: 518–30.

Hingst, A.G. 1981. "Children and Divorce: The Child's View." *Journal of Clinical Child Psychology* 3: 161–64.

Hodges, W.F. 1986. *Interventions for Children of Divorce: Custody, Access, and Psychotherapy.* N.Y.: John Wiley-Interscience Publications.

Hodges, W.F. & Bloom, B.L. 1984. "Parent's Report of Children's Adjustment to Marital Separation: A Longitudinal Study." *Journal of Divorce* 8: 33–49.

Jacobson, D.S. 1978. "The Impact of Marital Separation/Divorce on Children. III. Parent-Child Communication and Child Adjustment, and Regression Analysis of Findings from the Overall Study." *Journal of Divorce* 2: 175–94.

Johnston, J.R., Campbell, L.E.G. & Tall, M.C. 1985. "Impasses to the Resolution of Custody and Visitation Disputes." *American Journal of Orthopsychiatry* 55: 112–29.

Kinard, E.M. & Reinherz, H. 1986. "Effects of Marital Disruption on Children's School Aptitude and Achievement." *Journal of Marriage and the Family* 48: 285–93.

Kressel, K. 1985. *The Process of Divorce: How Professionals and Couples Negotiate Settlements.* N.Y.: Basic Books.

Kurdek, L.A. 1981. "An Integrative Perspective on Children's Divorce Adjustment." *American Psychologist* 36: 856–66.

Kurdek, L.A. & Blisk, D. 1983. "Dimensions and Correlates of Mothers' Divorce Experience." *Journal of Divorce* 6: 1–24.

Kurdek, L.A. & Siesky, A.E., Jr. 1980. "Children's Perceptions of Their Parents' Divorce." *Journal of Divorce* 3: 339–78.

Long, N., Forehand, R., Fauber, R. & Brody, G.H. 1987. "Self-Perceived and Independently Observed Competence of Young Adolescents as a Function of Parental Marital Conflict and Recent Divorce." *Journal of Abnormal Child Psychology* 15: 15–27.

Longfellow, C. 1979. "Divorce in Context: Its Impact on Children," in G. Levinger & O.C. Moles, eds., *Divorce and Separation: Context, Causes, and Consequences.* N.Y.: Basic Books.

Lowery, C.R. 1985. "Child Custody Evaluations: Criteria and Clinical Implications." *Journal of Clinical Child Psychology* 14: 35–41.

Luepnitz, D.A. 1986. "A Comparison of Maternal, Paternal, and Joint Custody: Understanding the Varieties of Post-Divorce Family Life." *Journal of Divorce* 9: 1–12.

Messinger, L. & Walker, K.N. 1981. "From Marriage Breakdown to Remarriage: Parental Tasks and Therapeutic Guidelines." *American Journal of Orthopsychiatry* 5: 429–38.

Mueller, C. & Pope, H. 1977. "Marital Instability: A Study of Its Transmission Between Generations." *Journal of Marriage and the Family* 39: 83–93.

Neal, J.J. 1983. "Children's Understanding of their Parents' Divorces," in L.A. Kurdek, ed., *Children and Divorce*. New Directions for Child Development, No. 19. San Francisco: Jossey-Bass.

O'Leary, K.D. & Emery, R.E. 1984. "Marital Discord and Child Behavior Problems," in M.D. Levine & P. Satz, eds., *Middle Childhood: Development and Dysfunction*. Baltimore: University Park Press.

Pedro-Carroll, J.L. & Cowen, E.L. 1985. "The Children of Divorce Intervention Project: An Investigation of the Efficacy of a School-Based Prevention Program." *Journal of Consulting and Clinical Psychology* 53: 603–11.

Pedro-Carroll, J.L., Cowen, E.L., Hightower, A.D. & Guare, J.C. 1986. "Preventive Intervention with Latency-Aged Children of Divorce: A Replication Study." *American Journal of Community Psychology* 14: 277–90.

Peterson, J.L. & Zill, N. 1986. "Marital Disruption, Parent-Child Relationships, and Behavior Problems in Children." *Journal of Marriage and the Family* 48: 285–93.

Rutter, M. 1979. "Protective Factors in Children's Responses to Stress and Disadvantage," in M.W. Kent & J.E. Rolf, eds., *Primary Prevention of Psychopathology*. Vol. 3. *Social Competence in Children*. Hanover, N.H.: University Press of New England.

Reynolds, W.M. 1985. "Depression in Childhood and Adolescence: Diagnosis, Assessment, Intervention Strategies and Research," in T.R. Kratochwill, ed., *Advances in School Psychology*. Vol. 4. Hillsdale, N.J.: Lawrence Erlbaum, Assoc. Publ.

Santrock, J.W., Warshak, R.A. & Elliott, G.L. 1982. "Social Development and Parent-Child Interaction in Father Custody and Stepmother Families," in M. Lamb, ed., *Nontraditional Families: Parenting and Child Development*. Hillsdale, N.J.: Lawrence Erlbaum Assoc. Publ.

Shiller, V.M. 1986. "Joint Versus Maternal Custody for Families with Latency Age Boys: Parent Characteristics and Child Adjustment." *American Journal of Orthopsychiatry* 56: 486–89.

Steinman, S. 1981. "The Experience of Children in a Joint-Custody Arrangement: A Report of a Study." *American Journal of Orthopsychiatry* 51: 403–14.

Stolberg, A.L. & Anker, J.M. 1984. "Cognitive and Behavioral Changes in Children Resulting From Parental Divorce and Consequent Environmental Change." *Journal of Divorce* 7: 23–41.

Stolberg, A.L. & Bush, J.P. 1985. "A Path Analysis of Factors Predicting Children's Divorce Adjustment." *Journal of Clinical Child Psychology* 14: 49–54.

Stolberg, A.L. & Cullen, P.M. 1983. "Preventive Interventions for Families of Divorce: The Divorce Adjustment Project," in L.A. Kurdek, ed., *Children and Divorce*. New Directions for Child Development, No. 19. San Francisco: Jossey-Bass.

Wallerstein, J.S. 1983a. "Children of Divorce: Stress and Developmental Tasks," in N. Garmezy & M. Rutter, eds., *Stress, Coping, and Development in Children*. N.Y.: McGraw-Hill Book Co.

Wallerstein, J.S. 1983b. "Separation, Divorce, and Remarriage," in M.D. Levine, W. Carey, A.C. Crocker & R.T. Gross, eds., *Developmental-Behavioral Pediatrics.* Philadelphia: W.B. Saunders Co.

———. 1984. "Children of Divorce: Preliminary Report of a Ten-Year Follow-Up of Young Children." *American Journal of Orthopsychiatry* 54: 444–58.

———. 1985a. "Children of Divorce: Preliminary Report of a Ten-Year Follow-Up of Older Children and Adolescents." *Journal of the American Academy of Child Psychiatry* 24: 545–53.

———. 1985b. "The Overburdened Child: Some Long-Term Consequences of Divorce." *Social Work* 30: 116–23.

———. 1987. "Children of Divorce: Report of a Ten-Year Follow-Up of Early Latency-Age Children." *American Journal of Orthopsychiatry* 57: 199–211.

Wallerstein, J.S. & Kelly, J.B. 1980. *Surviving the Breakup.* N.Y.: Basic Books.

Warren, N.J. & Amara, I.A. 1984. "Educational Groups for Single Parents: The Parenting After Divorce Program." *Journal of Divorce* 8: 79–96.

Weitzman, L. & Dixon, R. 1979. "Child Custody Awards, Legal Standards, and Empirical Patterns for Child Custody, Support, and Visitation after Divorce." *University of California Davis Law Review* 12: 473–521.

Wolchik, S.A., Braver, S.L. & Sandler, I.N. 1985. "Maternal versus Joint Custody: Children's Postseparation Experiences and Adjustment." *Journal of Clinical Child Psychology* 14: 5–10.

Zemmelman, S.E., Steinman, S.B. & Knoblauch, T.M. 1987. "A Model Project on Joint Custody for Families Undergoing Divorce." *Social Work* 32: 32–37.

5

Childhood Stress and Youth Suicide

Childhood Stress

On 27 October 1986, the cover article appearing in *U.S. News and World Report* was "Children Under Stress." The article, primarily based on interviews with child development experts, detailed a long list of stresses facing children in the 1980s: both parents working, drugs in the schoolyard, experience with sex at alarmingly early ages, a barrage of violence on the ever present television screen (see chapter 3). Infants and toddlers are sent off to day care (see chapter 2), often poor quality and unregulated, where they must cope with daily separations, multiple caregivers, and an adultlike world of schedules and structure. Today, the article continues, children are pushed into self-reliance before necessary coping skills are developed, and "quality" time with harried parents must be "scheduled" because quantity time is simply not available.

Further stress, it is pointed out, is inflicted by status-conscious parents. Children must attend the "right" schools, be dressed the "right" way, and occupy their time constructively. Not even sports are played for fun. Academics are introduced in preschool, and the first-grade curriculum has been moved down to kindergarten. The academic push continues despite research demonstrating that it is the younger children in the classroom who are more likely to experience learning problems, suggesting that their push into academics preceded their readiness (e.g., DiPasquale, Moule & Flewelling 1980).

The typical American family is now one in which rushed family members each go their separate ways and television substitutes for conversation. Even greater stress, the article points out, has fallen on the 16.3 million children whose lives have been disrupted during the past fifteen years by divorce. Their unique stress has been substantial, resulting in long-term consequences for many (see chapter 4). Required adjustments to subsequent stepparents and blended families heightens their stress still further.

It appears that stress has had its consequences for children. The *U.S. News* article reports that stress-related health problems are experienced by up to 35 percent of American children. Other research suggests that children have additional stress-related problems. A national health survey revealed that between 40 and 48 percent of their sample of 7,000 6- to 11-year-old children were moderately tense or high strung (see Brown & Rosenbaum 1984). On the basis of epidemiological investigations, it has been estimated that 1 in 14 children and 1 in 7 adolescents are seriously depressed (Reynolds 1985). Over the past twenty-five years, the adolescent suicide rate has increased 230 percent (Frederick 1985).

The *U.S. News* article is not unique in the popular press. Each year, new articles on childhood stress appear in popular magazines. Bookstores display books such as *The Hurried Child: Growing Up Too Fast Too Soon* (Elkind 1981), *Children Without Childhood* (Winn 1983), *All Grown Up and No Place to Go: Teenagers in Crisis* (Elkind 1984), and *Why Isn't Johnny Crying: Coping With Depression in Children* (McKnew, Cytryn & Yahraes 1983).

How has the professional literature dealt with childhood stress? Interestingly, the study of stress in children has been a relatively neglected area. Only recently has a piecemeal literature begun to emerge (Garmezy 1985a). Nevertheless, some fascinating findings are emerging from this new literature, which increase our understanding of childhood stress, children's diverse responses to it, its varied consequences for them, and how youngsters' can be helped to cope.

The study of stress has been a difficult one for researchers, partly because of problems conceptualizing the concept. As Rutter (1983) points out, everyone "understands" what stress is—in a very general way. But when precision is required, the few who are able to define stress do so quite differently. Garmezy and Tellegen (1984) point out that stress has been equated with "anxiety, conflict, frustration, emotional distress, tension, arousal, harsh environments, interpersonal deprivations, ego and physical threat, physical trauma, illness, and injury" (pp. 245–46).

We do not need as precise a definition as do researchers. For the purposes of this discussion, stress will be defined as: (1) situations that induce emotional tension in the average person (often called stressors), and (2) feelings of upset or concern caused by these situations. It is a simple and practical definition, combined from several sources (Garmezy 1985a, Longfellow & Belle 1984), which adequately deals with the kinds of stress discussed in the popular press and the kinds discussed in the professional literature.

Measures of Children's Stress and Their Correlates

Stress researchers have not yet dealt with some of the stresses discussed in the popular press, such as pushing children to grow up too fast and early exposure to the world of competitiveness and sex. It is not that these stresses are considered unimportant. They are too elusive to isolate and to measure.

The professional literature focuses on specific stressful life events. Many studies have conceptualized stress in terms of events that cause change and require some degree of coping and adaptation (see Johnson 1982). Based upon this conceptualization, life stress inventories have been developed, which are lists of a wide variety of events experienced by children and adolescents. Each event is weighted for its impact on most children, usually determined by a large number of professionals (for example, pediatricians, clinicians, teachers) who rate how much readjustment each event would require of the average child. A child's life stress score is derived from the sum of the values assigned to each event that he has experienced within a specified recent period of time. The most widely used of these life stress instruments has been the Life Events Record developed by Coddington (1972).

Examples of events judged as highly stressful for children of all ages (whether judged by professionals or by children themselves) are parental death, parental divorce, and death of a sibling (Chandler 1981, Coddington 1972, Hutton et al. 1987, Yeaworth et al. 1980). Examples of other stressful events typically included are grade retention, suspension from school, family relocating, birth of a sibling, mother beginning to work, change in acceptance by peers, and so forth. Some events are weighted as more stressful at one age range than at another. Other events are included only for specific age ranges; for example, unwed pregnancy, leaving school, and breakup with a boyfriend or girlfriend.

Other studies have not used life stress scores but have looked at the effects on children of a specific stressful life event, such as parental death, divorce, discord, or psychiatric illness, family poverty, hospitalization of the child, and so forth. (Examples of this type of research, as well as the long-term problems experienced by some children as a consequence of the stress related to parental discord and divorce, are discussed in chapter 4.)

It is now well documented that children can suffer a wide range of negative consequences as a result of stress (Brown & Rosenbaum 1984, Johnson 1982, O'Grady & Metz 1987, Wertlieb et al. 1987). For example, there are significant positive correlations between children's stress and the following:

1. Anxiety, depression, emotional maladjustment, behavior problems, and delinquency (see Brown & Rosenbaum 1984, Johnson 1982)

2. Onset, severity, and duration of a wide range of physical illnesses (see Brown & Rosenbaum 1984, Johnson 1982)

3. Children's accident proneness (see Brown & Rosenbaum 1984, Johnson 1982)

Even when stress is measured by the level of daily family hassles that children experience, it is positively correlated with symptoms of behavioral problems (Wertlieb et al. 1987). Additionally, highly stressful environments appear to place a cap on youngsters' intellectual functioning (Barocas, Seifer & Sameroff 1985; Brown & Rosenbaum 1984) and have been implicated as a risk factor in children's suicide behavior (Cohen-Sandler, Berman & King 1982; Smith & Crawford 1986; Teicher, cited in McConville 1983).

Differences in Children's Response to Stress

It appears indisputable that many children experience considerable stress and that an array of negative consequences can follow. But, as Rutter (1983) points out, research must progress beyond the "banal conclusion that bad experiences may have bad effects" (p. 6).

A number of researchers have pursued other directions of study in the area of childhood stress. For example, it is abundantly clear, once one looks at individual children rather than at large groups, that children's response to stress is highly varied. Efforts, therefore, have been directed towards identifying why some children cope with stress more successfully than do others. With this information, we may be in a better position to help all children cope more successfully with the stress they inevitably encounter. A number of conditions have been identified that mitigate the effects of stress in some children and exacerbate it in others.

Characteristics of the Child. It is not surprising that children's response to stress is influenced by various attributes within themselves. What may be surprising is the role played by some of these attributes. Characteristics found to be important include sex, temperament, intelligence, and age and developmental level.

Sex. It is a recurrent finding in the literature that boys are more adversely affected than are girls by a wide array of stressful situations, including parental conflict, parental divorce, maternal employment, and the birth of a sibling (see Rutter 1983, Zaslow & Hayes 1986). (See chapters 2 and 4 for relevant discussions.)

Why boys are more vulnerable is a matter of speculation. Biological factors may play a role. But, according to Rutter (1985b,c), they are not likely to be the entire answer. It seems that boys elicit more negative behaviors from others in many of these circumstances in which they fare so poorly. For example, parents quarrel more in the presence of their sons than their daughters. Boys generally receive less parental and outside support than do girls when parents are divorcing (see chapter 4). And sons are described more negatively than are daughters by mothers who are employed (see chapter 2). Boys must cope not only with the stress of the situation but the additional stress caused by others' behavior towards them.

Temperament. Temperamental differences play a role in whether children develop emotional or behavioral problems in response to stress (Rutter 1985b). Temperament not only influences a child's immediate response to stress but also the likelihood that stress-related problems will persist (Dunn 1985).

Temperament plays a role in two ways. The more obvious of the two is that some children simply are more flexible, adaptable, and easygoing than are others. The second, which is very important, is that the difficult and unadaptable child is far more likely to elicit criticism and hostility from others, thereby compounding her stress in stressful situations. The adaptable child, on the other hand, is more likely to be the recipient of positive responses, which are likely to ease the stress he experiences in the same situations (Rutter 1985c).

Intelligence. There is some data suggesting that IQ is a pervasive influence on children's ability to deal with stress (see Garmezy & Tellegen 1984, Rutter 1983).

Rutter (1983) suggests that IQ could play a role in three ways. Intelligent children are likely to have higher self-esteem, they are likely to have better problem-solving skills, and they may be more resilient constitutionally.

Age and Developmental Level. There seems to be no age at which children are more vulnerable or less vulnerable to stress in general. However, children's perceptions, interpretations, and coping abilities do change with their developmental level. Therefore, children can be more vulnerable to a specific type of stress at one age level than at another (Maccoby 1983, Masten & Garmezy 1985).

One type of stress is hospitalization. It causes the greatest distress for children between the ages of 6 months and 4 years (Rutter 1983). Why? Perhaps because prior to 6 months, infants have not yet formed selective attachments and therefore separations are not difficult. And beyond the age of 4, children appear to have developed the cognitive skills necessary to realize that relationships will endure despite periods of separation (Rutter 1983).

Developmental level also plays a role in a child's response to her own personal inadequacies. Young children are buffered from much of the stress caused by personal inadequacy. They generally do not evaluate their performance by comparing it with the performance of others, they are not sensitive to others' appraisals of them, and they do not perceive failures as reflections of their personal attributes (Garmezy 1985a, Maccoby 1983, Rutter 1985c).

How children's developmental level influences their response to parental divorce has been discussed in chapter 4.

Appraisal of Stress and Attributional Styles. It is clear that children's interpretation of a stressful situation affects their response to it (Brown & Rosenbaum 1984; Felner, Farber & Primavera 1983; Rutter 1983). In fact, a child's subjective appraisal of stress plays a larger role in determining his response than does its objective nature (Lundberg 1986). As Rutter (1983) points out, different children may define the same event as irrelevant, benign, or threatening. Similarly, the persistence of stress-related problems is likely to be influenced by the degree of importance the child attaches to the stressful event.

As previously discussed, a child's developmental level sometimes influences her appraisal of stressful situations. However, a more pervasive influence is her perceptions of how much control she has over her environment and her appraisal of her own general effectiveness or helplessness (Dunn 1985; Felner, Farber & Primavera 1983; Rutter 1983). The extent to which a child generally attributes events to controllable or uncontrollable factors is sometimes referred to as an *attributional style.* If a child generally feels that she is at the mercy of fate, she is far less likely to develop successful coping strategies than if she feels she has some control over her destiny (Rutter 1985c).

Understandably, many children who experience chronic stress and adversity develop such a helpless stance (Rutter 1985c). But feelings of helplessness do not only stem from the environmental stress a child encounters. Feelings of helplessness can, for example, be modeled by parents. They also can begin to develop very early through parent-child interaction. A German study, conducted by Trudewind and Husarek (see Garmezy 1985a), demonstrates how this might happen. The children selected for this study had either become very confident or had developed a serious fear of failure during their first year in school. Although no differences were found in the children intellectually, important differences were observed between the two groups in parent-child interactions. In marked contrast to the confident children, the "fearful" children were given little autonomy and independence. Their mothers held high aspirations for them but, at the same time, failed to notice their successes. Their failures, on the other hand, were not only noted but criticized and blamed on the child's inadequacies. It is not difficult to see how these children developed their fear of failure and how they may eventually develop feelings of helplessness. In contrast, it has been found that children who develop a belief in their own efficacy generally experience environments that are warm, praising, and supportive (see Garmezy 1981).

Family Functioning. To understand the impact of stress on a child, we must look at its impact on his parents, on the functioning of his family, and on his relationships with his parents (Dunn 1985, Felner et al. 1985, Rutter 1985c). Some families are highly effective in buffering children from the impact of stressful life events. Others are less effective. Some exacerbate the negative effects stressful events have on youngsters. This was clearly demonstrated by wartime studies. A prime factor influencing children's response to wartime stress was the way their parents characteristically behaved—for example, with intense anxiety versus a calm demeanor or with an attributional style reflecting personal control versus one reflecting helplessness (see Garmezy 1983, Masten & Garmezy 1985).

Rutter suggests that the primary reason that children are adversely affected by family stress may be the disruption of family functioning that is caused by the stress, rather than the stressful event itself (Rutter 1981). One of the most commonly found factors associated with the development of serious emotional problems in children is a disturbance of parent-child relationships (see Masten & Garmezy 1985). Often it is the parent's behavior in the stressful situation that provides the missing critical link in understanding why a stressful life event leads to emotional or behavioral problems in some children (Dunn 1985). For example, as demonstrated in chapter 4, studies on divorce find that the adverse outcomes experienced by some children are not caused by the divorce per se but by disruptions of parent-child relationships, the poor parenting received from stressed parents, parental conflict in the child's presence, and so forth.

Disrupted family functioning may also explain the puzzling sleeper effects that are sometimes found for children as a consequence of stressful events. (Sleeper effects are consequences that do not appear until long after the event has occurred.) An example of a sleeper effect is the recurrent finding that individuals who experienced the death of a parent during early childhood are at greater risk to experience depression in adulthood. Recent research, however, suggests that the critical factor in the link between early parental death and adult depression is not the childhood loss per se. Rather, it is the nature of the care and the family stability that the child experienced subsequent to the death. A parent's death often results in long-term family breakdown, which is likely to have a greater impact on a younger child than on an older one (see Rutter 1985b).

Coping Style. Still another important key to understanding children's response to stress is their repertoire of coping skills (Rutter 1983). Coping ability is another variable that could prove to be more important to children's functioning than is the nature of the stress itself (see Rutter 1983).

Coping includes both direct action strategies (attempts to change the stressful environment) and cognitive strategies (attempts to alter the appraisal of the environment) (Rutter 1983). There are many effective coping strategies. Some are more appropriate for specific situations, and some are more comfortable for one person than for another. However, there also are many ineffective and maladaptive coping strategies which may even increase a child's risk of subsequent problems (Rutter 1983).

A study conducted by Brown and his colleagues (1986) studied children's and adolescents' strategies for coping with both stress and pain. Not surprisingly, the repertoire of children's coping skills increased with age. Common effective coping strategies were positive self talk, task orientation, problem-solving, and diverting attention from inescapable pain. However, the predominant response of 64 percent of this sample was to catastrophize the situation. Catastrophizing included focusing on the negative aspects of the situation and ruminating about them. Although the tendency to catastrophize decreased with age (as the repertoire of effective coping strategies increased), it was still the predominant response of 54 percent of the 16- to 18-year-old group. Furthermore, the catastrophizers also had higher overall anxiety scores. This suggested to the researchers that catastrophizers may be more likely to perceive a wider array of situations as stressful, in addition to responding to each stress with greater anxiety. Research with adults has, in fact, found that catastrophizers report experiencing more stress than do those who employ cognitive coping strategies (see Brown et al. 1986).

We know very little about the ways in which children develop effective coping strategies (Rutter 1985c). Undoubtedly, a highly influential factor, says Rutter, is the general coping style of parents. Examples are responding to frustration with aggression versus problem solving, or responding to stress with an attributional style reflecting personal control versus helplessness.

Multiple Stresses. The likelihood that stress will have negative consequences for children is markedly increased if children experience multiple stressful life events (Sterling et al. 1985). Multiple stresses are more likely to overtax youngsters' coping abilities.

Rutter (1983, 1985b) points out that the effects of stress are not additive but interactive; the combined effects of several stresses are greater than the sum of their individual effects. In a study of chronic family adversities (such as parental discord, parental psychiatric disorder, overcrowding, and low socioeconomic status), Rutter (1979) found that the presence of a single adversity did not appreciably increase a child's risk of developing subsequent psychiatric problems. However, the risk increased fourfold for children who experienced two or three of these longstanding adversities.

In some circumstances, stress seems to increase an individual's vulnerability to future stress. This is called the sensitizing effect of stress. The interactive and sensitizing nature of stress help to explain many findings reported in the literature. Four examples follow.

1. Perinatal trauma (low birth weight, anoxia, and so on) increases a child's risk to develop long-term problems if her later environment is an adverse or deprived one but not if her later environment is a supportive, unstressful one (Kopp & Krakow 1983, O'Grady & Metz 1987, Sameroff & Chandler 1975).

2. Parental discord has more adverse effects on children from high-risk groups (who usually face other types of stress) than it has on children from more favorable environments (Emery & O'Leary, cited in Rutter 1985c).

3. Stressful life events consistently have more pronounced negative effects on individuals of low socioeconomic status, who usually face a number of other adversities (Masten & Garmezy 1985, Sandler & Block 1979).

4. According to World War II studies, some people who had survived concentration camps and were functioning adequately after the war had subsequent breakdowns in response to minor changes in life situations (see Garmezy 1983).

In his review, Rutter (1980) concluded that long-term damage from stress is most likely for individuals who experience multiple acute stresses along with chronic adversity. Long-term damage is less likely for individuals who experience a series of multiple acute stresses without chronic adversity, and it is least likely for those who experience a single isolated stress in early life.

The following is a look at what may prove to be the most fascinating aspect of the study of stress that is reported in the professional literature—the study of stress-resistant children.

Stress-Resistant Children

During World War II, millions of children were displaced from their homes, lost contact with their families, experienced bombings, starvation, and concentration camps, and were deprived of any sense of physical or emotional security (Garmezy 1981, 1983). Millions of children currently are raised in ghettos in chronic poverty and inadequate, overcrowded housing. Millions more are physically or sexually abused or neglected. Others are raised by schizophrenic parents and find themselves emotionally and socially isolated and economically disadvantaged (Garmezy 1981, 1983; Langmeier & Matêjcêk 1975; Werner 1986). The literature is full of case reports of children such as these who function competently despite their harsh circumstances and who develop into healthy adults, who "work well, play well, love well, and expect well" (see Garmezy 1981, Hetherington 1984).

In recognition of such children, the term *invulnerable children* became popular in the seventies. It was believed that some children were so tough that they were invulnerable to even the most severe adversity and stress (Rutter 1985c).

Why didn't these children succumb to the severe and chronic stress they faced? What protected them from the harsh realities of their lives? The study of stress-resistant children is a relatively new field (Garmezy 1985b). Researchers have been searching heterogeneous studies for children whose functioning and outcomes do not conform to predictions based on their adverse life circumstances. These investigators have then looked for common correlates of these children's coping abilities, in order to glean some clues about resiliency and stress resistance (Garmezy 1985b). This search has revealed some interesting findings:

First, it is now apparent that the term *invulnerable* is inappropriate. There do not appear to be children who are invulnerable to any magnitude of stress. The resistance to stress is not absolute but relative. Although some children show startling psychological strength and coping ability compared with their counterparts in similar circumstances, a child's vulnerability to stress can vary with circumstances and with the severity of stress. For this reason, the term *invulnerable* has been largely replaced with the terms *stress-resistant* or *resilient* (Rutter 1985c).

Second, resilient children are not uncommon. Recently published longitudinal studies, which have studied children from infancy on, have found that a "significant proportion" of children endure environments of severe stress and emerge with unusual psychological strength (Werner 1986).

Third, although there may be a stereotype of the resilient child as a self-made wonder who pulls himself up by the bootstraps, this is not the case. Instead, resilience comes from the presence of "social cushions that soften the blows" of stress (Pakizegi 1985). These cushions or buffers that protect the resilient child from stress and adversity have come to be called *protective factors* (Rutter 1979).

Protective Factors

Protective factors can be conceptualized as a sort of reserve bank account. Their influence on a day-to-day basis in a stress-free environment may not be a significant. However, in the presence of marked adversity, they assume great importance (Rutter 1985b). Rutter (1983), who pioneered the study of protective factors, conceives of them as catalysts that function to increase the likelihood of adaptive coping. One can better understand the concept of a protective factor by imagining a very young child in a highly anxiety provoking situation—and then imagining her in the same situation holding her calm mother's hand. The presence of her mother, a rather ordinary event, assumes immense importance in the stressful situation and affects her reaction significantly (Rutter 1985c).

A number of protective factors have been identified. These factors are associated with better-than-expected outcomes for children raised in adverse environments (Masten & Garmezy 1985). They appear to buffer children from the hazards they face. Garmezy has categorized most of these factors into three categories which he calls the *triad of protective factors*. This triad emerges over and over again in heterogeneous studies dealing with very different types of severe stress and adversity (Garmezy 1985b, Masten & Garmezy 1985). The triad consists of (1) attributes of the child, (2) a warm, supportive family environment, and (3) resources outside the family, such as outside support systems and compensatory experiences.

Attributes of the Child. These include many temperamental factors, such as hardiness, positive mood, and flexibility. Basically, they include the types of personal qualities that elicit positive responses from others and foster harmonious interactions with others. Not all protective attributes are constitutional in nature, points out Rutter (1985c). Children can be helped to develop many adaptive behaviors. Other attributes that can buffer children from adversity in their environments include self-esteem, social problem-solving skills that are flexible and varied, and an attributional style that reflects a sense of personal effectiveness and control (Garmezy 1981, Rutter 1985c).

Supportive Family Environment. In the search for resilient children, a correlate that has almost always emerged is a warm and supportive relationship with parents (see Masten & Garmezy 1985).

A powerful example of the protective effects of a supportive family was provided by studies of British children during the World War II bombing of England. Britain conducted mass evacuations of its children from large cities to safe rural areas. Among the children who were evacuated, an estimated 25 to 50 percent developed neurotic symptoms. The children who fared the poorest were those who had had previous conflict in their relationships with parents, whereas the children who had good relationships with parents handled the evacuation the best. Interestingly, the group of children who developed the fewest emotional difficulties were those who had remained in the cities with their parents right through the bombings and air raids. The security they found with their families apparently compensated for the trauma of the bombings (Langmeier & Matêjcêk 1975; see Garmezy 1983).

Even a good relationship with only one parent can go a long way in buffering a child from stress. For example, in a study of children from conflict-ridden homes, Rutter found that three-fourths of the children who had poor relationships with both parents developed conduct disorders, such as aggressiveness and destructiveness. Of the children who had a good relationship with one parent, only one-fourth developed such problems (Rutter 1979).

Resources Outside the Family. The third category of protective factors that has recurrently emerged includes compensatory relationships and experiences outside the home that foster children's coping efforts and the development of positive values. Felner and his colleagues (1985) point out that for a child whose family is disrupted or unsupportive, these external sources of support and stability assume a crucial importance in times of stress. A few examples of extrafamilial resources follow.

In a longitudinal study of high-risk children, Werner and Smith (1982) found that grandparents, older siblings, aunts, uncles, parents of friends, and peers played important roles in the lives of the resilient children they studied. Werner (1985) writes, "The emotional support of such elders or peer friends was a major ameliorative factor in the midst of poverty, parental psychopathology and serious disruptions of the family unit" (p. 351).

In a study of high-risk adolescents in inner-city schools, teacher support was found to be one of two important factors associated with positive outcomes. The second was family cohesiveness (Felner et al. 1985).

In a study of institutionally raised girls, positive experiences in school played a critical role in the outcome for these girls (Quinton & Rutter 1985). Although success was rarely achieved in academics, it was achieved in social relationships, music, athletics, and so forth. These researchers point out that schools can provide a rich source of compensatory experiences. They recommend that a conscious effort be made to use schools to provide children opportunities for success and positive experiences.

Required Helpfulness. In addition to the triad of protective factors that consistently emerge, at least two other factors appear to operate as protective factors, able to buffer children from stressful environments. One of these centers around a concept introduced by Rachman (1979), that of *required helpfulness*. The concept refers to the phenomenon that people often carry out difficult or dangerous tasks without strain when there is a social necessity to do so. Entering a burning building to save a child is an example.

It appears that required helpfulness may play an important role in some children's resistance to stress (Garmezy 1985b, Hetherington 1984). Studies suggest that children who are successfully fulfilling a task that is important to the needs of others often experience very adverse environments as less stressful than do other children. While fulfilling their task, they seem to develop personal resources that help to buffer them from stress (Garmezy 1985b). Some examples follow.

Elder found that many of the older children raised during the depression who had to take on part-time jobs and additional home responsibilities often emerged with enhanced strength. This was particularly true for children from cohesive families (see Rutter 1985c). In their longitudinal study of at-risk children living in adverse family circumstances, Werner and Smith (1982) found that many of the "invincible" children had assumed responsibility for younger siblings. And Bleuler (1978) reported the tremendous amounts of responsibility assumed by many of the resilient children he studied who had been raised by a schizophrenic parent in an environment of emotional, social, and financial deprivation (see Garmezy 1981).

Why should required helpfulness act as a protective factor when it involves the child assuming an increased load on his already overburdened shoulders? Garmezy (1985b) calls it therapy through helping others. Says Garmezy, it increases the child's competence, coping skills, morale, sense of accomplishment, and his tolerance for discomfort.

The Steeling Effect. A fifth protective factor that buffers a child from stress and adversity is not altogether different from required helpfulness. In some circumstances, stress itself toughens a child against future stress. This has been called the *steeling* or *inoculation effect* of stress (see Masten & Garmezy 1985, Rutter 1980, Rutter 1985c).

Recall that stress also can have a sensitizing effect in which it increases vulnerability to future stress. The crucial question, of course, is when stress sensitizes a child to future stress and when it inoculates her. The study of sensitizing and steeling effects is another field in its infancy (Rutter 1985c). However, it is widely hypothesized that steeling effects stem from stressful experiences that are manageable and with which the child has coped successfully. Such experiences are likely to increase a child's coping skills, self-esteem, and sense of effectiveness and personal control. On the other hand, it is hypothesized that stress experiences that leave a child distraught, unable to cope, and feeling helpless are likely to have a sensitizing effect, increasing the child's vulnerability to future stress (Rutter 1980).

Steeling effects are important because they imply that the most effective way to foster resilience and stress resistance is not to shield a child from stress altogether. Rather, it is to allow him to encounter stress in appropriate doses so that he can successfully cope and thereby increase his self-confidence and competence (Masten & Garmezy 1985, Rutter 1985c). Masten and Garmezy (1985) write:

> There is a widely held view that the most favorable circumstances for promoting stress resistance may not be a life without adversity, but rather a life with graduated challenges that enhance the development of mastery skills, flexible coping strategies, and adaptive personality attributes (p. 13).

How Protective Factors Buffer Children from Stress

Protective factors can operate rather directly, as in the case of the British children who remained with their parents through the bombing of their cities. Sometimes protective factors operate less directly. For example, they may enhance self-esteem, problem-solving skills, and a sense of self-effectiveness, all of which appear to be involved in coping and resilience. The effects of protective factors may be quite indirect, such as fostering harmonious relationships and interactions with others. And sometimes the effects of protective factors can be observed only over time, through some sort of chain of events (Rutter 1985c). A demonstration of such a chain reaction was found in a longitudinal study reported by Quinton and Rutter (1985), who followed institutionally raised girls into adulthood. As adults, these women were highly vulnerable to all sorts of stress, with the exception of women who had supportive husbands and harmonious marriages. A harmonious marriage appeared to buffer these women from stress, and their adjustment was similar to that of a control group reared consistently in a family. In general, the women with good marriages had not merely drifted into their marriages. As a group, they were more likely to plan for the marriage (indicated by the duration of the relationship before cohabiting and the reasons given for their decisions). Their counterparts with less successful marriages, on the other hand, appeared to drift into their relationships at the mercy of fate. Who were these women who were able to choose appropriate spouses and make successful marriages? Detailed analysis revealed that they had not distinguished themselves by superior functioning while growing up. However, there was something that did distinguish them as a group. Generally, they had had some type of positive experiences in school, such as in music, athletics, or social relationships. Quinton and Rutter suggested that these positive experiences in one area of their lives may have increased their self-esteem and sense of self-effectiveness so that they were later able to take charge of their lives and determine the direction of their futures (see Quinton & Rutter 1985, Rutter 1985c). Chains of events are discussed further in chapter 1.

Protective factors appear to be capable of buffering children from a wide array of stresses. Their influence, however, is not absolute; they do not buffer children from any magnitude of stress. Werner (1986) reports that it is the balance between protective factors, stressful life events, and risk factors which determines how successfully a child will cope with stress. (Risk factors are those that increase vulnerability to stress, such as low socioeconomic status, having a difficult temperament, having poor relations with parents, coming from a conflict-ridden home, and so forth.) In a longitudinal study of high-risk children, Werner and Smith (1982) found that the more stress children were exposed to and the more risk factors they were exposed to, the more protective factors they required to buffer them from their adverse circumstances.

The role that protective factors play in mitigating the effects of child abuse is discussed in chapter 6.

Depression in Children and Adolescents

One consequence of stress appears to be depression. Studies find that stressful life events are associated with depressive symptoms in children, adolescents, and adults (see Mullins, Siegel & Hodges 1985).

Depression generally involves feelings of unhappiness, misery, and rejection, as well as diminished vigor and a negative self-image (Rutter 1985a). Depression in children is not always obvious. Most studies comparing parent reports and child reports of children's depression find little correspondence between the two, according to Reynolds (1985). And Rutter and Garmezy (1983) report that both parents and teachers often are unaware of adolescents' depression, even when it is quite severe.

Perhaps the reason childhood depression may elude observers is because it is so often associated with other problems which may be far more obvious, such as aggression, behavior and conduct problems, poor academic achievement, poor peer relations, anxiety, somatic complaints, hyperactivity, suicide, anorexia nervosa, delinquency, and truancy (see Jacobsen, Lahey & Strauss 1983; McConville 1983; Reynolds 1985; Stroufe & Rutter 1984). Reynolds (1985) points out that childhood depression should not be thought of as a single symptom, such as feeling sad, but as a cluster of symptoms.

Prevalence

Presently, there are no precise figures of the prevalence of depression among children (Seligman & Peterson 1985). Assessing its presence in young children is difficult because of their limited ability to express their feelings (Rutter 1985a).

Studies of preadolescents, however, suggest that "feelings of misery and unhappiness are relatively common" in normal populations (Rutter & Garmezy 1983). Furthermore, self-reports of depression among this age group are highly stable over at least a six-month period, suggesting that these are not transient feelings (Seligman & Peterson 1985).

In adolescent populations, the prevalence of depression increases markedly. A study of almost 3,000 high school students revealed that 34 percent were mildly to severely depressed (Reynolds 1985). Depression appears to be related to puberty, at least for boys. Rutter (1985a) reports that among his 14- and 15-year-old boys, about one-third who had reached puberty showed depressive symptoms, whereas few who had not reached puberty did so. Data is not available for girls.

Why does depression escalate in adolescence? Rutter (1985a) suggests several reasons. Hormonal changes, of course, are a likely candidate. Other contributing causes may include increased stress during this period, as well as decreased family support which previously had served as a protective factor. Rutter also suggests there are developmental changes in the adolescent's capabilities to attribute her failures to enduring shortcomings within herself. These might make her more vulnerable to feelings of helplessness.

Depression and Learned Helplessness

Rutter's last point is quite important because depression appears to be strongly related to feelings of helplessness to control life events (e.g., Fincham, Diener & Hokoda 1987; Leon, Kendall & Garber 1980; Mullins, Siegel & Hodges 1985;

Seligman & Peterson 1985). For example, Seligman and Peterson (1985) found that 9- to 13-year-old depressed children more often expected that bad things would happen to them which they would be unable to deal with or to avoid. Furthermore, these feelings were consistent over the six-month period in which the children were tested, suggesting that they were not fleeting whims. Instead, they may have been a learned attributional style which affected the children's approach to life. Similar findings were reported by Fincham and his colleagues (1987).

It is not suggested that a child's attributional style *alone* causes depression (Fincham, Diener & Hokoda 1987; Seligman & Peterson 1985). It is suggested that it is a child's belief in his helplessness (sometimes called *learned helplessness*) in conjunction with aversive events which may lead to depression. The relationship between feelings of helplessness and depression is found at all ages, but it is even stronger in children than in adults (Seligman & Peterson 1985).

A problem will now be considered which is highly correlated with depression in adolescence and which currently is a source of intense concern in both the professional literature and popular press—adolescent suicide.

Youth Suicide

Concern about adolescent suicide is far more prevalent in the lay community than is concern for childhood stress. During 1985 and 1986, 31 articles on teen suicide appeared in popular magazines. Television networks have featured full-length films and documentaries. The U.S. House of Representatives conducted hearings on the problem in October of 1983 (Maris 1985). And an increasing number of secondary schools are including suicide prevention programs and seminars in their curricula.

Each new publicized case of adolescent suicide increases anxieties and raises questions among the lay and professional communities alike. What are the factors that place some teens at risk for taking their own lives? What signs indicate that a teen might make a suicide attempt? Are teens who make threats and attempts likely to complete suicide one day? How can troubled adolescents best be helped?

The Facts about Youth Suicide

Since the mid-fifties, the suicide rate for 10- to 14-year-old youths has increased 166 percent, and the increase for 15- to 19-year-olds has been 230 percent (Frederick 1985).

The United States is not alone; European nations have reported similar increases (Hawton & Osborn 1984). Nor is this the first time in U.S. history that youth suicide rates have risen markedly. Around 1910 there was a sharp increase, and the rate of youth suicide then was only slightly lower than it is today. The highest rate in history for suicides among young people was in 1977 (Hendin 1985).

Quoting only the increase in suicide rates, as the popular press often does, does not offer a clear picture of the problem. For this, one must look at both official statistics and unofficial estimates. Current official statistics for the United States indicate that among 10- to 14-year-old children, eight per million take their own lives yearly. Among 15- to 19-year-old youths, seventy-six per million complete suicide yearly (Rutter 1985a). This translates into somewhat fewer than 2,000 youths each year in the 15- to 19-year-old age bracket (Hawton & Osborn 1984).

Official statistics are misleading however. Because of the stigma attached to suicide and the potential grief caused parents, it appears that a great many youth suicides are classified as "undetermined whether death is accidental or purposefully inflicted" (Shaffer 1985). It also is suspected that many "accidents" actually are suicides, such as one car motor vehicle accidents, pedestrian accidents, drug overdoses, and so forth (Cantor 1983, Sheras 1983). The actual youth suicide rate is estimated to be at least twice the official rate. Some estimates are three times the official statistics (Emery 1983, Sommer 1984).

When one adds the number of attempted suicides each year, the figures weave an alarming picture. For every completed suicide, there is estimated to be anywhere from 50 to 120 attempted suicides among young people (Garfinkel, Froese & Hood 1982; Khan 1987; Pfeffer 1984a). Estimates of attempted suicide escalate still further when they are derived from surveys of high school students rather than medical reports. Studies of randomly selected high school students have found that between 8 and 15 percent report they have made a suicide attempt (see Ross 1985, Smith & Crawford 1986). If one can reliably extrapolate these figures to the general high school population, between 1 1/2 million and 2 1/2 million adolescents have made a suicide attempt (Smith & Crawford 1986).

Firearms or explosives are used by over 60 percent of youths (under age 24) who complete suicide. The next most common means is hanging or strangulation, which accounts for about 16 percent (mostly boys). Poisoning accounts for another 8.6 percent (primarily girls) (Frederick 1985). In contrast, 80 to 90 percent of attempted suicides are by poisoning (for example, overdoses), a method less likely to be lethal than firearms or hanging (Hawton 1982). Poisoning is more often used by girls (Sheras 1983), which may account for the reversed sex ratios found in completed and attempted suicides. Although boys complete suicide three times more than girls, girls attempt suicide three times more than boys (Frederick 1985).

Suicide is very rare in children younger than 10 (Shaffer 1985). Between the ages of 10 and 12, there begins a steady increase which continues through age 19 (Holinger & Luke 1984).

Attempted Suicide

Although completed suicide is rare for the very young, threats and attempts are not rare (Cohen-Sandler, Berman & King 1982; Kosky 1983; Pfeffer 1981; Rosenthal & Rosenthal 1984). About 12,000 children between the ages of 5 and 14 are admitted to psychiatric hospitals each year because of suicidal behavior (see Cohen-Sandler, Berman & King 1982). Several researchers have studied very young suicide attempters. Kosky (1983) reported on a 5-year-old who tried to hang himself, and 7- and 8-year-olds who purposefully ran into traffic. Pfeffer and her colleagues (1979) studied 15 suicide attempters, ages 6 through 12, who most frequently jumped from high places, stabbed themselves, or poisoned themselves. Rosenthal and Rosenthal (1984) reported on 16 preschool children who attempted suicide. Thirteen had made multiple attempts, most usually running into fast traffic, jumping from high places, or ingesting poison. All of these preschoolers reportedly had profound feelings of abandonment and despair; many had been abused. In a stratified random sampling of normal 6- to 12-year-old school children, it was found that 3 percent of these youngsters had made suicide attempts and another 8.9 percent either had had suicidal ideas or had made suicidal threats (Pfeffer et al. 1984).

Motivation for Suicide Attempts. Some professionals argue that attempted suicide is one step from completed suicide. Others, however, argue that suicide attempters are a different population from suicide completers. Although the suicide completer is hopeless, the attempter may be hopeful that her act will communicate her desperation and will instigate changes for the better (see Emery 1983, Farberow 1985).

In a study of adolescent suicide attempters, Hawton and his colleagues (1982) concluded their motives were complex and multifaceted. Motives most frequently reported by the adolescents were relief from a terrible state, escape from an impossible situation, or communication of their desperation to others. Less frequently given motives were making others sorry or trying to influence someone. Clinicians who interviewed the youths assessed that these latter two reasons played a greater motivating role for many of the youths than the youths had admitted.

Two different groups of suicide attempters were identified recently by Brent (1987). One group was characterized by hopelessness and depression. Youths in this group planned ahead and appeared to have a strong intent to kill themselves. The second group, on the other hand, was not hopeless but impulsive. They tended to have adjustment problems or conduct disorders and to overdose on readily available pills.

The impulsive nature of many youth suicide attempts has been noted by other researchers (see Hawton & Osborn 1984). In one study (Hawton et al. 1982) over half the youths under study had thought seriously about the attempt for less than 15 minutes! Only 8 percent had seriously considered the attempt for longer than 24 hours. However, as Hawton and Osborn (1984) point out, these youths may have seriously entertained suicidal thoughts in the past, making it easier for them to act quickly under severe stress.

Evidence suggests that suicidal thoughts are not uncommon in adolescents. For example, one survey of high school students found that 25 percent had thought about suicide enough to form a suicide plan (Smith & Crawford 1986).

The Risk Involved in Threats and Attempts. Professionals in the field advise taking any suicide threat or attempt as a danger signal. Even if an attempt does not appear to be serious, it does not mean there is no future danger. The lethality of an attempt may not reflect the youth's seriousness as much as it may reflect the availability of a lethal means (Brent 1987) or the youth's knowledge of what constitutes a lethal act (Garfinkel, Froese & Hood 1982).

In a study of youths who had completed suicide, Shaffer (1974) found that 40 percent had either specifically discussed, threatened, or attempted suicide earlier. Other studies report similar findings (see Rotheram 1987). Robbins and Alessi (1985) found that all their youths who made serious attempts had made less serious attempts in the past. According to the statistics, 1 in every 10 youth attempters will make a second attempt within a year (Hawton & Osborn 1984).

Undoubtedly, an important factor in whether a second attempt (perhaps more serious or fatal) will be made is whether the youth's problems are addressed and others' respond to his unhappiness, desperation, and inability to cope (Cantor 1983, Hawton & Osborn 1984).

Cultural Factors

Researchers suggest that cultural factors could play a critical role in the current youth suicide problem (Hendin 1985; Shaffer 1985; Sheras 1983; Sudak, Ford & Rushforth 1984). The past three decades have witnessed marked cultural changes which may be important contributors. Examples include the decreased quality of family life; family disorganization caused by rising divorce and remarriage rates; increased population which has intensified the competition for grades, school admissions, jobs, and recognition; increased mobility; alcohol and drug consumption; exposure to violence; and increased child abuse (Hendin 1985; Sudak, Ford & Rushforth 1984). It is not difficult to see how each of these cultural changes can contribute to stress, feelings of helplessness, and lowered self-esteem, three factors implicated in youth suicide.

The media may play some role in youth suicide (Bollen & Phillips 1982, Shaffer 1985, Sheras 1983). Bollen and Phillips (1982) followed suicide rates and media stories of suicides for a five-year period. For approximately ten days following media stories, suicide rates increased significantly in the geographic areas reached by the publicity. Peaks were obvious on days 0 and 1 and on days 6 and 7. It is feared that through media exposure, teens will come to see suicide as a reasonable way to deal with crisis.

There is some indication that today's youth already are more accepting of suicide as an alternative to other methods of dealing with adversity. A European study found that European teens gave significantly higher probabilities than did older populations that they themselves or others would commit suicide in the face of adverse social conditions (see Diekstra 1985). The more that suicide is implicitly accepted in a society as a reasonable way to deal with overwhelming stress, the more we are likely to see increased suicide rates (Diekstra 1985).

Behavioral Correlates of Youth Suicide

Depression. Not surprisingly, studies consistently find that a significant proportion of youths who complete, attempt, or threaten suicide are seriously depressed (see Cantor 1983; Farberow 1983; Maris 1985; Pfeffer 1981, 1984a; Reynolds 1985). According to Cantor (1983), depression is the symptom that is most frequently observed. However, not all suicidal children have symptoms of depression (Bettes & Walker 1986; Carlson & Cantwell 1982; Cohen-Sandler, Berman & King 1982).

A book that teens may find useful in understanding their depression is *Down Is Not Out* (Lee & Wortman 1986).

Antisocial Behavior. Studies also find that a significant number of suicidal children have symptoms of conduct disorders, such as aggressiveness, provocative and defiant behavior, stealing, truancy, drug abuse, and delinquency (see Bettes & Walker 1986, Carlson & Cantwell 1982, Frederick 1985, Hendin 1985, Pfeffer et al. 1982, Shaffer 1974). Behavior disorders characterize many of the children who do not have symptoms of depression (Carlson & Cantwell 1982). Some children have symptoms of both depression and behavior disorders (Shaffer 1974).

Social Isolation. Withdrawal and social isolation characterize a substantial number of youths who have completed or attempted suicide (see Cantor 1983, Farberow 1983, Maris 1985, Shaffer 1974, Sheras 1983). Undoubtedly, isolation can play a role. Not only does the youth lack social support in times of stress, but she is more likely to perceive that no one cares and that her problems are unique and unsolvable (Sheras 1983). The youth's poor communication and strained relationships often encourage others to stay at arm's length rather than to reach out with help, according to Sheras (1983). About one-third of youth suicide attempters have left school, increasing their social isolation even further (see Sheras 1983).

Substance Abuse. A high rate of alcohol and drug abuse has been associated with all forms of suicidal feelings and behavior (Crumley 1979; Garfinkel, Froese & Hood 1982; Maris 1985; Robbins & Alessi 1985). Substance abuse not only increases the likelihood of an attempt but it increases the likelihood of a medically serious attempt (Robbins & Alessi 1985).

Warning Signs. There is no widely accepted risk profile for suicidal youths (Bettes & Walker 1986), but lists of danger signs have been published from time to time. As one may now suspect, the warning signs make up a heterogeneous list. The following are frequently mentioned. (Blomquist 1974; Schneider, cited in Sommer 1984):

1. Loss of interests
2. Sadness
3. Withdrawal and uncommunicativeness

4. Sleeping or eating disturbances
5. Unusual neglect of personal appearance
6. Sudden personality changes
7. Problems concentrating
8. Problems with schoolwork
9. Weight loss
10. Physical complaints
11. Rebelliousness
12. Alcohol and drug use
13. Truancy
14. Promiscuity
15. Giving away possessions
16. Expressing suicidal thoughts

Factors Distinguishing Suicidal Youths

Many teens are depressed and socially isolated. Many have symptoms of behavior disorders and are alcohol or drug users. Yet most do not seek to end their lives. What distinguishes the youth who is at risk for suicide? This question has been the impetus for much research. The following factors appear to be useful in distinguishing youths who are at risk.

Disturbed Family Environments. Evidence of some kind of disturbance in family relationships or family environment is found so consistently among suicidal youths that some reviewers have referred to this as a universal finding (see Farberow 1985, Hendin 1985, Litman & Diller 1985, Robbins & Alessi 1985). Most often found are broken homes (due to divorce, separation, or death), family conflict, and family disorganization (see Cantor 1983; Cohen-Sandler, Berman & King 1982; Farberow 1983, 1985; Hawton & Osborn 1984; Sheras 1983; Sommer 1984). Some studies have found difficulties in parent-child relationships, excessively high parental standards for children's performance, or parental rejection or maltreatment (see Cantor 1983, Farberow 1985, Sheras 1983). Other studies have found parental substance abuse, suicidal behavior in other family members, and excessive mobility (see Cantor 1983, Farberow 1985, Hawton & Osborn 1984, Sheras 1983).

In a review of the youth suicide literature from ten countries, Farberow (1983) concluded that "family interaction contributed the greatest number of significant factors" to our understanding of teen suicide.

Stress and Loss. Several studies have found that suicidal youths have been subjected to significantly more stressful life events in their lives (Cohen-Sandler, Berman & King 1982; Smith & Crawford 1986; Teicher, cited in McConville 1983). Some studies report that the types of stresses experienced are more likely to involve losses of some kind (Cantor 1983; Cohen-Sandler, Berman & King 1982;

Kosky 1983). For example, Cohen-Sandler and others (1982) compared suicidal children (ages 5 to 14) with both depressed nonsuicidal children and a psychiatric control group. They reported that it was not behavioral symptoms which distinguished the suicidal group but the amount and types of stress they had experienced. They repeatedly experienced losses of all kinds—people, objects, only-child status, self-esteem, sense of security, and so forth. Their losses and separations frequently were caused by disruptive and chaotic family problems. Although their stress was longstanding and repetitive, generally it had increased during the year prior to the suicide attempt.

Hopelessness, Helplessness, and Low Self-Esteem. Hopelessness has emerged in a number of studies as a critical factor (see Beck, Kovacs & Weissman 1975; Farberow 1983; Khan 1987; Maltsberger 1986; Maris 1985; Pfeffer 1981). Beck and his colleagues (1975) report that hopelessness is a far stronger predictor of suicide than is depression.

Hopelessness may be the critical missing link in explaining suicidal behavior (Beck, Kovacs & Weissman 1975). It can explain why only some depressed children are suicidal and why some children with no depressive symptoms are suicidal (Beck, Kovacs & Weissman 1975).

Associated with hopelessness are low self-esteem and feelings of worthlessness and helplessness. All are commonly found in suicidal youths (see Farberow 1985; Maris 1985; Pfeffer et al. 1979; Robbins & Alessi 1985; Shaffer 1974; Khan 1987).

Concept of Death. It appears that many suicidal children may not grasp the finality of death. Pfeffer and her colleagues (1979) found that suicidal youngsters (ages 6 through 12) perceived death as a pleasant and temporary state. In a second study, compared to a control group, 10- to 12-year-old suicidal children more often believed that life processes (for example, sleeping and feeling) continued after death (Orbach & Glaubman, cited in Stambrook & Parker 1987).

Even many adolescents who fantasize about death may not fully appreciate its finality. One study found that teens with suicidal tendencies tended to deny that death was final (McIntire et al., cited in Pfeffer 1981). Another found that suicidal teens had less fear of death than did their peers (Lister, cited in Sheras 1983).

Exposure to Suicidal Behavior. A number of studies have found that suicidal adolescents have a higher probability of having a family member, relative, or acquaintance who completed, attempted, or threatened suicide (see Garfinkel, Froese & Hood 1982; Shaffer 1985; Sheras 1983; Smith & Crawford 1986; Walker 1980). For example, Walker (1980) found this true for one-third of his suicidal children. Garfinkel and others (1982) found that suicidal children were eight times more likely to have a family member who attempted or completed suicide than were controls.

It is possible that this previous exposure validates suicide as a means of coping with stress and problems. Or it may demonstrate to the youth that attempted suicide is an effective way to instigate concern and change within others (Sheras 1983).

Precipitating Conditions

Recently Khan (1987) has warned against conceptualizing suicidal youths as a single group. Rather, he points out, they are a heterogeneous population. This is an important point which should be kept in mind. It has been amply demonstrated by the diverse behavioral correlates typical of this group. It has been demonstrated by the diverse types of family disturbances and stress experienced by suicidal youths. It also can be demonstrated by cases of crisis suicides, in which the long-standing problems characteristic of most youth suicides are not evident. The term *crisis suicides* describes cases in which the youth has had a fairly normal development but encounters a significant loss (relationship, self-esteem, and so on) during a highly vulnerable period of his life. The suicide follows a dramatic change in personality, loss of interest in life, confusion, disorganization, hostility, and aggression. Crisis suicides appear to account for a relatively small percentage of youth suicides (Peck 1985).

Despite the wide variability in youth suicide, a three-stage progression occurs in many cases (Teicher, cited in McConville 1983): (1) a history of problems (losses, separations, family discord, environmental stresses, and so on); (2) a recent escalation of stress; and (3) a final precipitant.

The final precipitant often is trivial, such as disciplinary actions, losing face with peers, arguments with parents, school problems, and breaking up with a boyfriend or girlfriend (Hawton et al. 1982; Mattsson, Siese & Hawkins 1969; Shaffer 1974). Hawton and Osborn (1984) point out the relatively high frequency with which the disruption of a romantic relationship is the precipitant, particularly among girls. They suggest that the lack of family support experienced by many suicidal youths makes the loss of a love relationship particularly devastating.

Intervention

Prevention Efforts

Some researchers in the field believe that intervention should begin at the prevention level, teaching children how to cope with stressful life events (see Brown & Rosenbaum 1984, Humphrey 1984, Ross & Ross 1985, Sterling et al. 1985). Stress management is successfully used with adults, and there is an emerging literature indicating its effectiveness with children as well (Brown & Rosenbaum 1984). A book edited by Humphrey (1984) includes a number of stress management techniques for children. It has been suggested that stress management programs could be introduced through the schools (Ross & Ross 1985).

Reynolds (1985) suggests that it is practical to screen an entire school of students for depression. Measures such as the Child Depression Scale, the Children's Depression Inventory, or the Adolescent Depression Scale can be inexpensively administered in large groups in 10 to 15 minutes. Students who are identified as depressed should be screened with a second measure, suggests Reynolds; a single test should not be relied upon. Students with high depression scores on both measures should be followed up with clinical intervention. Many measures that have been developed over the past few years to assess depression in children and adolescents are discussed in Reynold's review (1985).

Studies suggest that adolescents with moderate to severe levels of depression can be treated successfully in groups within school settings (see Reynolds 1985). Both short-term cognitive-behavioral therapy and relaxation training have been found to be effective (Reynolds 1985, Reynolds & Coats 1986).

Other professionals believe that students should be screened for suicide potential. Screening devices are available. Most depression measures include an assessment of suicidal tendencies (Reynolds 1985). A screening checklist for the use of family physicians has been provided by Corder and Haizlip (1982). The Scale for Suicide Ideation has been developed by Beck and his colleagues (1979). A new evaluation procedure that can be implemented in school settings to determine whether a youth is in imminent danger for suicide has been developed by Rotheram and Bradley of the College of Physicians and Surgeons, Columbia University (Rotheram 1987).

Although screening devices are available, at present there is no foolproof way to predict whether a youth will one day try to end her life (Maltsberger 1986). Frederick (1985) warns that every suicide attempt, threat, and comment should be taken seriously. The potential significance of comments was underscored by Ross (1980), who reported on a student who had completed suicide. Several days before his suicide, he had asked a teacher whether a person had to be crazy to shoot himself. And just a few hours before he ended his life, he commented to a friend that he would be in heaven very soon.

A number of suicide prevention programs currently are being conducted in secondary school settings. Some programs train teachers, counselors, and administrators to identify and help adolescents who may be at risk (Ross 1980). Some focus on teens themselves. These programs help adolescents to learn about themselves, to learn that their feelings are not unique, to communicate their feelings to others, and to learn the facts about youth suicide. Programs also teach students to recognize suicidal symptoms in themselves and others and ways to help themselves or a friend who is at risk (Ross 1980, Sheras 1983). This latter knowledge is very important. Many cases have been reported in the literature in which a youth confided in a friend before committing suicide. The friend, either unwilling to betray the confidence or not knowing what to do, remained silent (Ross 1985). In a survey of adolescents conducted by Ross (1985), 91 percent said they would confide in a friend if they felt suicidal rather than a parent, counselor, teacher, minister, and so forth. Ross (1985) believes that adolescents must be trained both as potential victims and potential rescuers. Training programs both for school personnel (Ross 1980) and for teens (Ross 1985) have been developed by Charlotte Ross and her colleagues at the Suicide Prevention and Crisis Center of San Mateo County. Excellent pamphlets on youth suicide have been written for school personnel and for students (Ross & Lee, n.d., Ross, n.d.).

Once help and support are initiated, many youths who are at risk can be helped very quickly, reports Frederick (1985). There are over 200 crisis intervention and suicide prevention centers in the United States, as well as 700 community mental health centers, which can provide expertise in working with suicidal youths.

Treatment for the Youth Suicide Attempter

A common theme throughout the treatment literature is that any suicide attempt, even one which appears trivial, must be taken seriously. If not, it may lead to a more serious attempt or to a completed suicide (Sheras 1983). A second theme is that a suicide attempt is a desperate communication, used when other means of communicating are closed (Sheras 1983). Attempts should never be interpreted as manipulative, warns Ross (1985). To the youth, a suicide attempt may represent his belief that he is so powerless to bring about any changes, he has only his life with which to bargain.

The short-term prognosis for most youth suicide attempters is relatively good if their underlying problems are confronted and dealt with (Cantor 1983, Hawton 1982). According to Hawton and Osborn (1984), the small percentage of crisis suicide attempters, who have had normal lives until the precipitating crisis, probably need no specific treatment, if the crisis is resolved. Most youth suicide attempters, however, require both crisis intervention in response to the precipitating crisis and long-term intervention to deal with their underlying problems (Sands & Dixon 1986).

There is little research evaluating the effectiveness of various treatments for youth suicide attempters (Hawton 1982, Pfeffer 1984b). Frequently, the first treatment step is hospital admission. This protects the youth from a further attempt and assures her that her plea has been heard. It also provides time to evaluate both the youth and her family and to make decisions about treatment (Motto 1985, Pfeffer 1984b, Sheras 1983). If a hospital is not used, a support system must be available, warns Motto (1985).

Once the youth is released from the hospital, treatment is variable (Hawton 1982). Many mental health professionals suggest that initial treatment follow a crisis intervention approach, so that the precipitating crisis can be resolved before a further attempt is made (e.g., Sands & Dixon 1986, Sheras 1983). An example of a crisis intervention model is provided by Dixon (1979). A wide range of caring adults should be utilized in treatment who will interact with the youth, listen to her, and offer support—family members, teachers, guidance counselors, family doctor, minister, and so forth (Cantor 1983, Pfeffer 1984b, Sheras 1983). An important early step, suggests Orbach, is exploring the youth's perceptions of her own death (cited in Motto 1985). For children and adolescents, abstract conceptualizations of death are sometimes different than perceptions of their *own* death (e.g., Carlson, Asarnow & Orbach 1987). Clarification of misconceptions about death may delay another attempt long enough for the immediate crisis to be resolved. Another means of delaying a second attempt is a "no-suicide contract," in which the youth agrees that she will not kill herself for a certain period of time, no matter what. If she does not have confidence in her ability, the length of agreed-upon time is shortened. The more explicit and legal-sounding the contract, the more effective it generally is (see Sheras 1983).

Once the crisis is over, long-term treatment is recommended in order to deal with underlying problems (Sands & Dixon 1986). Terminating therapy once the crisis is over is a mistake made by some therapists and may account for repeated suicide attempts, say Sands and Dixon (1986). Although there are few special techniques for working with suicidal youths, it is generally agreed that the therapist should be a warm, supportive, caring person who is available at all times (Cantor 1983, Pfeffer 1984b). It is also widely accepted that enhancing the youth's self-image is critical (Motto 1985, Sheras 1983).

Beck and his colleagues (1975) suggest that therapy also focus on reducing the youth's feelings of hopelessness. Identifying the sources of these feelings will suggest starting points for constructive change. Beck uses a cognitive therapy approach to identify and deal with feelings of hopelessness. It appears to be a promising approach with suicidal youths. A detailed discussion of this approach and its specific techniques is provided by Bedrosian and Epstein (1984).

There is wide agreement that in most cases the family *must* be involved in a treatment program (Cantor 1983, Hawton 1982, Motto 1985, Pfeffer 1984b, Reynolds 1985, Sands & Dixon 1986, Sheras 1983). Family involvement should be enlisted as soon after the attempt as is possible, and therapy should focus on improving family communication (British Medical Journal 1981, Pfeffer 1981, Sheras 1983). Family therapy techniques recommended in the literature include those of Minuchin and Fishman (1981) and Richman (1979). A helpful approach for the initial family interview has been suggested by Haley (1976). Special problems encountered by therapists when working with youth suicide attempters and their families (who frequently are angry and resistant to participating in treatment) are discussed by Motto (1985).

Hawton and Catalán (1982) have written a practical guide for managing cases of attempted suicide.

Recurring Themes in the Literature

Some recurring themes emerge throughout the stress literature, the depression literature, and the youth suicide literature. One of these is the devastating consequences to children caused by a sense of helplessness to influence their environments and destinies. Feelings of helplessness increase children's vulnerability to stress and are significantly correlated with depression. Likewise, they have been associated with hopelessness, an important determinant of suicide risk. A sense of self-efficacy, on the other hand, serves as a protective factor, making effective coping more likely and buffering children from the negative impact of stress. Seligman and Peterson (1985) speculate that an important intervention strategy with children may be to focus on changing the "insidious attributional style" of helplessness.

A second theme which has emerged with startling clarity in the literature is the pervasive and pivotal role played by parents at all stages of children's development. It is disturbed parent-child relationships that are most often associated with serious emotional problems in children. It is parental death and divorce that children themselves rate as most stressful. It is the parent's level of functioning in stressful situations that often provides the missing link in understanding the immediate and long-term consequences of stressful events for children. It is good relationships with supportive parents that can provide a powerful protective factor for a child, buffering him from the impact of stressful life events. It is, perhaps, the parent who can be most influential in fostering a child's sense of self-effectiveness or sense of helplessness. Even for adolescents, a close, cohesive family is related to fewer psychophysiological symptoms and to good adjustment (Felner et al. 1985, Walker & Greene 1987). And it is a disturbed family environment that so consistently emerges in the background of suicidal youths.

The literature discussed in this chapter suggests, according to Werner (1986), that intervention with high-risk children can take two approaches. The first is attempting to reduce the stress in their lives. The second is attempting to increase the number of protective factors they can draw upon, either within themselves or within their environment. The first approach is not always possible, but the stress literature offers many suggestions for the second approach (Garmezy 1981, 1985b). If a child's family is not available, bonds can be encouraged with other supportive figures within his environment. Compensatory experiences outside the family can help to reduce the impact of adversities on the home front. An important and necessary task for a child to fulfill may be engineered in order to enhance his personal resources. Coping and problem-solving skills can be taught, and self-esteem and feelings of efficacy can be gradually developed.

The implications of the stress literature are perhaps exemplified by a quote from Robert Louis Stevenson: "Life is not a matter of holding good cards but of playing a poor hand well" (see Garmezy 1981).

References

Barocas, R. Seifer, R. & Sameroff, A.J. 1985. "Defining Environmental Risk: Multiple Dimensions of Psychological Vulnerability." *American Journal of Community Psychology* 13: 433–47.

Beck, A.T., Kovacs, M. & Weissman, A. 1975. "Hopelessness and Suicidal Behavior, An Overview." *Journal of the American Medical Association* 234: 1146–49.

——. 1979. "Assessment of Suicidal Intention: The Scale for Suicide Ideation." *Journal of Consulting and Clinical Psychology* 47: 343–52.

Bedrosian, R.C. & Epstein, N. 1984. "Cognitive Therapy of Depressed and Suicidal Adolescents," in H. Sudak, A.B. Ford & N.B. Rushforth, eds., *Suicide in the Young.* Boston: John Wright PSG, Inc.

Bettes, B.A. & Walker, E. 1986. "Symptoms Associated with Suicidal Behavior in Childhood and Adolescence." *Journal of Abnormal Child Psychology* 14: 591–604.

Bleuler, M. 1978. *The Schizophrenic Disorders: Long-Term Patient and Family Studies.* New Haven: Yale University Press.

Blomquist, K.R. 1974. "Nurse, I Need Help—The School Nurse's Role in Suicide Prevention." *Journal of Psychiatric Nursing and Mental Health Services* 12: 22–26.

Bollen, K.A. & Phillips, D.P. 1982. "Imitative Suicides: A National Study of the Effects of Television News Stories." *American Sociological Review* 47: 802–9.

Brent, D.A. 1987. "Correlates of the Medical Lethality of Suicide Attempts in Children and Adolescents." *Journal of the American Academy of Child and Adolescent Psychiatry* 26: 87–91.

British Medical Journal 1981. "Children and Parasuicide." 283: 337–38.

Brown, B. & Rosenbaum, L. 1984. "Stress and Competence," in J.H. Humphrey, ed., *Stress in Childhood.* N.Y.: AMS Press.

Brown, J.M., O'Keeffe, J., Sanders, S.H. & Baker, B. 1986. "Developmental Changes in Children's Cognition to Stressful and Painful Situations." *Journal of Pediatric Psychology* 11: 343–57.

Cantor, P. 1983. "Depression and Suicide in Children," in C.E. Walker & M.C. Roberts, eds., *Handbook of Clinical Child Psychology.* N.Y.: John Wiley and Sons.

Carlson, G.A., Asarnow, J.R. & Orbach, I. 1987. "Developmental Aspects of Suicidal Behavior in Children: I." *Journal of the American Academy of Child and Adolescent Psychiatry* 26: 186–92.

Carlson, G.A. & Cantwell, D.P. 1982. "Suicidal Behavior and Depression in Children and Adolescents." *Journal of the American Academy of Child Psychiatry* 21: 361–68.

Chandler, L.A. 1981. "The Source of Stress Inventory." *Psychology in the Schools* 18: 164–68.

Coddington, R.D. 1972. "The Significance of Life Events as Etiologic Factors in the Diseases of Children." *Journal of Psychosomatic Research* 16: 7–18.

Cohen-Sandler, R., Berman, A.L. & King, R.A. 1982. "Life Stress and Symptomatology: Determinants of Suicidal Behavior in Children." *Journal of the American Academy of Child Psychiatry* 21: 178–86.

Corder, B.G. & Haizlip, T.P. 1982. "Recognizing Suicidal Behavior in Children." *Medical Times* (Sept.): 25S–30S.

Crumley, F.E. 1979. "Adolescent Suicide Attempts." *Journal of the American Medical Association* 241: 2404–07.

Diekstra, R.F.W. 1985. "Suicide and Suicide Attempts in the European Economic Community: An Analysis of Trends with Special Emphasis upon Trends among the Young." *Suicide and Life-Threatening Behavior* 15: 27–42.

DiPasquale, G., Moule, A. & Flewelling, R. 1980. "The Birthdate Effect." *Journal of Learning Disabilities* 13: 234–38.

Dixon, S.L. 1979. *Working With People in Crisis.* St. Louis, Mo.: C.V. Mosby.

Dunn, J. 1985. "Stress, Development, and Family Interaction," in M. Rutter, C.E. Izard & P.B. Read, eds., *Depression in Young People: Developmental and Clinical Perspectives*. N.Y.: The Guilford Press.

Elkind, D. 1981. *The Hurried Child: Growing Up Too Fast Too Soon*. Reading, Mass.: Addison-Wesley Publ. Co.

———. 1984. *All Grown Up and No Place to Go: Teenagers in Crisis*. Reading, Mass.: Addison-Wesley Publ. Co.

Emery, P.E. 1983. "Adolescent Depression and Suicide." *Adolescence* 18: 245–58.

Farberow, N.L. 1983. "Adolescent Suicide," in H. Golombek & B. Garfinkel, eds., *The Adolescent and Mood Disturbance*. N.Y.: International Universities Press.

———. 1985. "Youth Suicide: A Summary," in M.L. Peck, N.L. Farberow & R.E. Litman, eds., *Youth Suicide*. N.Y.: Springer Publishing Co.

Felner, R.D., Aber, M.S., Primavera, J. & Cauce, A.M. 1985. "Adaptation and Vulnerability in High-Risk Adolescents: An Examination of Environmental Mediators." *American Journal of Community Psychology* 13: 365–79.

Felner, R.D., Farber, S.S. & Primavera, J. 1983. "Transition and Stressful Events: A Model for Primary Prevention," in R.D. Felner, L.A. Jason, J.N. Moritsugu & S.S. Farber, eds., *Preventive Psychology: Theory, Research, and Practice*. N.Y.: Pergamon Press.

Fincham, F.D., Diener, C.I. & Hokoda, A. 1987. "Attributional Style and Learned Helplessness: Relationship to the Use of Causal Schemata and Depressive Symptoms in Children." *British Journal of Social Psychology* 26: 1–7.

Frederick, C.J. 1985. "An Introduction and Overview of Youth Suicide," in M.L. Peck, N.L. Farberow & R.E. Litman, eds., *Youth Suicide*. N.Y.: Springer Publ. Co.

Garfinkel, B.D., Froese, A. & Hood, J. 1982. "Suicide Attempts in Children and Adolescents." *American Journal of Psychiatry* 139: 1257–61.

Garmezy, N. 1981. "Children Under Stress: Perspectives on Antecedents and Correlates of Vulnerability and Resistance to Psychopathology," in A.I. Rabin, J. Aronoff, A.M. Barclay & R.A. Zucker, eds., *Further Explorations in Personality*. N.Y.: John Wiley & Sons.

———. 1983. "Stressors of Childhood," in N. Garmezy & M. Rutter, *Stress, Coping, and Development in Children*. N.Y.: McGraw-Hill Book Co.

———. 1985a. "Developmental Aspects of Children's Responses to the Stress of Separation and Loss," in M. Rutter, C.E. Izard & P.B. Read, eds., *Depression in Young People: Developmental and Clinical Perspectives*. N.Y.: The Guilford Press.

———. 1985b. "Stress-Resistant Children: The Search for Protective Factors," in J.E. Stevenson, ed., *Recent Research in Developmental Psychopathology*. Oxford: Pergamon Press.

Germezy, N. & Tellegen, A. 1984. "Studies of Stress Resistant Children: Methods, Variables, and Preliminary Findings," in F. Morrison, C. Lords & D. Keating, eds., *Applied Developmental Psychology*. Vol. 1. N.Y.: Academic Press.

Haley, J. 1976. *Problem-Solving Therapy: New Strategies for Effective Family Therapy*. San Francisco: Jossey-Bass.

Hawton, K. 1982. "Attempted Suicide in Children and Adolescents." *Journal of Child Psychiatry* 23: 497–503.

Hawton, K. & Catalán, J. 1982. *Attempted Suicide: A Practical Guide to its Nature and Management*. Oxford: Oxford University Press.

Hawton, K., Cole, D., O'Grady, J. & Osborn, M. 1982. "Motivational Aspects of Deliberate Self-Poisoning in Adolescents." *British Journal of Psychiatry* 141: 286–91.

Hawton, K. & Osborn, M. 1984. "Suicide and Attempted Suicide in Children and Adolescents," in B.B. Lahey & A.E. Kazdin, eds., *Advances in Clinical Child Psychology.* Vol. 7. N.Y.: Plenum Press.

Hendin, H. 1985. "Suicide Among the Young: Psychodynamics and Demography," in M.L. Peck, N.L. Farberow & R.E. Litman, eds., *Youth Suicide.* N.Y.: Springer Publ. Co.

Hetherington, E.M. 1984. "Stress and Coping in Children and Families," in A.B. Doyle, D. Gold & D.S. Moskowitz, eds., *Children in Families Under Stress.* San Francisco: Jossey-Bass.

Holinger, P.C. & Luke, K.W. 1984. "The Epidemiologic Patterns of Self-Destructiveness in Childhood, Adolescence, and Young Adulthood," in H. Sudak, A.B. Ford & N.B. Rushforth, eds., *Suicide in the Young.* Boston: John Wright PSG, Inc.

Humphrey, J.H., ed. 1984. *Stress in Childhood.* N.Y.: AMS Press.

Hutton, J.B., Roberts, T.G., Walker, J. & Zuniga, J. 1987. "Ratings of Severity of Life Events by Ninth-Grade Students." *Psychology in the Schools* 24: 63–68.

Jacobsen, R.H., Lahey, B.B. & Strauss, C.C. 1983. "Correlates of Depressed Mood in Normal Children." *Journal of Abnormal Child Psychology* 11: 29–40.

Johnson, J.H. 1982. "Life Events as Stressors in Childhood and Adolescence," in B.B. Lahey & A.E. Kazdin, eds., *Advances in Clinical Child Psychology.* Vol. 5. N.Y.: Plenum Press.

Khan, A.U. 1987. "Heterogeneity of Suicidal Adolescents." *Journal of the American Academy of Child and Adolescent Psychiatry* 26: 92–96.

Kopp, C. & Krakow, J.B. 1983. "The Developmentalist and the Study of Biological Risk: A Review of the Past with an Eye Toward the Future." *Child Development* 54: 1086–1108.

Kosky, R. 1983. "Childhood Suicidal Behavior." *Journal of Child Psychology and Psychiatry* 24: 457–68.

Langmeier, J. & Matêjcêk, Z. 1975. *Psychological Deprivation in Childhood.* N.Y.: The Psychohistory Press.

Lee, E.E. & Wortman, R. 1986. *Down Is Not Out.* N.Y.: Julian Messner.

Leon, G.R., Kendall, P.C. & Garber, J. 1980. "Depression in Children: Parent, Teacher, and Child Perspectives." *Journal of Abnormal Child Psychology* 8: 221–35.

Litman, R.E. & Diller, J. 1985. "Case Studies in Youth Suicide," in M.L. Peck, N.L. Farberow & R.E. Litman, eds., *Youth Suicide.* N.Y.: Springer Publ. Co.

Longfellow, C. & Belle, D.B. 1984. "Stressful Environments and Their Impact on Children," in J.H. Humphrey, ed., *Stress in Childhood.* N.Y.: AMS Press.

Lundberg, Ulf, 1986. "Stress and Type A Behavior in Children." *Journal of the American Academy of Child Psychiatry* 25: 771–78.

Maccoby, E.E. 1983. "Social-Emotional Development and Response to Stressors," in N. Garmezy & M. Rutter, eds., *Stress, Coping, and Development in Children.* N.Y.: McGraw-Hill Book. Co.

Maltsberger, J.T. 1986. *Suicide Risk: The Foundation of Clinical Judgment.* N.Y.: N.Y. University Press.

Maris, R. 1985. "The Adolescent Suicide Problem." *Suicide and Life Threatening Behavior* 15: 91–109.

Masten, A.S. & Garmezy, N. 1985. "Risk, Vulnerability, and Predictive Factors in Developmental Psychopathology," in B.B. Lahey & A.E. Kazdin, eds., *Advances in Clinical Child Psychology.* Vol. 8. N.Y.: Plenum Press.

Mattsson, A., Siese, L.R. & Hawkins, J.W. 1969. "Suicidal Behavior as a Child Psychiatric Emergency: Clinical Characteristics and Follow-up Results." *Archives of General Psychiatry* 20: 100–109.

McConville, B. 1983. "Depression and Suicide in Children and Adolescents," in P.D. Steinhauer & Q. Rae-Grant, eds., *Psychological Problems of the Child in His Family.* N.Y.: Basic Books.

McKnew, D.H., Cytryn, L. & Yahraes, H. 1983. *Why Isn't Johnny Crying: Coping With Depression in Children.* N.Y.: Norton.

Minuchin, S. & Fishman, H.C. 1981. *Family Therapy Techniques.* Cambridge, Mass.: Harvard University Press.

Motto, J.A. 1985. "Treatment Concerns in Preventing Youth Suicide," in M.L. Peck, N.L. Farberow & R.E. Litman, eds., *Youth Suicide.* N.Y.: Springer Publ. Co.

Mullins, L.L., Siegel, L.J. & Hodges, K. 1985. "Cognitive Problem-Solving and Life Event Correlates of Depressive Symptoms in Children." *Journal of Abnormal Child Psychology* 13: 305–314.

O'Grady, D. & Metz, J.R. 1987. "Resilience in Children at High Risk for Psychological Disorder." *Journal of Pediatric Psychology* 12: 3–23.

Pakizegi, B. 1985. "Maladaptive Parent-Infant Relationships." *Journal of Applied Developmental Psychology* 6: 199–246.

Peck, M.L. 1985. "Crisis Intervention with Chronically and Acutely Suicidal Adolescents," in M.L. Peck, N.L. Farberow & R.E. Litman, eds., *Youth Suicide.* N.Y.: Springer Publ. Co.

Pfeffer, C.R. 1981. "Suicidal Behavior of Children: A Review with Implications for Research and Practice." *American Journal of Psychiatry* 138: 154–59.

——. 1984a. "Clinical Assessment of Suicidal Behavior in Children," in H. Sudak, A.B. Ford & N.B. Rushforth, eds., *Suicide in the Young.* Boston: John Wright PSG, Inc.

——. 1984b. "Modalities of Treatment for Suicidal Children: An Overview of the Literature on Current Practice." *American Journal of Psychotherapy* 38: 364–72.

Pfeffer, C.R., Conte, H.R., Plutchik, R. & Jerrett, I. 1979. "Suicidal Behavior in Latency Age Children: An Empirical Study." *Journal of the American Academy of Child Psychiatry* 18: 679–92.

Pfeffer, C.R., Solomon, G. Plutchik, R., Mezruchi, M.S. & Weiner, A. 1982. "Suicidal Behavior in Latency-Age Psychiatric Patients: A Replication and Cross Validation." *Journal of the American Academy of Child Psychiatry* 21: 564–69.

Pfeffer, C.R., Zuckerman, S., Plutchik, R., et al. 1984. "Suicidal Behavior in Normal School Children: A Comparison with Child Psychiatric Inpatients." *Journal of the American Academy of Child Psychiatry* 23: 416–23.

Quinton, D. & Rutter, M. 1985. "Parenting Behaviour of Mothers Raised 'In Care'," in A.R. Nicol, ed., *Longitudinal Studies in Child Psychology and Psychiatry.* Chichester: John Wiley and Sons.

Rachman, S.J. 1979. "The Concept of Required Helpfulness." *Behavior Research and Therapy* 17: 1–6.

Reynolds, W.M. 1985. "Depression in Childhood and Adolescence: Diagnosis, Assessment, Intervention Strategies and Research," in T.R. Kratochwill, ed., *Advances in School Psychology.* Vol. 4. Hillsdale, N.J.: Lawrence Erlbaum, Assoc. Publ.

Reynolds, W.M. & Coats, K.I. 1986. "A Comparison of Cognitive-Behavioral Therapy and Relaxation Training for the Treatment of Depression in Adolescents." *Journal of Consulting and Clinical Psychology* 54: 653–60.

Richman, J. 1979. "Family Therapy of Attempted Suicide." *Family Process* 18: 131–42.

Robbins, D.R. & Alessi, N.E. 1985. "Depressive Symptoms and Suicidal Behavior in Adolescents," *American Journal of Psychiatry* 142: 588–92.

Rosenthal, P.A. & Rosenthal, S. 1984. "Suicidal Behavior by Preschool Children." *American Journal of Psychiatry* 141: 520–25.

Ross, C.P. n.d. *Suicide in Youth and What You Can Do About It—A Guide for Students.* Pamphlet by the Suicide Prevention and Crisis Center of San Mateo County, Burlingame, Calif.

———. 1980. "Mobilizing Schools for Suicide Prevention." *Suicide and Life Threatening Behavior* 10: 239–43.

———. 1985. "Teaching Children the Facts of Life and Death: Suicide Prevention in the Schools," in M.L. Peck, N.L. Farberow, & R.E. Litman, eds., *Youth Suicide.* N.Y.: Springer Publ. Co.

Ross, C.P. & Lee, R. n.d. *Suicide in Youth and What You Can Do About It—A Guide for School Personnel.* Pamphlet by the Suicide Prevention and Crisis Center of San Mateo County, Burlingame, Calif.

Ross, D.M. & Ross, S.A. 1985. "Pain Instruction with Third and Fourth Grade Children: A Pilot Study." *Journal of Pediatric Psychology* 10: 55–63.

Rotheram, M.J. 1987. "Evaluation of Imminent Danger for Suicide among Youth." *American Journal of Orthopsychiatry* 57: 102–10.

Rutter, M. 1979. "Protective Factors in Children's Responses to Disadvantage," in M.W. Kent & J. Rolf, eds., *Primary Prevention of Psychopathology.* Vol. 3: *Social Competence in Children.* Hanover, N.H.: University Press of New England.

———. 1980. "The Long-Term Effects of Early Experience." *Developmental Medicine and Child Neurology* 22: 800–15.

———. 1981. "The City and the Child." *American Journal of Orthopsychiatry* 51: 610–25.

———. 1983. "Stress, Coping, and Development: Some Issues and Some Questions," in N. Garmezy & M. Rutter, eds., *Stress, Coping, and Development in Children.* N.Y.: McGraw-Hill Book Co.

———. 1985a. "The Developmental Psychopathology of Depression: Issues and Perspectives," in M. Rutter, C.E. Izard, & P.B. Read, eds., *Depression in Young People: Developmental and Clincial Perspectives.* N.Y.: The Guilford Press.

———. 1985b. "Family and School Influences: Meanings, Mechanisms and Implications," in A.R. Nicol, ed., *Longitudinal Studies in Child Psychology and Psychiatry.* Chichester: John Wiley and Sons.

———. 1985c. "Resilience in the Face of Adversity: Protective Factors and Resistance to Psychiatric Disorder." *British Journal of Psychiatry* 147: 598–611.

Rutter, M. & Garmezy, N. 1983. "Developmental Psychopathology," in P.H. Mussen, ed., *Handbook of Child Psychology.* Vol. 4. N.Y.: John Wiley and Sons.

Sameroff, A.J. & Chandler, M.J. 1975. "Reproductive Risk and the Continuum of Caretaking Casualty," in F.D. Horowitz, M. Hetherington, S. Scarr-Salapatek & G. Siegel, eds., *Review of Child Development Research.* Vol. 4. Chicago: University of Chicago Press.

Sandler, J.N. & Block, M. 1979. "Life Stress and Maladaptation of Children." *American Journal of Community Psychology* 7: 425–40.

Sands, R.G. & Dixon, S.L. 1986. "Adolescent Crisis and Suicidal Behavior: Dynamics and Treatment." *Child and Adolescent Social Work* 3: 109–22.

Seligman, M.E.P. & Peterson, C. 1985. "A Learned Helplessness Perspective on Childhood Depression: Theory and Research," in M. Rutter, C.E. Izard & P.B. Read, eds., *Depression in Young People: Developmental and Clinical Perspectives.* N.Y.: The Guilford Press.

Shaffer, D. 1974. "Suicide in Childhood and Early Adolescence." *Journal of Child Psychology and Psychiatry* 15: 275–91.

Shaffer, D. 1985. "Developmental Factors in Child and Adolescent Suicide," in M. Rutter, C.E. Izard, & P.B. Read, eds., *Depression in Young People: Developmental and Clinical Perspectives*. N.Y.: The Guilford Press.

Sheras, P.L. 1983. "Suicide in Adolescence," in C.E. Walker & M.C. Roberts, eds., *Handbook of Clinical Child Psychology*. N.Y.: John Wiley and Sons.

Smith, K. & Crawford, S. 1986. "Suicidal Behavior Among 'Normal' High School Students." *Suicide and Life Threatening Behavior* 16: 313–25.

Sommer, B. 1984. "The Troubled Teen: Suicide, Drug Use, and Running Away." *Women and Health* 9: 117–41.

Stambrook, M. & Parker, K.C.H. 1987. "The Development of the Concept of Death in Childhood: A Review of the Literature." *Merrill-Palmer Quarterly* 33: 133–57.

Sterling, S., Cowen, E.L., Weissberg, R.P., Lotyczewski, B.S. & Boike, M. 1985. "Recent Stressful Life Events and Young Children's School Adjustment." *American Journal of Community Psychology* 13: 87–98.

Stroufe, L.A. & Rutter, M. 1984. "The Domain of Developmental Psychopathology." *Child Development* 55: 17–29.

Sudak, H.S., Ford, A.B. & Rushforth, N.B. 1984. "Adolescent Suicide: An Overview." *American Journal of Psychotherapy* 38: 350–63.

Walker, L.S. & Greene, J.W. 1987. "Negative Life Events, Psychosocial Resources, and Psychophysiological Symptoms in Adolescents." *Journal of Clinical Child Psychology* 16: 29–36.

Walker, W.L. 1980. "Intentional Self-Injury in School Age Children." *Journal of Adolescence* 3: 217–28.

Werner, E.E. 1985. "Stress and Protective Factors in Children's Lives," in A.R. Nicol, ed., *Longitudinal Studies in Child Psychology and Psychiatry*. Chichester: John Wiley and Sons.

———. 1986. "The Concept of Risk from a Developmental Perspective," in B.K. Keogh, ed., *Advances in Special Education*. Vol. 5. Greenwich, Conn.: JAI Press.

Werner, E.E. & Smith, R.S. 1982. *Vulnerable But Invincible: A Study of Resilient Children*. N.Y.: McGraw-Hill Book Co.

Wertlieb, D., Weigel, C., Springer, T. & Felstein, M. 1987. "Temperament as a Moderator of Children's Stressful Experiences." *American Journal of Orthopsychiatry* 57: 234–45.

Winn, M. 1983. *Children Without Childhood*. N.Y.: Pantheon Books.

Yeaworth, R.C., York, J., Hussey, M.A., Ingle, M.E. & Goodwin, T. 1980. "The Development of an Adolescent Life Change Event Scale." *Adolescence* 15: 91–98.

Zaslow, M.J. & Hayes, C.D. 1986. "Sex Differences in Children's Response to Psychosocial Stress: Toward a Cross-Context Analysis," in M.E. Lamb, A.L. Brown & B. Rogoff, eds., *Advances in Developmental Psychology*. Vol. 4. Hillsdale, N.J.: Lawrence Erlbaum Assoc. Publ.

6
Child Abuse

C hild abuse is more than an internal family problem. It is a problem that is intricately linked with societal conditions. Most often, it has lasting consequences for its millions of victims. And, importantly, it is a problem that seems to be responsive to societal intervention.

The child abuse field is one in which misconceptions abound, some of which have been repeated so often, they are accepted as fact (S.L. Smith 1984). The misconceptions originated with research reported in the sixties, when child abuse first captured widespread professional concern as a major problem. This early research primarily consisted of clinical impressions, formed without the benefit of validated measures, large samples, or control groups for comparison (Starr 1979). During the seventies, serious efforts were directed toward conducting methodologically sound studies and developing a knowledge base of informed data (Gelles 1980). Many of the early misconceptions have been refuted; others required further scrutiny (S.L. Smith 1984). Yet many of the myths linger, not only within the media and lay community but among practitioners as well (S.L. Smith 1984).

Child Abuse and Its Occurrence

What constitutes child abuse? Definitional ambiguities prevent us from having a clear picture. Although there is wide consensus about extreme cases, only a small percentage of child abuse cases fall into headline-making categories (Straus & Gelles 1986). A larger percentage of cases raise a number of definitional problems. How much violence is necessary before it is considered abuse? How hurt does a child have to be before she is considered abused? Where is the line drawn between discipline and abuse? This distinction varies considerably from one cultural group to another, each with its own social norms. Additionally, there are many different types of abuse—physical, sexual, emotional, and neglect (Straus & Gelles 1986).

Another obstacle to grasping an accurate picture of child abuse is practical problems in collecting reliable data. No accurate statistics exist since most figures reflect only reported or "caught" cases (Belsky, Lerner & Spanier 1984). A different approach was recently attempted by Straus and Gelles (1986), who surveyed, by telephone, a nationally representative sample of over 1,400 two-parent households with children between the ages of 3 and 17. Straus and Gelles defined abuse as kicking, biting, punching, beating up, or either using or threatening to use a gun or knife on a child. If survey results can be reliably extrapolated to the general population, a minimum of 1 million children are kicked, bitten, punched, beaten up, or either threatened or attacked with a gun or knife by their parents each year. This estimate, however, is probably a conservative one. Not only would some reluctance to admit such violence be expected, but Straus and Gelles omitted from the survey two groups within which abuse is particularly high: children under the age of 3 and single-parent families. They also limited their survey to physical abuse. Child abuse estimates have been as high as 6 million children per year (see Meddin 1985).

Few statistics have been reported outside the United States. Child abuse is most common in developed nations. It is a recognized problem in Canada, Australia, England, and many West European countries. However, it is believed to be rare in China, Japan, the Soviet Union, Poland, and Scandinavia (Gelles & Cornell 1983).

The focus of this chapter will be physical abuse. The literature is far too extensive to attempt to include a review of each type of abuse (physical, sexual, emotional, and neglect). And from available evidence, it appears that the causes and impact of the different types of abuse are too different to be grouped together (Berger 1980a, Pakizegi 1985, S.L. Smith 1984, Wolfe 1985a).

Definitions of physical abuse vary from state to state and from study to study. A review of the literature by Valentine and her colleagues (1984) revealed that definitions generally have two characteristics in common: (1) identifiable harm or injury to a child inflicted by a caregiver, and (2) evidence that the injury was nonaccidental. A definition commonly cited in the literature is the following: "non-accidental physical injury (or injuries) as a result of acts (or omissions) on the part of parents or guardians that violate the community standards concerning the treatment of children" (Parke & Collmer 1975, p. 513).

Researchers generally select child-abusing populations on the basis of protective service agency reports that indicate the parent met both statutory and community criteria for abuse. Unfortunately, researchers often do not take into consideration the chronicity of abuse (Wolfe 1985a) when selecting study populations. However, studies have found that half to two-thirds of their populations of abused children are the victims of recurrent abuse that is serious enough to be investigated (see Friedrich & Einbender 1983).

Risk Factors Leading to Abuse

For many years, simplistic answers were sought to explain child abuse (Gelles 1982). However, the search has revealed that the causes of child abuse are far from simple.

Usually, they are intricately woven into a complex web that is somewhat unique in each individual case. Rather than specific causes, research has identified a number of risk factors which combine to increase the likelihood that a child will be abused (Pakizegi 1985). The appearance of a single risk factor, by itself, does not appear to be sufficient to explain the phenomenon of child abuse (Berger 1980b, Pakizegi 1985). And there is no consensus that any single risk factor is necessary for abuse to occur (Pakizegi 1985). Instead, abuse stems from combinations of risk factors which can vary from case to case (Berger 1980b; Pakizegi 1985; Starr 1979).

The risk factors that have been identified not only lie within the parent, child, and family. Social factors have been implicated as strongly in child abuse as have psychological factors (Gelles 1982). Risk factors embedded in our society will be looked at first, because it is these factors that create the broad conditions that allow child abuse to occur.

The Cultural Backdrop of Abuse

There is an emerging consensus that child abuse cannot be fully understood without considering the attitudes, values, and philosophy that are prevalent in the society in which it occurs—in this case the United States (Belsky 1980, Bittner & Newberger 1982, Garbarino 1980, Gil 1979, Pakizegi 1985).

America is a nation that tolerates violence. It is evident in our crime statistics, films, television programs, magazines, and sports (Belsky 1980, Garbarino 1980, Straus 1974). Available statistics suggest that our most violent institution or social group is the family (Allan, cited in Pakizegi 1985; Gelles 1982).

More directly relevant to child abuse is our sanctioning of physical punishment as a form of discipline for children (Belsky 1980). Where does discipline end and abuse begin? The majority of child abuse takes place within the context of discipline (Gil 1979). Yet, in excess of 90 percent of American families physically punish their children at some age level (Straus, cited in Garbarino 1980). Professional concern about corporal punishment is consistently expressed in the child abuse literature (e.g., Belsky 1980, Bittner & Newberger 1982, Burgess 1978, Gil 1979, Libbey & Bybee 1979, Williams 1983). In fact, Yale's Edward Zigler 1979) calls our willingness to inflict corporal punishment on children the single most important determinant of child abuse today. Interestingly, child abuse is reported to be very rare among peoples who use physical punishment infrequently, such as the Chinese, the Japanese, and the Tahitians (Parke & Collmer 1975).

It has been suggested that other attitudes currently prevalent in our society also contribute to child abuse. Children are considered the property of parents, to be raised as parents see fit. The privacy of the nuclear family is protected, discouraging the intervention of outsiders. The role of caring for children is devalued in comparison with earning money or pursuing self-fulfillment. Finally, there is generally poor support for public social service programs from which child-abusing families could benefit (Belsky 1980, Bittner & Newberger 1982, Friedman et al. 1981, Pakizegi 1985, Zigler 1979).

Parent Risk Factors

Early reports attributed child abuse to pathological parents who were either seriously emotionally disturbed or had a personality disorder (see Newberger 1982, Wolfe 1985a). However, these early conceptualizations have not been supported by empirical data (Bittner & Newberger 1982). It is now widely recognized that fewer than 5 percent of abusing parents have symptoms of serious disturbance (Friedman et al. 1981, Wolfe 1985a). With the exception of a few characteristics, empirical studies have also failed to identify much similarity in the personalities of abusing parents. They appear to be a heterogeneous population with widely varying traits which are also found in successful parents (see Friedman et al. 1981, Newberger 1982, Oates 1986, S.L. Smith 1984, Wolfe 1985a).

The data suggest that a combination of other risk factors in parents play a more important role in child abuse than do personality variables. These risk factors are both social and individual.

Social Risk Factors in Parents. The following social factors are among the most consistently found parent risk factors associated with child abuse: social isolation, socioeconomic status, and environmental stress.

Social Isolation. Interestingly, the characteristic of abusing parents that has most frequently emerged in the child abuse literature is social isolation (S.L. Smith 1984). In fact, Garbarino (1977) has pointed out that social isolation has been associated with child abuse in every study in which it was examined. Furthermore, Turner and Avison (1985) found it to be the most powerful factor they found to distinguish between maladaptive and normal mothers.

Abusive parents generally are isolated both from community contacts and informal supports (See Belsky, Lerner & Spanier 1984; Gaudin & Pollane 1983; Pakizegi 1985). Not only do they have fewer relatives and friends, but those they have are seen infrequently and are seldom asked for help. When a spouse is present, it is usually an unsupportive spouse (see Pakizegi 1985).

A few examples will illustrate the social isolation of these lives. In one sample, 95 percent of abusive parents had no continuing relationships with anyone outside the family (Young, cited in Wood-Shuman & Cone 1986). In another, 89 percent of abusers had unlisted telephone numbers and 81 percent preferred not to seek help in a crisis, compared with 12 percent and 43 percent of nonabusers, respectively (Garbarino & Gilliam cited in Pakizegi 1985).

What role does social isolation play in child abuse? Several have been suggested. Kempe pointed out that abusing families, because of their isolation, lacked a lifeline by which to escape during times of stress (see Belsky 1980); they have nowhere to turn for either emotional assistance or child care relief. Secondly, social isolation denies abusing parents role models from whom to learn parenting skills. Along the same line, social isolation results in little feedback about their inappropriate parenting (Belsky, Lerner & Spanier 1984). Finally, social isolation appears to have a negative effect on both the quality of parenting and the quality of children's experiences in the home. Conversely, the presence of social supports appears to enhance both. The convergence of many separate findings suggests this last conclusion. Several of these findings follow.

In a comparison of two comparable neighborhoods with very different rates of child abuse, the low-incident community was characterized by strong social support systems which were notably absent in the high-abuse neighborhood (Garbarino & Sherman 1980).

In an interesting study conducted with mothers and children who had behavior problems, Wahler (1980) found that daily fluctuations in mothers' yelling and coercive behavior could be predicted by the amount and quality of the mothers' daily social contacts.

In a study of parents who had been abused as children, one of the most obvious differences between those who abused their own children and those who did not was the absence or presence of social supports in their adult lives (Hunter & Kilstrom 1979).

In an anthropological study, Korbin (see S.L. Smith 1984) reported that one of the factors associated with more severe child rearing was the nuclear family, with its relative isolation and shortage of strong support systems and alternative caregivers.

The question remains why abusive parents are social isolates. It is often suggested that poor interpersonal skills are responsible (Pakizegi 1985). Abusers are also found to have negative attitudes towards people in general (see S.L. Smith 1984). Additionally, they tend to move frequently and perhaps fail to establish roots (see S.L. Smith 1984).

As with any of the factors that increase the risk of child abuse, social isolation is not a sufficient condition to cause abuse. Nor is it a necessary condition, as was demonstrated by Caplan and her colleagues (1984) and by Seagull (1987). Social isolation must be combined with other risk factors.

Socioeconomic Status. The early literature reported child abuse to be evenly distributed across all social classes. However, later research identified socioeconomic status as an important variable. Although child abuse can be found across the spectrum of socioeconomic levels, it is now widely recognized that it is far more common among the poor, uneducated, and unskilled (see Evans 1981, Friedrich & Einbender 1983, Gelles 1982, Oates 1986, Pakizegi 1985, Pelton 1978, S.L. Smith 1984, Williams 1983). An exception is adolescent abuse, which is more common in affluent families than is the abuse of younger children (see Garbarino 1980).

Much concern has been expressed that the observed prevalence of child abuse in low-income populations is due to biased detection and reporting. Researchers have found that the social class of the victim affects both perceptions and labeling in abuse cases. For example, physicians who were asked to judge a series of mock cases were more likely to label an injury "abuse" if the victim was described as lower-class or black (O'Toole, Turbett & Nalepka 1983). Katz and others (1986) reported that injuries were more likely to be labeled "accidents" when families were affluent and more likely to be labeled "abuse" when families were poor. And physicians in emergency rooms (where low-income individuals typically seek help) are more likely to diagnose injuries as abuse than are private physicians who have continuing contact with a family (see Gelles 1982).

Although sampling bias clearly plays a role, it cannot account for all the data. Some reviewers have pointed out that child abuse is related to the degree of poverty (see Friedrich & Wheeler 1982, Pakizegi 1985, Williams 1983). The poorest families tend to have the highest incidence of abuse and the most serious abuse. Furthermore, the incidence and severity of child abuse has been found to rise in periods of economic stress and unemployment.

People who are faced with basic needs of survival are likely to have higher levels of stress and frustration, leaving them more vulnerable and with less energy to cope (Pakizegi 1985). However, most low-income people do not abuse their children. Low socioeconomic status is a risk factor which raises the risk of abuse when combined with other risk factors.

Environmental Stress. Environmental stress, independent of that caused by low socioeconomic status, has also been found to play an important role in child abuse. Some studies have found that abusive families have more life changes, requiring them to constantly readjust (see Berger 1980b, Friedrich & Wheeler 1982). Other studies have found that abusive families experience a similar number of life changes as do other families, but the changes are more serious and disruptive (see Egeland, Breitenbucher & Rosenberg 1980). Still other data suggest that abusive families interpret stress as more aversive and debilitating than do comparison families (see Wolfe 1985a). Belsky and his colleagues (1984) point out that a family's ability to cope with adversity probably influences its tolerance of stress as much as does the absolute level of stress experienced. Wolfe (1985a) concurs; he identified family management skills and competence in handling daily stress to be an important discriminator between abusing and nonabusing parents.

Many variables found to be associated with child abuse can be interpreted as environmental stress. For example, significant correlations are found between child abuse and unemployment (Krugman et al. 1986; Steinberg, Catalano & Dooley 1981). Child abuse is also associated with single-parent homes, large families, families in which the children are spaced closely together (see Belsky 1980, Gelles 1982, Pakizegi 1985), and poor parental health (see Oates 1986). Additionally, the lives of many abusive families have been described as out of control (Pakizegi 1985). Households are disorganized, there are fewer routines, neither parent takes responsibility for decisions, and pregnancies are frequently unplanned (see Belsky 1978,

Pakizegi 1985). Studies out of the child abuse area have found that parents who feel overwhelmed and out of control tend to be more punitive than are those who feel in control of their lives (see Friedrich & Wheeler 1982). Perhaps parents perceive punitiveness as a means of swift control in at least one area of life.

Although there is strong evidence linking stress with child abuse, stress appears to be neither a necessary nor sufficient cause of abuse, concluded Friedrich and Wheeler (1982) from their literature review. Stress places a family at risk but other conditions must be present, such as parents who have a proclivity to use violence to resolve conflicts (Justice, Calvert & Justice 1985).

Individual Risk Factors in Parents. Although most abusive parents are neither very seriously disturbed nor similar in personality, individual parental risk factors have been identified that, combined with other conditions, raise the risk of a parent abusing his child.

A Childhood History of Abuse. Among the most widely held beliefs about child abusers is that they were abused as children and, conversely, that abused children will grow into abusing adults. Although there is some truth in this, the extent of the relationship is more modest than is widely believed (Kaufman & Zigler 1987; Potts & Herzberger, cited in Gelles 1982). Studies typically have found that between 20 to 50 percent of abusive parents experienced mistreatment as children (see Oates 1986). And Kaufman and Zigler (1987) have estimated from the research that approximately one-third of the children who are maltreated will one day abuse their own children.

Although the finding that abuse begets abuse is far from universal, there is consensus among many reviewers that abusing parents are more likely than are nonabusers to have been maltreated as children (Belsky 1980, Gelles 1982, Pakizegi 1985).

A childhood history of abuse is clearly a risk factor that may predispose a parent to abuse her own child. Why this is so is a matter of speculation. One hypothesis suggests that a childhood of rejection and abuse disrupts healthy development and creates an adult who is aggressive, insensitive, and noncaring (Belsky 1978). Another suggests that abusing parents are repeating the parenting patterns learned from their own abusive parents. The fact that abusive parents often do not believe they have acted inappropriately supports this latter hypothesis (Belsky 1978). Belsky (1978) suggests these two hypotheses are not mutually exclusive. Each probably contributes to our understanding of what has become to be called the *intergenerational cycle of maltreatment* (Pakizegi 1985).

Like other risk factors, a childhood history of abuse is neither a necessary nor sufficient condition to cause abuse (Belsky 1980, Berger 1980a). Most abusive parents do not report a history of abuse (see Oates 1986), and most parents who were abused as children do not abuse their own children (Conger et al., cited in Belsky 1980; Hunter & Kilstrom 1979). Clearly, other risk factors must also be present for a parent who experienced abuse to abuse his own child.

Personal Characteristics of Abusing Parents. Many studies have found personality differences between abusing parents and controls, but there is little consistency from study to study in the differences found (see Friedrich & Wheeler 1982, Pakizegi 1985, Wolfe 1985a). For example, studies using the Minnesota Multiphasic Personality Inventory (MMPI) all report significant differences on a number of MMPI scales between abusive and nonabusive parents (see Friedrich & Wheeler 1982). But the scales on which differences are found differ from study to study. In the Friedrich and Wheeler (1982) review, some scales seemed to show up with *some* frequency, such as the Sc (cold, indifferent), Pd (emotional shallowness, asocial, amoral), and Ma (emotionally excitable). Gabinet (see Friedrich & Wheeler 1982) points out that the MMPI profiles of abusing parents are quite similar to those of many nonabusing parents who seek help in psychiatric clinics.

Although abusing parents seem to represent a heterogeneous population, many seem to share at least a few characteristics. Those most frequently mentioned by reviewers of this literature follow.

Low self-esteem and a *lack of empathy* are mentioned most frequently (Berger 1980a, Friedrich & Wheeler 1982, Oates 1986, Pakizegi 1985). A lack of empathy may explain why the child's pain does not stop the abuse, why the abusing parent usually is not the one to seek help for the hurt child, and why abusing parents often justify their actions and minimize the significance of the abuse (Pakizegi 1985). Belsky (1980) suggests that the lack of empathy observed in many abusers may stem from an emotionally deprived childhood.

Perhaps significant are findings that abusing parents are more easily physiologically aroused by child behavior than are nonabusing parents (see Berger 1980a, Friedrich & Wheeler 1982, Wolfe 1985a). This becomes obvious when parents' physiological responses (for example, heart rate, blood pressure) are measured while the parents view videotapes of children's behavior. It may help to explain the difficulty that abusing parents have controlling their violent reactions toward their offspring (Wolfe 1985a). Interestingly, there is evidence that the child behavior does not need to be aversive to elicit stronger physiological responses in this population. Abusing parents, compared to controls, have stronger physiological responses to videotapes of crying *and* smiling infants and to videotapes of aversive *and* pleasant parent-child interactions (Disbrow et al., cited in Frodi & Lamb 1980; Doerr, Disbrow & Caulfield, cited in Friedrich & Wheeler 1982; Frodi & Lamb 1980). It will be helpful to keep in mind this characteristic of many abusive parents.

Parental alcohol and drug addiction each raise the risk that children will be abused (see Famularo et al. 1986, Oates 1986, Zigler 1979). Alcoholic and drug-dependent parents are overrepresented in abusing populations, and abusive parents are overrepresented in alcohol- and drug-addicted populations.

There have been conflicting findings about the intelligence of abusing parents. Some studies have reported abusers more likely to have borderline intelligence, whereas others have reported no significant IQ differences (see Oates 1986). These conflicting findings undoubtedly reflect the heterogeneity of the population.

A characteristic of abusing parents that was frequently reported in the early clinical literature was strong dependency needs. These hypothesized needs were the basis for the now well-known role-reversal hypothesis. According to this hypothesis, unmet dependency needs cause the abusive parent to turn to the child for love and nurturance. It is because the child is unable to satisfy strong parental needs that the parent strikes out in anger (see Berger 1980a, S.L. Smith 1984). The hypothesis, however, needs further testing before any conclusions can be reached. The literature supporting it is inferential (Berger 1980a), and the few empirical studies that have included measures of dependency have yielded mixed results (see S.L. Smith 1984).

Parenting Skills. Early clinical studies reported that a distinguishing characteristic of abusive parents was their ignorance about child rearing and children's development (Friedrich & Wheeler 1982). In a review of empirical studies which assessed abusers' knowledge about children, Friedrich and Wheeler (1982) concluded that results were rather mixed. Some studies reported abusers had less accurate information than did controls, whereas others reported no significant differences.

Although studies have not necessarily found abusing parents' knowledge to be inadequate, they have found their parenting behavior to be inadequate (Friedrich & Wheeler 1982). Studies of mothers with infants have found abusing mothers, in general, to be less able to identify with their infants' emotional signals (for example, pain, anger, surprise, interest), to be unresponsive to their initiative, to interfere more in their infants' behavior, and to be overly sensitive to their crying (Kropp & Haynes 1987, Lyons-Ruth et al. 1987, see Pakizegi 1985). Compared to nonabusers, abusing mothers show less positive emotion toward their infants and offer them less eye contact, less interaction, and less stimulation (see Burgess 1979, Pakizegi 1985, Starr 1979). Beyond the infancy period, abusing parents generally show less warmth and support and more negative behavior with their children. Compared to their nonmaltreating counterparts, abusing parents interact less with their offspring and reason with them less. At the same time, they value parental power more and believe more in the necessity of physical punishment (Friedrich & Wheeler 1982, Pakizegi 1985). Poor child management skills is a characteristic of abusive parents that has been found in many studies (see Friedman et al. 1981, Wolfe 1985a).

It could be, as has been suggested, that abusive parents cannot act on the knowledge or information they appear to have (Polansky et al. 1981, cited in Pakizegi 1985). This may explain some findings that abusive parents have either unrealistic or distorted perceptions of children (see Berger 1980a, Pakizegi 1985, Wolfe 1985a). For example, abusive mothers rate an infant's cry (heard on audiotape) as significantly more demanding, angry, and annoying than do nonabusive mothers (Friedrich, cited in Friedrich & Wheeler 1982; Frodi & Lamb 1980). They attribute more provocation to "normal" child behavior than do nonabusing parents (see Wolfe 1985a). They rate scenes depicting mildly aversive child behavior more negatively than do controls (Wood-Shuman & Cone 1986). And they rate a greater variety of child behavior as negative, including many normal child activities (Wood-Shuman & Cone 1986). Abusive parents' interpretations of children's behavior may help to explain why they are more easily physiologically aroused by all types of child behavior. They appear to overreact to children's behavior and to perceive a wider range of behavior as bad (Wood-Shuman & Cone 1986).

Child Risk Factors

Not every child in an abusing family is abused or is equally vulnerable to abuse. For example, Gil (1970) found abuse of more than one child in only 27 percent of his families. Other studies have reported abuse of more than one youngster in up to 56 percent of their study families (see Friedman et al. 1981, Friedrich & Einbender 1983). Researchers, therefore, have asked what makes one child more vulnerable to abuse than her siblings?

Some groups of children are overrepresented in populations of abused youngsters, such as children who were born prematurely or those with difficult temperaments or chronic illness. Youngsters who are mentally retarded, physically handicapped, developmentally delayed, or behaviorally deviant are also overrepresented (see Berger 1980b, Friedrich & Boriskin 1976, Gelles 1980, Newberger 1982, S.L. Smith 1984). However, since most studies are retrospective, investigating children who have already been abused, it is difficult to separate cause from effect. Does a difficult temperament, chronic illness, or developmental delay elicit abuse? Or does abuse cause a difficult temperament, chronic illness, or developmental delay? Even when characteristics precede the abuse, they may be exacerbated by the abuse and the type of care the child receives (Belsky, Lerner & Spanier 1984; Berger 1980b).

Some characteristics that are associated with abuse clearly precede it, such as hereditary or congenital birth defects, prematurity, and low birth weight. Three recent reviews have looked at handicaps that are present at birth and have concluded that the research has not sufficiently substantiated their role as major causal factors of abuse (S.L. Smith 1984, Starr et al. 1984, White et al. 1987). Prematurity and low birth weight have been the subjects of most of this research, discussion, and speculation. Retrospective studies have reported a higher percentage of premature and low-birth-weight children in child abuse samples than are found in the population at large (see Friedrich & Boriskin 1976). It has been suggested that these children are more vulnerable to abuse because of their unattractive physical characteristics, high-pitched cries, the special care they require, and their early separation from parents due to their extended hospital care. This separation, it is speculated, may disrupt the formation of parent-infant bonds (Friedrich & Einbender 1983). (See chapter 1.) The importance of prematurity and low birth weight is an issue of debate, however. Their relationships with child abuse become less obvious when the data are carefully scrutinized, say several reviewers (e.g., Berger 1980b; Newberger 1982; Oates 1986). The relationships are not found in all studies, the relationships are less obvious when control groups are used, and prematurity does not contribute to the *prediction* of abuse (Berger 1980b, Oates 1986). Furthermore, when relationships are found, they are not necessarily causal relationships. Premature and low-birth-weight infants are more likely to be born in populations marked with poverty, poor education, and poor access to prenatal care. These are the same populations in which child abuse is most likely to occur (Newberger 1982). Nevertheless, Friedman and his colleagues (1981) contend that most authorities continue to consider prematurity and low birth weight to be risk factors, along with other conditions requiring intensive care after birth.

It appears that any number of minor child problems, as opposed to major handicaps, are associated with abuse. This was the conclusion of Starr and others (1984), on the basis of prospective studies that followed children from birth. Their conclusion concurs with Martin's earlier suggestion (see Berger 1980b) that children at risk are not those who are obviously different because such obvious differences would elicit social support for the mother. Martin contended that it is the children who are more subtly difficult to care for who elicit abuse. Any number of attributes can make a youngster difficult to care for or elicit ambivalence in particular parents. For example, in one sample of abused children, 64 percent had been unplanned, 46 percent were born out of wedlock, 32 percent had been born at a "bad time," and 31 percent had had a negative impact on the abusers' relationships with their partners. Mothers had had difficult pregnancies with 34 percent and difficult deliveries with 43 percent. Forty-eight percent were identified with a person the abuser disliked (Kadushin & Martin 1981). Abusing parents also reportedly perceive their abused infants as different, difficult, fussy, prone to excessive crying, or unresponsive (see Pakizegi 1985).

In summary, any number of minor child problems are associated with abuse but none are high-risk factors in and of themselves. Only when they are considered in relation to a particular parent do they begin to make sense. A different parent would not have abused the child. And a different child may not have elicited abuse. It is a mismatch between parent and child that increases the risk of abuse (Berger 1980b, Belsky 1980). In conjunction with other risk factors, this mismatch may be sufficient to tip a delicate balance.

Later in this chapter it will be shown that abused children do have a number of personality and emotional characteristics that play an important role in their abuse. However, it appears likely that these characteristics either develop or are seriously exacerbated as a result of abuse and then function to ignite further abuse. Therefore these personality and emotional characteristics will be considered under "The Sequelae of Abuse." Some of these characteristics will be obvious in the following discussion of dysfunctional family interactions.

Dysfunctional Family Interaction

The relationship between the perpetrator of the abuse and the abused child generally is not the only dysfunctional relationship in abusing families. Marital conflict is common. Often physical and verbal aggression are as evident in the spousal relationship as in the relationship between parent and abused child (see Belsky, Lerner & Spanier 1984; Berger 1980a; Gelles 1982).

In general, members of abusing families interact with one another significantly less frequently than do members of nonabusing families. Furthermore, the limited interaction which does occur is dominated by aversive and coercive exchanges, such as yelling, complaints, threats, humiliation, noncompliance, and physical aggression (see Koverola, Manion & Wolfe 1985; Reid, Taplin & Lorber 1981; Wolfe 1985a). Aversive exchanges are particularly severe between the abusing parent and the abused child, with the nonabusing parent usually assuming a passive role, even during the abusive incidents (see Friedman et al. 1981).

The abused child usually is not a passive participant in his abuse (see Friedrich & Wheeler 1982). The behavior of abused children generally is more disruptive, problematic, and negative than the behavior of their nonabused counterparts. It cannot be determined, of course, to what degree their aversive behavior causes their abuse and to what degree previous abuse causes their aversive behavior (Wolfe 1985a). Both undoubtedly feed upon the other in a vicious cycle.

Although it may be logical to assume that abusing parents rely on harsh punitive methods as a response to a child's disruptive and aversive behavior, the situation is not quite so simple. For example, in one study of abuse incidents, 86 percent of the parents first intervened in a nonpunitive manner, such as scolding, threatening, or leaving the situation. Five percent intervened with a mild shaking, slap, or spanking. Only 8 percent first responded with more severe corporal punishment (Kadushin & Martin 1981).

How then does an incident culminate in abuse? Several studies offer a possible key. It appears that abusing parents do not rely on harsh forms of punishment so much as they rely on ineffective child management methods (see Wolfe 1985a). Studies have found that abusing parents do not reinforce prosocial behavior, they have difficulty setting limits, and they rely on coercive methods of discipline, such as threats. In general, their discipline is inconsistent and ineffective, with little corrective value (see Berger 1980b; Koverola, Manion & Wolfe 1985; Reid, Taplin & Lorber 1981; Wolfe 1985a). In one study, inconsistent and ineffective discipline characterized all the seriously abusing families and 91 percent of the moderately abusing families under study (Young, cited in Reid, Taplin & Lorber 1981).

Abusing parents are generally ineffective in stopping children's aversive behavior, perhaps because of their poor disciplinary techniques (see Koverola, Manion & Wolfe 1985; Reid, Taplin & Lorber 1981). Furthermore, compared to other parent-child dyads, abusing parent and abused child are more likely to become involved in a spiraling confrontation in which each reciprocates the other's threats and aversive responses (see Burgess 1979; Reid, Taplin & Lorber 1981; Wolfe 1985a). Perhaps the easier physiological arousal of abusing parents plays a role here. A detailed analysis of 66 abuse incidents (Kadushin & Martin 1981) revealed an escalating cycle in which children's repeated defiance or *perceived* defiance (challenging, badmouthing, ignoring or perceived ignoring) fueled increasingly higher levels of parental anger and punitiveness. Almost invariably, it was in this volatile context of escalating anger, conflict, and retaliation that the children were abused (Kadushin & Martin 1981).

The Abuse

The Triggering Incident

Although child abuse most frequently occurs within a disciplinary context precipitated by some behavior on the part of the child (Gil 1970, Kadushin & Martin 1981), often the original infraction is one that would be considered common behavior at that child's developmental level (Berger 1980b, Friedman et al. 1981). One study reported minor aversive behaviors, such as crying, bedwetting, and failure to eat as the precipitating incident in almost half the cases studied (Thomson et al. 1971). In another analysis of 830 incidents, behaviors involving food, sleeping, eliminating, crying, whining, and aggression were the most frequent precipitating behaviors in the most serious abuse cases. Other infractions which preceded abuse included persistent disobedience, unacceptable habits, failure to do chores, stealing, lying, and truancy (Kadushin & Martin 1981). A third analysis revealed the precursors of abuse to include fighting, refusals, accidental occurrences, inconveniences due to the child, and dangerous or immoral behavior (Herrenkohl, Herrenkohl & Egolf 1983).

By themselves, it is unlikely that any of these behaviors would trigger abuse. They must be considered within the context of a combination of other risk factors that increase the probability that abuse will be triggered:

Parents who are easily emotionally aroused by child behaviors

Parents whose perceptions of child behaviors are often distorted (for example, infants' cries perceived as angry and demanding, or provocativeness attributed to normal child behavior)

Parents who have little empathy

Parents who value the use of parental power

Parents who are under continual stress from many fronts

Parents who have poor coping skills and who are predisposed to solve conflicts with violence

Parents who have no one to turn to for perspective, emotional support, or child care relief from a child perceived to be difficult

It is a combination of such multiple risk factors that interact with the immediate setting—most often a child persisting in aversive behavior, despite parental demands and threats to stop—that comprises the triggering incident.

The importance of multiple risk factors is also evident in the parental child abuse incidents that are not precipitated by child behavior. Some incidents are precipitated by parental intoxication, general resentment of the child, or parental battles in which the child, in some way, is in the middle (Gil 1970, Thomson et al. 1971).

The Children and Injuries

Minor injuries, such as bruises and welts, are inflicted ten times more frequently than are major injuries, such as bone fractures and burns (Friedrich & Einbender 1983). These major injuries are most often found in infants, toddlers, and preschoolers, probably because of their greater fragility and because of the greater demands they place upon parents (Friedrich & Einbender 1983). Infants, who are most vulnerable to injury from shaking and impact, have the highest incidence of fatalities, broken bones, and skull and brain injuries (Fischler 1984, Johnson & Showers 1985). The highest incidence of water burns (and genitalia injuries) are found in 1- to 3-year-olds, perhaps because of parental frustration with toilet training and accessibility to hot water during diaper changing (Johnson & Showers 1985). Six- to twelve-year-old children are most likely to receive injuries from belts, cords, and paddles, whereas fists are responsible for 70 percent of the injuries in children over ten (Johnson & Showers 1985).

Most studies have found boys and girls equally likely to be abused. There is some evidence, however, that abused children under the age of 12 are overrepresented by boys, whereas abused teens are overrepresented by girls. This shift to girls in the teen years is perhaps due to parental anxiety and parent-daughter conflicts over issues of sexuality. Adolescent sons, on the other hand, may be less likely to elicit abuse because of their physical strength and potential to retaliate (see Gil 1970).

Most generally, child abuse is not an isolated incident. A large-scale survey of parents reported that "one-time abuse" occurred in only 6 percent of cases. The median number of assaults on one child during a single year was 4.5, with a mean of 10.5 (see Straus & Gelles 1986). Studies find half to two-thirds of abused children to be the victims of recurrent abuse that is serious enough to be investigated (Friedrich & Einbender 1983). Although abuse sometimes is a long-time pattern, it often lasts for only one to three years (see Pakizegi 1985), perhaps because of parents' hypersensitivity to a particular developmental stage. There is evidence, for example, that adolescent abuse generally is not a continuation of an established pattern but begins *in* adolescence (see Libbey & Bybee 1979).

The Sequelae of Abuse

Determining the consequences of child abuse is an area fraught with methodological difficulties. By the age of 2, abused children are substantially different from their nonabused counterparts cognitively, emotionally, and socially (Friedrich & Einbender 1983, Roscoe 1985). However, because most studies are initiated after the child has been abused, it is difficult to determine whether these differences precipitated the abuse or whether they developed as a consequence of the child's abuse and care. As a simple example, abused infants are sick more often than their nonabused siblings. They also are more likely to receive erratic treatment for their illnesses (see Pakizegi 1985). Does their chronic illness precipitate their abuse or is it caused by their erratic medical care?

The recurrent patterns found in abused children are so highly consistent, however, that it can safely be said that abuse is likely to at least intensify problems in children's cognitive, emotional, and social development.

Cognitive Development

Studies consistently find impaired intellectual abilities, language delays, poor verbal skills, learning disorders, and poor school adjustment and performance in abused children (see Friedrich & Einbender 1983, Lamphear 1985, Newberger 1982, Oates 1986, Pakizegi 1985, Roscoe 1985).

Usually abused children function within the normal range of cognitive functioning except when the abuse has led to permanent neurological damage (Pakizegi 1985). Follow-up studies conducted by Martin revealed that 53 percent of his sample had some neurological damage. Thirty-one percent of these had impairments serious enough to handicap their everyday functioning (see Salter 1985).

Emotional Development

The emotional development of abused children has been the area least studied because it is the most difficult to assess (Roscoe 1985). Research that has been conducted has found the following.

Compared to their nonabused counterparts, abused infants are less likely to have secure attachments to parents. They appear to be sad, distressed, fearful, and often angry. Their play is characterized by aimlessness and a lack of pleasure (see Belsky, Lerner & Spanier 1984; Pakizegi 1985).

Older abused children generally are found to have a number of emotional problems, although problems are not always consistent from child to child (Friedrich & Einbender 1983). Perhaps most commonly reported by reviewers of the research are low self-esteem and poor self-concepts with concomitant feelings of depression, unhappiness, and sadness (Friedrich & Einbender 1983, Kinard 1980, Oates 1986, Roscoe 1985). According to some studies, the more severe the abuse, the poorer the child's self-concept generally is (see Kinard 1982). A poor self-concept is not surprising, given findings that abused children blame their abuse on their own bad behavior (Dean et al. 1986, see Weinbach & Curtiss 1986). All abused children, however, do not have poor self-concepts, suggesting that other life experiences can outweigh the effects of abuse (Weinbach & Curtiss 1986).

Other emotional problems mentioned with some frequency by reviewers of this research are a lack of trust, poor emotional investment in other people, difficulty giving and receiving affection, and impaired empathy (Friedrich & Einbender 1983, Kinard 1980, Lamphear 1985, Oates 1986, Roscoe 1985). Several studies have reported that child abuse victims are overrepresented in the populations of children and adolescents who have attempted suicide (Deykin, Alpert & McNamarra 1985; Green 1978; Kosky 1983; Rosenthal & Rosenthal 1984). Kosky (1983) suggests that risk for suicide be added to the possible sequelae of abuse. Relevant discussions can be found in chapter 5.

Social Development

Consistently reported is the finding that the majority of abused children are more aggressive than comparison children. Their aggressiveness is directed towards their caretakers, other adults, peers, and themselves (for example, self-biting). Their aggression is evident in both fantasy and actual behavior, such as hitting, kicking, harassing, threatening, angry outbursts, and severe temper tantrums. Increased aggression is observed in abused children as young as toddlers in their interactions with both peers and adults (see Belsky 1980, Kinard 1980, Lamphear 1985, Newberger 1982, Oates 1986, Roscoe 1985).

There is a second pattern observed in some abused children: social and emotional withdrawal. Apathy, avoidance of social contacts, and excessive compliance are all characteristic of this pattern (see Belsky, Lerner & Spanier 1984; Berger 1980b; Oates 1986). Even many of these children, however, express a good deal of violence (Belsky, Lerner & Spanier 1984).

It is believed that the violence expressed by abused children stems from two separate sources: from the frustration, despair, and anger caused by their abuse and, secondly, from "lessons" taught by parents that conflicts are solved with aggression (Newberger 1982).

Given their characteristic responses, it is not surprising to learn that abused children generally have poor social skills and poor relationships with both peers and adults (see Friedrich & Einbender 1983, Kinard 1980, Lamphear 1985, Roscoe 1985). There is some evidence that abused children as young as toddlers are already showing characteristic ambivalent patterns in their interactions with others, such as avoidance of friendly overtures, less contact with peers, and aggression and harassment (see Belsky, Lerner & Spanier 1984; Main 1981; Roscoe 1985). It is a pattern not unlike that of their abusing parents.

Some studies have found a strong relationship between childhood abuse and later juvenile delinquency (see Garbarino 1980, Lamphear 1985). Studies of truants, runaways, prostitutes, and violent criminals also report a high incidence of childhood abuse. Causal relationships, however, cannot be determined (Fischler 1984, Libbey & Bybee 1979).

Survivors of Abuse

The sequelae of abuse are not equally poor for all children. Researchers, therefore, have searched for the factors that mediate the final outcome for abused children. In her review, Kinard (1980) concluded that the severity of abuse and the age at the time of abuse are important factors. Abuse during the infant and toddler years is associated with greater emotional problems, perhaps because these young children are more likely to be set on a lifelong course that requires more direct intervention than most abused children receive. On a positive note, however, Beezley, Martin & Kempe (see Pakizegi 1985) reported that when children receive treatment, improvement occurs faster for those of younger age.

A crucial factor pointed out by many reviewers is the quality of the environment subsequent to the period of abuse (Friedrich & Einbender 1983, Garbarino 1982, Oates 1986). Poorer outcomes are associated with the continuation of the poor environment and continued inadequate mothering (see Garbarino 1982, Oates 1986). Poorer outcomes are also associated with bouncing from one foster home to another (see Kinard 1980).

Pointing out that there are many factors in an abusive environment, Augoustinos (1987) suggests that all these factors interact to determine the outcome for abused youngsters. Some current evidence indicates that the negative consequences of abuse can be mitigated somewhat by other factors in a child's environment and in a child herself. For example, a good relationship with a caring person seems able to mitigate the negative effects of abuse. And so can some personal attributes of a child, such as above-average intelligence (see Augoustinos 1987). Augoustinos's point is consistent with the stress literature which finds there are many factors within a child's environment and within the child herself that can buffer her from the negative consequences of severe adversity. These buffering factors, called *protective factors,* are discussed in chapter 5 and in chapter 1. The role of protective factors in mitigating the negative consequences of child abuse was demonstrated in a study reported by Zimrin (1986).

Zimrin followed a group of abused Israeli children into adulthood and compared those who had serious adult emotional problems with those who "survived." None of the children or families had received any help over the years, and many of the children were subjected to severe abuse throughout their childhoods. Emotional problems were evident in all of these young adults, so survival was defined modestly: adjustment at school or work, the absence of severe emotional problems, and constructive plans for the future.

Zimrin found only two childhood situational differences between the survivors and nonsurvivors. The survivors generally had some adult who took an interest in them, encouraged them, and treated them with empathy. These adults, frequently teachers, did not necessarily spend a great deal of time with the abused children, but their interest was a stable presence in the children's lives. The second situational difference was the presence of a younger sibling or pet whom the abused child nurtured and protected. This, says Zimrin, appeared to provide children with an additional inner resource. (Zimrin suggests that abused children be allowed to care for a pet at school.) The stress literature also suggests the importance of a caring person and of having an important task that the child can perform successfully (for example, protecting and nurturing a sibling) as factors that can buffer children from the consequences of severe adversity.

Beyond these situational differences, the survivors and nonsurvivors themselves responded very differently to their abuse. The nonsurvivors appeared to avoid positive information about themselves. In fact, they generally discontinued activities in which they were successful and initiated ones in which they were doomed to fail. The survivors, on the other hand, seemed able to utilize whatever positive information they received from other sources. Not surprisingly, they had many more positive experiences and better self-images. Both these are found in the stress literature to be important protective factors.

There were other personal attributes that distinguished the two groups. The survivors, for example, were above average in cognitive ability. Interestingly, the survivors were more provocative and belligerent, and this belligerence seemed to be part of an overall pattern that distinguished them from the nonsurvivors. The nonsurvivors passively accepted their abuse with despair, feeling helpless to influence their own lives. The survivors, on the other hand, refused to be fatalistic. They were characterized by a determination to fight back and by a hopefulness for the future (usually expressed in fantasies of what life might be like one day). Above-average cognitive ability and the belief that one has some control over one's fate have also been reported in the stress literature as protective factors that can buffer children from the negative consequences of severe adversity. For a more complete discussion of protective factors, see chapter 5.

Intervention

The bulk of child abuse research has been focused on prevalence, causes, and consequences of abuse (Belsky, Lerner & Spanier 1984). Because the early research indicated that parental pathology was the cause of abuse, it had been assumed that psychotherapy was the most effective avenue of treatment. However, now that the complexity of child abuse is unraveling, researchers are rising to the challenge and developing an array of promising treatment strategies. Because child abuse is a multidimensional problem, effective intervention must be multidimensional as well, addressing the many risk factors involved in each case. The interventions that have been developed are in use to varying degrees around the country, with scattered reports of their effectiveness. However, there have been inadequate systematic evaluations of their long-term effectiveness or relative merits.

In practice, at this point in time, intervention efforts in child abuse cases are highly subjective and variable (Wasserman & Rosenfeld 1986). Depending upon the particular family and the agencies and community involved, a family may receive only one or two standard types of interventions or a combination of many innovative approaches that address that family's unique problems.

The best advice to practitioners who are involved with treatment, says Gelles (1982), is to avoid simplistic thinking based upon the many misconceptions about abuse. Treatment must be based upon careful assessment and available knowledge. And it must address the many risk factors involved in each case. To give an oversimplified example, abuse that primarily stems from poor child management skills, distorted perceptions of children's behavior, and belief in the value of physical punishment and parental power requires different intervention than does abuse that primarily stems from overwhelming stress with which the parent cannot cope. The first parent may benefit from training in parenting skills and participation in Parents Anonymous. The second may need help such as improved housing, food stamps, homemaker services, relief child care, and a shelter for battered wives before she can turn her attention to the quality of her parenting. Similarly, an abusing parent who is addicted to drugs requires different treatment from one who cannot control explosive bursts of anger (see Dubanoski, Evans & Higuchi 1978). Practitioners should not think in terms of what treatment works for child abuse but in terms of what combinations of interventions will best help this family in this set of circumstance with this particular set of problems (Blythe 1983).

Before looking at specific treatments, assessment, the first step in intervention, will be discussed.

Assessment

The key to intervention is careful assessment. Oates (1986) states this more emphatically: treatment without thorough assessment is irresponsible and unlikely to succeed. According to Friedman and his colleagues (1981), the parents, the child, and the abuse incident should each be assessed. Included in assessment should be parents' child management skills, their ability to manage stress and anger, their existing social and community supports, their marital relations, the overall family environment, and their perceptions of the child and the abuse situation. Child characteristics, behavior, and functioning should also be assessed. Friedman and his colleagues offer a wealth of concrete information to help practitioners in the assessment process, including specific interview and observation techniques. Particularly helpful is information on specific screening instruments developed to assess parents' social supports, psychopathology, knowledge and expectations of children, ability to handle stress, the situations that elicit anger, and so forth.

Some communities now have the benefit of *multidisciplinary teams* that consist of a group of professionals from different fields who pool their expertise and resources to assess and treat child abuse cases (Totah & Wilson-Coker 1985). Usually there is a core team, perhaps a social worker, physician, child development specialist, and psychiatrist (Fischler 1984). Other professionals may be available on a case-to-case basis, such as an attorney, a representative from juvenile court, a public health nurse, a teacher, a police officer, and paraprofessionals who work with abusing parents (Totah & Wilson-Coker 1985).

The first multidisciplinary teams were hospital based. They were established to identify and to help, without duplication of effort, the maltreated children brought to emergency rooms. Now multidisciplinary teams can be found within other agencies. At times, they consist of an informal group of professionals who are willing to volunteer their time, expertise, and unique perspectives (Totah & Wilson-Coker 1985).

Besides providing better assessment and broader intervention programs, multidisciplinary teams are found to get more of their recommendations followed and more of their recommended services delivered. Apparently they have more "clout" than individual child protective service workers (Hochstadt & Harwicke 1985). A discussion of some of the interventions used in child abuse cases follows.

Intervention with Children

It is now widely recognized in the literature that help is needed by abused children to reverse the detrimental consequences of their abuse (Cohn 1982; Kinard 1980; Oates 1986; Perry, Doran & Wells 1983). However, in practice, treatment most often is confined to the parent (Kinard 1980, Roscoe 1985). Some children receive some type of supportive counseling or are placed in therapeutic day care programs or in early stimulation programs (Fischler 1984). Research suggests these programs are beneficial in improving children's self-image, happiness, social competence, and their ability to give and to receive affection (Cohn 1979a). However, in the majority of communities, the reality of limited funds and the absence of programs restrict concern for the child to concern for his physical safety (Pakizegi 1985). If he is in danger, usually he is removed from the home.

Foster Home Placement. Fischler (1984) reports that about 10 percent of abused children are placed in foster care or receiving homes. This provides a child a safe environment while the parent is treated and tells the youngster that someone will protect her (Wasserman & Rosenfeld 1986). However, foster care has created much controversy because of its potential harm to abused children (Fischler 1984, Katz et al. 1986, Oates 1986, Wasserman & Rosenfeld 1986, Williams 1983). Although some studies report foster care's benefits to some children in terms of intellectual, social, and physical growth (see Wald et al. 1983), other studies have documented its inadequacies, its many failures, and its high costs (see Katz et al. 1986). The term *foster care drift* originated from studies finding that "short-term" foster care all too often turned into a prolonged limbo in which the child awaited his fate (Whittaker 1983). Studies found that if children were not returned home within three months, they were likely to remain in foster care for long periods and were likely to bounce from home to home (see Fischler 1984).

Foster home placement failure is common among abused children (Oates 1986). For example, the maltreated children studied by Bolton had an average of 5.2 different foster homes in the three years they averaged in foster care (see Fischler 1984). Other studies suggest that approximately one-third of the abused children who are placed in foster care move a minimum of three times (see Cooper, Peterson & Meier 1987). Cooper and others (1987) found that some children had been in as many as a dozen foster homes.

Why is placement failure so common? Being uprooted and placed in foster care is confusing and unsettling for many abused children. They often feel a sense of failure and loss, and they refuse to accept the court's decision. The foster care situation commonly exacerbates the emotional and behavioral problems that stem from their abuse. Foster parents, many of whom have had no specialized training, frequently are unable to deal with these problems. Of course each move serves to disrupt the child again and makes it less likely that she will establish relationships. It is more adaptive for her to avoid relationships (Wasserman & Rosenfeld 1986).

What is the answer to the foster care dilemma? Fischler (1984) warns that children should be placed in foster care only after the risks of physical harm are carefully weighed. Removal of the abusing parent should always be considered first. Both Hess (1987) and Whittaker (1983) cite evidence indicating the importance of contact and regular visits between the biological parents and the child while he is in foster care (assuming the goal is to return the child to the parents). Studies consistently demonstrate that frequent visiting has a positive effect on the child's well-being (Hess 1987). Williams (1983) advocates a somewhat different approach to the foster care dilemma: legal changes that would facilitate the adoption of the child in cases with a very poor prognosis. She points to studies that have reported favorable outcomes for abused children who have been adopted. Adoptions are less likely to be successful, however, after multiple foster care placements (see Fischler 1984).

Therapeutic Day Care. Placing young abused children in good-quality day care settings is becoming a highly recommended intervention, with benefits for both child and parent (Main 1981, Oates 1986). For the child, it provides both compensatory relationships and contact with normally developing children from whom to learn social skills. For the parent, it provides relief from the continuous strains of child care.

Studies have supported the effectiveness of day care as an intervention with maltreated children. Howes and Espinosa (1985), for example, found that abused children in these programs were more competent interacting with peers than were abused children who were not enrolled in programs. In fact, while interacting in well-established groups, abused children were as socially competent as their nonabused peers. Similar beneficial outcomes have been reported in other studies (Bradley et al. 1986, Lewis and Schaeffer 1979). A study conducted by Carter (see Oates 1986) suggested additional benefits. Abusing parents reported that they had benefited from meeting other parents and that their own children were easier to manage since attending the day care programs.

Not any day care setting will foster the social development of abused children, however. Bradley and his colleagues (1986), studying abused children in settings of varying quality, found wide variability in their social behavior. More competent and positive behavior was associated with good-quality care, providing, for example, warm, responsive, and consistent caregivers, good facilities, and well-organized programs. (See chapter 2 for a complete discussion of the empirically determined standards that define quality day care.)

Oates (1986) recommends that help be given day care providers who work with abused children. They must be prepared to be rejected and be willing to respond with steady support and affection. Many techniques for working with abused children that may be helpful to day care providers and foster parents have been suggested by Salter and her colleagues (1985). These children, they point out, need more individual attention, more consistency, more patience, and more clarity than do most children. It is suggested that children be talked to at eye level and be provided with clearly defined options from which to make choices. Limits should be set and enforced, relying (whenever possible) on logical consequences for misbehavior. Building children's self-esteem and developing their language, motor, and social skills should be a high priority. Salter and her associates also suggest that children be helped to label feelings and to substitute assertiveness for aggressiveness.

Psychotherapy with Abusing Parents

At one time, psychotherapy was the preferred treatment for abusing parents and it is still used (Gelles 1982). In some cases, group therapy or family therapy are recommended. There has been little systematic evaluation of the effectiveness of therapy with abusive parents (Pakizegi 1985). In one major evaluation study in which demonstration intervention programs were compared, those relying exclusively on individual counseling were the least effective programs (compared to programs combining group therapy with parent education and to programs adding lay services, which will be discussed shortly). However, what constituted counseling was not specifically defined; it varied from program to program (Cohn 1979b).

Programs in Parenting and Child Management

In light of the poor parenting skills, distorted perceptions and poor child management strategies characteristic of abusing parents, parent education programs are a logical intervention strategy and are widely used (Egan 1983, Gaudin & Kurtz 1985). Parent Effectiveness Training (PET) (Gordon 1975), Systematic Training for Effective Parenting (STEP) (Dinkmeyer & McKay 1982), supportive discussion groups, and behavioral approaches have all been employed (see Gaudin & Kurtz 1985).

Behavioral approaches have been the most heavily researched and have received the best support. Behavioral programs usually focus on two major changes that are believed necessary to turn these families around: teaching parents nonphysical child management skills and reducing children's aversive behavior (Reid, Taplin & Lorber 1981). Parents are instructed in the new parenting techniques and why they are more effective than their old methods. Both modeling and role playing are used in training (Gaudin & Kurtz 1985). Common skills taught are:

1. How to identify problem behavior, how to chart and monitor behavior, and how to implement a behavior change program.

2. Nonphysical forms of discipline, such as time-out (isolating the child for a short period of time when she engages in aversive behavior), ignoring undesirable behavior, and using positive reinforcement to shape appropriate behavior.

3. How to use techniques such as family contracts and token programs. How to be consistent.

Parenting programs based on behavioral approaches have been found to be both effective and economical for some abusing parents (see Koverola, Manion & Wolfe 1985; Szykula & Fleischman 1985; Wolfe 1984). Positive outcomes reported by studies have included improved child management skills *and* reduced conflict and hostility in abusing homes (see Reid, Taplin & Lorber 1981; J.E. Smith 1984). One study found behaviorally based parenting programs to be successful in reducing, though not eliminating, the rate of foster care placements (Szykula & Fleischman 1985). Twelve-month follow-ups suggest the improvements are stable, although some families require a two-hour refresher class (see Isaacs 1982, Parke & Collmer 1975, J.E. Smith 1984). It is recognized that longer term follow-ups must be undertaken.

Not all abusing parents benefit from parent skills training. Parents most likely to succeed are those whose continuation in training is ensured by external sources, such as a court order or the offer of tangible rewards (J.E. Smith 1984). It is also critical that parent training be incorporated into a broader intervention program that deals with other problems within the family (Gaudin & Kurtz 1985; Reid, Taplin & Lorber 1981).

A complete description of a treatment program found to be effective with abusing parents can be found in Patterson, Reid, Jones, and Conger (1975). Also, see Becker's excellent and easily readable book *Parents Are Teachers* (1971), which has been used in several programs.

Teaching Coping Skills to Abusing Parents

Sometimes coping skills are taught to abusing parents in order to provide them with alternatives to aggressive behavior. Skills in stress management, anger control, and problem-solving have all been taught (e.g., Denicola & Sandler 1980, Nomellini & Katz 1983, Wolfe 1985b). Examples are deep breathing and muscle relaxation, desensitization to anger-eliciting situations, and learning (through modeling and role playing) how to express anger assertively rather than aggressively. Cognitive restructuring skills also have been taught. These involve teaching parents how to recognize when they are interpreting feelings and situations negatively.

Parents are then taught how to use self-verbalizations to reduce their stress and anger (Egan 1983, Gaudin & Kurtz 1985, Parke & Collmer 1975). See D'Zurilla and Goldfried (1971) and Meichenbaum (1977) for anger control techniques.

Empirical studies have supported the effectiveness of teaching coping skills to abusive parents (see Gaudin & Kurtz 1985). Positive outcomes reported by various studies have included increases in positive parent-child interactions, fewer child behavior problems, less parental coercion, and no subsequent abuse. Improvements are reportedly maintained at follow-ups (see Gaudin & Kurtz 1985), although very long term follow-ups are still needed.

Coping skills programs also can be cost-effective. Nomellini and Katz (1983) reported their anger control program involved an average of 10-1/2 hours of a therapist's time for each family.

Community-Based Programs for Families

In an effort to keep children out of foster care, there is now a large emphasis on providing services to abusing families that will strengthen the family unit (Gentry 1985, Katz et al. 1986, Stehno 1986). Efforts are directed toward linking abusing families with formal as well as informal support networks. They are also directed at providing families with practical help to relieve the overwhelming situational demands they so often face (Oates 1986, Whittaker 1983).

It is now recognized that informal social supports can play an important role in the prevention of further child abuse (Garbarino et al. 1980, Whittaker 1983). For example, a study conducted by Zimrin (1984) found a significant reduction in abusive behavior when abusing mothers were visited by a woman from the same community for 3 hours a day, 3 days a week. The woman functioned only as a friend and human contact. Some agencies now include an assessment of the parents' social supports outside the family and attempt to involve them in the intervention program. These supporting persons are encouraged to call the parent regularly, provide emotional support, encourage parents to keep appointments for treatment, provide transportation if needed, and so forth (Fischler 1984, Garbarino 1982). Methods to identify parents' informal social supports have been developed by Bertsche, Clark and Iverson (1981) and by Gaudin and Pollane (1983). Many suggestions for using social support networks can be found in Garbarino and others (1980). A model for developing social networks has been offered by Rueveni (1979).

More common than developing informal support systems are efforts toward developing formal support networks for abusing families. Families are linked with community agencies and programs that provide the practical help they need. Examples include Parents Anonymous programs, the use of lay therapists, and crisis nurseries. The availability of community services is highly variable from community to community and state to state. Practitioners working with abusing parents must have a "social map" of the community and its services, must be able to coordinate them, and must be an advocate for both the child and family (Gelles 1982; Gentry 1985).

Following are examples of services available in some communities that have been found to be effective with abusing parents.

Paraprofessionals. The use of trained volunteers and paid paraprofessionals in child abuse intervention is an idea whose time has come (Garbarino 1980). There are many innovative programs across the country (Whittaker 1983). How paraprofessionals are used varies somewhat from program to program. Usually they are people living in the community whom the abusing parent can trust, identify with, and relate to without feeling threatened, as is often the case with an authority figure (Miller et al. 1985).

Many communities have lay therapists who are trained in the area of child abuse, children's needs, and parenting skills. They go into the home and become a friend, emotional supporter, and a model of appropriate behavior who is understanding, giving, and nonjudgmental. They help the parent to understand the child's needs, to develop better parenting skills, and to cope with daily problems. They are usually accessible by phone 24 hours a day and parents are encouraged to call them in a crisis. In a sense, they parent the parent (Miller et al. 1985, Parke & Collmer 1975, Paulson 1985).

Some programs focus on homemaker services to temporarily relieve a stressed mother from housekeeping and child care burdens. Homemakers tactfully teach homemaking skills and help the parent to assume responsibility more effectively (Brown 1981).

An innovative program in California uses trained volunteers to act as lay advocates for abused children. They represent the child, focus on his welfare, and make sure he doesn't get "lost in the system" (Garbarino 1980).

Paraprofessionals such as lay therapists have been found to be highly effective supplements to treatment programs. The comparison of demonstration intervention programs, mentioned previously, revealed that when lay services were added to treatment programs, the effectiveness of the programs markedly increased (Cohn 1979b).

Parents Anonymous. Parents Anonymous (PA) is a self-help group for abusing parents with over 1,000 chapters in the United States, Canada, England, Australia, and several other countries (Lieber 1983).

Parents Anonymous provides a safe and supportive setting in which abusing parents can share their common problems, stresses, and concerns. Groups encourage parents to help one another, they help put problems in perspective, and they foster self-esteem. They also expect members to work hard to change their abusing patterns (Cohn 1979b, Lieber 1983). When the group feels it is ready, parent programs, such as PET and STEP, are introduced (Gordon 1975, Dinkmeyer & McKay 1982). Although groups formally meet only once a week, further contact between members is encouraged, and groups often function as an extended family. A volunteer professional serves as a nonauthoritarian consultant and resource person, but meetings are led by an established parent member (Lieber 1983).

Parents Anonymous has been highly effective with a substantial number of abusing parents (see Garbarino 1982, Lieber 1983). However, it is not for every parent. The dropout rate is 20 to 30 percent (Lieber 1983). According to Lieber, a parent who participates in a PA group for a year is unlikely to return to his abusive behavior. Participation for three years generally results in a better-than-average parent and a paraprofessional who can successfully help others.

Parents Anonymous groups offer telephone hot-line services that counsel parents in crisis situations and encourage them to get help. Treatment programs for children are in the process of being developed (Lieber 1983).

The process of starting a PA group and acting as its sponsor/consultant has been described by Moore (1983).

Respite Care. Some communities have a variety of facilities that provide respite care for abusing families. Crisis nurseries provide 24-hour emergency short-term care for infants whose parents are in a crisis situation and at risk of abusing their child. Drop-off centers provide care for older children (Parke & Collmer 1975). Subramanian (1985), measuring parents' stress levels, found significant reductions after they had used respite care.

Short-term residential treatment for abusing families or for mother and child is available in some communities (Starr 1979). In some of these programs, abusing parents are helped to learn parenting skills (see Pakizegi 1985).

Multifaceted Programs

Across the country, there are a number of innovative multifaceted child abuse intervention programs. Some have been developed by universities which then receive contracts from state agencies to work with abusing families (e.g., Lutzker, Wesch & Rice 1984; Van Meter 1986). These excellent programs benefit not only the families but the universities because they attract qualified graduate students and provide an accessible research population (Van Meter 1986). Other multifaceted programs are community based. The following is a very brief look at two of these multifaceted programs.

Project 12 Ways (Lutzker, Wesch & Rice 1984) is in operation at Southern Illinois University at Carbondale and offers an array of treatment services individually tailored to each family's needs. Available services include parent training, marital counseling, stress reduction training, self-control training, and alcohol treatment referral. Help is also given with money management, health and nutrition, home safety, and job finding. Children who have developmental delays also receive help. Lutzker and his colleagues report that their data persuasively argues for the effectiveness of the program.

Oliver (1980) describes the development and implementation of a community-based intervention program largely supported by local industry. It employs multidisciplinary teams and offers a wide array of services, including emergency homemakers, emergency funds, respite day care, family and child counseling, parenting classes, and job and home finding. Paulson (1985) suggests it should serve as a model program to be developed by other communities.

The Social Problem of Child Abuse

By 1973, every state had passed laws that mandated the reporting of child abuse (Oates 1986). Professionals from virtually every area involved with children are now required to report suspected cases of abuse: physicians, nurses, mental health professionals, teachers, day care providers, law enforcement personnel, and so forth (Bittner & Newberger 1982, Faller 1985). As a result of reporting requirements, public awareness campaigns, and hot line numbers, there has been an astronomical increase in the reported number of suspected child abuse cases (Faller 1985, Gelles 1982). Unfortunately, this astronomical increase in reported cases has coincided with national cutbacks in social services. A survey by the House Select Committee on Children, Families, and Youth, released in March of 1987, revealed that reported cases of child abuse and neglect had increased nearly 55 percent between 1981 and 1985; during this same period, resources to deal with child abuse had increased only 1.9 percent (*San Diego Union*, March 3, 1987).

There now is a situation in which social workers are swamped with double the number of case loads that are recommended by standard-setting boards (Williams 1983). Out of sheer necessity, their time is relegated to investigation, child protection, and the accompanying paperwork. There is an abysmal shortage of time and resources for the systematic assessment and treatment of troubled families and for implementing the types of innovative programs that have been developed (Faller 1985, Meddin & Hansen 1985, Wolfe 1984).

What is the result? "Cure" rates of "treated" parents have typically ranged from 30 percent to 70 percent (Garbarino 1980). Is it because child abuse is so difficult to treat, or is it because abusing families do not receive the services they require to turn their lives around? It is a misnomer, says Wolfe (1984), to label the services received by most parents as "treatment."

What is the solution to this national dilemma? Faller (1985) suggests that one small step is to train professionals to accurately identify child abuse. Currently, fewer than one-half the reported cases of abuse are substantiated (American Humane Association, cited in Faller 1985). A reduction in the number of reported erroneous cases would represent a substantial savings in time and resources allocated to investigation—time and resources that could be devoted to treatment.

Some suggest that a realistic approach in this era of inadequate fiscal resources is a greater reliance on the community and on social resources (e.g., Garbarino 1982, Whittaker 1983). This view encourages communities to develop community-based programs, such as that described by Oliver (1980), discussed previously. Programs would then enlist and train volunteers and systematically build social support networks within high-risk communities (see Garbarino et al. 1980, for examples).

Reliance on community efforts and volunteers is resisted by others, however, who point out society's responsibility to ensure its children a safe environment (e.g., Faller 1985). More responsible government involvement, they say, is the answer. The kinds of efforts going on in some communities are impressive and inspiring. But other communities are relatively impoverished in terms of available services. Children's welfare cannot wait until individuals in their community assume the initiative and mobilize others into action. What is needed, says Faller (1985) are (1) increased funds to develop and implement innovative treatments that address the needs of abusing families at all levels and (2) greater numbers of trained caseworkers. (The need for more trained caseworkers has been supported by research. For example, in the comparison of demonstration child abuse programs, Cohn [1979b] found that an important predictor of a low reincidence rate of abuse was employing highly trained and experienced professionals to conduct intakes, plan treatment, and manage cases. Working conditions for caseworkers have also been found to be important. Dissatisfied workers, high turnover, and high rates of "burnout" are associated with less satisfactory outcomes for families [see Fischler 1984].)

Other professionals in the field point to a different answer to the child abuse problem. They suggest that *prevention* of child abuse is the area in which emphasis and resources should be increased (e.g., Rickel 1986).

Prevention

The past several years have witnessed a rapid growth in child abuse prevention programs (Barth, Ash & Hacking 1986). Some programs are aimed at the population at large and are called *primary prevention*. Other prevention programs are aimed specifically at high-risk individuals; these are called *secondary prevention*.

There has been little systematic research conducted on the effectiveness of either primary or secondary prevention programs. Studies which have been conducted have yielded equivocal findings (Barth, Ash & Hacking 1986) that some have interpreted to be encouraging (Helfer 1982).

Secondary Prevention Programs. In these types of programs, parents who are at a high risk for child abuse are identified, and some type of intervention is attempted with them before abuse occurs. High-risk parents are identified on the basis of referrals or on the basis of a number of screening devices which have been developed. Further information on screening devices can be found in McMurtry (1985) and Murphy, Orkow and Nicola (1985).

Secondary prevention programs usually are based in hospitals, community agencies, and sometimes in public child welfare agencies. Many rely on paraprofessionals and volunteers (Barth, Ash & Hacking 1986).

The approach receiving the most attention and greatest endorsement in the literature is the home visitor program (see Barth, Ash & Hacking 1986; Garbarino 1986; Halpern 1986; Rosenberg & Reppucci 1985). This usually is a hospital-based program in which a trained paraprofessional or nurse visits new mothers on a regular basis for up to two years after the birth of their infants (and sometimes during pregnancy as well). Programs differ (e.g., Gray et al. 1977, Olds 1986). Most home visitors, however, work to establish a personal relationship with the parent, to strengthen her coping skills, and to impart information about child rearing. They sometimes become involved in linking mothers with social networks or obtaining necessary services, such as adequate housing or food stamps (Halpern 1986).

Other secondary prevention programs have been reported in the literature. O'Connor and associates (1980) reported success with a "rooming-in" program, in which high-risk mothers shared their hospital room with their infants after delivery. It was hoped that this would facilitate early parent-infant bonding (O'Connor et al. 1980).

The University of Western Ontario is the site of the Parent/Child Early Education Program (Wolfe & Manion 1984). In it, high-risk, poorly motivated mothers are successfully learning new parenting and coping skills. A number of incentives are being used to motivate these mothers and to involve them in the program, such as videotaped feedback, working with problems chosen by parents, and rewarding parent participation with gifts of their choice.

Andrews and Linden (1984) report in detail on a successful prevention program developed by joint community effort in a rural Kentucky community which had been plagued by alarming increases in child abuse and little money for services. Public service announcements and information about children's needs were provided by the media. Community organizations were recruited to raise money. A Parents Anonymous group was established. A cooperative day care center was started in church-donated space. (Mothers were eligible for four free hours of child care for each hour they volunteered. They also received training in child management skills as part of the parent participation day care program.) A separate program was developed for expectant mothers who were recruited for classes that dealt with stress management, infant care, and children's development. Informal support networks were encouraged as well.

Although secondary prevention programs are recommended enthusiastically by many, they have certain practical problems. Many high-risk mothers are reluctant to become involved, either refusing outright or canceling appointments (Barth, Ash & Hacking 1986). Hence, a motivational component often needs to be built into these programs. Additionally, screening devices used to identify potential child-abusing parents yield a high number of false positives. This means that services also must be provided to many parents who would not actually require them (Gelles, cited in Garbarino 1986). Although these interventions are likely to improve the quality of life and parenting for any parent in a high-risk category, the reality of diminishing fiscal resources must be faced. In many communities, the limited monies must be allotted to the most cost effective programs.

Primary Prevention Programs. Some prevention programs are aimed at the population at large. Examples include child abuse hot lines, high school parenting classes, and media campaigns to increase awareness of the child abuse problem and the availability of help. Also in this category are videotaped skits that portray appropriate parenting or the successful resolution of family crises. These are often played in well-child clinics, shopping centers, military bases, and so forth (Rosenberg & Reppucci 1985).

Some professionals in the field believe that a multifaceted primary prevention program, designed to fight child abuse at all levels, would be highly effective in reducing abuse. There have been numerous suggestions (Cohn 1982, Helfer 1982, Pakizegi 1985), such as:

Expansion of health services to include training for all new parents

A national perinatal support program (such as a home visitor program)

Parent-infant centers that provide films, books, and classes for parents, as well as answers to parenting questions

Neighborhood parenting groups organized by YMCAs and community mental health organizations

Neighborhood support groups

Family support services, such as family planning, subsidized child care, marriage counseling and job training

Child screening for the early detection and treatment of developmental problems

The Potential Role for Child Specialists

There is a phenomenal amount of work that needs to be done to make a marked impact on reducing child abuse. But research has offered clear directions. Many professionals are in a unique position to make their own impact in some way, perhaps establishing a self-help group or linking isolated parents with formal support systems. Prevention and intervention programs can be developed within high-risk communities. Volunteers can be recruited and trained for home visitor programs, parenting classes can be initiated, or a cooperative day care program can be organized. Universities are in the unique position to develop programs which can be implemented with graduate students. At the same time, they will have an accessible research population with which to conduct much needed evaluation research. Some professionals are in the position to raise public consciousness against the use of corporal punishment for children. Others can raise the public's awareness of the need to mobilize their own communities to develop child abuse programs. Krugman (1985) points out that when mothers decided in 1957 to march for dimes in the fight against polio, there were only 57,000 cases of polio in the United States. Today there are millions of children who are emotionally crippled as a consequence of child abuse. They need the same kind of concern and concerted effort. Faller (1985) points out that we as a society have the responsibility of ensuring every child an environment free of harm. This is not a privilege—it is a child's right.

Child abuse is not someone else's problem. It is everyone's problem. Millions of children each year fall victim to it, often with disastrous consequences—increased aggressiveness, impaired empathy, impaired cognitive ability, an unwillingness to trust or to become involved with people, a proclivity to resolve conflicts with violence, and so on. Yet, these children are tomorrow's adults. As Garmezy (1987) pointed out, "Simply stated, the long-term well-being of a nation is a function of the long-term well-being of its people."

References

Andrews, D.D. & Linden, R.R., 1984. "Preventing Rural Child Abuse: Progress in Spite of Cutbacks." *Child Welfare* 63, 443–52.

Augoustinos, M., 1987. "Developmental Effects of Child Abuse: Recent Findings." *Child Abuse and Neglect* 11: 15–27.

Barth, R.P., Ash, J.R. & Hacking, S. 1986. "Identifying, Screening, and Engaging High-Risk Clients in Private Non-Profit Child Abuse Prevention Programs." *Child Abuse and Neglect* 10: 99–109.

Becker, W.C., 1971. *Parents Are Teachers:* A Child Management Program. Champaign, Ill.: Research Press.

Belsky, J. 1978. "Three Theoretical Models of Child Abuse: A Critical Review." *Child Abuse and Neglect* 2: 37–49.

——. 1980. "Child Maltreatment: An Ecological Integration." *American Psychologist* 35: 320–35.

Belsky, J., Lerner, R.M. & Spanier, G.B., 1984. *The Child in the Family.* Reading, Mass.: Addison-Wesley.

Berger, A.M., 1980a. "The Child Abusing Family: I. Methodological Issues and Parent-Related Characteristics of Abusing Families." *The American Journal of Family Therapy* 8 (3): 53–66.

——. 1980b. "The Child Abusing Family: II. Child and Child-Rearing Variables, Environmental Factors, and Typologies of Abusing Families." *The American Journal of Family Therapy* 8 (4): 52–68.

Bertsche, J.W., Clark, F.W. & Iversen, M.A. 1981. *Using Informal Resources in Child Protective Services.* Missoula: University of Montana School of Social Work.

Bittner, S. & Newberger, E.H., 1982. "Pediatric Understanding of Child Abuse and Neglect," in E.H. Newberger, ed., *Child Abuse.* Boston: Little Brown.

Blythe, B. 1983. "A Critique of Outcome Evaluation in Child Abuse Treatment." *Child Welfare* 62: 325–35.

Bradley, R.H., Caldwell, B.M., Fitzgerald, J.A., Morgan, A.G. & Rock, S.L., 1986. "Experiences in Day Care and Social Competence Among Maltreated Children." *Child Abuse and Neglect* 10: 181–89.

Brown, H.F., 1981. "Effective Use of Caretakers as an Alternative to Placement," in M. Bryce & J.C. Lloyd, eds., *Treating Families in the Home: An Alternative to Placement.* Springfield, Ill.: Chas. C. Thomas Publ.

Burgess, R.L., 1978. "Child Abuse: A Behavioral Analysis," in B.B. Lahey & A.E. Kazdin, eds., *Advances in Child Clinical Psychology,* Vol. 1. N.Y.: Plenum Press.

——. 1979. "Child Abuse: A Social Interactional Analysis," in B.B. Lahey & A.E. Kazdin, eds., *Advances in Clinical Child Psychology.* Vol. 2 N.Y.: Plenum Press.

Caplan, P.J., Watters, J., White, G., Parry, R. & Bates, R., 1984. "Toronto Multiagency Child Abuse Research Project: The Abused and the Abuser." *Child Abuse and Neglect* 8: 343–51.

"Child Abuse, Neglect Rise 55%, Funding up 1.9%." *The San Diego Union.* 3 March 1987, p. A2.

Cohn, A.H., 1979a. "An Evaluation of Three Demonstration Child Abuse and Neglect Treatment Programs." *Journal of the American Academy of Child Psychiatry* 18: 283–91.

————. 1979b. "Essential Elements of Successful Child Abuse and Neglect Treatment." *Child Abuse and Neglect* 3: 491–96.

————. 1982. "Stopping Abuse Before It Occurs: Different Solutions for Different Population Groups." *Child Abuse and Neglect* 6: 473–83.

Cooper, C.S., Peterson, N.L. Meier, J.H., 1987. "Variables Associated with Disrupted Placement in a Select Sample of Abused and Neglected Children." *Child Abuse and Neglect* 11: 75–86.

Dean, A.L., Malik, M.M., Richards, W. & Stringer, S.A. 1986. "Effects of Parental Maltreatment on Children's Conceptions of Interpersonal Relationships." *Developmental Psychology* 22: 617–26.

Denicola, J. & Sandler, J. 1980. "Training Abusive Parents in Child Management and Self Control Skills." Behavior Therapy 11: 263–70.

Deykin, E.Y., Alpert, J.J. & McNamarra, J.J. 1985. "A Pilot Study of the Effect of Exposure to Child Abuse or Neglect on Adolescent Suicidal Behavior." *American Journal of Psychiatry* 142: 1299–1303.

Dinkmeyer, D. & McKay, G., 1982. *The Parent's Handbook: Systematic Training for Effective Parenting.* Circle Pines, Minn.: American Guidance Service.

Dubanoski, R.A., Evans, I.M. & Higuchi, A.A. 1978. "Analysis and Treatment of Child Abuse: A Set of Behavioural Propositions." *Child Abuse and Neglect* 2: 153–72.

D'Zurilla, T.J. & Goldfried, M.R., 1971. "Problem Solving and Behavior Modification." *Journal of Abnormal Psychology* 78: 107–26.

Egan, K.J. 1983. "Stress Management and Child Management with Abusive Parents." *Journal of Clinical Child Psychology* 12: 292–99.

Egeland, B., Breitenbucher, M. & Rosenberg, D., 1980. "Prospective Study of the Significance of Life Stress in the Etiology of Child Abuse." *Journal of Consulting and Clinical Psychology* 48: 195–205.

Evans, A.L., 1981. *Personality Characteristics and Disciplinary Attitudes of Child-Abusing Mothers.* Saratoga, Calif.: Century Twenty One Publishing.

Faller, K.C., 1985. "Unanticipated Problems in the United States Child Protective System." *Child Abuse and Neglect* 9: 63–69.

Famularo, R., Stone, K., Barnum, R. & Wharton, R. 1986. "Alcoholism and Severe Child Maltreatment." *American Journal of Orthopsychiatry* 56: 481–85.

Fischler, R.S., 1984. "Child Abuse Treatment and Follow-Up: Can the Pediatrician Help Improve Outcome?" *Child Abuse and Neglect* 8: 361–68.

Friedman, R.M., Sandler, J., Hernandez, M. & Wolfe, D., 1981. "Child Abuse," in E.J. Mash & L.G. Terdal, eds., *Behavioral Assessment of Childhood Disorders.* N.Y.: The Guilford Press.

Friedrich, W.N. & Boriskin, J.A., 1976. "The Role of the Child in Abuse: A Review of the Literature." *American Journal of Orthopsychiatry* 46: 580–90.

Friedrich, W.N. & Einbender, A.J., 1983. "The Abused Child: A Psychological Review." *Journal of Clinical Child Psychology* 12: 244–56.

Friedrich, W.N. & Wheeler, K.K., 1982. "The Abusing Parent Revisited: A Decade of Psychological Research." *Journal of Nervous and Mental Disease* 170: 577–87.

Frodi, A.M. & Lamb, M.E., 1980. "Child Abusers' Responses to Infant Smiles and Cries." *Child Development* 51: 238–41.

Garbarino, J., 1977. "The Human Ecology of Child Maltreatment." *Journal of Marriage and the Family* 39: 721–35.

———. 1980. "Meeting the Needs of Mistreated Youths." *Social Work* 25: 122–26.

———. 1982. "Healing the Social Wounds of Isolation," in E.H. Newberger, ed., *Child Abuse.* Boston: Little Brown.

———. 1986. "Can We Measure Success in Preventing Child Abuse? Issues in Policy Programming and Research." *Child Abuse and Neglect* 10: 143–56.

Garbarino, J. & Sherman, D. 1980. "High-Risk Neighborhoods and High-Risk Families. The Human Ecology of Child Maltreatment." *Child Development* 51: 188–98.

Garbarino, J., Stocking, S., and Associates, 1980. *Protecting Children from Abuse and Neglect: Developing and Maintaining Effective Support Systems for Families.* San Francisco: Jossey-Bass.

Garmezy, N., 1987. "Stress, Competence, and Development: Continuities in the Study of Schizophrenic Adults, Children Vulnerable to Psychopathology, and the Search for Stress-Resistant Children." *American Journal of Orthopsychiatry* 57: 159–74.

Gaudin, J.M. & Kurtz, D.P., 1985. "Parenting Skills Training for Child Abusers." *Journal of Group Psychotherapy, Psychodrama and Sociometry* 38: 35–54.

Gaudin, J.M., & Pollane, L., 1983. "Social Networks, Stress, and Child Abuse." *Children and Youth Services Review* 5: 91–102.

Gelles, R.J., 1980. "Violence in the Family: A Review of Research in the Seventies." *Journal of Marriage and the Family* 42: 873–85.

———. 1982. "Child Abuse and Family Violence: Implications for Medical Professionals," in E.H. Newberger, ed., *Child Abuse.* Boston: Little Brown.

Gelles, R.J. & Cornell, C.P., 1983. "International Perspectives on Child Abuse." *Child Abuse and Neglect* 7: 375–86.

Gentry, C.E., 1985. "Treatment of Child Physical Abuse," in C.M. Mouzakitis & R. Varghese, eds., *Social Work Treatment with Abused and Neglected Children.* Springfield, Ill.: Chas. C. Thomas Publ.

Gil, D.G., 1970. *Violence Against Children.* Cambridge, Mass.: Harvard University Press.

———. 1979. "Unraveling Child Abuse," in R. Bourne & E.H. Newberger, eds., *Critical Perspectives in Child Abuse.* Lexington, Mass.: Lexington Books.

Gordon, T. 1975. *PET: Parent Effectiveness Training.* N.Y.: New American Library.

Gray, J.D., Cutler, C.A., Dean, J.G. & Kempe, C.H., 1977. "Prediction and Prevention of Child Abuse and Neglect." *Child Abuse and Neglect* 1: 45–53.

Green, A.H., 1978. "Psychopathology of Abused Children." *Journal of the American Academy of Child Psychiatry* 17: 92–104.

Halpern, R., 1986. "Home Based Early Intervention: Dimensions of Current Practice." *Child Welfare* 65: 381–98.

Helfer, R.E., 1982. "A Review of the Literature on the Prevention of Child Abuse and Neglect." *Child Abuse and Neglect* 6: 251–61.

Herrenkohl, R.C., Herrenkohl, E.C. & Egolf, B.P., 1983. "Circumstances Surrounding the Occurrence of Child Maltreatment." *Journal of Consulting and Clinical Psychology* 51: 424–31.

Hess, P.M., 1987. "Parental Visiting of Children's Foster Care: Current Knowledge and Research Agenda." *Children and Youth Services Review* 9: 29–50.

Hochstadt, N.J. & Harwicke, N.J., 1985. "How Effective is the Multidisciplinary Approach? A Follow-Up Study." *Child Abuse and Neglect* 9: 365–72.

Howes, C. & Espinosa, M.P., 1985. "The Consequences of Child Abuse for the Formation of Relationships with Peers." *Child Abuse and Neglect* 9: 397–404.

Hunter, R.S. & Kilstrom, N., 1979. "Breaking the Cycle in Abusive Families." *American Journal of Psychiatry* 136: 1320–22.

Isaacs, C.D., 1982. "Treatment of Child Abuse: A Review of the Behavioral Interventions." *Journal of Applied Behavior Analysis* 15: 273–94.

Johnson, C.F. & Showers, J., 1985. "Injury Variables in Child Abuse." *Child Abuse and Neglect* 9: 207–15.

Justice, B., Calvert, A., & Justice, R., 1985. "Factors Mediating Child Abuse as a Response to Stress." *Child Abuse and Neglect* 9: 359–63.

Kadushin, A. & Martin, J.A., 1981. *Child Abuse: An Interactional Event*. N.Y.: Columbia University Press.

Katz, M.H., Hampton, R.L., Newberger, E.H., Bowles, R.T. & Snyder, J.C., 1986. "Returning Children Home: Clinical Decision Making in Cases of Child Abuse and Neglect." *American Journal of Orthopsychiatry* 56: 253–62.

Kaufman, J. & Zigler, E., 1987. "Do Abused Children Become Abusive Parents?" *American Journal of Orthopsychiatry* 57: 186–92.

Kinard, E., 1980. "Mental Health Needs of Abused Children." *Child Welfare* 59: 451–62.

———. 1982. "Experiencing Child Abuse: Effects on Emotional Adjustment." *American Journal of Orthopsychiatry* 52: 82–91.

Koverola, C., Manion, I., & Wolfe, D.A., 1985. "A Microanalysis of Factors Associated with Child Abusive Families." *Behaviour Research and Therapy* 23: 499–506.

Kosky, R., 1983. "Childhood Suicide Behavior." *Journal of Child Psychology and Psychiatry* 24: 457–68.

Kropp, J.P. & Haynes, O.M., 1987. "Abusive and Nonabusive Mothers' Ability to Identify General and Specific Emotion Signals of Infants." *Child Development* 58: 187–90.

Krugman, R.D., 1985. 'The Coming Decade: Unfinished Tasks and New Frontiers." *Child Abuse and Neglect* 9: 119–21.

Krugman, R.D., Lenherr, M., Betz, L. & Fryer, G.E., 1986. "The Relationship Between Unemployment and Physical Abuse in Children." *Child Abuse and Neglect* 10: 415–18.

Lamphear, V.S., 1985. "The Impact of Maltreatment on Children's Psychosocial Adjustment: A Review of the Research." *Child Abuse and Neglect* 9: 251–63.

Lewis, M. & Schaeffer, S., 1979. "Peer Behaviour and Mother-Infant Interaction in Maltreated Children," in M. Lewis & L. Rosenbaum, eds., *The Uncommon Child: The Genesis of Behaviour*. Vol. 3. N.Y.: Plenum Press.

Libbey, P. & Bybee, R., 1979. "The Physical Abuse of Adolescents." *Journal of Social Issues* 35: 101–26.

Lieber, L.L., 1983. "The Self-Help Approach: Parents Anonymous." *Journal of Clinical Child Psychology* 12: 288–91.

Lutzker, J.R., Wesch, D. & Rice, J., 1984. "A Review of Project 12 Ways: An Ecobehavioral Approach to the Treatment and Prevention of Child Abuse and Neglect." *Advances in Behaviour Research and Therapy* 6: 63–73.

Lyons-Ruth, K., Connell, D.B., Zoll, D. & Stahl, J., 1987. "Infants at Social Risk: Relations Among Infant Maltreatment, Maternal Behavior, and Infant Attachment Behavior." *Developmental Psychology* 23: 223–32.

Main, M., 1981. "Abusive and Rejecting Infants," in N. Frude, ed., *Psychological Approaches to Child Abuse.* Totowa, N.J.: Rowman & Littlefield.

Mann, P.A., Lauderdale, M. & Iscoe, I., 1983. "Toward Effective Community-Based Intervention in Child Abuse. Professional Community-Based Interventions in Child Abuse." *Professional Psychology: Research and Practice* 14: 729–42.

McMurtry, S.L., 1985. "Secondary Prevention of Child Maltreatment: A Review." *Social Work* 30: 42–48.

Meddin, B.J., 1985. "The Assessment of Risk in Child Abuse and Neglect Case Investigations." *Child Abuse and Neglect* 9: 57–62.

Meddin, B. & Hansen, I., 1985. "The Services Provided During a Child Abuse and/or Neglect Case Investigation and the Barriers that Exist to Service Provision." *Child Abuse and Neglect* 9: 175–82.

Meichenbaum, D., 1977. *Cognitive-Behavior Modification.* N.Y.: Plenum.

Miller, K., Fein, E., Howe, G.W., Goudo, C.P. & Bishop, G., 1985. "A Parent Aide Program: Record Keeping Outcomes and Costs." *Child Welfare* 64: 407–19.

Moore, J.B., 1983. "The Experience of Sponsoring a Parents Anonymous Group." *Social Casework* 64: 585–92.

Murphy, S., Orkow, B. & Nicola, R.M., 1985. "Prenatal Prediction of Child Abuse and Neglect: A Prospective Study." *Child Abuse and Neglect* 9: 225–35.

Newberger, C.M., 1982. "Psychology and Child Abuse," in E.H. Newberger, ed., *Child Abuse.* Springfield, Ill.: Chas. C. Thomas Publ.

Nomellini, S. & Katz, R.C., 1983. "Effects of Anger Control Training on Abusive Parents." *Cognitive Therapy and Research* 1: 57–68.

Oates, K., 1986. *Child Abuse and Neglect: What Happens Eventually?* N.Y.: Brunner/Mazel.

O'Connor, S., Vietze, P.M., Sherrod, K.B., Sandler, H.M. & Altemeier, W. 1980. "Reduced Incidence of Parenting Inadequacy Following Rooming-In." *Pediatrics* 66: 176–82.

Olds, D., Chamberlin, R., Henderson, C., & Tatelbaum, R., 1986. "The Prevention of Child Abuse and Neglect: A Randomized Trial of Nurse Home Visitation." *Pediatrics* 78: 65–78.

Oliver, D., 1980. *Bridging the Gap: Issues, Problems, and Program Designs of Six Community Based Child Abuse Treatment Programs.* Department of Social Services, Health and Welfare Agency, State of California.

O'Toole, R., Turbett, P. & Nalepka, C., 1983. "Theories, Professional Knowledge, and Diagnosis of Child Abuse," in D. Finkhelhor & R.J. Gelles, eds., *The Dark Side of Families: Current Family Violence Research.* Beverly Hills, Calif.: Sage.

Pakizegi, B., 1985. "Maladaptive Parent-Infant Relationships." *Journal of Applied Developmental Psychology* 6: 199–246.

Parke, R. & Collmer, C., 1975. "Child Abuse: An Interdisciplinary Review," in E.M. Hetherington, ed., *Review of Child Development Research.* Vol. 5. Chicago: University of Chicago Press.

Patterson, G.R., Reid, J.B., Jones, R.R. & Conger, R.E., 1975. *A Social Learning Approach to Family Intervention.* 1. *Families with Aggressive Children.* Eugene, Oreg.: Castolia Publ. Co.

Paulson, M.J., 1985. "Interdisciplinary and Community-Based Approaches to Treating and Preventing Child Assault," in J.H. Meier, ed., *Assault Against Children.* San Diego: College Hill Press.

Pelton, L.H., 1978. "Child Abuse and Neglect: The Myth of Classlessness." *American Journal of Orthopsychiatry* 48: 608–17.

Perry, M.A., Doran, L.D. & Wells, E.A., 1983. "Developmental and Behavioral Characteristics of the Physically Abused Child." *Journal of Clinical Child Psychology* 12: 320–24.

Reid, J.B., Taplin, P.S. & Lorber, R., 1981. "A Social Interactional Approach to the Treatment of Abusive Families," in R.B. Stuart, ed., *Violent Behavior: Social Learning Approaches to Prediction, Management, and Treatment.* N.Y.: Brunner/Mazel.

Rickel, A.U., 1986. "Prescriptions for a New Generation: Early Life Interventions." *American Journal of Community Psychology* 14: 1–15.

Roscoe, B., 1985. "Intellectual, Emotional, and Social Deficits of Abused Children: A Review." *Childhood Education* 61: 388–92.

Rosenberg, M.S. & Reppucci, N.D., 1985. "Primary Prevention of Child Abuse." *Journal of Consulting and Clinical Psychology* 53: 576–85.

Rosenthal, P.A. & Rosenthal, S., 1984. "Suicidal Behavior by Preschool Children." *American Journal of Psychiatry* 141: 520–25.

Rueveni, U., 1979. *Networking Families in Crisis.* N.Y.: Human Sciences Press.

Salter, A.C., Richardson, C.M. & Kairys, S.W., 1985. "Caring for Abused Preschoolers." *Child Welfare* 64: 343–56.

Seagull, E.A., 1987. "Social Support and Child Maltreatment: A Review of the Evidence." *Child Abuse and Neglect* 11: 41–52.

Smith, J.E., 1984. "Non-accidental Injury to Children: 1. A Review of Behavioural Interventions." *Behaviour Research and Therapy* 22: 331–47.

Smith, S.L., 1984. "Significant Research Findings in the Etiology of Child Abuse." *Social Casework* 65: 337–46.

Starr, R.H., Jr., 1979. "Child Abuse." *American Psychologist,* 34: 872–78.

Starr, R.H., Jr., et al., 1984. "The Contribution of Handicapping Conditions to Child Abuse." *Topics in Early Childhood Special Education* 4: 55–69.

Stehno, S.M., 1986. "Family-Centered Child Welfare Services: New Life for a Historic Idea." *Child Welfare* 65: 231–40.

Steinberg, L.D., Catalano, R. & Dooley, D., 1981. "Economic Antecedents of Child Abuse and Neglect. *Child Development* 52: 975–85.

Straus, M.A., 1974. "Cultural and Social Organizational Influences on Violence Between Family Members," in R. Prince & D. Barrier, eds., *Configurations: Biological and Cultural Factors in Sexuality and Family Life.* Lexington, Mass.: Lexington Books.

Straus, M.A. & Gelles, R.J., 1986. "Societal Change and Change in Family Violence from 1975 to 1985 as Revealed by Two National Surveys." *Journal of Marriage and the Family* 48: 465–79.

Subramanian, K., 1985. "Reducing Child Abuse Through Respite Center Intervention." *Child Welfare* 64: 501–9.

Szykula, S.A. & Fleischman, M.J., 1985. "Reducing Out-of-Home Placements of Abused Children: Two Controlled Field Studies." *Child Abuse and Neglect* 9: 277–83.

Thomson, E., Paget, N., Bates, D., Mesch, M. & Putnam, T., 1971. *Child Abuse: A Community Challenge.* N.Y.: Henry Stewart.

Totah, N.L. & Wilson-Coker, P. 1985. "The Use of Interdisciplinary Teams," in C.M. Mouzakitis & R. Varghese, eds., *Social Work Treatment with Abused and Neglected Children.* Springfield, Ill.: Chas. C. Thomas Publ.

Turner, R.J. & Avison, W.R., 1985. "Assessing Risk Factors for Problem Parenting. The Significance of Social Support." *Journal of Marriage and the Family* 47: 881–92.

Valentine, D.P., Acuff, D.S., Freeman, M.L. & Andreas, T., 1984. "Defining Child Maltreatment: A Multidisciplinary Overview." *Child Welfare* 63: 497–509.

Van Meter, M.J., 1986. "An Alternative to Foster Care for Victims of Child Abuse/Neglect: A University-Based Program." *Child Abuse and Neglect* 10: 79–84.

Wahler, R.J., 1980. "The Insular Mother: Her Problems in Parent-Child Treatment." *Journal of Applied Behavior Analysis* 13: 207–19.

Wald, M., Carlsmith, M., Leiderman, P.H. & Smith, C., 1983. "Intervention to Protect Abused and Neglected Children," in M. Perlmutter, ed., *Development and Policy Concerning Children with Special Needs. The Minnesota Symposia on Child Psychology*. Vol. 16. Hillsdale, N.J.: Lawrence Erlbaum Assoc. Publ.

Wasserman, S. & Rosenfeld, A., 1986. "Decision-Making in Child Abuse and Neglect." *Child Welfare* 65: 515–29.

Weinbach, R.W. & Curtiss, C.C., 1986. "Making Child Abuse Victims Aware of Their Victimization: A Treatment Issue." *Child Welfare* 65: 337–46.

White, R., Benedict, M., Wulff, L. & Kelley, M., 1987. "Physical Disabilities as Risk Factors for Child Maltreatment: A Selected Review. *American Journal of Orthopsychiatry* 57: 93–101.

Whittaker, J.K., 1983. "Social Support Networks in Child Welfare," in J.K. Whittaker, J. Garbarino & Associates, eds., *Social Support Networks: Informal Helping in the Human Services*. N.Y.: Aldine Publ. Co.

Williams, G.J., 1983. "Child Abuse Reconsidered: The Urgency of Authentic Prevention." *Journal of Clinical Child Psychology* 12: 312–19.

Wolfe, D.A., 1984. "Treatment of Abusive Parents: A Reply to the Special Issue." *Journal of Clinical Child Psychology* 13: 192–94.

———. 1985a. "Child Abusive Parents: An Empirical Review and Analysis." *Psychological Bulletin* 97: 462–82.

———. 1985b. "Prevention of Child Abuse Through the Development of Parent and Child Competence," in R.J. McMahon & R. Peters, eds., *Childhood Disorders: Behavioral-Developmental Approaches*. N.Y.: Brunner/Mazel.

Wolfe, D.A. & Manion, I.G., 1984. "Impediments to Child Abuse Prevention: Issues and Directions." *Advances in Behaviour Research and Therapy* 6: 47–62.

Wood-Shuman, S. & Cone, J.D., 1986. "Differences in Abusive, At-Risk for Abuse, and Control Mothers' Descriptions of Normal Child Behavior." *Child Abuse and Neglect* 10: 397–405.

Zigler, E., 1979. "Controlling Child Abuse in America: An Effort Doomed to Failure," in R. Bourne & E.H. Newberger, eds., *Critical Perspectives in Child Abuse*. Lexington, Mass.: Lexington Books.

Zimrin, H., 1984. "Do Nothing But Do Something: The Effects of Human Contact with the Parent on Abusive Behavior." *British Journal of Social Work* 14: 475–85.

———. 1986. "A Profile of Survival." *Child Abuse and Neglect* 10: 339–49.

7

Learning Disabilities:
What Has Been Learned?

I n 1963, a small number of independent parent groups met in Chicago, hoping to join forces with one another and form a single organization. The common link among these parents was a child who had difficulty learning in school because of brain injury, neurological dysfunction, minimal brain damage, or perceptual handicaps, to mention but a few of the terms frequently used at the time. The keynote speaker at the meeting was Samuel Kirk, one of the leading researchers in the field. In his address, Kirk proposed the term *learning disabilities*, a term gratefully embraced by these parents who believed the current labels to be damaging to their children (Cruickshank 1981). This meeting launched the development of two milestones in the field of learning disabilities as we know it today: the establishment of the Association for Children and Adults with Learning Disabilities (ACLD) and the beginning of the widespread use of the current term learning disabilities. Since that time, the study of learning failure has evolved into a different field of study, its focus extended to a wider range of problems than those originally spurring the Chicago meeting. But progress in this field did not evolve smoothly, and to understand the current field, it is necessary to digress briefly.

A Brief Look Back

Historically, it was assumed that unexplained serious learning difficulties in children with normal intelligence were caused by some neurological dysfunction (Feagans 1983). Even in the beginning of this century, it had been noted that the reading problems of some children resembled those of brain-injured adults. The hypothesis that *behavioral* problems could be caused by brain dysfunction began to emerge in the twenties, and in the forties, the term *brain-injured child* was first introduced (Rutter 1983b). By the early sixties, conceptualizations of the brain-injured child were still influencing research and thinking, which helps to explain the enthusiastic acceptance by parents and educators of the newly introduced term learning disabilities. It did not have the negative connotations of brain-injured, and it implied that learning failure was reversible (Strichart & Gottlieb 1981).

However, the term learning disabilities proved to be more than just a term. It was to have far-reaching consequences for the future direction the field was to take. Because the term was so general, it gradually became attached to greater numbers of children and soon became an "explanation" for the many learning problems that once had baffled educators. "No wonder so many children couldn't learn. They had a learning disability!"

In 1969, Congress selected this very general term for usage in the Elementary and Secondary Act Amendments (PL 91-230) and created *learning disabilities* as an official category of exceptional children eligible for federal aid. Previously established categories included visual and auditory impairments, motor handicaps, mental retardation, emotional disturbance, and environmental disadvantage. The new category, learning disabilities, comprised learning problems that were not encompassed by these previously established categories. In other words, learning disabilities became a "wastebasket" category, encompassing a broad spectrum of diverse learning problems that could not be explained in any other way. Throughout the sixties and seventies, the number of children officially classified as learning disabled (LD) grew astronomically.

The new practice of encompassing many diverse problems under a single designation had serious repercussions for research in the field which were not generally recognized until many years later: definition, theory, and research became entangled in a mass of confusion and misconceptions (Cruickshank 1981). By the mid-sixties, researchers had no standard set of characteristics by which they selected learning disabled children for study (Radencich 1984). The crux of the problem, as Torgesen (1986) points out, was that learning disabilities developed as a political and social concept rather than as a scientific concept.

The political arena had a further impact on growth and direction of the field. The sixties was an era of massive federal funding to education, without stringent demands for accountability (Strichart & Gottlieb 1981). A plethora of remedial programs and materials were rapidly developed to help the growing population of LD children. Many of these programs were "based" on the theories and principles of the early pioneers in the field, such as Frostig (Frostig & Horne 1965) and Kephart (1960). However, as Smith (1985) points out, their theories were interpreted very narrowly and with a type of fanaticism. Many "experts" were so convinced that learning problems would be remedied by narrow training programs limited to, for example, perceptual training or motor training, that serious effort had not been made to empirically validate the effectiveness of the programs (Smith 1985, Strichart & Gottlieb 1981). Nevertheless, they were widely adopted in the schools because of slick marketing, their strong "theoretical" rationales, and a lack of alternatives.

By the seventies, some of the early leaders in the learning disabilities field were speaking out against the direction the field had taken (Strichart & Gottlieb 1981). Ames (1977) cautioned that it was time to jump off bandwagons and evaluate future directions. Several publications appeared at this time that reviewed and evaluated the available learning disabilities research. These reviewers found little empirical support for the training programs widely used in the schools at the time (e.g., Arter & Jenkins 1977, Larsen & Hammill 1975, Tarver & Dawson 1978, Vellutino et al. 1977).

Since the mid-seventies, the growth in this field has been extraordinary. Although there still is much to learn, researchers from the United States, England, Canada, and other Western nations have jointly made significant gains in understanding the broad range of learning problems that affect children throughout the world. This chapter looks at the population of children who currently are labeled learning disabled and at many of the underlying causes of learning failure. The following chapter looks at current remedial techniques. Each of the chapters should be read for a full appreciation of the other.

Learning Disabled Children

Children labeled learning disabled continue to be a heterogeneous population. General definitions lack preciseness because of the wide range of problems and causes encompassed by the term. The most recent and widely accepted definition, formulated and adopted by the National Joint Committee on Learning Disabilities (NJCLD 1981), is the following:

> Learning Disabilities is a generic term that refers to a heterogeneous group of disorders manifested by significant difficulties in the acquisition and use of listening, speaking, reading, writing, reasoning or mathematical abilities. These disorders are intrinsic to the individual and presumed to be due to nervous system dysfunction. Even though a learning disability may occur concomitantly with other handicapping conditions (e.g., sensory impairment, mental retardation, social and emotional disturbance) or environmental influences (e.g., cultural differences, insufficient/inappropriate instruction, psychogenic factors), it is not the direct result of those conditions or influences (see NJCLD 1987, p. 108).

Prevalence and Assessment

The prevalence estimates of learning disabled children have varied widely. Some estimates of the number of schoolchildren who have serious academic problems that are not easily explained have occasionally ranged as high as 30 percent (see Feagans 1983, Lerner 1985). Currently, the number of schoolchildren "officially" classified as learning disabled, and therefore receiving special educational services, ranges from 2.3 percent to 8.9 percent, according to a 1986 survey of state educational services (McNutt 1986). The reason prevalence estimates vary so widely probably reflects the absence of precise and universally accepted criteria for identifying a child with a learning disability. States vary in their methods of identification and in their criteria for achievement discrepancy. It would be conceivable for a child to meet the criteria in one state and not in another (Frankenberger & Harper 1987).

Often, the first step in identification is a child's unexplained performance below grade-level expectancy by at least one year in the lower grades and two years in the upper grades (Houck 1984). Diagnosis usually is made on the basis of some combination of classroom observation, school records, parent interview, medical history, and diagnostic tests (Johnson 1981). These are used to rule out other possible causes of learning failure, such as visual or auditory handicaps, emotional disturbance, mental retardation, and so forth. However, distinguishing between a child who is learning disabled and one who is a low achiever is often very difficult. It is suspected that there is an overlap between the learning disabled and low-achiever populations (Feagans 1983, Forness & Kavale 1983b, Radencich 1984, Ysseldyke 1983).

Characteristics of Learning Disabled Children

A number of behavioral and learning characteristics have been associated with learning disabled children. However, no learning disabled child displays all of these characteristics and normally achieving children often display some. Additionally, some are more significant at one age level than at another. The following characteristics are mentioned with the greatest frequency in the literature (Dworkin 1985, Johnson 1981, Lerner 1985, McKinney 1984).

1. Language difficulties
2. Perceptual problems
3. Attentional problems (e.g., easily distracted, impulsive)
4. Poor conceptual thought, poor memory, and poor learning strategies
5. Deficits in basic academic skills
6. A poor grasp of *spatial concepts* (e.g., over, under), *time concepts* (before, after; days of the week), *sequential relationships* (multistep directions, order of letters in a word, steps to an arithmetic problem, and so on)
7. Poor motor ability (e.g., clumsiness, poor coordination)
8. Poor self-concept and emotional difficulties (e.g., easily excitable and discouraged, low frustration level)
9. Inappropriate social behavior (poor interpersonal skills, poor social perception, poor social awareness, and low social status)
10. Soft neurological signs. These are subtle indicators of mild neurological dysfunction (e.g., awkward gait, mild tremors, poor fine motor coordination, and slight reflex abnormalities).

Research is now reporting other factors that characterize our current learning disabled population, some of which do not fit the stereotype of these youngers.

For example, it was commonly believed that learning disabled children have average to superior intelligence. However, although they score within the normal range of intelligence, learning disabled children, as a group, score 5 to 10 points below their normally achieving peers. Their IQ scores generally are closer to 90 than to 100 (see Feagans 1983, Stanovich 1986, Torgesen & Dice 1980, Wolford & Fowler 1984).

Socioeconomic status is proving to be strongly related to learning disabilities. Youngsters of lower socioeconomic status are more likely to develop learning disabilities and to have enduring learning problems (see Schonhaut & Satz 1983).

Finally, there is a higher incidence of learning disabilities in boys than in girls. Studies have varied in the ratios reported. A 1981 estimate from the U.S. General Accounting Office was approximately 72 percent boys and 28 percent girls (Lerner 1985).

Types of Learning Disabilities

Confusion exists in the learning disabilities literature because of a lack of agreed-upon terminology. On the one hand, some investigators group children with many types of learning disabilities and label them simply "learning disabled." At the same time, terms such as *learning disabled, reading disabled, dyslexic,* and *MBD* (minimal brain dysfunction) sometimes are used interchangeably. Some of this terminology will be clarified in order to avoid confusion.

It is now known that the LD population is not a homogeneous one (e.g., Pirozzolo & Campanella 1981). There are many distinctive types of learning disabilities: reading disabilities, writing disabilities, spelling disabilities, math disabilities, and nonverbal disabilities. A child with one disability may not have any others or may have several. The primary (although not exclusive) focus here will be reading disabilities because the bulk of the research has been with reading disabled children and because reading failure is the most common criterion used to refer children for learning disabilities services. (Reading disabilities characterize 60 to 80 percent of all LD children [see Jones, Torgesen & Sexton 1987].) More thorough information on other specific disabilities can be found in the following: writing disabilities (Cicci 1983), spelling disabilities (Cicci 1983, Sweeney & Rourke 1985), math disabilities (Badian 1983; Strang & Rourke 1985a,b), nonverbal disabilities (Ozols & Rourke 1985, Strang & Rourke 1985a).

The terms *dyslexia* and *MBD* cause many people considerable confusion and should be mentioned. The literal translation of dyslexia is "not" (dys) "read" (lexia). Dyslexia is simply a severe reading disability (Houck 1984). A popular definition, put forth by the World Federation of Neurology is:

> . . . a disorder manifested by difficulty in learning to read despite conventional instruction, adequate intelligence, and sociocultural opportunity. It is dependent upon fundamental cognitive disabilities which are frequently of constitutional origin (Pirozzolo & Campanella 1981, p. 179).

In this chapter, the simpler terms *reading failure* and *reading disability* are used rather than *dyslexia*.

The term MBD (minimal brain dysfunction) causes even more confusion. One child may be labeled learning disabled and another MBD. MBD refers to patterns of behavior that suggest neurological involvement; however, because the indications are so subtle, brain dysfunction cannot be firmly established (Johnson 1981). MBD is not a precise concept. Since its introduction in the forties, its conceptualization has often changed (Gaddes 1985). Currently, according to Rutter (1983b), there is no single concept of MBD nor agreed-upon diagnostic criteria. In fact, R.B. Johnson (1982) notes that whether a child is diagnosed as having minimal brain dysfunction may sometimes have more to do with the bias and philosophy of the diagnostician than with the specific characteristics of the child. The terms learning disabled and reading disabled are used in this chapter rather than the MBD term.

Causes of Learning Disabilities

The search for the causes of learning disabilities has spanned several decades. The numbers of theories put forth over the years are legion, and their diversity has been extraordinary. This is not surprising, given the number of different disciplines and subdisciplines that are researching learning problems. Psychology, education, psycholinguistics, neuropsychology, neurology, psychiatry, endocrinology, and pediatrics have contributed to our knowledge, and this is not an exhaustive list.

Many explanations of learning disabilities were originally put forth to deal with virtually all learning disabilities. However, calls to abandon the search for a single cause have become common in the literature (see McKinney 1984). There is now a rather broad consensus that the learning disabled population is so heterogeneous, it defies unification. Since the term learning disabilities encompasses a wide range of problems, learning disabilities are likely to stem from many different causes. Even a single learning disability, such as reading disability, appears to have many causes (Pirozzolo & Campanella 1981).

Many of the explanations proposed to date offer insights about specific subsets of children with learning problems. Consequently, each contributes valuable pieces to the complex puzzle of learning failure. Space prohibits a discussion of all the explanations proposed over the years. Those selected were done so on the basis of three criteria: their influence in the field, their practical value to practitioners, and their contribution to a balanced and comprehensive view of learning disabilities.

Remedial techniques are discussed in this chapter only insofar as they directly relate to an approach under discussion. The following chapter is devoted to the many remedial strategies developed for learning disabled children (as well as any child with a learning problem). Once again, these two chapters are intended to complement one another. Having a working knowledge of the potential causes of learning failure will allow remediation to be approached systematically rather than by trial and error.

Most attempts to explain learning disabilities can be conceptualized as belonging to one of two categories. In the first category are attempts to explain causation in a broad sense, such as neurologically, genetically, biochemically, nutritionally, or by a maturational delay. Of these, neurological and maturational lag approaches will be discussed. In the second category are attempts to explain learning disabilities by pinpointing specific deficits within the child (for example, perceptual or language deficits) that interfere with her ability to learn. Whether these deficits are caused by neurological impairments, biochemical imbalances, genetic transmission, or a maturational lag is not germane to this approach. Five of these approaches and the current evidence pertaining to each will be discussed. The deficiencies they focus upon are perceptual, linguistic, metacognitive, attentional, and information processing.

It should be noted that an alternative conceptualization of learning disabilities focuses upon the educational system. Adelman (1971), for example, attributes learning disabilities to a poor match between situational factors (such as instructional approaches) and a child's strengths and limitations. He suggests many learning problems are caused because instruction is not individualized enough to accommodate children's individual differences. This conceptualization is not discussed further in this chapter, but methods to personalize instruction are discussed in the following chapter.

Broad Approaches to Causation

The Neurological Approach. Stressing that the brain is the principal mediator of behavior, the neurological approach assumes that learning problems are caused by a specific brain dysfunction. Readers should not be tempted to dichotomize neurological functioning into impaired or normal. As Gaddes (1985) points out, there is a continuum of cerebral functioning ranging from exceptional to severely impaired. Many people have "imperfect" brains which impinge upon their ability to process information in one way or another. R.B. Johnson (1982), of Johns Hopkins University School of Medicine, believes it is useful to conceptualize the brain as a complex switchboard. Within this conceptualization, the learning disabled child may have a few disrupted connections while all else is intact.

There are limitless possibilities for the location of an impairment (Gaddes 1985). There are numerous causes of brain dysfunction as well. A long list of potential causes have been suggested over the years (Houck 1984, Lerner 1985). In prenatal development, maternal diseases, endocrine disorders, smoking, alcohol, medication, and blood incompatibility between mother and fetus have all been suggested. Perinatal causes include premature birth, low birth weight, and difficult labor and delivery. During childhood, brain injury may be caused by extremely high fevers, dehydration, encephalitis, meningitis, or head injuries incurred in accidents. Note, however, that these are only potential causes of brain inury. None of these events necessarily cause brain injury or dysfunction.

Cerebral dysfunction can also have limitless cognitive and behavioral sequelae. Neurological researchers in the learning disabilities field are working to discover the precise relationships between the brain and behavior so that effective intervention can be determined. This is an ambitious long-term goal, however, since there are rather limited conditions under which the brain can be studied directly. At this point in time, the science of brain-behavior relationships in children is still in its infancy (Chadwick & Rutter 1983). However, sophisticated neurological measurement techniques are developing rapidly, which are likely to contribute a great deal of information in the future. Examples are positron emission tomography and nuclear magnetic resonance (NMR) imaging (Benton 1985; Fisk, Finnell & Rourke 1985).

Parents often seek neurological assessment of their child, believing it will provide the answer to their offspring's school failure. In practice, however, the methods currently at our disposal to detect neurological impairment in LD children are far from precise. Since direct brain study is not feasible, a brain dysfunction must be conjectured. Several methods are used: (1) *The neurological exam* examines a child's nervous system via a wide range of measures that are believed to reflect brain functioning, such as reflexes, sensations, and motor abilities (R.B. Johnson 1982). (2) *The EEG* (electroencephalogram) measures the electrical activity of the brain. (3) *Neuropsychological assessment batteries* test a wide range of abilities that may be impaired by brain dysfunction. Examples include abstract concept formation, memory, language, perception, attention, and coordination. This last type of testing, which must be given by a trained neuropsychologist, has the advantage of providing useful information about a child's strengths and deficits in the wide range of areas tested (Chadwick & Rutter 1983).

Each of the preceding three assessment methods can distinguish children with indisputable neurological impairment. However, opinions differ on their ability to diagnose unequivocally the presence or absence of brain damage in most children with learning problems (see Abrams 1984, Chadwick & Rutter 1983, C. Johnson 1981, R.B. Johnson 1982).

For excellent discussions of neurological exams and EEGs, see R.B. Johnson (1982), and of neuropsychological assessment batteries, see Chadwick and Rutter (1983).

Although neurological explanations of learning disabilities dominated the field for over half a century, many theorists and investigators skirt the issue of whether learning disabilities are neurologically based (Feagans 1983). They suggest instead that attention be focused on treatment of the problems rather than on their cause. On the other hand, research being published since the mid-eighties suggests that children may respond differently to remedial programs depending upon the nature of neurological problems when they exist (see Lyon 1985, Sweeney & Rourke 1985). Presently, research in this area is flourishing and, reports Radencich (1984), there seems to be a new emphasis returning to the medical model.

The Maturational Lag Approach. Some theorists have argued that learning disabilities in some children are not caused by neurological impairments but by neurological immaturity (e.g., Goldstein & Myers 1980, Satz & Fletcher 1980, Satz & Van Nostrand 1973). Maturational lag theories suggest that some children have a developmental delay in some aspect(s) of neurological development required for academic learning. Hence, according to this approach, the cause of learning disabilities in some children is a temporary one that could be avoided. Learning problems develop only if the academic demands made upon these children are beyond their capabilities at a given time (Houck 1984, Johnson 1981, Lerner 1985).

The maturational lag hypothesis has received support in several forms:

1. Many children seem to outgrow their early learning problems (see Johnson 1981).

2. Younger children in a grade (whose birthdays are close to the cut-off date for school entrance) are more likely to experience learning problems than are their older classmates, suggesting they may be less ready developmentally for academic demands (see Lerner 1985).

3. Several studies have found that reading skills and errors displayed by failing readers are similar to those of much younger children (see Houck 1984, Johnson 1981).

4. Tests that are sensitive to children's level of maturation have been found to be good predictors of subsequent reading achievement (see Lerner 1985).

Satz and his colleagues propose that even many long-standing cases of learning disabilities may be due to maturational lags (e.g., Satz & Van Nostrand 1973). It is commonly thought that children who enter school without the appropriate skills eventually will catch up to their classmates. However, these theorists point out that skills required for reading and school achievement change from grade to grade, becoming progressively more complex. They suggest that perceptual skills play an important role during early stages of reading acquisition, whereas more complex conceptual and linguistic skills play a more important role at later stages.

These theorists suggest that a maturational lag in the left hemisphere of the brain will cause delayed perceptual and motor skills in a younger child as well as delayed linguistic and conceptual abilities when he is somewhat older. Hence, children with such maturational delays will be consistently behind their classmates, enmeshed in a losing game of catch-up throughout their school careers. Each year, required academic skills become more complex and also build on the foundation of earlier skills. By the time junior high school is reached, sophisticated reading skills are necessary for survival in almost all regular classes and these students are likely to fall even further behind.

The maturational lag hypothesis points out that it is critical for teachers, particularly those in the early grades, to become painstakingly sensitive to the maturity of each student in their class. Flexible programs must be provided for immature students, so that inappropriate requirements will not be demanded of them.

Deficit Approaches to Causation

Deficit approaches pinpoint underlying deficiencies that are characteristic of learning disabled children. They attempt to specify the role these deficits play in learning failure and how they can best be treated. Whether these underlying deficits are caused by neurological impairment, genetic transmission, maturational delay, or some other factor is not critical. Unlike neurological theorists, whose goal it is to understand the specific relationships between brain and behavior, theorists using this approach may refer to neurology only as an underlying explanation for the observed deficits (Haring & Bateman 1977).

Although some of these explanations were originally put forth as "general theories" of learning disabilities, few people in the field would now consider any of them adequate to explain the heterogeneous LD population. Instead, each deals with subgroups within this population and each offers specific implications for intervention.

Perceptual Deficits. Originally proposed by the pioneers of the field, it was perceptual deficit theories that preoccupied the learning disabilities field in the sixties. These theories are no longer playing a prominent role in the current learning disabilities research literature (Feagans 1983, Forness & Kavale 1983a). However, historically, they have had the greatest impact on remedial efforts for learning disabled children, and they continue to influence the instructional strategies of many teachers (Allington 1982). They therefore require some attention.

The perceptual deficit school hypothesizes that reading failure is caused by deficiencies in a child's perceptual processing abilities, caused by either an impairment or delay in her neurological development (Cruickshank 1981). According to this approach, the foundation for reading and other conceptual learning is adequate perceptual development.

Marianne Frostig (Frostig & Horne 1965) identified numerous visual perceptual problems that seem to be characteristic of many learning disabled children and made a good case for the role they played in reading failure. How can a child learn how to read if all he sees is a page of random printed symbols, rather than meaningful configurations that we call words? How can he learn to read when he cannot recognize the same letter or word just because it appears in different colors or sizes of print? How can he learn to read or write if he can't see the difference between "b" and "d," "p" and "q," was and saw, ton and not?

Others in this school of thought have implicated deficits in spatial perception as a cause of learning failure. They have pointed to the problems in spatial perception, spatial thinking, and spatial relationships that are so commonly observed in LD children, such as confusion with directions, with their left and right, with spatial concepts (such as over, near, or away from).

Many perceptual deficit theorists have gone a step further and hypothesize that the roots of reading failure extend down to deficits in motor ability. The rationale behind this is the hypothesis that adequate motor development lays the groundwork for both subsequent perceptual and cognitive development. Many different theories (perceptual-motor theories) are based on this premise (e.g., Delacato 1963, Kephart 1960). Generally, these theories hypothesize the following: first, that development occurs in a sequential fashion from motor development to perceptual development to higher order learning, and second, that each earlier level provides the foundation for the next level (Roberton 1981).

For a complete discussion of perceptual-motor theories and their critics, see Roberton (1981). Hallahan and his colleagues (1985) provide an excellent summary of perceptual deficit theories and the research investigating them.

The reason the perceptual deficit theories no longer play a prominent role in the literature is due to lack of research evidence supporting some of their premises. Most damaging has been research investigating the effectiveness of remedial programs based upon the theories. According to perceptual deficit theories, the most effective means of ameliorating reading disabilities is treatment of the *underlying* perceptual or perceptual-motor deficits. A large body of research now exists reporting no improvement in reading ability as a result of training these underlying perceptual and motor deficits (e.g., Arter & Jenkins 1977, Kavale & Mattson 1983, Larsen & Hammill 1975, Tarver & Dawson 1978, Vellutino et al. 1977). See the following chapter for a discussion of these programs and research.

According to Hallahan and his colleagues (1985), there currently is a movement in the field to discount not only perceptual deficit theories but also the importance of perceptual problems in learning disabilities. This movement, they hypothesize, may partially be an overreaction to the long-accepted belief in the LD field that perceptual problems were *the* cause of most, if not all, learning failure (Hallahan, Kauffman & Lloyd 1985). However, recent research has found there *is* a subgroup of reading disabled children who do appear to have a great deal of difficulty with visual-spatial perceptual processing (see Pirozzolo 1979). The size of this group is an issue of controversy. Some suggest it is quite small (e.g., Dworkin 1985; Feagans 1983; Stanovich 1982, 1986). Others believe it to be substantial (e.g., Pirozzolo 1979).

The remedial methods that are currently suggested for children with perceptual problems are discussed in the following chapter.

Language Deficits. Over the past decade and a half, accumulating research evidence has been implicating language deficits as an important cause of reading disabilities. The role of language was slow to be recognized because of the long-standing dominance in the learning disabilities field of perceptual deficit theories. There is now, however, a converging consensus that language plays an important role in a large percentage of cases of reading failure (see, e.g., *Harvard Educational Review*, August 1977; Rubin & Dworkin 1985; Scholl 1981; Stanovich 1986; Vellutino 1979).

The link between language-processing problems and early reading problems has been established not only in English-speaking children but also in Swedish,

Japanese, and Chinese children (see Mann 1986). Among English-speaking children, studies have found that deficient verbal skills in preschool and kindergarten youngsters are predictive of subsequent reading problems (see Rubin & Dworkin 1985). It fact, speech- and language-retarded children have been found to be up to six times more likely to experience reading problems than children without language difficulties (see Mann 1986). Retrospective studies also support the relationship between language and reading difficulties, finding that the early language of many reading disabled children either had been impaired or had been slow to develop (e.g., Ingram, Mason & Blackburn 1970; Rutter & Yule 1975).

Knowing there is a link between language deficits and reading disabilities is not sufficient, however. For appropriate remediation, we must know where in language the problems lie.

Frank Vellutino (1977, 1979, 1983), who has both conducted and stimulated extensive research in this area, suggests that the problems lie in a poor grasp of one or more of the three important components of language:

1. *Phonology*: how sounds are combined into meaningful units (such as words, prefixes, and so on)

2. *Syntax*: how words are combined into phrases and sentences

3. *Semantics*: how meaning is obtained from words and sentences

According to Vellutino, language is the best device we have to help us store information in our memory in such a way that we can quickly retrieve it. How can a youngster successfully read without the ability to rapidly retrieve letters, words, sounds, and word meanings? How can she successfully compete in school if she cannot quickly retrieve a vast array of information?

A simple example of beginning readers who are introduced to new words will illustrate his point. Remembering new words will be an easy task for a child with a firm grasp of phonology. He understands that words are made up of component sounds represented by letters. And he has a firm grasp of the sounds associated with letters. Therefore, he has many separate clues to help him remember the newly introduced words (the whole words, the initial, medial, and ending sounds, comparisons to other words he knows, and so forth). In a sense, he has many ways to code each word, to store it in his memory, and to retrieve it. A youngster without a firm grasp of phonology (of the implicit "rules" used to combine sounds into words) has far fewer clues to help him remember the word. He may have to resort to remembering each new word as a whole—sometimes a tricky task, especially if printed symbols have little meaning to him. (Every teacher has come across a child who approaches the same word every day as if it were the first time he saw it.)

The more that youngsters are "language-sophisticated," the more devices they will have at their disposal to help them remember new information. Beginning readers will have many more ways to remember a new word if it is already familiar, if they have used the word in conversation, and if they have understood its use in various contexts. These young readers will then be able to code the word by various context clues, in addition to letter and sound cues. In a sense, they can store the word in their memory by a cross-referenced system. If they can't retrieve it by sight, they can use letters and sounds. If it still eludes them, they can use context clues. This wide network of associations surrounding the word will help them to remember any new information about the word as well, such as its use in new contexts.

According to Vellutino, a child also needs to grasp the syntactic and semantic components of language in order to read. Often, the meaning of a sentence rests not in the summation of its individual words but in the structure of the sentence, such as the order of words and punctuation. A child with a poor grasp of syntax will have difficulty holding a string of words in her memory long enough to make sense of them. She may read the words but miss the meaning. The third component of language, semantics, becomes increasingly more important as reading material becomes more advanced, says Vellutino. For example, semantics plays a role in the storage and retrieval of abstract words and in distinguishing between irregular words that are similar (for example, cough, rough, dough, and bough).

The problems of language-deficient children do not end with reading. Each school day, children are bombarded with verbal information which they must remember. Since language provides the quickest and most versatile way to code and cross-reference information for quick retrieval, the language-deficient child is at a great disadvantage in the typical classroom.

Vellutino reports extensive research supporting various aspects of his theory (1979). Interesting support comes from studies reporting that younger reading disabled children perform more poorly on *some* memory tasks than do average readers. Which memory tasks? Those in which they must remember *verbal* material. When information to be remembered cannot be easily named (abstract figures, photographs of faces, Hebrew letters), reading disabled children and average readers perform somewhat similarly; the average readers no longer have the advantage of language (see Liberman & Shankweiler 1985, Mann 1984, Torgesen 1985). In other words, reading disabled children are at the largest disadvantage when they must rely on verbal devices to store and retrieve information. Unfortunately, the typical classroom situation is a verbally dependent environment.

Some of the more clever experiments conducted by Vellutino and other researchers from the language deficit school have tested language deficit hypotheses against perceptual deficit hypotheses. This research suggests that for many reading disabled children, problems that traditionally have been considered perceptual problems actually may be verbal problems. An example of this research follows. In experiments conducted by Vellutino and his colleagues (1972, 1975), both problem and normal readers were shown (very briefly) a series of 3- and 4-letter words that were easy to confuse, such as was/saw, from/form, calm/clam, and the like. As in past findings, problem readers, compared to normal readers, made many errors both reading the words and saying the letters that made up each word. However, when asked to write down what they saw, poor readers produced the confusing letters and words as accurately as did average readers. Their problem, therefore, did not seem to be a perceptual problem (which had been the traditional interpretation of such errors). What was their problem then? According to these theorists, the children could perceive words accurately, but they could not remember their names. (They wrote them accurately but could not say them accurately.) The root of their problem was poorly established associations between printed symbols (letters and words) and their correct names and sounds. Their problem was a labeling problem. This conclusion has received support from other types of experiments (e.g., Liberman et al. 1971, Shankweiler & Liberman 1972, Vellutino 1979).

A number of linguistic theorists maintain that the cause of language-based reading problems lies primarily in the phonological domain as opposed to the syntactic or semantic domains (Liberman & Shankweiler 1985, Mann 1986, Stanovich 1982, Wagner & Torgesen 1987, Wallach & Wallach 1982, Williams 1986). Competence at the phonological level, they point out, requires an awareness of a very abstract aspect of speech. The following will illustrate this point. At the phonological level, language is represented by phonemes. Phonemes are all the possible speech sounds that are represented by printed symbols. However, there are no one-to-one relationships between phonemes and letters. For example, English as spoken by midwesterners has 45 phonemes but only 26 letters in the alphabet to represent them (see Wagner & Torgesen 1987). Some letters (or combinations of letters) represent more than one phoneme (for example, "ou" as in dough, cough, bough, rough). And some phonemes are represented by more than one letter or letter combinations (for example, "w" and "wh"; "g" and "j"). Liberman and Shankweiler (1985) point out that words, in reality, are strings of "abstract phonological elements."

Phonological awareness is a necessary prerequisite for making sense out of the alphabet, and consequently, it is a necessary prerequisite for decoding words. However, although beginning reading programs often teach phonics, they generally do not teach the more basic phonemics (Williams 1984). Usually, beginning programs assume that children have some phonemic skills when they enter school (Wallach & Wallach 1982). For example, reading readiness exercises that require children to match the initial letters of words presuppose phonemic awareness. However, many children, upon entering school, seem to lack a basic understanding that words are comprised of component sounds. This has been the conclusion of Wallach and Wallach (1982) based upon their research. In one experiment they cite, for example, disadvantaged children who could not distinguish between the sounds "rr" and "cc," could distinguish between the words rake and cake. They could hear the sounds, but they seemed to respond to words as wholes, rather than tune in to their critical sound differences.

Tasks that test a child's phonemic awareness and skills include rhyming, counting the number of phonemes in familiar monosyllabic words (presented verbally), recognizing words with the same beginning, medial, or ending sounds, blending phonemes smoothly, reversing the order of phonemes (for example, top, pot), the use of pig latin, and so forth. These are all tasks with which reading disabled children often have difficulty (see Liberman et al. 1980).

Theorists from this school of thought suggest that poor phonological skills also can account for poor reading comprehension (Liberman & Shankweiler 1985). They point out that a poor ability to decode and/or recognize words results in a very slow reading pace. This slow pace, they maintain, prevents children from keeping the string of words in their memory long enough to make sense of them.

Of the extensive research that has supported the importance of language deficits in reading failure, the most compelling evidence supports the importance of phonological skills. Phonological skills have been causally linked with reading acquisition (see Wagner & Torgesen 1987), and poor phonological skills are strongly related to reading problems (see Stanovich 1986). Many disabled readers, both children and adults, do indeed have poor phonological skills (see Liberman & Shankweiler 1985, Mann 1986, Stanovich 1986).

There is some evidence that poor syntactic skills may be involved in reading problems also, but findings are equivocal. Studies have found that awareness of syntax and reading acquisition are related (Stanovich 1986; Tunmer, Nesdale & Wright 1987). And evidence suggesting that poor readers are developmentally delayed in syntactic awareness has recently been reported by Tunmer and others (1987). However, Liberman and Shankweiler (1985) report evidence to the contrary. The evidence that reading disabled children have difficulty at the semantic level has been least compelling (Mann 1986).

Teaching phonemic skills is currently considered to be a promising new technique for teaching reading (Torgesen, cited in Williams 1984). Many authors have suggested enjoyable ways in which children can be taught phonemic skills. (Interested readers are referred to Liberman 1982, Liberman et al. 1980, Mann 1984, Mann & Liberman 1984, Wallach & Wallach 1982.) A training program that has been effective in teaching LD children phonemic skills has been developed by Williams (1979).

Discussion of a third type of deficit theory follows. This theory, too, deals with a set of problems commonly found in reading disabled children (and many other learning disabled children as well). It will be clear how these problems are likely to contribute to learning failure.

Cognitive Strategy and Metacognitive Deficits. A common and frustrating characteristic of learning disabled children is their inability to remember information. One day they seemingly know material, the next day it's forgotten. Vellutino's language deficit approach offers a seemingly logical explanation for the poor memory so characteristic of learning disabled children. Research on cognitive strategy deficits contributes another dimension to our understanding of the memory problems, as well as the general academic problems, of many of these children.

Joseph Torgesen has been influential in focusing attention on the inefficient learning strategies characteristically used by learning disabled children. Unlike efficient learners, who have developed a repertoire of cognitive strategies to help them learn (organizing material, integrating it with previous learning, monitoring their understanding, attending to relevance, and so on), learning disabled children do not seem to know *how* to go about learning (Torgesen 1977, Torgesen & Licht 1983).

Perhaps the most effective way to explain LD children's difficulties is through some examples of research findings.

1. When given memory assignments, learning disabled children are less likely than normally achieving children to group items from similar categories together or to otherwise organize material (see Torgesen & Licht 1983).

2. Younger learning disabled children are less likely to verbally rehearse material they are asked to learn (determined by watching lip movements) (Torgesen & Goldman, cited in Torgesen & Licht 1983).

3. The memory performance of LD children has been improved dramatically by teaching them strategies to help them remember, such as grouping related items into categories (Torgesen, Murphy & Ivey 1979) and using mnemonic techniques (Mastropieri et al. 1985).

4. While reading, reading disabled children are unlikely to selectively attend to important information or to monitor their own understanding (see Ryan, Weed & Short 1986).

5. The reading comprehension of reading disabled students has shown marked improvement when they have been taught how to become actively involved in reading: how to organize material, look for main ideas, and ask themselves questions about the material (see Ryan, Weed & Short 1986). See chapter 8.

6. In a study of reasoning strategies, learning disabled children used fewer strategies and less efficient strategies than did controls (Kavale 1980).

7. Research conducted in the Soviet Union reports that learning disabled children are less likely than normal learners to provide structure and organization to tasks automatically. This is true for a wide variety of tasks, including those requiring plans of action and strategy. The performance of Soviet children also improves when they are given strategic help. Since the Soviet definitions and Western definitions of learning disabilities are quite similar, this research is very relevant (Torgesen & Licht 1983).

The composite of these research findings leaves one with the impression that the learning styles of learning disabled children either are very inactive or are maladaptive (Torgesen & Licht 1983).

Although the weight of the evidence suggests that strategy deficits are a fairly general characteristic of the LD population (Torgesen & Licht 1983), not all LD children are strategy deficient (see Torgesen 1985). For those who are, Torgesen points out that strategy deficits may be the primary cause of learning failure for some and the result of learning failure for others (Torgesen & Licht 1983). This latter group, according to Torgesen, may initially develop learning problems for diverse reasons (maturational delay, linguistic or perceptual deficits, home experiences that poorly prepared them for school, and so forth). But these diverse children all have one important thing in common: the experience of chronic school failure, which is almost certain to have consequences for them.

In conceptualizing what these consequences of chronic school failure may be, Torgesen and Licht (1983) drew upon the large body of learned helplessness research. This research indicates that the experience of chronic failure can foster a child's belief that failure is beyond his control (Weiner 1974). Once children believe their academic fate is beyond their control, they tend to accept failure as imminent. When faced with difficulty, they put forth little effort and concentration. When initial problem-solving attempts fail, they tend to give up rather than to try alternative strategies. "Why try? Nothing I do matters" (Dweck & Wortman 1982). This phenomenon is called *learned helplessness.*

Based upon this research, Torgesen and Licht suggest that early chronic failure begins a vicious cycle, continuing throughout a child's school career. Chronic failure leads to a type of learned helplessness. Withdrawal of effort and deteriorated problem-solving follow, which lead to further failure. A good deal of recent research has supported the hypothesis that LD children develop a type of learned helplessness. This research has been reviewed recently by Licht and Kistner (1986). (Chapter 5 contains more extensive discussions of the negative consequences of learned helplessness in nonacademic areas.)

Very similar to Torgesen's conceptualization of the LD child as a maladaptive or inactive learner is a current stream of research studying metacognitive deficits in LD children (Stanovich 1986). Metacognition is an awareness of how to go about learning effectively and how to go about performing tasks effectively. It includes planning, evaluating, and determining the appropriateness of an array of strategies, skills, and resources (Baker 1982). One can think of it as a person's savvy about learning, problem-solving, and her own capabilities and limitations.

Studies consistently have reported metacognitive deficits in LD children as a group (see Short & Ryan 1984, Swanson 1987). In general, these children are insensitive to the need to behave strategically in learning situations, and they can't judge the approriateness of one strategy over another. They also have a poor understanding of the purpose of reading (see Short & Ryan 1984). Their poor metacognitive functioning can be illustrated by a study of reading disabled children conducted by Forrest and Waller (see Ryan 1981). When questioned how they would study for a test, reading disabled children responded they would read the material once. And when asked how they would evaluate their test performance, they answered they would have to wait for their grade. In contrast, normal learners said they would study by reading the material several times while asking themselves questions, and they would evaluate their test performance by the difficulty of the questions.

The conceptualization of learning disabled children as inefficient learners has many implications for remediation. Even if strategy deficits were not the initial cause of a child's learning failure, they must be addressed if intervention is to be effective. Specific techniques to help children develop more efficient learning strategies are discussed in the following chapter.

The following section examines a fourth deficit theory. This theory focuses on problems with attention.

Attentional Problems. The attentional problems of learning disabled children have become a focus of study, and several theories have implicated them as a cause of learning failure. Referrals for learning disabled children usually include descriptive terms such as, short attention span, easily distracted, and impulsive. This anecdotal data has been supported by empirical evidence (see Krupski 1986). In fact, in her recent review of the literature, Krupski (1986) points out that the generality of attentional problems is rather impressive, given the heterogeneity of the population. Learning disabled children with attentional problems are not to be equated with hyperactive children. Hyperactive children are not necessarily learning disabled and those who are comprise only a small percentage of the LD population (Feagans 1983).

Attentional problems may be a primary cause of learning problems for some children. For others, they may be a reaction to chronic failure (Krupski 1986). In either case, attentional problems increase the likelihood of additional failure.

Several theories have focused on the role attentional problems may play in learning failure (e.g., Keogh & Margolis 1976, Koppell 1979, Ross 1976). Although these theories are quite different, only one will be discussed because it will provide sufficient rationale for some of the remedial techniques discussed in the following chapter. The Keogh and Margolis theory (1976) was selected because of its direct usefulness to practitioners working with learning disabled children.

Rather than treating attentional problems as a single problem, Keogh and Margolis have identified three separate components of attention: (1) coming to attention, (2) attention at the stage of decision making, and (3) ability to sustain attention throughout assignments. A child's attentional problems may lie in any one area or in all three. Each represents very different problems, each has very different consequences for school performance, and each has different implications for intervention.

Coming to Attention. A child with problems coming to attention is unable to zero in on the salient aspects of the task at hand. He can neither select what is relevant nor organize what he does select. It is not difficult to appreciate how a learning disabled child may be confused about tasks and their requirements when one remembers the problems so many have with language and with organizing information. Admonitions to "Get started and stop wasting time" are useless. Some seemingly inattentive behavior and "looking around" may, in fact, be a maladaptive effort to gain information. Keogh and Margolis provide some empirical evidence to support this suggestion. It is obvious that children with attentional problems such as these will have difficulty completing assigned tasks successfully.

According to Keogh and Margolis, a child with a coming-to-attention problem needs explicit guidance and direction with each new task. Time and effort needs to be spent ascertaining whether she understands the task and the directions and whether she possesses the strategies and information necessary to complete the task.

Does research support the contention that LD children have these kinds of attentional problems? Studies do find that these youngsters have difficulty attending to the salient aspects of a task and ignoring the task's irrelevant features (see Krupski 1986). A simple task used in laboratory studies can illustrate this point. Children are asked to sort cards into two piles, based upon whether or not the card contains a square. However, if one or two irrelevant features also appear on the card (a star and/or horizontal line), the LD child has increasing difficulty completing the task. He makes more errors and it takes him considerably longer.

It is a common impression that LD children are distracted by noise and other activities in the classroom. This, however, has not been substantiated by research. Apparently these youngsters can ignore such nontask stimuli as well as their classmates (see Krupski 1986).

Attention during Decision Making. According to the Keogh and Margolis theory, children with this type of attentional problem usually are labeled "impulsive." They respond too quickly, calling out an answer or forging ahead with a problem without any thought. They attend only to fragmentary information, do not weigh alternatives, and do not check for accuracy. The consequence, of course, is a high rate of errors and inaccuracy. Research has found that many LD children *do* have such impulsive response styles (see Blackman & Goldstein 1982, Krupski 1986).

This type of impulsive responding, according to Keogh and Margolis, may reflect limited problem-solving skills. General admonishments to "think before you speak" generally are useless. Teaching LD children to delay responding for a period of time usually is ineffective too, because they do not know what to do during the lapsed time. These children, say Keogh and Margolis, do need to learn to delay responding, but they also need to be taught how to gather all the relevant information, how to look for alternatives, how to weigh alternatives, how to check and confirm their choices, and how to correct their responses. Specific techniques for teaching these skills are discussed in the following chapter.

Sustaining Attention. Teachers frequently observe that learning disabled children are unable to sustain their attention long enough to complete a task, and Keogh and Margolis identify this as the third component of attention. It is obvious that attentional problems of this type would play a significant role in school failure.

Research employing various measures of sustained attention, including physiological measures, confirms that this is a fairly general characteristic of this heterogeneous population (see Keogh & Margolis 1976, Krupski 1986).

Although it is tempting to dismiss such attentional problems as a deficit in a youngster, Keogh and Margolis suggest approaching the problem from the perspective of a poor match between the child and assignments. These children need help in developing their ability to sustain attention. The first step is to assign short and easily completed tasks. These can become longer and more complex as children master easier levels. It is helpful for tasks to have well-defined outcomes. Increasing the interest of assignments and rewarding completed assignments are both obvious and useful techniques. Additional techniques are discussed in chapter 8.

The following section looks at the last of the deficit approaches that will be discussed.

Information Processing Deficiencies. An information processing framework is currently considered to be a promising way in which to examine learning disabilities (see the *Journal of Learning Disabilities* January, February, and March 1987). This perspective looks at the way sensory input is dealt with and used by the individual. In so doing, it incorporates a number of factors implicated in learning disabilities that have already been discussed, such as attentional problems, decoding and word recognition difficulties, memory problems, and cognitive strategy deficits (Kolligan & Sternberg 1987, Samuels 1987).

One example of this approach is that of LaBerge and Samuels (see Samuels 1987). Coverage will be brief because many of its individual components have already been discussed. However, such brief coverage necessarily oversimplifies a complex model. Interested readers are urged to read Samuels (1987) and Samuels and Kamil (1984).

Samuels (1987) points out that two things must occur in skilled reading: the text must be (1) decoded and (2) processed for meaning. Both steps require the reader's attention—which, it is maintained, is a limited resource.

A major factor in reading problems, according to this approach, is difficulty decoding and quickly recognizing words. Why? Because so much of the poor reader's attention is consumed by her slow, labored process of reading each word that she has little attentional capacity left to devote to the task of making sense of what she is reading. This means that she cannot decode/recognize and construct meaning simultaneously, as good readers do. She is therefore required to shift her attention back and forth between decoding and comprehension—a process which overtaxes her memory capacity. To better appreciate the problems of poor readers, try reading the following paragraphs by using a mirror to obtain a mirror image. Then try testing your comprehension. Or, imagine the difficulty a beginning language student has trying to translate passages written at a level above his ability.

The difficulties of poor readers can stem from many sources, including the inability to automatically process information at the phonological and visual levels. (Difficulties at the visual level result in the poor reader processing the print on a page in very small units, such as single letters, as opposed to larger units, such as clusters and whole words. This problem is characteristic of many poor readers.)

It is critical, points out Samuels, for poor readers to learn to decode/recognize words automatically. This will free their attention for comprehension. This automaticity, however, will occur only with very extensive practice.

The importance of automaticity is discussed further in the remediation chapter.

The Search for Subtypes of Learning Disabilities

The heterogeneity of the learning disabled population has plagued the field for over two decades. It has retarded progress in the precise definition of learning disabilities, in their accurate assessment, in the search for causation, and in the development of optimal remedial programs.

Currently, however, a number of researchers are channeling their efforts into empirically identifying and defining specific subtypes of learning disabled children. If valid and reliable subtypes can be identified, research can be directed toward each subtype separately. It is hoped that subtyping research will lead to precise assessment guidelines and, ultimately, to optimal remedial programs for each of the subgroups within this heterogeneous population. Subtyping research has gained increasing support over the past decade. The research, however, is still in its early stages (McKinney 1984).

Sophisticated statistical techniques are being employed in the search for learning disability subtypes. Studies take LD children's responses on a wide variety of neuropsychological and psychometric measures and apply statistical techniques, such as Q factor analysis or cluster analysis. A number of somewhat homogeneous clusters of children emerge, which it is hoped represent meaningful subgroups of learning disabilities (Satz & Morris 1981).

Subtyping research has confirmed suspicions that the LD population consists of different subgroups, characterized by different strengths and weaknesses. Research conducted by Byron Rourke and his associates illustrates this point (see Rourke 1983, Rourke & Strang 1983, Sweeney & Rourke 1985). These researchers found that reading, math, and spelling disabled children each displayed distinctive patterns of deficits on neuropsychological test batteries. Even more interesting are findings that spelling disabled children who are phonetically inaccurate spellers have different test profiles than others who are phonetically accurate (although equally impaired). This suggests that spelling disabled children who are impaired to the same degree may need very different types of remediation because their impairment stems from different deficits.

Among reading disabled children, at least two major subtypes have frequently emerged (see Pirozzolo 1979). The first is a language disabled subtype. This appears to be the largest group of disabled readers, and frequently several subtypes of language disorders emerge (Lyon 1983, Pirozzolo & Campanella 1981, Satz & Morris 1981, Van Der Vlugt & Satz 1985). The second is a visual-spatial subtype, which is less common. Evidence suggests that there are other subtypes as well (see Pirozzolo 1979, Pirozzolo & Campanella 1981). Additionally, some studies have found a group that performed normally on neuropsychological testing (Lyon 1985, Satz & Morris 1981). Perhaps these children are low achievers who have been incorrectly identified as learning disabled.

The identification of LD subtypes also has extended to the area of social-emotional functioning. There is a considerable body of research studying the social functioning of LD children. Much of it has reported that these youngsters, as a group, have poor interpersonal skills, poor social perception, and low social status. (See Bryan & Bryan [1983] and Gerber [1982] for discussions of the social-emotional problems of LD youngsters.) However, the evidence has not been consistent, and this has prompted subtyping research in this area (Porter & Rourke 1985). Studies have found relationships between LD subtypes and social behavior. For example, Ozols and Rourke (1985) found that two different subtypes of learning disabled children performed poorly in different areas of social sensitivity tests. This suggests that different patterns of neuropsychological weaknesses may not only lead to different academic problems but to different interpersonal problems as well. All LD children do not have social-emotional problems, however. Porter and Rourke (1985) found that over a third of their LD sample functioned adequately socially and emotionally.

At this point, it is difficult to compare the subtypes of disabilities found by different investigators because of methodological inconsistencies in studies. Investigators have used different criteria to select subjects, different test batteries, and different methods of collecting and evaluating data (Lyon 1983). Researchers do not yet agree about the number of subtypes that may exist or about their distinguishing charactersitics (Doehring 1984). However, efforts currently are geared in that direction (Lyon 1983). At least one study, for example, has been a joint effort between researchers in two countries, the United States and the Netherlands (Van Der Vlugt & Satz 1985). With standardized methodologies, these researchers found that 82 percent of the Dutch sample could be placed in subtypes that were very similar to those of the U.S. sample.

At this time, efforts also are being made within laboratories to validate the subtypes found in that laboratory (Fletcher 1985, Lyon 1985). One way to validate subtypes is to determine whether different subtypes respond differently to remedial techniques. Lyon (1985), for example, has found that the six reading disabled subtypes he has identified respond differently to teaching methods.

The current trend in subtyping research holds out promise to clarify many of the problems that have puzzled this field for decades and to simplify the practitioner's task in the future. McKinney (1984) points out that we may finally have the potential to precisely define subtypes of learning disabilities, to precisely specify assessment guidelines, and to distinguish between children with real disabilities and children who are low achievers. Finally, subtyping research has the potential to determine the most appropriate course of intervention for individual children (McKinney 1984).

At this time, available theory, evidence, and remedial techniques provide only broad guidelines for practitioners working with LD children. Each of the approaches discussed in this chapter, and its associated body of research, contributes to the understanding of the problems of subgroups within this heterogeneous population.

But the practitioner's job is a difficult one. He or she must systematically observe and test the individual child, form hypotheses about the nature of the child's specific problems, hypothesize which remedial techniques might best help her, and finally test the validity of those hypotheses with additional observation and testing. Detailed knowledge of remediation research is needed in order to match appropriate remediation with an individual child. The following chapter will discuss the remedial techniques that are dominating the current research literature.

References

Abrams, J. 1984. "Interaction of Neurological and Emotional Factors in Learning Disability." *Learning Disabilities* 3: 27–37.

Adelman, H.S. 1971. "The Not So Specific Learning Disability Population." *Exceptional Children* 37: 528–33.

Allington, R.L. 1982. "The Persistence of Teacher Beliefs in Facets of the Visual Perceptual Deficit Hypothesis." *Elementary Education* 82: 351–59.

Ames, L.B. 1977. "Time to Check Our Road Maps?" *Journal of Learning Disabilities* 10: 328–30.

Arter, J.A. & Jenkins, J.R. 1977. "Examining the Benefits and Prevalence of Modality Considerations in Special Education." *Journal of Special Education* 11: 281–98.

Badian, N.A. 1983. "Dyscalculia and Nonverbal Disorders of Learning," in H.R. Myklebust, ed., *Progress in Learning Disabilities*. Vol. 5. N.Y.: Grune & Stratton.

Baker, L. 1982. "An Evaluation of the Role of Metacognitive Deficits in Learning Disabilities." *Topics in Learning and Learning Disabilities* 2: 27–35.

Benton, A.L. 1985. "Child Neuropsychology: Retrospect and Prospect," in L. Costa & O. Spreen, eds., *Studies in Neuropsychology: Selected Papers of Arthur Benton*. N.Y.: Oxford University Press.

Blackman, S. & Goldstein, K.M. 1982. "Cognitive Styles and Learning Disabilities." *Journal of Learning Disabilities* 15: 106–15.

Bryan, J.H. & Bryan, T.H. 1983. "The Social Life of the Learning Disabled Youngster," in J.D. McKinney & L. Feagans, eds., *Current Topics in Learning Disabilities*. Norwood, N.J.: Ablex Publ. Corp.

Chadwick, O. & Rutter, M. 1983. "Neuropsychological Assessment," in M. Rutter, ed., *Developmental Neuropsychiatry*. N.Y.: The Guilford Press.

Cicci, R. 1983. "Disorders of Written Language," in H.R. Myklebust, ed., *Progress in Learning Disabilities*. Vol. 5. N.Y.: Grune & Stratton.

Cruickshank, W.M. 1981. *Concepts in Learning Disabilities: Selected Writings*. Vol. 2. Syracuse: Syracuse University Press.

Delacato, C. 1963. *The Diagnosis and Treatment of Speech and Reading Problems*. Springfield, Ill.: Chas. C. Thomas Publ.

Doehring, D.G. 1984. "Subtyping of Reading Disorders: Implications for Remediation." *Annals of Dyslexia* 34: 205–15.

Dweck, C.S. & Wortman, C.B. 1982. "Learned Helplessness, Anxiety, and Achievement Motivation," in H.W. Krohne & L. Laux, eds., *Achievement, Stress, and Anxiety*. Washington, D.C.: Hemisphere Publishing Corp.

Dworkin, P.H. 1985. *Learning and Behavior Problems in School Children.* Philadelphia: W.B. Saunders Co.

Feagans, L. 1983. "A Current View of Learning Disabilities." *Journal of Pediatrics* 102: 487–93.

Fisk, J.L., Finnell, R. & Rourke, B.P. 1985. "Major Findings and Future Directions for Learning Disability Subtype Analysis," in B.P. Rourke, ed., *Neuropsychology of Learning Disabilities: Essentials of Subtype Analysis.* N.Y.: The Guilford Press.

Fletcher, J.M. 1985. "External Validation of Learning Disability Typologies," in B.P. Rourke, ed., *Neuropsychology of Learning Disabilities: Essentials of Subtype Analysis,* N.Y.: The Guilford Press.

Forness, S.R. & Kavale, K.A. 1983a. "Remediation of Reading Disabilities, Part 1: Issues and Concepts." *Learning Disabilities* 2: 141–52.

———. 1983b. "Remediation of Reading Disabilities, Part 2: Classification and Approaches." *Learning Disabilities* 2: 153–63.

Frankenberger, W. & Harper, J. 1987. "States Criteria and Procedures for Identifying Learning Disabled Children: A Comparison of 1981/1982 and 1985/1986 Guidelines." *Journal of Learning Disabilities* 20: 118–21.

Frostig, M. & Horne, D. 1965. "An Approach to the Treatment of Children with Learning Disorders," in J. Hellmuth, ed., *Learning Disorders.* Vol. 1. Seattle: Special Child Publications.

Gaddes, W.H. 1985. *Learning Disabilities and Brain Function: A Neuropsychological Approach.* 2d ed. N.Y.: Springer-Verlag.

Gerber, P.J. 1982. "Social Perceptual Processing Problems," in W.M. Cruickshank & J.W. Lerner, eds., *Coming of Age: Vol. 3, The Best of ACLD.* Syracuse, N.Y.: Syracuse University Press.

Goldstein, D. & Myers, B. 1980. "Cognitive Lag and Group Differences in Intelligence." *Child Study Journal* 10: 119–32.

Hallahan, D.P., Kauffman, J.M. & Lloyd, J.W. 1985. *Introduction to Learning Disabilities.* 2d ed. Englewood Cliffs, N.J.: Prentice-Hall.

Haring, N.G. & Bateman, B. 1977. *Teaching the Learning Disabled Child.* Englewood Cliffs, N.J.: Prentice-Hall.

Houck, C.K. 1984. *Learning Disabilities: Understanding Concepts, Characteristics, and Issues.* Englewood Cliffs, N.J.: Prentice-Hall.

Ingram, T.T.S., Mason, A.W. & Blackburn, I. 1970. "A Retrospective Study of 82 Children with Reading Disability." *Developmental Medicine and Child Neurology* 12: 271–81.

Johnson, C. 1981. *The Diagnosis of Learning Disabilities.* Boulder, Colo.: Pruett Publ. Co.

Johnson, R.B. 1982. "Neurological Assessment of the Learning-Disabled Child." *Learning Disabilities* 1: 137–49.

Jones, K.M., Torgesen, J.K. & Sexton, M.A. 1987. "Using Computer-Guided Practice to Increase Decoding Fluency in Learning Disabled Children: A Study Using the Hint and Hunt I Program." *Journal of Learning Disabilities.* 20: 122–28.

Kavale, K.A. 1980. "The Reasoning Abilities of Normal and Learning Disabled Readers on Measures of Reading Comprehension." *Learning Disabilities Quarterly* 3: 34–45.

Kavale, K.A. & Mattson, P. 1983. "One Jumped Off the Balance Beam. Meta-Analysis of Perceptual Motor Training." *Journal of Learning Disabilities* 16: 165–73.

Keogh, B.K. & Margolis, J. 1976. "Learn to Labor and to Wait: Attentional Problems of Children with Learning Disorders." *Journal of Learning Disabilities* 9: 276–86.

Kephart, N.C. 1960. *The Slow Learner in the Classroom.* Columbus, Ohio: Charles E. Merrill.

Kolligan, J., Jr. & Sternberg, R.J. 1987. "Intelligence, Information Processing, and Specific Learning Disabilities: A Triarchic Synthesis." *Journal of Learning Disabilities* 20: 8–17.

Koppell, S. 1979. "Testing the Attentional Deficit Notion." *Journal of Learning Disabilities* 12: 43–48.

Krupski, A. 1986. "Attention Problems in Youngsters with Learning Handicaps," in J.K. Torgesen & B.Y.L. Wong, eds., *Psychological and Educational Perspectives on Learning Disabilities.* Orlando: Academic Press, Inc.

Larsen, S.C. & Hammill, D.D. 1975. "The Relationship of Selected Visual-Perceptual Abilities to School Learning." *Journal of Special Education* 9: 281–91.

Lerner, J.W. 1985. *Learning Disabilities: Theories, Diagnosis, and Teaching Strategies.* Boston: Houghton Mifflin Co.

Liberman, A.M. 1982. "On Finding That Speech Is Special." *American Psychologist* 37: 148–67.

Liberman, I.Y. 1983. "A Language-Oriented View of Reading and Its Disabilities," in H.R. Myklebust, ed., *Progress in Learning Disabilities.* Vol. 5. N.Y.: Grune & Stratton.

Liberman, I.Y. & Shankweiler, D. 1985. "Phonology and the Problems of Learning to Read and Write." *Remedial and Special Education (RASE)* 6: 8–17.

Liberman, I.Y., Shankweiler, D., Camp, L., Blackman, B. & Werfelman, M. 1980., "Steps Toward Literacy: A Linguistic Approach," in P. Levinson & C. Sloan, eds., *Auditory Processing and Language: Clinical and Research Perspectives.* N.Y.: Grune & Stratton.

Liberman, I.Y., Shankweiler, D., Orlando, C., Harris, K.S. & Berti, F.B. 1971. "Letter Confusion and Reversals of Sequence in the Beginning Reader: Implications for Orton's Theory of Developmental Dyslexia." *Cortex* 7: 127–42.

Licht, B.G., & Kistner, J.A. 1986. "Motivational Problems of Learning-Disabled Children: Individual Differences and Their Implications for Treatment," in J.K. Torgesen & B.Y.L. Wong, eds., *Psychological and Educational Perspectives on Learning Disabilities.* Orlando: Academic Press, Inc.

Lyon, G.R. 1983. "Learning Disabled Readers: Identification of Subgroups," in H.R. Myklebust, ed., *Progress in Learning Disabilities.* Vol. 5. N.Y.: Grune & Stratton.

———. 1985. "Educational Validation Studies of Learning Disability Subtypes," in B.P. Rourke, ed., *Neuropsychology of Learning Disabilities: Essentials of Subtype Analysis.* N.Y.: The Guilford Press.

Mann, V.A. 1984. "Longitudinal Prediction and Prevention of Early Reading Difficulty." *Annals of Dyslexia* 34: 117–51.

———. 1986. "Why Some Children Encounter Reading Problems: The Contribution of Difficulties with Language Processing and Phonological Sophistication to Early Reading Disability," in J.K. Torgesen & B.Y.L. Wong, eds., *Psychological and Educational Perspectives on Learning Disabilities.* Orlando: Academic Press, Inc.

Mann, V.A. & Liberman, I.Y. 1984. "Phonological Awareness and Verbal Short Term Memory: Can They Presage Early Reading Success?" *Journal of Learning Disabilities* 17: 592–99.

Mastroprieri, M.A., Scruggs, T.E. & Levin, J.R. 1985. "Maximizing What Exceptional Students Can Learn: A Review of Research on the Keyword Method and Related Mnemonic Techniques." *Remedial and Special Education (RASE)* 6: 39–45.

McKinney, J.D. 1984. "The Search for Subtypes of Specific Learning Disability." *Journal of Learning Disabilities* 17: 41–50.

McNutt, G. 1986. "The Status of Learning Disabilities in the States: Consensus or Controversy?" *Journal of Learning Disabilities* 19: 12–16.

National Joint Committee on Learning Disabilities. 1981. "Learning Disabilities: Issues on Definition." A Position Paper of the National Joint Committee on Learning Disabilities. 30 Jan. 1981.

———. 1987. "Learning Disabilities: Issues on Definition." *Journal of Learning Disabilities* 20: 107–109.

Ozols, E.J. & Rourke, B.P. 1985. "Dimensions of Social Sensitivity in Two Types of Learning-Disabled Children," in B.P. Rourke, ed., *Neuropsychology of Learning Disabilities: Essentials of Subtype Analysis.* N.Y.: The Guilford Press.

Pirozzolo, F.J. 1979. *The Neuropsychology of Developmental Reading Disorders.* N.Y.: Praeger.

Pirozzolo, F.J. & Campanella, D.J. 1981. "The Neuropsychology of Developmental Speech Disorders, Language Disorders, and Learning Disabilities," in G.W. Hynd & J.E. Obrzut, eds., *Neuropsychological Assessment and the School-Age Child: Issues and Procedures.* N.Y.: Grune & Stratton.

Porter, J.E. & Rourke, B.P. 1985. "Socioemotional Functioning of Learning-Disabled Children: A Subtype Analysis of Personality Patterns," in B.P. Rourke, ed., *Neuropsychology of Learning Disabilities: Essentials of Subtype Analysis.* N.Y.: The Guilford Press.

Radencich, M.C. 1984. "The Status of Learning Disabilities: The Emergence of a Paradigm or a Paradigm Shift?" *Learning Disabilities* 3: 79–89.

Roberton, M.A. 1981. "Motor Development in Learning Disabled Children," in J. Gottlieb & S.S. Strichart, eds., *Developmental Theory and Research in Learning Disabilities.* Baltimore: University Park Press.

Ross, A.L. 1976. *Psychological Aspects of Learning Disabilities and Reading Disorders.* N.Y.: McGraw-Hill Book Co.

Rourke, P.B. 1983. "Outstanding Issues in Research on Learning Disabilities," in M. Rutter, ed., *Developmental Neuropsychiatry.* N.Y.: The Guilford Press.

Rourke, B.P. & Strang, J.D. 1983. "Subtypes of Reading and Arithmetical Disabilities: A Neuropsychological Analysis," in M. Rutter, ed., *Developmental Neuropsychiatry.* N.Y.: The Guilford Press.

Rubin, H. & Dworkin, P.H. 1985. "The Language-Impaired Student," in P.H. Dworkin, ed., *Learning Problems in Schoolchildren.* Philadelphia: W.B. Saunders Co.

Rutter, M. 1983a. "Introduction: Concepts of Brain Dysfunction Syndromes," in M. Rutter, ed., *Developmental Neuropsychiatry.* N.Y.: The Guilford Press.

———. 1983b. "Issues and Prospects in Developmental Neuropsychiatry," in M. Rutter, ed., *Developmental Neuropsychiatry.* N.Y.: The Guilford Press.

Rutter, M. & Yule, W. 1975. "The Concept of Specific Reading Retardation." *Journal of Child Psychiatry* 16: 181–97.

Ryan, E.B. 1981. "Identifying and Remediating Failures in Reading Comprehension: Toward an Instructional Approach for Poor Comprehenders," in G. Makinnon & T. Waller, eds., *Reading Research: Advances in Theory and Practice.* Vol. 3. N.Y.: Academic Press.

Ryan, E.G., Weed, K.A. & Short, E.J. 1986. "Cognitive Behavior Modification: Promoting Active, Self-Regulatory Learning Styles," in J.K. Torgesen & B.Y.L Wong, eds., *Psychological and Educational Perspectives on Learning Disabilities.* Orlando: Academic Press, Inc.

Samuels, S.J. 1987. "Information Processing Abilities and Reading." *Journal of Learning Disabilities* 20: 18–22.

Samuels, S.J. & Kamil, M.L. 1984. "Models of the Reading Process," in P.D. Pearson, ed., *Handbook of Reading Research.* N.Y.: Longman.

Satz, P. & Fletcher, J. 1980. "Minimal Brain Dysfunction: An Appraisal of Research Concepts and Methods," in H. Rie & E. Rie, eds., *Handbook of Minimal Brain Dysfunctions: A Critical View.* N.Y.: Wiley Interscience Press.

Satz, P. & Morris, R. 1981. "Learning Disability Subtypes: A Review," in F.J. Pirozzolo & M.C. Wittrock, eds., *Neuropsychological and Cognitive Processes in Reading.* N.Y.: Academic Press.

Satz, P. & Van Nostrand, G.K. 1973. "Developmental Dyslexia: An Evaluation of a Theory," in P. Satz & J. Ross, eds., *The Disabled Learner: Early Detection and Intervention.* Rotterdam, The Netherlands: Rotterdam University Press.

Scholl, H.M. 1981. "Language Disorders Related to Learning Disabilities," in J. Gottlieb & S.S. Strichart, eds., *Developmental Theory and Research in Learning Disabilities.* Baltimore: University Park Press.

Schonhaut, S. & Satz, P. 1983. "Prognosis for Children with Learning Disabilities: A Review of Follow-Up Studies," in M. Rutter, ed., *Developmental Neuropsychiatry.* N.Y.: The Guilford Press.

Shankweiler, D. & Liberman, A.M. 1972. "Misreading: A Search for Causes," in J.F. Kavanagh & I.G. Mattingly, eds., *Language by Ear and by Eye: The Relationships Between Speech and Reading.* Cambridge, Mass.: The MIT Press.

Short, E.J. & Ryan, E.B. 1984. "Metacognitive Differences Between Skilled and Less Skilled Readers: Remediating Deficits Through Story Grammar and Attribution Training." *Journal of Educational Psychology* 76: 225–35.

Smith, C.R. 1985. "Learning Disabilities: Past and Present." *Journal of Learning Disabilities* 18: 513–17.

Stanovich, K.E. 1982. "Individual Differences in the Cognitive Process of Reading: I. Word Decoding." *Journal of Learning Disabilities* 15: 485–93.

——. 1986. "Cognitive Processes and the Reading Problems of Learning Disabled Children: Evaluating the Assumption of Specificity," in J.K. Torgesen & B.Y.L. Wong, eds., *Psychological and Educational Perspectives on Learning Disabilities.* Orlando: Academic Press, Inc.

Strang, J.D. & Rourke, B.P. 1985a. "Adaptive Behavior of Children Who Exhibit Specific Arithmetic Disabilities and Associated Neuropsychological Abilities and Deficits," in B.P. Rourke, ed., *Neuropsychology of Learning Disabilities: Essentials of Subtype Analysis.* N.Y.: The Guilford Press.

——. 1985b. "Arithmetic Disability Subtypes: The Neuropsychological Significance of Specific Arithmetic Impairment in Childhood," in B.P. Rourke, ed., *Neuropsychology of Learning Disabilities: Essentials of Subtype Analysis.* N.Y.: The Guilford Press.

Strichart, S.S. & Gottlieb, J. 1981. "Learning Disabilities at the Crossroads," in J. Gottlieb & S.S. Strichart, eds., *Developmental Theory and Research in Learning Disabilities.* Baltimore: University Park Press.

Swanson, H.L. 1987. "Information Processing Theory and Learning Disabilities: A Commentary and Future Perspectives." *Journal of Learning Disabilities* 20: 155–66.

Sweeney, J.E. & Rourke, B.P. 1985. "Spelling Disability Subtypes," in B.P. Rourke, ed., *Neuropsychology of Learning Disabilities: Essentials of Subtype Analysis.* N.Y.: The Guilford Press.

Tarver, S.G. & Dawson, M.M. 1978. "Modality of Preference and the Teaching of Reading: A Review." *Journal of Learning Disabilities,* 11: 5–17.

Tatham, S. 1970. "Reading Comprehension of Materials Written with Select Oral Language Patterns." *Reading Research Quarterly* 5: 402–26.

Torgesen, J.K. 1977. "The Role of Non-Specific Factors in the Task Performance of Learning Disabled Children: A Theoretical Assessment." *Journal of Learning Disabilities* 10: 27–35.

———. 1981. "The Study of Short-Term Memory in Learning Disabled Children: Goals, Methods, and Conclusions," in K. Gadow and I. Bailer, eds., *Advances in Learning and Behavioral Disabilities*. Greenwich, Conn.: JAI Press.

———. 1985. "Memory Processes in Reading Disabled Children." *Journal of Learning Disabilities* 18: 350–57.

———. 1986. "Learning Disabilities Theory: Its Current State and Future Prospects." *Journal of Learning Disabilities* 19: 399–407.

Torgesen, J.K. & Dice, C. 1980. "Characteristics of Research on Learning Disabilities." *Journal of Learning Disabilities* 13: 531–35.

Torgesen, J.K. & Licht, B.G. 1983. "The Learning Disabled Child as an Inactive Learner: Retrospect and Prospects," in J.D. McKinney and L. Feagans, eds., *Current Topics in Learning Disabilities*. Norwood, N.J.: Ablex Publ. Corp.

Torgesen, J.K., Murphy, H. & Ivey, C. 1979. "The Effects of an Orienting Task on the Memory Performance of Reading Disabled Children." *Journal of Learning Disabilities* 12: 396–401.

Tunmer, W.E., Nesdale, A.R. & Wright, D. 1987. "Syntactic Awareness and Reading Acquisition." *British Journal of Developmental Psychology* 5: 25–34.

Van Der Vlugt, H. & Satz, P. 1985. "Subgroups and Subtypes of Learning-Disabled and Normal Children: A Cross-Cultural Replication," in B.P. Rourke, ed., *Neuropsychology of Learning Disabilities: Essentials of Subtype Analysis*. N.Y.: The Guilford Press.

Vellutino, F.R. 1977. "Alternative Conceputalizations of Dyslexia: Evidence in Support of a Verbal-Deficit Hypothesis." *Harvard Educational Review*, 47: 344–54.

———. 1979. *Dyslexia: Theory and Research*. Cambridge, Mass.: The MIT Press.

———. 1983. "Childhood Dyslexia: A Language Disorder," in H.R. Myklebust, ed., *Progress in Learning Disabilities*. Vol. 5. N.Y.: Grune & Stratton.

Vellutino, F.R., Smith, H., Steger, J.A. & Kaman, M. 1975. "Reading Disability: Age Differences and the Perceptual Deficit Hypothesis." *Child Development* 46: 487–93.

Vellutino, F.R., Steger, J.A. & Kandel, G. 1972. "Reading Disability: An Investigation of the Perceptual Deficit Hypothesis." *Cortex* 8: 106–18.

Vellutino, F.R., Steger, B.M., Moyer, S.C., Harding, C.J. & Niles, J.A. 1977. "Has the Perceptual Deficit Hypothesis Led Us Astray?" *Journal of Learning Disabilities* 10: 375–85.

Wagner, R.K. & Torgesen, J.K. 1987. "The Nature of Phonological Processing and Its Causal Role in Acquisition of Reading Skills." *Psychological Bulletin* 101: 192–212.

Wallach, L. & Wallach, M.A. 1982. "Phonemic Analysis Training in the Teaching of Reading," in W.M. Cruickshank & J.W. Lerner, eds., *Coming of Age: Vol. 3, The Best of ACLD*. Syracuse, N.Y.: Syracuse University Press.

Weiner, B. 1974. *Achievement Motivation and Attribution Theory*. Morristown, N.J.: General Learning Press.

Williams, J.P. 1979. "The ABD's of Reading: A Program for the Learning Disabled," in L.B. Resnick & P.A. Weaver, eds., *Theory and Practice of Early Reading*. Vol. 3. Hillsdale, N.J.: Lawrence Erlbaum Assoc. Publ.

———. 1984. "Phonemic Analysis and How It Relates to Reading." *Journal of Learning Disabilities* 17: 240–45.

——. 1986. "The Role of Phonemic Analysis in Reading," in J.K. Torgesen & B.Y.L. Wong, eds., *Psychological and Educational Perspectives on Learning Disabilities.* Orlando: Academic Press, Inc.

Wolford, G. & Fowler, C. 1984. "Differential Use of Partial Information by Good and Poor Readers." *Developmental Review* 4: 16–35.

Ysseldyke, J.E. 1983. "Current Practices in Making Psychoeducational Decisions About Learning Disabled Students." *Journal of Learning Disabilities* 16: 226–33.

8
Learning Disabilities: Steps to Remediation

O ver the years, learning disabilities have been attributed to a host of causes. (See chapter 7.) Often the hypothesized causes have provided the impetus for the development of new remedial programs. At one time or another, each of the following methods of remediation has been touted as an effective means to ameliorate learning disabilities: vision training, perceptual training, perceptual-motor training, psycholinguistic training, medication, behavior modification, cognitive behavior modification, and countless varieties of direct instruction. And this is not an exhaustive list.

This chapter will survey the research evaluating remedial programs and techniques, emphasizing those that are dominating the current research literature. Although the focus will often be on children with reading problems, it will be clear that many of these interventions are appropriate for children with different types of learning problems, including children not officially classified as *learning disabled*. A number of the treatment approaches that will be discussed are not commonly used in schools at this time, but it is predicted they will be by the mid-1990s (Torgesen & Wong 1986).

Within each remedial approach, the problems that it was designed to deal with will be discussed. Recall from the previous chapter that the population of children labeled learning disabled (most often on the basis of reading failure) is a very heterogeneous one with a wide range of disabilities. Even children who have the same types of learning disabilities (reading, arithmetic, spelling, and so forth) have different combinations of deficits, and they have them to varying degrees.

Generally, there have been three broad approaches to the remediation of learning disabilities: the process training approach, the holistic approach, and the direct skills approach (see Lloyd, Epstein & Cullinan 1981; Tarver 1986; Zadig & Meltzer 1983). Each approach will be looked at, along with current research evidence associated with each. A fourth approach—the neuropsychological approach, which is presently receiving much attention—will also be discussed.

The Process Training Approach to Remediation

This approach dominated remedial programs for many years. It assumes that reading failure is caused by some deficiency in a child's ability to process information. According to this approach, the best way to treat reading disabilities is to train these underlying processing deficits. Until these are improved, academic instruction will not be effective; once they are improved, reading will improve as well (see Gittelman 1983; Hallahan, Kauffman & Lloyd 1985).

The chief advocates of this approach have been perceptual deficit theorists, which were discussed in chapter 7. Recall that these theories focus on deficits in a child's perceptual processing abilities. They maintain that: (1) adequate perceptual and motor development are the foundations for reading acquisition and other conceptual learning, (2) primary causes of reading failure are deficits in perceptual and/or motor abilities, and (3) the most effective way to treat reading failure is to work with the underlying perceptual and motor deficits.

Teaching strategies, teaching materials, and a plethora of commercially available kits and programs have been developed on the preceding three premises. Remediation has most frequently involved training an array of perceptual, perceptual-motor, and motor abilities. Examples of remedial activities might be finding and tracing shapes embedded in complex pictures, copying designs, completing puzzles, practice with spatial relationships, working on balance beams, exercises in body movement, practice with eye-hand coordination, practice catching balls, skipping, and so forth (Gittelman 1983; Hallahan, Kauffman & Lloyd 1985).

There is now a large body of literature studying the effectiveness of remedial programs based upon the process training approach, and many reviewers have thoroughly examined this research. These reviewers (e.g., Gittelman 1983, Goodman & Hammill 1973, Hammill 1972, Hammill & Larsen 1974, Kavale and Mattson 1983, Vellutino et al. 1977) have concluded that the weight of the evidence does not support the effectiveness of the process training approach in remediating reading problems. Hallahan and his colleagues (1985) recently wrote: "The best that can be said is that perceptual training based on a process training model may have some effect on perceptual skills. However, it does not increase reading achievement" (p. 72).

Many perceptual training kits and programs are still commercially available and claim to be effective. Gittelman (1983), however, points out that much of the literature cited by these programs "does not meet minimum scientific standards" (p. 526).

There *is* a subgroup of reading disabled children who appear to have a great deal of difficulty with visual-perceptual processing (see Pirozzollo 1979). However, there seems to be a rather strong consensus in the field that treating only their underlying deficits, in isolation, is not an effective remedial strategy. It is also recognized that a child who has perceptual problems may also have other problems that contribute to his learning failure. What remediation is suggested?

Some investigators now recommend that time and effort be directed toward academic content directly and exclusively (see "The Direct Skills Approach to Remediation"). A child with perceptual problems should be given help and practice discriminating between letters and words, not shapes and designs. Learning to discriminate between shapes and other nonverbal material does not necessarily generalize to reading skills. In fact, correlations are quite low between the ability to visually discriminate nonverbal material and subsequent reading skill. On the other hand, correlations are much higher between the ability to visually discriminate verbal material (letters and words) and subsequent reading skill (see Johnson 1981). Hallahan and others (1985) point out that behavioral principles are helpful in remedial programs for children with perceptual problems. These, along with examples, will be discussed shortly. Additional suggestions can be found in Hallahan, Kauffman, and Lloyd (1985).

Others in the field suggest that remedial programs for children with perceptual problems be broadly based. They suggest that remedial programs address both academic skill deficits and perceptual and motor deficits, in either separate or integrated remedial programs (e.g., Benton 1984, Gaddes 1985, Zadig & Meltzer 1983).

The Holistic Approach to Remediation

Whereas the process training approach focuses on deficits within the child, the holistic approach points to some of our best minds who reportedly encountered serious learning problems during their school careers (Poplin 1984). The holistic school of thought, according to Poplin, attributes learning disabilities not to children's "deficits" but to an interaction between child, school, and societal variables. Adherents to this approach do not deny there are "variations" within children, but they place much of the blame for children's school failure on the way that "learning" is conceptualized and implemented in our educational system. The learning process, they maintain, cannot be reduced and segmented into deficits and abilities. And what is to be learned cannot be reduced and segmented into instructional objectives, sequential steps, or predetermined experiences (Poplin 1984). In fact, there are neither definitive stages nor schedules that learning should follow, although there are guidelines (McNutt 1984). To be effective, learning must come from within the child. It needs to be generated from her own experiences and involvement and her attempts to make sense of new information by integrating it with that already learned (Poplin 1984). This position can be succinctly stated in a quote from a child in a traditional classroom, "When are we gonna' stop readin' and start readin' something?" (Poplin 1984).

The holistic approach suggests a basic language experience approach for the remediation of reading disabilities (Tarver 1986). This involves basing reading instruction, as much as possible, on a child's own experiences and his expression of those experiences. Reading is seen as an extension of thinking and talking and is thoroughly integrated with speaking, listening, writing, and spelling. Further information on a language experience approach may be obtained in Stauffer (1980) or Hall (1981).

An example of a holistic language experience approach used with learning disabled children was reported by Kerchner and Kistinger (1984). These researchers established a writing program for fourth- through sixth-grade learning disabled children to be conducted in their resource room. Students selected their own topic, first discussing ideas with the teacher in a prewriting conference. Stories were composed on a word processor so that changes could be made painlessly. The initial writing stage emphasized the expression of ideas. In a subsequent editing conference, students and teacher edited the story on a predetermined criteria, such as sentence structure, spelling, or punctuation. The students, who formed a writers' club and read their stories to audiences, maintained their enthusiasm throughout the seven-month experimental period. Their scores on a standardized test of written language significantly improved on vocabulary, thematic maturity, and style. Their gains in reading scores were similar to those of a control group in a more conventional program.

A more complete holistic program for the resource room has been offered by McNutt (1984). This program involves students virtually 100 percent of the time in reading, writing, speaking, and listening activities. Children frequently work in groups. There is group collaboration on writing, group discussion of reading material to improve comprehension skills, and group discussion to develop listening and speaking skills. Effective study skills, writing skills, and questioning techniques are also learned and practiced in groups. Children work independently on individualized work as well, and records are kept of individual progress. Reading is a high priority in the program. A wide range of materials is used, including library books, texts, newspapers, magazines, and students' work. Meaningfulness is the key. (Commercially available instructional materials that are designed to avoid a fragmented approach to reading might be welcomed in this kind of program. Examples are those published by Scholastic TAB Publications, Ltd. or Richmond Hill of Ontario, Canada [see Poplin 1984].) McNutt recognizes that students need specific instruction in certain skills they lack. For this, she includes "strategy lessons" that are tied, if possible, to a student's own work. For example, a lesson on punctuation could use samples of a youngster's past writing rather than worksheets of meaningless sentences. Finally, for resource rooms that must employ required texts for content courses, McNutt suggests that texts be adapted for easier reading (for example, main ideas can be highlighted or material can be rewritten at a simpler level).

There has been a negligible amount of research studying the effectiveness of the holistic approach. The studies that have assessed children's progress in a language experience program generally have not provided encouraging support for their academic gains (see Hallahan, Kauffman & Lloyd 1985). Research with learning disabled children is even more scarce. Disadvantaged children were studied in Project Follow Through, a national study that evaluated the effectiveness of different model educational programs; several of the programs were based on a language experience approach. Over a period of several years (kindergarten through third grade), disadvantaged children in language experience programs made few if any gains over control groups, and they performed more poorly than controls in many academic areas (Abt Associates 1976, 1977).

Advocates of the holistic approach, however, maintain that the approach is difficult to evaluate because meaningful learning is too elusive to measure (see Tarver 1986). Additionally, with an approach that is as loosely defined as this one, it is difficult to know whether poor scores reflect failure of the approach or failure to implement it effectively.

Readers who wish to pursue this school of thought in more detail are referred to Hall (1981), Reid and Hresko (1981), Smith (1983), Stauffer (1980), and the fall issue of Learning Disability Quarterly (1984), which was devoted to the holistic approach.

The Direct Skills Approach to Remediation

The thrust of current research has been on the direct skills approach, which has a completley different emphasis than either the process training or the holistic school of thought. Its focus is not primarily on the learner's underlying processing deficits, interests, or the cause of her disabilities. Instead, it focuses on the specific academic skills in which the learner is deficient and the most effective way those skills can be taught (Lloyd, Epstein & Cullinan 1981; Zadig & Meltzer 1983). This approach does not deny that learning disabled children have underlying deficits. But it maintains that the most effective treatment of a problem may not be directly related to its origin (Ryan, Weed & Short 1986; Treiber & Lahey 1983).

There are many direct skills approaches. Each is able to deal more effectively with some skill deficiencies than with others. Practitioners often can select techniques from different approaches and combine them as needed. If one looks at the problems commonly found in reading disabled children, virtually all of them are in some way addressed by some direct skills approach. Common problems include:

1. Poor oral reading, with omissions, additions, and distortions of words (American Psychiatric Assoc. 1980)
2. Poor reading comprehension (American Psychiatric Assoc. 1980)
3. Language deficits (Stanovich 1986)
4. Poor listening skills (Stanovich 1986)
5. Poor usage of cognitive strategies (Torgesen & Licht 1983, Stanovich 1986)
6. Poor short-term memory—which appears to stem from language deficits and cognitive strategy deficits (Stanovich 1986, Torgesen 1985)
7. Attentional problems (Krupski 1986)

Many techniques developed by direct skills approaches are not limited to reading disabled children. It will be obvious that many can be used with any child who has difficulty learning in a number of areas. The following sections look at three broad approaches to remediation that can be considered direct skills approaches. Each of these has generated extensive interest, intervention techniques, and a body of research evaluating its effectiveness. These approaches are direct instruction, applied behavior analysis, and cognitive-behavior modification.

Direct Instruction

During the mid-seventies, the term *direct instruction* began to be used simultaneously by a number of researchers (Rosenshine 1978). The term refers to a variety of different programs and learning situations with a common premise and common characteristics (Rosenshine 1978). The common premise: the best way to teach reading and other academic skills is to analyze the task into its component skills and then teach each of these components directly and systematically. In this way, each new component is built on a foundation that is carefully laid and controlled (Becker et al. 1981). Common characteristics of direct instruction programs are: (1) learning is teacher directed, (2) learning materials are structured and sequenced, and (3) students are involved in direct learning activities for a high ratio of their class time (Rosenshine 1978).

The best known of the direct instruction programs are those developed by Siegfried Engelmann and his colleagues (see Engelmann & Carnine 1982). Engelmann pioneered the concept and was the first to use the term in 1969 (Rosenshine 1978, Tarver 1986). He believed that many children failed to learn because basal programs assumed skills that many low-performance children simply lacked (Becker et al. 1981). He set out to design an approach that could both prevent and remediate skill deficiencies (Becker et al. 1981, 1982). Today, the term direct instruction is sometimes used synonymously with the many programs developed by Engelmann and his colleagues (Tarver 1986). It is these that will be discussed. They are referred to as DI.

DI programs are packaged multilevel programs that are appropriate for all ability levels, including learning disabled children. Programs have been developed in reading, decoding skills, comprehension, language, spelling, and math. Others, in expository and cursive writing, vocabulary, library and reference skills, and science, are at various stages of development and use (Becker et al. 1982, Tarver 1986). Each is broadly based, teaching numerous skills and concepts.

The goal of DI programs is to teach more in less time (Becker et al. 1982). To accomplish this, every aspect of a program is meticulously planned and extensively researched. Each begins with a detailed logical analysis that identifies the concepts and skills to be taught, breaks them down into their component parts, and identifies the relationships of each component with the others.

Once the content of programs is determined, analysis shifts to the most effective way to teach each of the component concepts and skills. Each is systematically taught so it builds upon the foundation of those preceding it. Individual concepts and skills are then intricately interrelated with one another, not only within a single program but across all DI programs. In this way, higher level strategies are developed that can be applied to a wide range of situations and problems. Higher level thinking skills are also taught. Examples are organizational skills, reasoning, identifying faulty logic, making inferences, and so forth (Tarver 1986). All DI programs are extensively tested for their effectiveness and modified accordingly (Tarver 1986).

Perhaps the best descriptive statement to summarize DI programs is that they leave nothing to chance. For example: (1) Teachers are given scripted lessons, pretested for their effectiveness. (2) Strategies to facilitate and maintain student motivation and interest are incorporated into lessons. (3) Instructional sequences and materials are designed to maximize success. (For example, each component skill is taught individually to develop readiness for more complex skills.) (4) Meaningfulness is consistently maximized. (For example, relationships between new and previously learned material are always stressed.) (5) The teaching techniques used have been demonstrated empirically to be effective. (6) Generalization of material is specifically taught rather than assumed. (7) Assessment of students' progress is made every two weeks, so that potential problems are corrected before they can spiral. (8) Finally, implementation of DI programs is easy. Groups of between 5 and 15 students can be taught effectively, and aides can be trained in one or two weeks to use programs (Becker et al. 1981, 1982).

The research evaluating DI programs has led many authors to conclude there is strong support for their effectiveness across a variety of populations, including learning disabled children (e.g., Becker et al. 1982; Forness & Kavale 1983; Gerstein 1982, 1983; Koorland 1986; Lloyd, Epstein & Cullinan 1981; Tarver 1986). Two examples of research studying DI effectiveness may help to explain the enthusiasm some have shown for these programs.

Project Follow Through was a large-scale national study comparing thirteen model educational programs designed to teach economically disadvantaged children (Abt Associates 1976, 1977). Children were evaluated from kindergarten through third grade on tests of reading, language, word knowledge, spelling, math computation, math concepts, math problem-solving, and self-esteem. Stanford Research Institute collected the data and Abt Associates analyzed it. Of the thirteen model programs studied, the positive gains made by children in DI programs generally were the largest and most consistent across all measures.

The second example is an eight-year series of studies conducted in Australia by Maggs and Maggs (see Becker et al. 1982). These studies tested the effectiveness of the DI program *Distar* with a diverse population of children, ranging from the very brightest to those with a variety of learning problems. The program was reported to be effective (by both norm-referenced and criterion-referenced measures) across populations, whether used in regular classrooms or special classes. In one study, Distar was found to produce marked year-end gains in skills for all groups of children in a class that was so heterogeneous that most American educators would find it incomprehensible. The class consisted of 35 children, ages 7 to 9, whose IQs ranged from borderline defective to very superior and whose basic skills had a six-year spread!

DI programs are published by Science Research Associates. Additional information about DI programs can be found in Becker and others (1981, 1982), Carnine and Silbert (1979), and Engelmann and Carnine (1982).

The following section discusses a second broad approach within the direct skills school of thought.

Applied Behavior Analysis

As in other direct skills approaches, applied behavior analysis focuses on the learner's deficient academic skills and how these skills can best be taught, rather than on deficits underlying his learning problems. Adherents to this approach do not deny that such deficits exist, but they deny that the deficits must be the focus of remediation (Treiber & Lahey 1983).

Applied behavior analysis is not a remedial program per se. Rather, it offers procedures for remediation. Basically, it is the systematic application of learning principles and can be used in conjunction with many types of remedial instruction to make them more effective (Neeper & Lahey 1984). As Treiber and Lahey (1983) point out:

> Because learning disabled children are, by definition, less able than most children to benefit from classroom instruction, it is necessary to maximize the conditions of learning for them. This means that the teaching method must be based more precisely on the principles of learning than is necessary for other children (p. 114).

This approach is sometimes called academic behavior therapy (Neeper & Lahey 1984).

The applied behavior analysis approach has three characteristics (Treiber & Lahey 1983):

1. Academic skills are taught directly.
2. Children are individually assessed on academic skills, learn at their own pace, and master one skill before proceeding to the next.
3. Performance is repeatedly measured to determine progress.

A more detailed look at applications of this approach will clarify its use in the remediation of learning problems. These applications will be discussed within the framework of the three common characteristics just mentioned. However, these characteristics will be discussed slightly out of order. Measurement will be discussed first since it is basic to a discussion of the other two characteristics.

Measurement. The frequent measurement of performance is an integral part of applied behavior analysis that distinguishes it from other programs (Koorland 1986). Measurement is not difficult and the measure taken can be quite simple. It can be the number of correct answers or errors in arithmetic, spelling, comprehension, oral reading, punctuation, or any other academic skill.

Each time a measure is taken, it is plotted on a graph. This provides a clear picture of whether the learner is progressing or not. Measurement should be frequent (daily is ideal, but perhaps not feasible). A measure of a youngster's initial performance level should, of course, be taken so that her progress can be judged against it (Koorland 1986).

Measurement is used not only to assess children's progress. It is used to assess the effectiveness of the teaching strategy or type of instruction currently in use. With progress objectively assessed on a frequent basis, day-to-day instructional decisions can be made. If a particular approach has not been proving effective, another can be tried. For example, a teacher may wonder if it is effective to teach children how to use mnemonic techniques to help them remember new material. She may, perhaps, wish to know whether a different method of teaching multiplication would be more effective than her standard one. Or she may wish to know if her use of flash cards is improving a child's ability to recognize words.

Measurement provides practitioners with objective information about the effectiveness of a particular strategy with a particular child. It also allows a comparison of the effectiveness of different strategies (Lloyd, Epstein & Cullinan 1981). Thus, although this approach focuses on skills, it is very responsive to the individual child.

Skills Are Taught Directly. Applied behavior analysis maintains that skills should be taught directly. It does not recommend specific teaching techniques but recognizes that there are a plethora of strategies, curricula, techniques, and sequences that can be employed to teach academic skills directly. The approach points out that *any* curricula will be made more effective by applying basic learning principles. A number of behavioral interventions that have been researched with learning disabled children will be discussed, along with examples of the research.

Reinforcement. The frustration and demoralization that chronic school failure is likely to create in a child has been pointed out by several investigators (e.g., Torgesen & Licht 1983). As discussed in chapter 7, it is not difficult to see how a child may become trapped in a vicious cycle: chronic failure leading to poor motivation and withdrawal of effort, leading to further failure. Reinforcement is a way to break this vicious cycle and actively involve a child in learning.

The majority of behavioral studies have used some type of reinforcement, either alone or in conjunction with another intervention. Reinforcements have included verbal praise, pennies, desirable activities, and token systems (in which earned tokens, points, or even check marks could be traded for desirable objects or activities [Koorland 1986]).

An example is a study conducted by Lahey and his colleagues (1973), in which children's correct answers to reading comprehension questions were reinforced with praise and pennies. Children's accuracy was increased two grade levels by this program. In another study, Schumaker and her colleagues (1977a) found that junior high school students improved their grades (both in resource rooms and in mainstream classrooms) when they could exchange points earned in school for privileges at home. These investigators went on to demonstrate that the reinforcement program could be gradually faded and finally eliminated for some of the students without their grades decreasing (1977b).

Many teachers find it unfeasible to consistently reinforce each child for his or her correct performance. They may be relieved to know that intermittent reinforcement (that is, reinforcement given on an unpredictable schedule) also improves children's performance levels. Although consistent reinforcement may be needed for LD children while they are initially learning skills (Treiber & Lahey 1983), intermittent reinforcement may be more effective at later stages because it keeps alive their interest in the rewards (Koorland 1986). Koorland (1986) suggests interesting ways to implement intermittent schedules of reinforcement: reinforcement can be given on the basis of the average performance of the group, for the work of a randomly selected individual in the group, or on the basis of whether a card is selected from a container that says "points today" or "no points today."

Performance Feedback. Providing learning disabled children with a visual display of their progress (graph or chart) has significantly improved their performance in diverse areas, such as oral reading, arithmetic computation, science test scores, and the formation of cursive letters (see Thorpe, Chiang & Darch 1981). Usually some type of reinforcement is given for improved performance.

Although many teachers find the procedure time consuming, performance feedback does not have to be provided at the individual level. Group feedback is also effective, and it is much easier to implement: the number of correct or incorrect answers for the group are merely tallied and transferred to a single graph. Reinforcement can be given either for the average performance of group members or for the performance of randomly selected members (Thorpe, Chiang & Darch 1981).

A study conducted by Thorpe and his colleagues (1981) found that group and individual performance feedback were equally effective in improving the oral reading accuracy of fifth-grade students in an LD resource room. These authors point out that, when feasible, graphs should reflect success rates rather than errors.

Prompts and Fading Techniques. The use of "prompts" has been found to be effective with learning disabled children (Neeper & Lahey 1984). A prompt is more or less a crutch that a child can use to help him learn unfamiliar material. An example is pairing a picture with each new word he must learn. Another common example is exaggerating the distinguishing characteristics of similar letters (for example, with color or size), so that the child's attention will be drawn to the minor dissimilarities rather than to the many similarities in the letters.

Of course, there is the danger that children will simply rely on the prompt and never learn the material. To prevent this, the prompt is faded gradually. For example, if the stem of the letter "R" has been marked in red to help a child distinguish it from the letter "P," the red stem can be faded by gradually covering the red with black so that it becomes increasingly similar in color to the remainder of the "R."

Modeling, Practice, and Reinforcement. This strategy has been found effective for teaching learning disabled children highly specific skills, such as multiplication, forming letters, phonics, and identifying sight words (see Neeper & Lahey 1984). Simply, students watch the teacher perform the skill to be learned. Students are then given ample opportunity to practice and rehearse the new skill while they are given immediate feedback about their accuracy. If youngsters are accurate, they are rewarded. If they are inaccurate, the procedure is repeated: teacher demonstration of the procedure, student practice, and teacher feedback about performance.

Blankenship and Baumgartner (1982) improved learning disabled children's accuracy on subtraction problems by using this simple but systematic procedure for a six-day period. (Although children received consistent feedback, their accuracy was reinforced on an intermittent schedule.) The children's initial accuracy on problems was only 18.2 percent. During the six-day learning period, it reached 100 percent. A follow-up found their accuracy to be 76 percent (below that of the training period but well above their initial level).

The measurement and direct teaching characteristics of applied behavior analysis have now been discussed. The following looks at the performance characteristics of this approach.

Individual Assessment, Pacing, and Mastery Learning. In applied behavior analysis, children are individually assessed on skills, they learn at their own pace, and they master one skill before proceeding to the next.

There are a number of ways in which a learner's skill deficiencies can be assessed. Neeper and Lahey (1984) recommend using standardized achievement tests in order to obtain a broad picture of academic functioning. To be most useful, a test should measure a broad range of skills and should yield information about very specific skills that can be targeted for improvement. Test items, suggest Neeper and Lahey, should be similar to tasks performed in the classroom. A standardized test of language functioning is also recommended. This should also be a test that offers information about specific targetable skills. Samples of written work and teacher observations offer good supplemental information.

Once a learner's academic deficits are identified, the question becomes which skills should be targeted for treatment and in what sequence. An obvious question is whether complex skills should be broken into subskills as is done in DI programs. Applied behavior analysis seems to take the stance, "Do what works." As has already been seen, some rather complex skills (reading comprehension, oral reading) have been improved simply by applying behavioral techniques, without first dealing with component skills. Treiber and Lahey (1983) recommend a pragmatic approach. First target global skills that are important in the classroom (oral reading, comprehension, accuracy in written assignments). If intervention is not successful at this level, and for many children it will not be, then focus on subskills with which the child is having difficulty (word attack skills, strategies to improve comprehension, and so forth). Skills should be broken down as far as necessary to ensure a high probability of success. Throughout the process of targeting appropriate skills, measurement will be an invaluable aid.

Measurement will be just as important in determining progress. Gains will be smaller and slower than those of normal achievers, but graphing will provide a clear picture of progress and suggest appropriate instructional strategies. If no progress is made, a new technique can be tried. But keep in mind that very slow progress may indicate a need to increase instructional time.

A recommendation that appears frequently in the LD field is that LD children should learn skills to a level of (1) *mastery* (a high level of accuracy) and (2) *automaticity* (a high level of speed). Over and over again, investigators strongly emphasize that children be given as much practice on skills as needed until they can perform skills accurately and quickly (e.g., Deshler et al. 1983, Goldman & Pellegrino 1987, Liberman et al. 1980, Samuels 1987, Torgesen 1986). Both accuracy and speed on basic skills (for example, word recognition) are necessary before more complex skills can be tackled (for example, comprehension). This, of course, contrasts with the approach of many reading programs that provide only a few pages of skill practice before moving on to a new skill (Liberman et al. 1980). The necessity for accuracy and speed in basic skills was discussed in chapter 7.

The Issue of Generalization. The application of general learning principles has been effective in improving a number of academic skills in learning disabled children, including reading comprehension, oral reading, sight word vocabulary, letter identification, spelling, handwriting, and arithmetic (see Gadow, Torgesen & Dahlem 1983; Koorland 1986; Treiber & Lahey 1983). However, enthusiasm must be tempered because most of the research has looked at improvement only on a short-term basis. Additionally, most experiments have employed very small numbers of children.

Two important issues now must be addressed (Koorland 1986): Will learned skills be maintained? (Will they continue to be used for long periods of time?) And, will skills generalize? (Will a skill learned in a resource room be used in the regular classroom? Will learning sight words in isolation make reading more fluent?) Researchers are now addressing these questions and designing experiments to answer them. Investigators are beginning to include follow-up and generalization measures, such as determining if the skill is being used several months later in the regular classroom. Recent studies report that some generalization does occur. However, the improvement in the generalized setting has not been as dramatic as that in the experimental setting (see Gadow, Torgesen & Dahlem 1983).

Many object to a behavioral approach, arguing that it is too superficial. It has been criticized because of its focus on behavior and because of its reliance on externally imposed events (see Rooney & Hallahan 1985). Prompts, fades, feedback charts, reinforcement, and so forth are effective teaching devices, but they are events that are external to the learner. In a sense, the learner is a passive participant in the learning process. For this reason, some question the extent to which youngsters will apply newly learned skills in new situations.

The discussion will now turn to an approach that developed in response to these objections. This approach also falls within the direct skills school of thought and has been responsible for a good share of the current research in the area of LD remediation.

Cognitive-Behavior Modification

Cognitive-behavior modification addresses the criticisms raised against a strict behavioral approach (Rooney & Hallahan 1985). Rather than relying on external events to improve academic skills, it entices the child into being an active participant in charge of her own learning. Rather than influencing only her academic skills, it attempts to change her thinking about learning.

This approach is championed by some of its supporters as a way in which LD children may compensate for their deficits (Ryan, Weed & Short 1986). Like other direct skills approaches, it does not deny that these children have underlying deficits, but it maintains that the most effective treatment of a problem may not be directly related to its origin (see Ryan, Weed & Short 1986).

The cognitive-behavior modification approach (CBM) addresses many problems commonly observed in LD children, but primarily it focuses on their deficient strategic behavior in learning situations. As discussed in chapter 7, it has been a recurrent finding that a large percentage of the LD population are deficient in learning strategies. For example, in memory tasks, they are unlikely to verbally rehearse material, group similar items together, or employ mnemonic devices. When reading, they are unlikely to monitor their understanding of material or to selectively attend to important information. When faced with a problem that requires strategic behavior, they commonly seem at a loss. They are unaware of the variety of learning strategies available. They are unable to judge whether a strategy is appropriate to a task. In fact, many seem to be unaware that strategic behavior is necessary (see Hallahan, Kneedler & Lloyd 1983; Hallahan & Sapona 1983; Ryan, Weed & Short 1986; Short & Ryan 1984; Swanson 1987a,b; Torgesen & Licht 1983). Such strategy deficits would interfere with school performance in many areas, including all those involving memory, problem-solving, or reading. CBM also addresses two other problems commonly found in LD children: attentional problems (see Krupski 1986) and impulsiveness when responding to tasks (see Blackman & Goldstein 1982). Once again, all learning disabled children do not have these characteristics, but a large percentage do.

Basically, CBM techniques teach children how to behave strategically in learning situations. They teach children how to approach tasks slowly and systematically, how to guide themselves through a step-by-step plan that will lead to the successful solution of a problem, and how to keep themselves attending to the task. It is reasoned that this self-guiding process should help LD children grasp the relationships between the task, their actions, and successful outcomes of their actions. Additionally, children are taught how and why strategies are useful to them (Hallahan, Kneedler & Lloyd 1983; Ryan, Weed & Short 1986). Some researchers recommend that strategy instruction become an integral part of instructional programs for LD children (e.g., Palincsar & Brown 1987).

CBM incorporates numerous programs and strategies. Most fall within the framework of three general procedures: self-instruction, self-monitoring, and cognitive strategy training. Each of these, its applications, and the research evidence that has been gathered to date will be discussed.

Self-Instruction. Self-instruction, the first CBM technique to be used with learning disabled children, was pioneered by Meichenbaum (see Meichenbaum 1977). Children have been taught to guide themselves through various academic tasks using this technique. It is somewhat akin to a think-aloud training program (Ryan, Weed & Short 1986).

The set of self-instructions generally has five components. (These steps and many of the examples appear in Ryan, Weed & Short [1986].)

1. *Planning.* This first step prevents children from responding impulsively. (For example, "How do I begin? I think about what I have to do. I need to work slowly and carefully.")

2. *Strategy instruction.* In this step, children must focus on the requirements of a problem. (For example, "What kind of problem is this? I look at the sign. It is a multiplication problem. What is it I do?" Any type of strategy can be taught here. Strategies are step-by-step procedures which children follow to complete a task. Examples of strategies are given later in this section.

3. *Self-monitoring.* Here the child monitors his own progress. ("Am I following my plan?" or "Is the answer right?")

4. *Correcting errors.* ("I made a mistake. I'll try again.") Sometimes instructions are also included to help children cope with failure and frustration. (For example, "I made a mistake, but it's OK. I can do it again.")

5. *Self-reinforcement.* ("I finished. My answer is right. I did a good job.") Self-reinforcement is an important last step. Evidence suggests that self-reinforcement may be more effective than reinforcement given by a teacher and even more effective than tangible rewards.

See Hallahan, Kauffman, and Lloyd (1985) for specific guidelines to develop and teach a set of self-instructions.

How effective has self-instruction been? This research has been reviewed by Hallahan, Kneedler, and Lloyd (1983) and by Ryan, Weed, and Short (1986). Generally, attempts to teach learning disabled children very broad strategies have not resulted in improved academic performance. A broad strategy consists of a plan of attack for virtually any task and therefore has very general steps. An example is a "Stop, Look, Listen, Think" strategy (Lloyd 1980). The ineffectiveness of such a broad strategy is not really very surprising, according to Hallahan and his colleagues (1983). For it to be effective, a child must already have the skills required for a specific task. And even if she does have the skills, she must be able to recognize that they are needed in a situation. Such broad strategies may be too general to be successfully applied by learning disabled children.

Using the self-instruction technique to teach specific strategies has been more successful in improving academic performance. Examples of specific strategies will be given shortly; basically, they guide the child through specific academic tasks. Reading comprehension, math performance, handwriting, and homework completion are examples of academic skills which have been improved by teaching LD children specific strategies through self-instruction (Fish & Mendola 1986; Leon & Pepe, cited in Wong 1985; see Ryan 1981).

Self-Monitoring. Recall that self-instruction procedures included a self-monitoring component in which the child monitored his own performance. "Am I keeping to my plan?" "Is my answer right?" Self-monitoring is sometimes used as a treatment procedure by itself (Hallahan, Kneedler & Lloyd 1983).

When self-monitoring alone is used, the learner not only evaluates whether she is keeping to her plan but keeps a record as well (Rooney & Hallahan 1985). Once again, children are involved actively, and the relationships between their actions and the outcomes of their actions are made very salient to them.

By far the most well known and heavily researched application of self-monitoring with LD children has been to reduce attentional problems and increase on-task behavior. This has been an ongoing research endeavor of Daniel Hallahan and his colleagues at the University of Virginia Learning Disabilities Research Institute (e.g., Hallahan, Kneedler & Lloyd 1983; Hallahan, Lloyd & Stoller 1982; Hallahan & Reeve 1980; Hallahan & Sapona 1983; Rooney & Hallahan 1985).

The attentional problems that are often characteristic of children with a variety of learning problems were discussed in chapter 7 and have been reviewed by Krupski (1986). It is not unreasonable to assume that these attentional problems play a role in school failure. Hallahan's self-monitoring procedure was designed to reduce these problems, with the expectation that improved academic performance will follow.

There are several variations of the procedure. Basically, an audio cue is sounded at intervals throughout the time children are working. (The cue is provided by a timer or a tape recorder with prerecorded beeps.) At the sound of the cue, each child records on a sheet (in a "yes" or "no" column) whether he or she is paying attention. (Teachers train children how to recognize whether they are paying attention by modeling examples of on-task and off-task behavior. They also "test" children's understanding.)

Hallahan's self-monitoring program has been successful in increasing LD children's attentional behavior (validated by independent observers). It also has been successful in increasing youngsters' academic productivity. Improvements have continued at least throughout a ten-week follow-up period (Hallahan, Kneedler & Lloyd 1983). Evidence suggests that the procedure can be implemented in a mainstream classroom with children as young as second-graders. However, when used in this larger context, reinforcement is likely to be needed to induce children to use the procedure consistently (see Hallahan & Sapona 1983).

Procedures also have been developed to wean children from their dependence on the audio cue and the self-recording procedure. Eventually, the cue is replaced by the child asking herself (whenever she thinks of it), "Am I paying attention?" Self-recording is replaced by the youngster praising herself if she is on-task and instructing herself to pay attention if she is off-task.

Hallahan and his colleagues believe the attention-monitoring procedure works most effectively when children already have the skills necessary to stay on-task. They do not recommend its use when children are first learning skills (Hallahan, Kneedler & Lloyd 1983). Hallahan, Lloyd, and Stoller (1982) have written a manual for teachers who wish to implement self-monitoring of attention in their classroom.

Cognitive Strategy Training. Children also have been trained to use strategy skills without resorting to elaborate use of self-instruction and self-monitoring, although these usually are used to some extent. This approach is called cognitive strategy training or attack strategy training (Lloyd 1980). Strategy training has been used effectively with LD children in the areas of arithmetic, problem-solving, test-taking, reading comprehension, and memory performance (see Deshler, Schumaker, Lenz & Ellis 1984; Mastropieri, Scruggs & Levin 1985; Ryan, Weed & Short 1986).

Mnemonic techniques are examples of attack strategies that have been used successfully with LD children (Elliott & Gentile 1986; Mastropieri, Scruggs & Levin 1985). Mastropieri and her colleagues (1985) report good success with a mnemonic technique called the *Keyword Method.* In their 1985 article, they describe the method fully and review the relevant research.

Examples of many other strategies to improve performance in a variety of areas can be found in Alley and Deshler (1979) and in Palincsar and Brown (1987).

Examples of strategies to improve reading comprehension will be looked at. Several types of cognitive strategies have improved the comprehension of reading disabled students. Examples include teaching children to ask themselves questions about the text before reading, teaching them to paraphrase each section of the text as they read it, and teaching them how to organize the material through the use of visual imagery (see Ryan, Weed & Short 1986). Following are two examples of comprehension strategies reported in the literature. Carnine and Silbert (1979) provide others.

In a study conducted by Short and Ryan (1984), children were required to verbalize a set of five questions to themselves, to find and underline the answers in the text, and to indicate in the margin the question answered. The five questions follow:

1. *Who* is the main character?
2. *Where* and *when* did the story take place?
3. *What* did the main characters do?
4. *How* did the story end?
5. *How* did the main characters feel?

The questions provided a framework to organize the information in the story. This is something reading disabled children generally do not do on their own and therefore must be specifically taught. When used, the comprehension performance of these poor readers did not differ significantly from that of skilled readers.

A second example was provided by Wong and Jones (1982), who taught eighth- and ninth-grade reading disabled students a five-step self-questioning procedure to monitor their reading comprehension. This procedure is appropriate for reading textbooks in subject areas as well as stories. In the five steps, students were to:

1. Determine why they were reading or studying the material
2. Find the main ideas and underline them
3. Think of questions about the main (underlined) ideas
4. Learn the answers to their questions
5. Determine how each of their questions and answers provided them with information

Once again, training was effective in improving comprehension for these reading disabled children.

The Issue of Generalization. CBM researchers are now focusing their attention on the issue of generalization. They are asking how they can ensure that newly learned strategies will be used in new situations. Generally, when strategies are taught in isolation, poor generalization has been found (Ryan, Weed & Short 1986). However, many procedures have been developed that increase the likelihood that students will use the newly learned strategies in new situations (see Deshler et al. 1983; Ellis, Lenz & Sabornie 1987a,b; Palincsar & Brown 1987; Ryan, Weed & Short 1986; Schumaker, Deshler & Ellis 1986). Some examples follow:

1. Make the usefulness of a strategy very salient to the student. One way to do this is to give students specific feedback about their improved performance when they use the strategy. Graphing their performance is one good approach.

2. Combine a self-monitoring procedure with strategy training. Students then learn to plan and self-check their strategy use. The more that students take over the strategy as their own, the more likely they are to use it in new situations.

3. Specifically teach students how to generalize strategies and provide them with many generalization experiences. Students also can be asked to think of additional situations in which the strategy will be useful to them. Have them practice strategies in their mainstream classrooms and discuss their progress with the LD teacher.

4. Enlist the aid of mainstream teachers to remind and encourage students to use strategies.

5. Have the student practice the strategy until it is overlearned and therefore can be used automatically.

Ellis and others (1987a,b) point out that generalization should be a major focus at all phases of strategy instruction: prior to instruction, during instruction, and subsequent to instruction. In a very extensive treatment of the topic, these investigators provide many suggestions of how generalization can be focused upon at each instructional phase (Ellis, Lenz & Sabornie 1987a,b). Additionally, Ryan and her colleagues (1986) suggest that reinforcement be used initially in order to encourage student use of strategies.

The following is an example of a comprehensive program, designed on cognitive-behavior modification principles, that has been the focus of extensive research and interest.

The Strategies Intervention Model. This program is the brainchild of Donald Deshler and Jean Schumaker and their colleagues at the University of Kansas Institute for Research in Learning Disabilities. One of the five learning disabilities research institutes funded by the U.S. Department of Education, the Kansas Institute has devoted its research efforts to developing an effective and feasible intervention program for learning disabled adolescents (Schumaker, Deshler & Ellis 1986).

The strategies intervention model is based on practical grounds. Researchers asked in what way the greatest impact could be made on the lives of learning disabled adolescents in their few remaining years in school. The fact is that most LD adolescents are in resource rooms for only one to two hours a day (Deshler, Lowrey & Alley 1979). For the remainder of the day, most are mainstreamed in regular classes where, in order to cope, they need skills in listening, memory, problem-solving, note-taking, writing, and functioning independently (Deshler et al. 1983).

These researchers decided that the greatest impact could be made by teaching learning disabled teens how to learn. A complete description of the program can be found in Deshler and others (1983) and Schumaker, Deshler and Ellis (1986). Only a very brief description will follow.

The program systematically teaches (1) specific learning strategies, (2) general strategies, and (3) how to generalize strategies to new situations.

Specific learning strategies have been designed to develop skills in reading, writing, math, listening, speaking, and thinking. They include some strategies already discussed, such as paraphrasing, self-questioning, and visual imagery (see Clark et al. 1984 for descriptions). Other specific strategies deal with sentence-writing, paragraph organization, listening, note-taking, error-monitoring, and obtaining information from textbook chapters.

The strategies that are taught depend upon a student's deficiencies and school needs. The Kansas group teaches strategies in a step-by-step procedure in which the strategy is described, its rationale is given, and its steps are modeled. Students rehearse the steps verbally and extensively practice until the strategy is learned to a level of mastery and automaticity. While practicing, students are given immediate feedback on their performance. Of course, pre- and post-testing are always included (see Deshler et al. 1983, p. 267). Strategies are taught to students in groups within the resource room.

Since LD children have difficulty determining when a specific strategy should be used, general strategies are taught after several specific strategies have been learned. The specific strategies can be thought of as the tools and the general strategies (sometimes called *executive strategies*) as the means by which to determine when and where to use which tools and why. Executive strategies help students to assess a situation and to determine its requirements.

One such executive strategy is SMART, a self-instructional strategy in which students must question themselves about the situation and determine (as well as verbalize) the appropriate answers. In SMART, a student sets a goal (S), makes a plan (M), attempts the plan (A), reviews the plan, assessing progress made and whether additional work is needed to reach the goal (R), and assesses how hard he tried (T).

Recall that attempts to teach LD children *only* very broad strategies generally have not resulted in improved academic performance. Before general strategies can be effective, students must have the specific skills needed for a task. It is believed that the procedure of teaching specific strategies before general strategies eliminates this shortcoming of general strategies for many students.

The Kansas research group places a heavy emphasis on generalization. Many of the procedures developed to increase the likelihood of generalization were developed and researched by this group.

Every attempt is made in the program to involve students at every phase of the learning process, including instructional decisions. This increases the likelihood that students will have a vested interest in the program and that they will assume "ownership" of the strategies they learn. The more students feel that the strategies are their own, the more likley they are to use them spontaneously.

The strategies intervention model is an ongoing research effort. Although it continues to be developed, modified, and validated, it is being used successfully in schools, with teachers and students generally reporting their satisfaction. In general, research has yielded favorable results. Not only can LD adolescent students learn the strategies (both specific and executive), but they can appropriately apply strategies to grade-level material (see Deshler et al. 1983; Deshler, Schumaker, Lenz & Ellis 1984; Schumaker, Deshler & Ellis 1986). Furthermore, strategy use by LD students is found to improve both course grades and scores on standardized tests (Deshler, Schumaker, Lenz & Ellis 1984). Some research results have been rather startling. Schumaker and her colleagues (1986) reported that some LD students who had mastered particular strategies earned A and B grades in regular classrooms. Strategy training has improved basic skills as well. Students who were receiving strategy training 75 percent of their time in the resource room showed twice the improvement in basic skills (measured by standardized tests) as did LD students in other programs (Schumaker, Deshler & Ellis 1986).

Some youngsters benefit from strategy training more than others do. Since generalization of skills is not consistently found for all students, generalization remains a significant focus of research conducted by the Kansas group (Deshler et al. 1983; Deshler, Schumaker & Lenz 1984).

The following approach is currently attracting wide attention in the learning disabilities field and is beginning to make its mark on remedial efforts.

The Neuropsychological Approach: Fine-Tuning Remediation

Given the recent emphasis in the literature on learning disabilities subtypes (see chapter 7), it may seem strange that no mention has been made of prescribing remedial programs for different subtypes of children. Unfortunately, subtyping research is only in the preliminary stages of generating specific remedial programs for different types of learning disabilities.

However, neuropsychologists appear to be making some progress towards fine-tuning remediation. They can, to some degree, do this on the basis of a child's neuropsychological profile. Profiles are obtained from extensive neuropsychological test batteries that measure a child's functioning across a wide range of abilities, such as abstract concept formation, reasoning, memory, ability to categorize, language, perception, attention, coordination, and so forth. Testing provides information about possible neuropsychological involvement, if any, and about a child's level of performance. But most importantly, it will delineate patterns of her strengths and deficits in each of the areas tested (Chadwick & Rutter 1983; Hynd, Snow & Becker 1986; Knights & Stoddart 1981).

Some neuropsychologists are now beginning to step beyond their traditional role as diagnosticians and become directly involved in developing remedial programs for individual learning disabled children. Although they have no crystal balls, neuropsychologists can form educated hunches about what will work effectively with a particular child on the basis of his diagnostic profile. Neuropsychologists use combinations of all remedial techniques, trying to match an appropriate teaching strategy with a child's abilities and disabilities (Gaddes 1985). Although there is some theoretical disagreement about whether remediation should take a deficit-based approach (trying to improve a child's weaknesses) or a strength-based approach (working with a child's strengths), most neuropsychologists, in practice, use a combination of the two.

Hartlage and Reynolds (1981) believe the neuropsychological approach has the potential to reduce the anxiety, frustration, and humiliation so commonly caused by chronic school failure, because it can capitalize on a child's identified strengths. And when neuropsychological deficits are very severe, the neuropsychologist can often recommend untraditional ways to approximate educational goals for a child. Hartlage and Telzrow (1983) refer to this as an instructional detour. An example is using a calculator for math problems, which may be the only realistic solution for some severely disabled students. Gaddes (1985) points out that solutions may be rather creative at times, as in the case of a child who cannot learn the alphabet due to a left hemisphere dysfunction. The solution? Teach him to sing it.

The neuropsychological approach is a promising one. For example, one study (cited in Hartlage & Telzrow 1983) found that when children were assigned to an instructional program matched to their neuropsychological strengths, they made significantly greater gains than did students randomly assigned to the same programs.

In spite of its promise, however, this approach is not yet widely employed. Neuropsychologists are only recently becoming involved in remediation. Moreover, there is considerable expense involved since testing is very time consuming and must be done by a highly trained neuropsychologist (Gaddes 1981). Some (e.g., Gaddes 1981) suggest that neuropsychological testing be used selectively with certain children who can particularly benefit from it. Examples are a child who is obviously neurologically impaired or a child who cannot seem to progress in the remedial program in which she has been placed.

The neuropsychological batteries most widely used are the Halstead-Reitan and the Luria-Nebraska (Hynd, Snow & Becker 1986). The Halstead-Reitan consists of the Halstead Neuropsychological Test Battery for children (ages 9 to 14) and the Reitan-Indiana Neuropsychological Test Battery (ages 5 to 8). Research suggests the Halstead-Reitan is more effective in differentiating LD children than is the Luria-Nebraska (Hynd, Snow & Becker 1986). In practice, most neuropsychologists use a neuropsychological battery as a core but also administer many other tests as well.

There Are No Remedial Shortcuts

If there is any agreement in the learning disabilities field at this point, it is probably that there are no shortcuts to remediation. Evidence is accumulating that for learning disabled children to make gains, a substantial amount of time must be devoted to systematic remediation (see Forness & Kavale 1983). According to Forness and Kavale, the growing consensus from research is that: (1) instruction should be intense, individualized, and focused on direct instruction of academic skills the child lacks, and (2) specific instructional decisions should be guided by ongoing observation and measurement.

That learning disabled children require large amounts of time devoted to remediation has been clearly demonstrated (see Gutherie, Martuza & Seifert 1979; Torgesen 1986). For example, Gutherie and his colleagues (1979) concluded, both from their own research and that of others, that gains made by poor readers are affected more by the amount of instruction than by the specific reading program used. They firmly state that amount of instruction has emerged as an important variable in determining the progress made by reading disabled children.

Conclusions that remedial efforts should be very intense are fueled by findings such as those reported by Finucci and her colleagues (1985). These investigators conducted a long-term follow-up of over 500 men who, as children, had been identified as dyslexic. These men had all attended a private boarding school for dyslexic boys at some time during their junior high or high school years. In addition to content courses, the school provided intense and systematic instruction and practice in reading skills, language skills, language structure, phonics, and word roots. As adults, more than 50 percent of this large sample had graduated from four-year colleges. About 50 percent were engaged in managerial work, and another 18 percent held professional and technical positions. Sixty percent reported they enjoyed leisure reading. These findings are in marked contrast to most longitudinal studies which have found generally poor outcomes in adulthood for learning disabled children (see Schonhaut & Satz 1983). It is obvious that children with the opportunity to attend such a school did not comprise a representative LD sample. Nevertheless, results hold out promise for what is potentially achievable by some reading disabled children who receive the benefit of intense and systematic instruction.

The educational experience of these 500 dyslexic men was in marked contrast to that available to most reading disabled children today. The most common form of help provided LD students in this country is special assistance in a resource room (McNutt 1986), generally for one to two hours a day (Deshler, Lowrey & Alley 1979). During the remainder of the day, students are mainstreamed in regular classrooms.

Several investigators have asked how much instruction LD students actually receive. To determine this, they have conducted observational studies and have recorded the amount of time learning disabled students actually spent on remedial activities (Haynes & Jenkins 1986; Leinhardt, Zigmond & Cooley 1981; Schumaker et al., n.d.; Thurlow et al. 1982). Consider the results of these studies: In one study, only 44 percent of the time specifically scheduled for reading instruction was actually spent on reading activities (only 25 percent for direct reading and 19 percent for supportive reading activities). The remaining 56 percent of the time was spent in off-task behavior, waiting, management activities, and "academic other" (Haynes & Jenkins 1986). Observations of resource rooms revealed that students spent only 18 minutes of each hour actively engaged in remedial work (Schumaker et al., n.d.). Observations of elementary self-contained LD classrooms revealed that children received an average of 16 minutes per day in general reading instruction and another 14 minutes in silent reading (Leinhardt, Zigmond & Cooley 1981). A fourth study reported that LD students spent only 12 percent of their day actively engaged in academic tasks (Thurlow et al. 1982); this was estimated to be 45 minutes per day (Ysseldyke 1983).

Academic Engaged Time

The reason the time spent on remediation is so abysmally small in some of these studies is that it reflects *academic engaged time*. Although it is true that amount of time allotted to instruction is related to progress, not surprisingly, what is done during that time is more critical (see Gutherie, Martuza & Seifert 1979; Rosenshine 1978). You might think of academic engaged time as the quality of time, and amount of time as the quantity. Academic engaged time, sometimes called *academic response time*, has been found to be highly related to achievement (see Schumaker, Deshler & Ellis 1986).

Just what exactly is academic engaged time? Basically, it is the proportion of instructional time that students are actively responding to academic tasks—that is, tasks in which they can be expected to learn skills or content (Gutherie & Seifert 1978; Stanley & Greenwood, cited in Schumaker, Deshler & Ellis 1986). For example, of the activities often included within the allotted time for reading instruction, the following have been found to be related to reading achievement: phonics, word drill, and reading itself. Many other activities included during reading instruction have been found to be unrelated to reading achievement, such as discussion of stories, dramatization, writing, and artwork (Harris & Serwer 1966), although they probably increase motivation and interest. According to Schumaker and her colleagues, passive activities, such as listening to a lecture or watching a movie, should not be considered as academic engaged time. And obviously, the time devoted to management and organizational activities (which Leinhardt, Zigmond, and Cooley [1981] found to be almost an hour a day) is irrelevant to learning. Once again, academic engaged time is reported to be highly related to achievement.

One method of ensuring a high degree of academic engaged time is tutoring, which, incidentally, has resulted in impressive progress with reading disabled children. In a review of research studying remedial reading programs, Gutherie and his colleagues (1979) reported that the major variable that marked effective programs was tutoring. When children learned in groups of three or less, their average reading grade level increased at the rate of 3.7 years for each year of instruction.

Although working intensively with such small groups of children is not always feasible, there are other ways to increase academic engaged time. From the data collected in their large-scale observational study of instructional time in self-contained LD classrooms, Leinhardt and his colleagues (1981) estimated that increasing actual reading instruction only 5 to 10 minutes a day would make a difference to reading disabled children. They pointed out that this small amount of time could easily come from the one hour a day typically devoted to management chores and waiting for teacher-initiated activity. Or it could come from the 50 minutes a day typically devoted to indirect reading activities (discussion of stories, and so forth).

A very realistic means of providing learning disabled students with a high degree of academic engaged time is the use of computers.

The Use of Computers

A recent survey found that 88 percent of school districts currently use computers with learning disabled children (Makros & Russell 1986). If used properly, computers can be a valuable asset in a remedial program. In fact, many researchers take the position that computers are a crucial contribution to LD remediation. Why? Because they are able to provide large amounts of practice on skills already introduced by the teacher (Goldman & Pellegrino 1987, Torgesen 1986).

In general, learning disabled children are deficient in the subskills necessary for academic success (for example, rapid recognition of words, word analysis skills, ability to quickly solve single-digit arithmetic problems, and so forth). Furthermore, it is well documented that these youngsters generally learn these skills at a much slower rate than do normal learners (see Goldman & Pellegrino 1987, Torgesen 1986).

These basic skills must be learned to a level of mastery and automaticity. Otherwise, the learner must focus his attentional capacity on these rather than on more complex tasks, such as reading comprehension (Goldman & Pellegrino 1987). For LD students to achieve a level of mastery and automaticity, extensive practice is required. Such extensive practice via worksheets or drill is drudgery. Computers, on the other hand, are fun. They provide an enjoyable, active, and nonthreatening way for LD children to practice skills until they reach a level of mastery and automaticity (Goldman & Pellegrino 1987, Kolich 1985, Torgesen 1986). With a computer, a student can progress at her own pace, maintain a high level of attention, and receive immediate feedback about the accuracy of her performance (Kolich 1985). Immediate feedback is important so the student does not "practice" incorrect responses (Goldman & Pellegrino 1987).

A study conducted by Young and others (1983) suggests that a substantial amount of time must be devoted to such practice. On the basis of their data, these investigators estimated that for academic skills to be significantly and broadly impacted, LD students should spend approximately one and one-half hours a day practicing basic skills on the computer.

Of course, computers are only as good as their programs, and programs vary widely in their effectiveness in delivering practice. To provide appropriate practice, a program should do the following, according to Torgesen (1986). In the early stages of learning, practice should be limited to a single skill and should be spaced over the course of many days for short periods of time. During the later stages of learning, mixed practice is found to be effective. In mixed practice, several skills already learned are practiced during the same sitting. Finally, a program should gradually increase the speed with which a skill must be performed. This is so that students can reach a level of automaticity (Torgesen 1986). The Hint and Hunt program is reportedly an effective program for increasing both accuracy and speed of word analysis skills (Jones, Torgesen & Sexton 1987). Learning disabled children showed substantial improvements in reading both practice and new words, both in isolation and in context, after using the program for 10 weeks, 15 minutes each day, 5 days per week. The program is published by DLM (Beck & Roth 1984).

Learning Disabilities Subtypes Revisited

The previous chapter ended with the issue of subtypes, and so will this chapter, in order to emphasize the issue's potential importance to the remediation of learning disabilities. It is widely recognized (e.g., Forness & Kavale 1983, Rourke 1983) that the reason more clear-cut results have not been found for the effectiveness of one type of instruction over another is probably due to the fact that the learning disabled population consists of many subtypes. An instructional program may help one subgroup, have no effect on a second, and perhaps be harmful to a third (Rourke 1983). Deshler, Schumaker, Lenz, and Ellis (1984) warn against the temptation to look for the "right" approach to remediation. Rather, attention should be focused on identifying the conditions under which an approach is effective or ineffective.

At this point, the brunt of determining the effectiveness of a given approach for an individual child rests on practitioners. Applied behavior analysis techniques should provide an invaluable tool in this difficult process. Currently, however, it appears that insufficient effort is made, in practice, to gear remediation to the needs of a given child. The University of Minnesota Institute for Research on Learning Disabilities has conducted an ongoing research project studying the assessment and decision-making practices at the elementary school level across the country (e.g., Algozzine & Ysseldyke 1986, Ysseldyke 1983). Ysseldyke (1983) reports that during professional team meetings in which individual children are assessed as learning disabled, typically fewer than five minutes are devoted to the issue of intervention for any given child. Generally, the same intervention (instruction, materials, and techniques) is prescribed, regardless of the child involved.

Until the time that subtyping research has advanced its knowledge to the point of matching subtypes of LD children with treatment programs, or until the time that funds are available for extensive neuropsychological testing of each child, practitioners must be sensitive to the diverse nature of learning disabled children and try to match an appropriate intervention with a given child. Neeley and Lindsley (1978) suggest hedging one's bets with reading disabled children and using two or more reading programs at a time, each with a different emphasis. In this way, diverse needs, strengths, and weaknesses will be met. Forness and Kavale (1983) suggest that the key for practitioners lies in detailed knowledge of remediation research, so that particular treatments can be matched to the needs and characteristics of individual children, as well as conditions in the classrooms. In its admittedly limited space, this chapter has attempted to provide the practitioner with an overview of this research and to furnish additional sources that contain a more detailed treatment of each approach.

References

Abt Associates, Inc. 1976, 1977. *Education as Experimentation: A Planned Variation Model.* Vols. 3, 4. Cambridge, Mass.: Abt Books.

Algozzine, B. & Ysseldyke, J.E. 1986. "The Future of the LD Field: Screening and Diagnosis." *Journal of Learning Disabilities* 19: 394–98.

Alley, G.R. & Deshler, D.D. 1979. *Teaching the Learning Disabled Adolescent: Strategies and Methods.* Denver: Love Publ. Co.

American Psychiatric Association, Committee on Nomenclature and Statistics. 1980. *Diagnostic and Statistical Manual of Mental Disorders.* 3d. ed. (DSM III) Washington, D.C.: American Psychiatric Association.

Beck, J. & Roth, S.F. 1984. *Hint and Hunt I. Teacher's Manual.* Allen, Tex.: Developmental Learning Materials/Teaching Resources.

Becker, W.C., Engelmann, S., Carnine, D.W. & Maggs, A. 1982. "Direct Instruction Technology: Making Learning Happen," in P. Karoly & J.J. Steffen, eds., *Improving Children's Competence: Advances in Child Behavioral Analysis and Therapy.* Vol. 1. Lexington, Mass.: Lexington Books.

Becker, W.C., Engelmann, S., Carnine, D.W. & Rhine, W.R. 1981. "Direct Instruction Model," in W. Ray Rhine, ed., *Making Schools More Effective: New Directions from Follow Through.* N.Y.: Academic Press.

Benton, A.L. 1984. "Dyslexia and Spatial Thinking." *Annals of Dyslexia* 34: 69–85.

Blackman S. & Goldstein, K.M. 1982. "Cognitive Styles and Learning Disabilities." *Journal of Learning Disabilities* 15: 106–15.

Blankenship, C.S. & Baumgartner, M.D. 1982. "Programming Generalization of Computational Skills." *Learning Disability Quarterly* 5: 152–62.

Carnine, D. & Silbert, J. 1979. *Direct Instruction Reading.* Columbus, Ohio: Charles C. Merrill.

Chadwick, O. & Rutter, M. 1983. "Neuropsychological Assessment," in M. Rutter, ed., *Developmental Neuropsychiatry.* N.Y.: The Guilford Press.

Clark, F.L., Deshler, D.D., Schumaker, J.B. & Alley, G.R. 1984. "Visual Imagery and Self Questioning: Strategies to Improve Comprehension of Written Materials." *Journal of Learning Disabilities* 17: 145–49.

Deshler, D.D., Lowrey, N. & Alley, G.R. 1979. "Programming Alternatives for Learning-Disabled Adolescents: A Nationwide Survey." *Academic Therapy* 14: 389–97.

Deshler, D.D., Schumaker, J.B. & Lenz, B.K. 1984. "Academic and Cognitive Interventions for LD Adolescents: Part I." *Journal of Learning Disabilities* 17: 108–17.

Deshler, D.D., Schumaker, J.B., Lenz, B.K. & Ellis, E. 1984. "Academic and Cognitive Interventions for LD Adolesents: Part II." *Journal of Learning Disabilities* 17: 170–79.

Deshler, D.D., Warner, M.M., Schumaker, J.B. & Alley, G.R. 1983. "Learning Strategies Intervention Model: Key Components and Current Status," in J.D. McKinney & L. Feagans, eds., *Current Topics in Learning Disabilities.* Norwood, N.J.: Ablex Publ. Corp.

Elliott, J.L. & Gentile, J.R. 1986. "The Efficacy of a Mnemonic Technique for Learning Disabled and Nondisabled Adolescents." *Journal of Learning Disabilities* 19: 237–41.

Ellis, E.S., Lenz, B.K. & Sabornie, E.J. 1987a. "Generalization and Adaptation of Learning Strategies to Natural Environments: Part I: Critical Agents." *Remedial and Special Education (RASE)* 8(1): 6–20.

———. 1987b. "Generalization and Adaptation of Learning Strategies to Natural Environments: Part 2: Research into Practice." *Remedial and Special Education (RASE)* 8(2): 6–23.

Engelmann, S. & Carnine, D. 1982. *Theory of Instruction: Principles and Applications.* N.Y.: Irvington.

Finucci, J.M., Gottfredson, L.S. & Childs, B. 1985. "A Follow-up Study of Dyslexic Boys." *Annals of Dyslexia* 35: 117–36.

Fish, M.C. & Mendola, L.R. 1986. "The Effect of Self Instruction Training on Homework Completion in an Elementary Special Education Class." *School Psychology Review* 15: 268–76.

Forness, S.R. & Kavale, K.A. 1983. "Remediation of Reading Disabilities, Part 2: Classification and Approaches." *Learning Disabilities* 2: 153–63.

Gaddes, W.H. 1981. "An Examination of the Validity of Neuropsychological Knowledge in Educational Diagnosis and Remediation," in G.W. Hynd & J.E. Obrzut, eds., *Neuropsychological Assessment and the School-Age Child: Issues and Procedures.* N.Y.: Grune & Stratton.

———. 1985. *Learning Disabilities and Brain Function: A Neuropsychological Approach.* 2d ed. N.Y.: Springer-Verlag.

Gadow, K.D., Torgesen, J.K. & Dahlem, W.E. 1983. "Learning Disabilities," in M. Hersen, V.B. Hasselt, & J.L. Matson, eds., *Behavior Therapy for the Developmentally and Physically Disabled: A Handbook.* N.Y.: Academic Press.

Gerstein, R. 1982. "A Review of Evaluation Research, Part I." *Direct Instruction News* 2: 11–13.

———. 1983. "A Review of Evaluation Research, Part II." *Direct Instruction News* 2: 11–16.

Gittelman, R. 1983. "Treatment of Reading Disorders," in M. Rutter, ed., *Developmental Neuropsychiatry.* N.Y.: The Guilford Press.

Goldman, S.R. & Pellegrino, J.W. 1987. "Information Processing and Educational Microcomputer Technology: Where Do We Go From Here?" *Journal of Learning Disabilities* 20: 144–54.

Goodman, L. & Hammill, D. 1973. "The Effectiveness of the Kephart-Getman Activities in Developing Perceptual-Motor and Cognitive Skills." *Exceptional Children* 4: 1–10.

Gutherie, J.T., Martuza, V. & Seifert, M. 1979. "Impacts of Instructional Time in Reading," in L. Resnick & P. Weaver, eds., *Theory and Practice in Early Reading.* Vol. 3. Hillsdale, N.J.: Lawrence Erlbaum Assoc. Publ.

Gutherie, J.T. & Seifert, M. 1978. "Education for Children with Reading Disabilities," in H.R. Myklebust, ed., *Progress in Learning Disabilities.* Vol. 4. N.Y.: Grune & Stratton.

Hall, M. 1981. *Teaching Reading as a Language Experience.* 3d ed. Columbus, Ohio: Charles Merrill.

Hallahan, D.P., Kauffman, J.M. & Lloyd, J.W. 1985. *Introduction to Learning Disabilities.* 2d ed. Englewood Cliffs, N.J.: Prentice Hall.

Hallahan, D.P., Kneedler, R.D. & Lloyd, J.W. 1983. "Cognitive Behavior Modification Techniques for Learning Disabled Children: Self-Instruction and Self-Monitoring," in J.D. McKinney & L. Feagans, eds., *Current Topics in Learning Disabilities.* Norwood, N.J.: Ablex Publ. Corp.

Hallahan, D.P., Lloyd, J.W. & Stoller, L. 1982. *Improving Attention with Self-Monitoring: A Manual for Teachers.* Charlottesville, Va.: U. of Va. Learning Disabilities Research Institute.

Hallahan, D.P. & Reeve, R.E. 1980. "Selective Attention and Distractibility," in B.K. Keogh, ed., *Advances in Special Education.* Vol. 1. Greenwich, Conn.: JAI Press.

Hallahan, D.P. & Sapona, R. 1983. "Self-Monitoring of Attention with Learning Disabled Children: Past Research and Current Issues." *Journal of Learning Disabilities* 16: 616–20.

Hammill, D.D. 1972. "Training Visual Perceptual Processes." *Journal of Learning Disabilities* 5: 552–59.

Hammill, D.D. & Larsen, S.C. 1974. "The Relationship of Selected Auditory Perceptual Skills and Reading Ability." *Journal of Learning Disabilities* 7: 429–35.

Harris, A. & Serwer, B. 1966. "The CRAFT Project: Instructional Time in Reading Research." *Reading Research Quarterly* 2: 27–57.

Hartlage, L.C. & Reynolds, C.R. 1981. "Neuropsychological Assessment and the Individualization of Instruction," in G.W. Hynd & J.E. Obrzut, eds., *Neuropsychological Assessment and the School-Age Child: Issues and Procedures.* N.Y. Grune & Stratton.

Hartlage, L.C. & Telzrow, C.F. 1983. "The Neuropsychological Basis of Educational Intervention." *Journal of Learning Disabilities* 16: 521–28.

Haynes, M.C. & Jenkins, J.R. 1986. "Reading Instruction in Special Education Rooms." *American Educational Research Journal* 23: 161–91.

Hynd, G.W., Snow, J. & Becker, M.G. 1986. "Neuropsychological Assessment in Clinical Child Psychology," in B.B. Lahey & A.E. Kazdin, eds., *Advances in Clinical Child Psychology.* Vol. 9. N.Y.: Plenum Press.

Johnson, C. 1981. *The Diagnosis of Learning Disabilities.* Boulder, Colo.: Pruett Publ. Co.

Jones, K.M., Torgesen, J.K. & Sexton, M.A. 1987. "Using Computer Guided Practice to Increase Decoding Fluency in Learning Disabled Children: A Study Using the Hint and Hunt I Program." *Journal of Learning Disabilities* 20: 122–28.

Kavale, K.A. & Mattson, P. 1983. " 'One Jumped Off the Balance Beam': Meta-Analysis of Perceptual Motor Training." *Journal of Learning Disabilities* 16: 165–73.

Kerchner, L.B. & Kistinger, B.J. 1984. "Language Processing/Word Processing: Written Expression, Computers, and Learning Disabled Students." *Learning Disability Quarterly* 7: 329–35.

Knights, R.M. & Stoddart, C. 1981. "Profile Approaches to Neuropsychological Diagnosis in Children," in G.W. Hynd & J.E. Obrzut, eds., *Neuropsychological Assessment and the School-Age Child: Issues and Procedures.* N.Y.: Grune & Stratton.

Kolich, E.M. 1985. "Microcomputer Technology with the Learning Disabled: A Review of the Literature." *Journal of Learning Disabilities* 18: 428–31.

Koorland, M.A. 1986. "Applied Behavior Analysis and the Correction of Learning Disabilities," in J.K. Torgesen & B.Y.L. Wong, eds., *Psychological and Educational Perspectives on Learning Disabilities*. Orlando: Academic Press, Inc.

Krupski, A. 1986. "Attention Problems in Youngsters with Learning Handicaps," in J.K. Torgesen & B.Y.L. Wong, eds., *Psychological and Educational Perspectives on Learning Disabilities*. Orlando: Academic Press, Inc.

Lahey, B.B., McNees, M.P. & Brown, C.C. 1973. "Modification of Deficits in Reading for Comprehension." *Journal of Applied Behavior Analysis* 6: 475–80.

Leinhardt, G., Zigmond, N. & Cooley, W. 1981. "Reading Instruction and Its Effects." *American Educational Research Journal* 18: 343–61.

Liberman, I.Y., Shankweiler, D., Blackman, B.A., Camp, L. & Werfelman, M. 1980. "Steps Toward Literacy," in P. Levinson & C.H. Sloan, eds., *Auditory Processing and Language: Clinical and Research Perspectives*. N.Y.: Grune & Stratton.

Lloyd, J.W. 1980. "Academic Instruction and Cognitive Behavior Modification: The Need for Attack Strategy Training." *Exceptional Education Quarterly* 1: 53–63.

Lloyd, J., Epstein, M.H. & Cullinan, D. 1981. "Direct Teaching for Learning Disabilities," in J. Gottlieb & S.S. Strichart, eds., *Developmental Theory and Research in Learning Disabilities*. Baltimore: University Park Press.

Makros, J.R. & Russell, S.J. 1986. "Learner-Centered Software: A Survey of Microcomputer Use with Special Needs Students." *Journal of Learning Disabilities* 19: 185–90.

Mastropieri, M.A., Scruggs, T.E. & Levin, J.R. 1985. "Maximizing What Exceptional Students Can Learn: A Review of Research on the Keyword Method and Related Mnemonic Techniques." *Remedial and Special Education* 6: 39–45.

McNutt, G. 1984. "A Holistic Approach to Language Arts Instruction in the Resource Room." *Learning Disability Quarterly* 7: 315–20.

———. 1986. "The Status of Learning Disabilities in the States: Consensus or Controversy?" *Journal of Learning Disabilities* 19: 12–16.

Meichenbaum, D. 1977. *Cognitive-Behavior Modification: An Integrative Approach*. N.Y.: Plenum Press.

Neeley, M.D. & Lindsley, O.R. 1978. "Phonetic, Linguistic, and Sight Readers Produce Similar Learning with Exceptional Children." *Journal of Special Education* 12: 423–41.

Neeper, R. & Lahey, B.B. 1984. "A Critical Appraisal of Behavioral Interventions for Learning Disabilities: Which Behavior Should We Modify?" *Learning Disabilities* 3: 51–61.

Palincsar, A.S. & Brown, D.A. 1987. "Enhancing Instructional Time Through Attention to Metacognition." *Journal of Learning Disabilities* 20: 66–75.

Pirozzolo, F.J. 1979. *The Neuropsychology of Developmental Reading Disorders*. N.Y.: Praeger.

Poplin, M.S. 1984. "Toward a Holistic View of Persons with Learning Disabilities." *Learning Disability Quarterly* 7: 290–94.

Reid, D.K. & Hresko, W.P. 1981. *A Cognitive Approach to Learning Disabilities*. N.Y.: McGraw-Hill Book Co.

Rooney, K.J. & Hallahan, D.P. 1985. "Future Directions for Cognitive Behavior Modification Research: The Quest for Cognitive Change." *Remedial and Special Education (RASE)* 6: 46–51.

Rosenshine, B.V. 1978. "Academic Engaged Time, Content Covered, and Direct Instruction." *Journal of Education* 160: 38–66.

Rourke, B.P. 1983. "Outstanding Issues in Research on Learning Disabilities," in M. Rutter, ed., *Developmental Neuropsychiatry*. N.Y.: The Guilford Press.

Ryan, E.B. 1981. "Identifying and Remediating Failures in Reading Comprehension: Toward an Instructional Approach for Poor Comprehenders," in G. Mackinnon & T. Waller, eds., *Reading Research: Advances in Theory and Practice.* Vol. 3. N.Y.: Academic Press.

Ryan, E.B., Weed, K.A. & Short, E.J. 1986. "Cognitive Behavior Modification: Promoting Active, Self-Regulatory Learning Styles," in J.K. Torgesen & B.Y.L. Wong, eds., *Psychological and Educational Perspectives on Learning Disabilities.* Orlando: Academic Press, Inc.

Samuels, S.J. 1987. "Information Processing Abilities and Reading." *Journal of Learning Disabilities* 20: 18–22.

Schonhaut, S. & Satz, P. 1983. "Prognosis for Children with Learning Disabilities: A Review of Follow-Up Studies, in M. Rutter, ed., *Developmental Neuropsychiatry.* N.Y.: The Guilford Press.

Schumaker, J.B., Deshler, D.D. & Ellis, E.S. 1986. "Intervention Issues Related to the Education of LD Adolescents," in J.K. Torgesen & B.Y.L. Wong, eds., *Psychological and Educational Perspectives on Learning Disabilities.* Orlando: Academic Press, Inc.

Schumaker, J.B., Hovell, M.F. & Sherman, J.A. 1977a. "An Analysis of Daily Report Cards and Parent-Managed Privileges in the Improvement of Adolescents' Classroom Performance." *Journal of Applied Behavior Analysis* 10: 449–64.

———. 1977b. *A Home Based School Achievement Program.* Lawrence, Kans.: H. & H. Enterprises.

Schumaker, J.B., Warner, M.M., Deshler, D.D. & Alley, G.R. n.d. *The Evaluation of a Learning Strategies Intervention Model for LD Adolescents.* Research Report No. 67. Lawrence, Kans.: The Univ. of Kansas Institute for Research in Learning Disabilities.

Short, E.J. & Ryan, E.B. 1984. "Metacognitive Differences Between Skilled and Less Skilled Readers: Remediating Deficits Through Story Grammar and Attribution Training." *Journal of Educational Psychology* 76: 225–35.

Smith, F. 1983. "How Children Learn," in D. Carnine & D. Elkind, eds., *Interdisciplinary Voices in Learning Disabilities and Remedial Education.* Austin, Tex.: Pro-ed.

Stanovich, K.E. 1986. "Cognitive Processes and the Reading Problems of Learning-Disabled Children: Evaluating the Assumption of Specificity," in J.K. Torgesen & B.Y.L. Wong, eds., *Psychological and Educational Perspectives on Learning Disabilities.* Orlando: Academic Press, Inc.

Stauffer, R.G. 1980. *The Language Experience Approach to the Teaching of Reading.* 2d ed. N.Y.: Harper & Row.

Swanson, H.L. 1987a. "Information Processing Theory and Learning Disabilities: An Overview." *Journal of Learning Disabilities* 20: 3–7.

———. 1987b. "Information Processing Theory and Learning Disabilities: A Commentary and Future Perspective." *Journal of Learning Disabilities* 20: 155–66.

Tarver, S.G. 1986. "Cognitive Behavior Modification, Direct Instruction, and Holistic Approaches to the Education of Students with Learning Disabilities." *Journal of Learning Disabilities* 19: 368–74.

Thorpe, H.W., Chiang, B. & Darch, C.B. 1981. "Individual and Group Feedback Systems for Improving Reading Accuracy in Learning Disabled and Regular Class Children." *Journal of Learning Disabilities* 14: 332–34.

Thurlow, M.L., Graden, T., Greever, T.W. & Ysseldyke, J.E. 1982. *Academic Responding Time for Learning Disabled and Non-Learning Disabled Students.* Technical Report No. 72. Minneapolis, Minn: Institute for Research on Learning Disabilities.

Torgesen, J.K. 1985. "Memory Processes in Reading Disabled Children." *Journal of Learning Disabilities* 18: 350–57.

———. 1986. "Computer-Assisted Instruction with Learning-Disabled Children," in J.K. Torgesen & B.Y.L. Wong, eds., *Psychological and Educational Perspectives on Learning Disabilities*. Orlando: Academic Press, Inc.

Torgesen, J.K. & Licht, B.G. 1983. "The Learning Disabled Child as an Inactive Learner: Retrospect and Prospects," in J.D. McKinney & L. Feagans, eds., *Current Topics in Learning Disabilities*. Norwood, N.J.: Ablex Publ. Corp.

Torgesen, J.K. & Wong, B.Y.L., eds., 1986. *Psychological Perspectives on Learning Disabilities*. Orlando: Academic Press, Inc.

Treiber, F.A. & Lahey, B.B. 1983. "Toward a Behavioral Model of Academic Remediation with Learning Disabled Children." *Journal of Learning Disabilities* 16: 111–16.

Vellutino, F.R., Steger, B.M., Moyer, S.C. Harding, C.J. & Niles, J.A. 1977. "Has the Perceptual Deficit Hypothesis Led Us Astray?" *Journal of Learning Disabilities* 10: 375–85.

Wong, B.Y.L. 1985. "Issues in Cognitive-Behavioral Intervention in Academic Skill Areas." *Journal of Abnormal Child Psychology* 13: 425–42.

Wong, B.Y.L. & Jones, W. 1982. "Increasing Metacomprehension in Learning-Disabled and Normally Achieving Students Through Self Questioning Training." *Learning Disability Quarterly* 5: 228–39.

Young, K., Torgesen, J.K., Rashotte, C.A. & Jones, K.M. 1983. *Microcomputers in the Resource Room: A Handbook for Teachers*. Tallahassee, Fla.: Leon County Public Schools.

Ysseldyke, J.E. 1983. "Current Practices in Making Psychoeducational Decisions About Learning Disabled Students." *Journal of Learning Disabilities* 16: 226–33.

Zadig, J.M. & Meltzer, L.J. 1983. "Special Education," in M.D. Levine, W.B. Carey, A.C. Crocker, & R.T. Gross, eds., *Developmental-Behavioral Pediatrics*. Philadelphia: W.B. Saunders Co.

Index

Abelman, R., 58, 68, 73, 75, 76, 78
Academic behavior therapy. *See* Applied behavior analysis
Academic engaged time, 233–234
Achievement, academic: and aggressiveness, 66; low achievers, 184, 201, 202; and middle-class sons of employed mothers, 31; and parental divorce, 90, and television, 65, 66, 72–73, 77–78. *See also* Intellectual functioning
Adelman, H.S., 187
Adolescents: adjustment and cohesive families, 136; and child abuse, 147, 156, 158; coping styles, 117; and depression, 112, 123, 124, 133; and employed mothers, 30, 33; and parental divorce, 80–90, 93, 97–98, 105; and suicidal thoughts, 127; and television, 58, 59, 64, 69, 72, 76. *See also* Suicide, youth
Adoption: abused children, 163; older children, 10–11, 17, 20
Aggressive behavior: of abused children, 158, consistency throughout development, 16, 68; of day care children, 37, 38; and IQ, 66; and television violence, 62–68. *See also* Behavioral problems
American Academy of Pediatrics, 45
Ames, L., 182
Anger-control techniques, 100, 165, 166
Antisocial behavior, 3, 129. *See also* Conduct disorders
Applied behavior analysis, 218–223
Assessment: of academic deficits, 221–222; in child abuse cases,

161–162; of depression, 133; of learning disabilities, 183–184, 188, 202, 235; of parents at risk for child abuse, 170; of suicidal tendencies, 133; of teaching progress, 219. *See also* Intervention; Prevention; Remediation
Attachment(s): abused infants, 157; father-infant son, in employed mother homes, 29; influence of day care on, 34–36; lack of early opportunity to form and later social development, 3, 17, 20; secure versus anxious versus avoidant, 35
Attentional problems, 198–200, 225–226
Attributional style: and depression, 124–125, 136; and response to stress, 115–116, 136. *See also* Learned helplessness
Automaticity, level of, 200, 222, 234

Beck, A.T., 131, 135
Behavioral approaches, 164–166, 218–223
Behavioral problems: and neurological dysfunction, 181; and parental discord, 98–99; and parental divorce, 88, 89, 90, 95, 98. *See also* Aggressive behavior; Conduct disorders
Belsky, J., 37, 38, 43, 46, 48, 51, 145, 148, 149, 150
Berger, A.M., 145, 149, 151, 152, 153
Berkeley Growth Study, 13–14
Birth complications, 11, 87
Bleuler, M., 121
Block, J., 16
Block, Jeanne, 99
Bollen, K.A., 128

Bonding, parent-infant 11–13; and child abuse research 12, 152–153, 171
Bowlby, J., 2
Brain-behavior relationships, 188
Brain-injured child, 181. *See also* Minimal brain damage, Neurological dysfunction
Brazelton, T., 50
Bronfenbrenner, U., 27, 31, 46, 72
Brown, B., 112, 113, 115, 132
Brown, J.M., 117

Caldwell, B., 49, 50
Camara, K.A., 87, 88, 89, 91, 93, 95, 102
Cerebral dysfunction. *See* Neurological dysfunction
Chains of events, 5, 19–20, 123
Chandler, L.A., 113
Chess, S., 12, 15, 22, 49
Child abuse, 143–173; assessment in cases of 161–162; 166; caseworker overload, consequences of, 169, 170; characteristics of abused children, 152–153, 154, 156; characteristics of abusing parents, 146–155; and corporal punishment, 145, 151, 154, 172; cultural and social causal factors 145–149; and cutbacks in social services, 169–170; definitions of, 143–144; effects of, on children 156–160; family interaction in abusing families 153–154; incidents of, 155–156; intergenerational cycle of maltreatment, 149–150; limitations of research in the area of, 143–144, 152, 153, 156–157; misconceptions about, 143, 146, 147, 149, 151, 152, 153, 160; occurrence of, 143–144, 156; and parent-infant bonding, 12, 152, 171; prevention of, 170–173; and protective factors, 159–160; reporting laws for 169; treatment for children and parents, 162–168; treatment success rates, 169; unsubstantiated reports of, 169
Child Development Associate Credential, 45
Child Welfare League of America, and minimal day care standards, 41
Childhood stress. *See* Stress
Clarke, A.D.B., 1, 4, 5, 7, 17

Clarke, Ann, 1, 4, 5, 7, 17
Clarke-Stewart, A., 33, 35, 36–38, 47, 48, 51
Coddington, R.D., 113
Cognitive-behavior modification, 223–230
Cognitive-behavioral therapy, 133
Cognitive strategy deficits. *See* Learning disabilities
Cognitive strategy training, 226–227, 228, 229, 230
Cognitive therapy, 135
Cohen-Sandler, R., 126, 127, 129, 130, 131
Cohn, A.H., 162, 164, 167, 170, 172
Collins, R.C., 40, 43, 44
Community-based programs: for child abuse 166–168, 169, 170–171; for day care, 49
Comparative Licensing Study, 44
Computers, use of in schools, 234–235
Conduct disorders: and children of divorce, 90; consistency throughout development, 16; and parental discord, 120; and youth suicide, 129. *See also* Antisocial behavior; Behavioral problems
Coping skills, 19, 117, 118–123; and abusing parents, 148, 155, 161, 167, 171. *See also* Coping skills programs
Coping skills programs: for abusing parents, 156–166, 168; for children with divorcing parents, 100; for children's stress, 132; for youth suicide prevention, 133–134
Corder-Bolz, C.R., 74, 75, 76
Crisis intervention, 134
Crisis nurseries, 168
Critical periods, 3, 5, 22
Crouter, A., 27, 31, 92, 95, 100

Day care, 33–51; adaptation to, 46; conclusions of reviewers about effects of, 38; considerations before placement, 46–48; early entry, 35, 36, 46; and emotional development, 34–36; infant, 34–36, 38, 42, 43, 44, 46, 47; in-service training, 50; and intellectual development, 36–37; limitations of research in area of, 34, 39; national crisis in, 49–50; quality of, defined, 39–42; quality of, and effects

on children, 35, 36, 40–41, 42–43;
quality, minimal standards of, 41–42;
quality, minimal standards versus
state regulations, 43–45; sex differences in response to, 35, 46; and
social development, 37–38; and social
policy, 49–50, therapeutic, for abused
children, 163–164; types of, and comparisons, 33, 34, 37, 47–48
Dennis, W., 9
Department of Health, Education, and
Welfare, and minimal day care standards, 41, 42
Depression, youth, 123–125; assessment
and intervention, 133; prevalence of,
112, 124; and suicidal behavior, 129
Deshler, D.D., 226, 228, 229, 230, 232,
235
Direct instruction programs, 216–218
Distar, 217, 218
Divorce. *See* Parental divorce
Divorce mediation, 103
Dixon, S.L., 134, 135
Dunn, J., 114, 115, 116
Dyslexia. *See* Reading disabilities. *See
also* Learning disabilities; Reading;
Remediation

Early experience, 1–23; and chains of
events, 5, 19–20; conclusions of
reviewers about effects of, 5–6; controversy about effects of, 2–6, 16–18;
early trauma studies, 6–11; and environmental continuity/discontinuity,
5, 19, 22–23; factors increas-
ing/decreasing the influence of,
18–21; implications of research on
21–23; and IQ, 2, 3, 5, 6–10, 17, 23;
life span view of, 17–18; limitations
of research in area of, 4, 12, 16–17;
longitudinal studies, 13–16; parent-
infant bonding research, 11–13;
strong early influence view of,
16–17, 18
Early years. *See* Early experience
Easterbrooks, M.A., 29, 30, 33
Electroencephalogram (EEG), 188
Elementary and Secondary Act Amendments (PL 91–230), 182
Elkind, D., 112
Ellis, E.S., 228
Emery, R.E., 90, 91, 96, 98–99

Emotional Development: in abused
children, 157–158; and day care,
34–36
Employed mothers. *See* Maternal
employment
Engelmann, S., 216, 218
Eron, L., 64, 65, 67, 74
Ettema, J., 62, 74
Executive learning strategies, 225, 229

Fading techniques, 220–221
Faller, K.C., 169, 170, 172
Family influences, 19, 20, 21, 136; and
attributional style, 116; and emotion-
al problems, 116; and parental con-
flict and divorce, 88–93, 94, 98–99;
and response to stress, 116–117, 120,
136; and television, 68, 75–76; and
youth suicidal behavior, 128, 130,
131, 135, 136. *See also* Parent-child
interaction
Family therapy, 135
Felner, R.D., 88, 99, 116, 121, 136
Fels study, the, 14–15
Finucci, J.M., 232
Fischler, R.S., 161, 162, 163
Flint, B.M., 9
Forness, S.R., 191, 217, 232, 235,
236
Foster care placement, 159, 162–163,
165
Friedman, R.M., 146, 152, 153, 161
Friedrich, W.N., 148, 149, 150, 151,
154
Frostig, M., 182, 190

Gaddes, N.H., 186, 187, 231
Gamble, T.J., 35, 36, 38, 45
Garbarino, J., 145, 146, 147, 158, 159,
166, 167, 169
Garfinkel, B.D., 128, 129, 131
Garmezy, N., 112, 118, 119, 120, 121,
122, 173
Gelles, R.J., 144, 145, 148, 156, 160,
164, 166
Generalization of learned skills,
222–223, 227–228
Gil, D.G., 145, 152, 155
Gittelman, R., 212
Goldfarb, W., 2
Grief, J., 86, 91, 104
Gutherie, J.T., 232, 233

Hallahan, D.P., 191, 212, 213, 214, 223, 225, 226
Harlow, H., 2, 4
Hartlage, L.C., 231
Hawton, K., 127, 132, 134, 135
Head Start, 3, 5
Hetherington, E.M., 85, 87, 88, 89, 92–93, 94, 121
Hoffman, L.W., 29, 30, 32
Home visitor program, 170–171. *See also* Paraprofessionals
Hospitalization, 115
Huesmann, L.R., 64, 65, 66, 67, 68
Hunt, J. McVicker, 2, 23
Hyperactive children, 198

Imprinting, 3, 4
Impulsive children. *See* Remediation
Inactive learners. *See* Learning disabilities: Cognitive strategy deficits
Information processing perspective, 67–68, 200
Institutionally reared infants, 2, 3, 6–7, 9, 18; methodological flaws in studies, 4
Intellectual functioning: and abused children, 157, 159; and aggressiveness, 66; of children from discordant homes, 99; of day care children, 36–37; and early experience, 2, 3, 5, 6–11, 17, 23; and late adoptions, 17; of learning disabled children, 185; of middle-class boys with employed mothers, 31; and stress, 113, 114–115; and television, 66, 72, 73. *See also* Achievement, academic
Intervention: age at, 21, 22, 159; in child abuse cases, 160–168; with depressed youths, 133; with divorcing families, 100–101, 103; early stimulation, 3, 5, 23, 36–37; with learning disabled children, 202, 203, 211–236; to reduce negative effects of television, 74–78; with stressed children 132, 136; with suicidal youth, 134–135; suicide prevention programs, 133–134. *See also* Assessment; Prevention; Therapy
Invulnerable children. *See* Stress-resistant children

Johnson, R.B., 186, 187, 188
Johnston, J., 62, 74

Journal of Divorce, and handbook for clinicians, 101
Journal of Learning Disabilities, and information processing perspective, 220

Kadushin, A., 10–11, 17
Kagan, J., 6, 7–9, 14–15, 16, 17, 18, 19, 22, 46
Kaufman, J., 149
Kavale, K.A., 191, 212, 217, 232, 235, 236
Kennell, J.H., 12–13
Keogh, B.K., 198, 199, 200
Kephart, N.C., 182, 191
Kerchner, L.B., 214
Kinard, E., 157, 158, 159, 162
Kirk, S., 181
Klaus, M., 12–13
Koluchova, J., 10
Koorland, M.A., 217, 219, 220, 222
Kopp, C., 11, 118
Kosky, R., 127, 131, 158
Krakow, J.B., 11, 118
Krupski, A., 198, 199, 225
Kurdek, L.A., 88, 90, 94, 96

Lahey, B.B., 218, 220, 221, 222
Language, 191–195
Language experience approach, 213, 214, 215
Latchkey children, 49
Lay therapists, 167. *See also* Paraprofessionals
Lazar, I., 5
Learned helplessness: and abused children, 160; and depression, 124–125, 136; and school failure, 197, 219; and stress, 115–116; 136
Learning disabilities, 181–203; assessment, 183–184, 188, 202, 221, 235; and attentional problems, 198–200, 224; causes of, 186–201; characteristics of LD children, 183–185; and cognitive strategy deficits, 195–198, 200, 223; definition of, 183, 196; disciplines researching, 186; government-funded research institutions, 225, 228, 235; heterogeneity of LD population, 182, 183, 185, 186, 190, 201, 202, 211; history of field of, 181–183; and information processing deficiencies, 200; and

language deficits, 191–195, 196, 201; and low achievers, 184, 201, 202; math disabilities, 185, 201, 211, 221; maturational lag explanations of, 187, 188–189, 196; and memory, 193, 195, 196, 200, 223; and metacognitive deficits, 195, 197; neurological explanations of 187–188; nonverbal disabilities, 185, 202; perceptual deficit theories, 190–191, 212; and perceptual, perceptual/motor deficits, 184, 190–191, 193, 194, 201, 212; prevalence of, 183; research problems in area of, 182, 183, 185; significance of LD term, 181, 182; social-emotional functioning of LD children, 202; spelling disabilities, 185, 201, 211; subtyping research, 201–203; types of, 185–186; writing disabilities, 185. *See also* Hyperactive children; Minimal brain damage (MBD); Reading disabilities; Remediation

Learning Disability Quarterly, and holistic approach, 215
Leinhardt, G., 232, 233, 234
Leupnitz, D.A., 104, 105
Liberman, I.Y., 193, 194, 195, 222
Life-span approach, 18
Life stress inventories, 112–113
Low birth weight. *See* Prematurity
Lyon, G.R., 188, 201, 212

McCartney, K., 36, 41, 42, 43
Maccoby, E.E., 115
Macfarlane, J., 13–14
McKinney, J.D., 186, 201, 202
McNutt, G., 183, 213, 214
Margolis, J., 198, 199, 200
Marital conflict. *See* Parental conflict
Masten, A.S., 116, 120, 122
Maternal employment, 27–33; conclusions of reviewers about effects of, 27, 29, 30, 33, 49; effects on children, 30–33; effects on family relationships, 28–30; effects on household division of labor, 28, 30; effects on mothers, 28; full versus part-time employment, 32–33, 45; health professionals' attitudes toward, 27, 45; limitations of research in area of, 32–33; statistics of, 27

Maturational lag, 188–189
Meichenbaum, D., 165, 224
Memory, and language, 192–193. *See also* Learning disabilities
Messinger, L., 93, 102, 103, 105
Metacognition, 197
Minimial brain damage (MBD), 181, 185, 186. *See also* Learning disabilities; Neurological dysfunction
Minnesota Multiphasic Personality Inventory, 150
Mnemonic techniques, 219, 226
Montemayor, R., 31, 32, 33
Motor training. *See* Remediation: process training
MTV, 69, 70, 71
Multidisciplinary assessment teams, 161–162
Music videos, 69–71

National Association for the Education of Young Children (NAEYC), 41, 50
National Coalition on Television Violence, 69, 70
National Day Care Home Study, 39, 40, 41
National Day Care Study, 39–41
National Joint Committee on Learning Disabilities, 183
Neeley, M.D., 235–236
Neeper, R., 218, 220, 221
Neurological assessment techniques, 188
Neurological dysfunction, 181, 187–188. *See also* Minimal brain damage (MBD)
Neuropsychological assessment batteries, 188, 201, 230–231
Neuropsychologist, 230–231
New York Longitudinal Study, 15, 20
Newberger, C.M., 146, 152, 157, 158
Nuclear magnetic resonance (NMR) imaging, 188

Oates, K., 148, 149, 150, 157, 161, 163, 164
O'Bryant, S.L., 74, 75, 76
Oliver, D., 168, 169

Pakezegi, B., 119, 145, 146, 147, 149, 150, 157, 159, 164, 168
Paraprofessionals, 166–167, 170–171

Parent-child interaction: and child abuse, 151, 154, 165; and employed mother homes, 29–30, 31, 32, 33; and parental divorce, 87–88, 90, 91. *See also* Family influences

Parent education programs, 164–165, 171

Parent Effectiveness Training (PET), 164

Parental conflict, effects on children, 94, 98–99, 102, 120. *See also* Parental divorce

Parental death, in early childhood and adult depression, 19–20, 116–117

Parental divorce, 85–106; adjustment programs for children and parents, 100–101, 103; and age of child, 96–98; custodial home environment, 92–93, 101–102; and custody arrangements, 95–96, 103–105; effects on children, 87–90, 96–98; effects on parents, 86–87; experience of children during, 87–88, 95, 96–98; factors influencing children's adjustment to, 90–98, 99–100; how to reduce negative consequences for children, 99–106; and increased family conflict, 86, 94, 102; and non-custodial parent, 91, 102, 105–106; parent-child relationships in, 87–88, 90, 91–93; and sex of child, 88, 89–90, 95–96. *See also* Divorce mediation; Parental conflict

Parents Anonymous, 166, 167–168

Patterson, G.R., 165

Pedro-Carroll, J.L., 100

Perceptual, perceptual/motor deficits. *See* Learning disabilities. *See also* Remediation: for children with perceptual deficits

Perceptual, perceptual/motor training. *See* Remediation: process training

Performance feedback, 200

Perinatal trauma, 11, 187

Pfeffer, C.R., 126, 127, 129, 131, 134

Phillips, D., 41, 42, 49

Phillips, D.P., 128

Phonemic skills, 194–195

Phonology, and reading, 192–193, 194–195, 200

Pirozzollo, F.J., 185, 186, 191, 201, 212

Poplin, M.S., 213, 214

Positron emission tomography, 188

Prematurity: and bonding, 12–13; and child abuse, 12, 152–153; and neurological dysfunction, 187; and role in development, 11

Prevention: child abuse, 170–173; stress, depression, and suicide in youth, 132–134. *See also* Intervention

Process training. *See* Remediation

Project Follow Through, 215, 217

Prompts, 220–221

Prosocial behavior, 68–69

Protective factors, 20–21, 119–123, 136, 159–160

Psychotherapy. *See* Therapy. *See also* Assessment; Intervention

Quinton, D., 121, 123

Rachman, S.J., 21

Reading: activities correlated to reading achievement, 233; and attention, 198, 199, 200, 234; instructional materials/resources, 214, 216–218, 226–227, 235, 236; and language skills/deficits, 191–195; and memory, 200; and preschoolers, 23. *See also* Reading disabilities; Remediation

Reading disabilities, 185–186, 189, 211; characteristic problems of, 215: and cognitive strategy deficits, 196, 197, 223; dyslexia defined, 185; and language deficits, 191–195; and perceptual deficits, 190–191, 193–194, 201, 212; subtypes of, 201, 202, 235. *See also* Learning disabilities; Reading; Remediation

Reinforcement, 219–220, 221, 224

Relaxation training, 100, 133, 165

Remediation, educational, 211–236; amount of remedial instruction received by LD students, studies of, 232–233; applied behavior analysis, 218–223, 235; for attentional problems, 198, 199, 200, 225–226; automaticity, level of, 200, 222, 234; basic skills, 200, 216–217, 222, 234; for children with perceptual deficits, 213, 231, 236–237; cognitive-behavior modification, 211, 223–230; computers, use of, 234–235; direct instruction programs, 216–218; direct skills approach to, 211, 215–231; holistic approach to, 211, 213–215; with impulsive children, 199, 224; instructional resources, 218–222, 224–228, 229, 234–235; intensity of instruction required for success, 231–235; and learning disabilities, 186, 202, 203, 211–236; and mastery learning, 221, 222, 234; measuring progress in, 219; for memory deficiencies, 196, 226; neuropsychological approach to, 211, 230–231, 235; for children with perceptual deficits, 213, 231, 236–237; for phonemic skills deficiencies, 195; process training, 182, 183, 191, 211, 212–213; for reading comprehension, 196, 226–227; strategies to improve generalization of learned skills, 227–228; and subtypes of LD children, 202; targeting skill deficiencies, 221–222; tutoring, success with, 233

Required helpfulness, 121–122, 136
Resiliency, factors influencing, 17, 18–21
Resilient children, 4, 6–11. *See also* Stress: stress-resistant children
Respite care, 168
Reynolds, W.M., 124, 133
Risk factors, environmental, 20–21; and vulnerability to stress, 123
Rosenthal, P.A., 127, 158
Rosenthal, S., 127, 158
Ross, C.P., 133, 134
Rourke, B.P., 188, 201, 202
Rueveni, U., 166
Ruopp, R., 39, 40, 45
Rutter, M., 16, 21, 186, 188; continuity in development, 5, 19, 20, 23; maternal employment and day care, 38, 45, 46; stress, 112, 113–114, 115, 116, 118, 119, 123, 124
Ryan, E.B., 223, 224, 226, 227, 228

Sameroff, A.J., 5, 11, 17
Samuels, S.J., 200
Sands, R.G., 134, 135
Santrock, J.W., 93, 95–96
Satz, P., 189, 201
Scarr, S., 41, 44, 47, 48, 49, 50
Schools: assessment and treatment of depressed youths, 133; and children's divorce adjustment programs, 100; and day care potential, 49–50; early entry, 111, 189; learning disabled children in the, 183–184, 187, 228, 232–233, 234, 235; and stress management programs, 132; and suicide prevention programs, 133–134; and teaching phonemic skills, 195; and television literacy curricula, 77–78
Schumaker, J.B., 200, 228, 229, 230, 233, 235
Seagull, E.A., 147
Self-concept, 16, 19, 157, 160, 162, 184
Self-esteem, and child abuse, 150, 157; and parental divorce, 89, 92, 100, 104; and response to stress, 115, 120, 122, 123; and youth suicide, 128, 131, 132
Self-instruction, 224–225
Self-monitoring, 224, 225–226
Seligman, M.E.P., 124, 125, 136
Semantics, and reading, 192, 193, 194, 195
Sensitive periods, 22
Sex differences: in children's divorce adjustment, 88, 89–90, 95–96; in differential treatment of children in employed and nonemployed mother families, 31–32; in learning disabled children, 185; in response to day care, 35, 46; in response to maternal employment, 31–32; in response to parental discord, 98, 99; in response to stress, 114
Singer, D.G., 63, 64, 77, 78
Singer, J.L., 63, 64, 77, 78
Single-parent homes, 89, 93, 95, 100, 148
Skeels, H.M., 6–7
Sleeper effects, 33, 38, 116
Smith, S.L., 143, 146, 147, 151
Social development: in abused children, 158, 163, and day care, 37–38; and discordant homes, 99; and lack of opportunity to form early attachments, 3, 17, 20; in learning disabled children, 202
Social isolation: and child abuse, 146–147; and youth suicide, 129
Social policy: and child abuse, 169–170; and day care, 49–50; and learning disabilities, 182, 183; and plasticity of

Social policy: (*Continued*)
development, implications for, 8, 22; and television, 78
Social support: and parenting behavior, 147; role in divorce adjustment 100, 101; in treatment of child abuse, 166–168, 170–171; in treatment of youth suicide attempters, 134, 135
Socioeconomic status: and child abuse, 147–148; and learning disabilities, 185
Steinman, S., 91, 104–105
Stolberg, A.L., 92, 93, 96, 99, 100
Strategies intervention model, 228–230
Straus, M.A., 144, 145, 156
Stress, 111–123; and child abuse, 148–149; and children's divorce adjustment, 93–94; children's response to, factors influencing, 113–118; 120–122; consequences for children, 111–112, 113; definition of, 112; and depression, 123; family, and influence on day care infants, 35; limitations of research in area of, 112; long term damage from, 118; management techniques for children, 132; measures of, in children, 112–113; multiple stresses, 117–118; protective factors, 119–123; sensitizing effect of, 118, 122; steeling effect of, 122; stress-resistant children, 118–123; and youth suicidal behavior, 113, 128, 130–131
Stress-resistant children. *See* Stress
Stroufe, L.A., 16, 17, 124
Substance abuse: and child abuse 150; and suicidal behavior in youth, 129
Suicide, youth: 125–135; attempted suicide, 126–128, 133; characteristics of suicidal youths, 129–132; crisis suicides, 132, 134; and cultural factors, 128; and European youth, 125, 128; media and, 128; precipitating conditions, 132; prevention and screening, 133–134; statistics of, 125–126; treatment of attempted suicides, 134–135; warning signs of, 129–130; in young children, 126–127
Syntax, and reading, 192, 193, 194, 195
Systematic Training for Effective Parenting (STEP), 164

Tarver, S.G., 211, 213, 216, 217
Television, 57–78; children's understanding of, 58–60; conclusions of reviewers about effects of, on children, 57, 62, 63, 68, 69; how to reduce negative effects of, on children, 74–78; influence of, on children's perceptions, 60–62; intervention to reduce aggressive behavior of high violence viewers, 74; and IQ and achievement, 66, 72–73, 77; and music videos, 60–71; portrayal of the world on, 60–63; potential for positive influence of, 62, 68–69, 73; and television literacy skills curricula, 77–78; television violence and aggressive behavior, 62–68; viewing habits of children, 57–58
Temperament, 15–16, 20, 94–95; 114
Therapy: cognitive-behavioral therapy, 133; cognitive therapy, 135; crisis intervention, 134; family therapy, 135, relaxation training, 100, 133, 165. *See also* Anger control techniques; Assessment; Coping skills programs; Intervention
Thomas, A., 12, 15, 22, 49
Torgesen, J., 182, 194; 195, 196, 197, 234, 235
Treatment. *See* Assessment; Intervention; Therapy
Treiber, F.A., 218, 220, 222

Vellutino, F.R., 192–194, 195
Verbal deficits. *See* Learning disabilities: language deficits

Walker, K.N., 93, 102, 103, 105
Wallerstein, J.S., 87, 88–89, 92, 96–98, 101, 102, 105, 106
Werner, E., 121, 123, 136
Williams, P.A., 72, 73
Wolchik, S.A., 104
Wolfe, D.A., 144, 148, 151, 154, 169, 171
Wong, B.Y.L., 211, 227
World Federation of Neurology, 185

Young, K.T., 43, 44, 49
Ysseldyke, J.E., 184, 233, 235

Zigler, E., 21–22, 145, 149; and day care, 35, 36, 38, 43, 44, 45, 49, 50
Zimrin, H., 159, 160, 166

About the Author

Genevieve Clapp received the Ph.D. in psychology from the University of Iowa in 1968. Since that time, she has taught psychology courses and seminars at both the graduate and undergraduate level and has authored many chapters in a number of multiauthored psychology textbooks. A onetime associate publisher of psychology texts with CRM Books, she left the administrative side of publishing to become a consultant for two publishing companies that specialized in the area of psychology.

Her direct involvement with children has been varied—an elementary school teacher in an earlier career, an involved mother of two, and a parent active in educational issues and with the public schools.

Currently she is engaged in consulting and is with San Diego Research Consultants.